Encyclopedia of Blacks in European History and Culture

VOLUME 2: K–Z

Edited by Eric Martone

GREENWOOD PRESS
Westport, Connecticut • London

Library of Congress Cataloging-in-Publication Data

Encyclopedia of Blacks in European history and culture / edited by Eric Martone.
    p. cm.
  Includes bibliographical references and index.
  ISBN 978–0–313–34448–0 (set : alk. paper) — ISBN 978–0–313–34450–3 (v. 1 : alk. paper) —
  ISBN 978–0–313–34452–7 (v. 2 : alk. paper)
 1. Blacks—Europe—History—Encyclopedias.   I. Martone, Eric.
  D212.2.B53E53   2009
  940'.0496—dc22   2008030542

British Library Cataloguing in Publication Data is available.

Library of Congress Catalog Card Number: 2008030542
ISBN: 978–0–313–34448–0 (set)
     978–0–313–34450–3 (Vol. 1)
     978–0–313–34452–7 (Vol. 2)

First published in 2009

Greenwood Press, 88 Post Road West, Westport, CT 06881
An imprint of Greenwood Publishing Group, Inc.
www.greenwood.com

Printed in the United States of America

The paper used in this book complies with the
Permanent Paper Standard issued by the National
Information Standards Organization (Z39.48–1984).

10 9 8 7 6 5 4 3 2 1

Encyclopedia of Blacks
in European
History and Culture

Contents

Chronology

500s B.C.E.	Aesop, who might have been of African origin, creates his fables on the Greek island of Samos.
300s B.C.E.	Clitus "the Black," one of the Macedonian commanders under Alexander the Great, may have been of black African descent.
219 to 202 B.C.E.	During the Second Punic War between Rome and Carthage, Carthaginian general Hannibal invades Italy with many African soldiers, many of whom are black African.
200s B.C.E. to 476	The ancient Roman army uses African troops, which are stationed throughout Western Europe.
100s	African playwright Terentius Afer writes several pieces for the theater of the ancient Roman Empire.
100s to 200s	Five emperors from Africa rule ancient Rome: Septimius Severus, Geta, Caracalla, Marcus Opellius Macrinus, and Marcus Aemilius Aemilianus; the exact race of each of these emperors is often debated.
100s to 400s	Ancient Rome incorporates Africa into its empire; Africans become members of the Roman government.
600s to 900s	Muslims from Africa launch attacks and eventually occupy parts of Italy.
700s	Muslims from Africa begin to launch attacks and occupy parts of the Iberian peninsula; Muslims retain control over parts of the Iberian peninsula until 1492.

1000s to 1400s	Development of the Black Madonna tradition in Europe, which depicts Mary, the mother of Jesus, with dark skin tones.
1099	Nugaymath Turquia leads a contingent of 300 female Moorish archers, called "Amazons" during the Almoravid siege of Valencia, which led to the death of the Spanish hero El Cid.
1100s	Prester John, a mythical figure, is thought by Europeans to rule over a distant Christian empire beyond the Islamic world; over time, this empire is believed to be in Africa.
1194	Holy Roman Emperor Henry VI is accompanied by turbaned black trumpeters on his entry into Sicily.
1200	Feirefiz is a courtly knight and the biracial half-brother of the main character Parzival in the Middle High German epic poem *Parzival* by Wolfram von Eschenbach.
1200s	Sir Morien, a black Moorish knight, is the subject of a romantic epic poem written in medieval Dutch set in the mythical era of King Arthur of England and the Knights of the Round Table.
1200s	Mourana Gil, a Moor, becomes the mistress of King Afonso III of Portugal.
1200s to 1300s	Black Africans are used frequently in the iconography of the Holy Roman Empire to express the desire of particular emperors to extend their sovereignty beyond Europe.
1240s	Earliest surviving image of Maurice, the important soldier and Catholic saint, as a black African is made in Magdeburg, Germany.
Late 1200s	The *Romance of Palamedes* is written. Palamedes, a Moorish knight, is a member of the Knights of the Round Table in Arthurian legend and a prominent character in the tale of Tristan and Isolde.
Late 1200s	The heraldic symbol of the Moor's head, which depicts the profile of a black African Muslim, begins to appear on the traditional flags of many southern European regions.
Late 1200s	Many coats of arms in Europe begin to feature black Africans.
1300s	The Muslim community in Lucera in southern Italy, which included many black Africans, is suppressed by Charles II of Anjou.

1300s	One of the Three Magi who worshipped the infant Jesus of Nazareth begins to be shown as black in European art.
1300s to 1400s	Black Death results in the increase of slaves in Europe, many of whom come from Africa.
1400s to 1600s	The Age of Exploration takes place.
1400s to 1500s	Renaissance art features many representations of black African slaves and domestic servants and their often manumitted descendants in Europe.
1400s to 1800s	African pirates known as Barbary pirates or Ottoman corsairs attack southern European cities and ships in the Mediterranean.
1450s	Pope Nicholas V issues papal bulls granting the right to reduce pagans, Muslims, and other non-Christians to slavery.
1490s to early 1500s	The Kingdom of the Kongo converts to Christianity and begins to send delegations to Portugal.
1492	Pedro Alonso Niño, a Spanish navigator of black African descent, pilots the Niña during Columbus's first voyage to the Americas.
Early 1500s	Bartolomé de las Casas encourages the use of black African slaves in the New World instead of the native population.
1500s	The trans-Atlantic slave trade begins.
1500s	Leo Africanus, a former slave of Pope Leo X, publishes a multivolume survey of African geography.
1500s	John Blanke, a "Moor," has a long career as a trumpeter at the Tudor Court in England.
1513	Nuflo de Olano, a black slave, accompanies explorer Vasco Nuñez de Balboa when his expedition sights the Pacific Ocean.
1526	Benedict the Moor, the son of African slaves and patron saint of Palermo, is born in Sicily.
1537	Alessandro de Medici, whose mother was a black servant, dies; he was the last of the senior branch of the Italian Medici family to rule Florence and the first to become a hereditary duke.
1574 to 1585	Juan Latina, a black Spanish poet, publishes three volumes of poetry in Latin.

1590s	Luce Negro, a famous black courtesan who ran a brothel in London, may have been the inspiration for the "Dark Lady" of Shakespeare's sonnets.
Early 1600s	Leonardo Ortíz works as an Afro-Spanish lawyer of the Royal Court in Spain.
1600s	Henrique (or Enrique) Dias, a black African soldier from Brazil, serves in the Portuguese army during several colonial campaigns.
1603	William Shakespeare writes *Othello*.
1603	Andrés de Claramonte publishes *El Valiente Negro de Flandes* ("The Valiant Negro of Flanders").
1640s	António Vieira, a biracial Jesuit missionary and Portuguese diplomat during the seventeenth century, becomes an advisor to the king of Portugal.
Mid-1600s	Sebastian Gomez, a former slave, becomes a student of Bartolomé Esteban Murillo, a famous Spanish painter.
Mid-1600s	Juan de Pareja, a slave of African descent who worked in the household of Spanish painter Diego Velázquez, eventually earns his freedom and becomes a noted painter.
1665	Nabo the Moor, a favorite at the court of Queen Marie-Teresa of France, disappears; he is speculated to be the infamous Man in the Iron Mask.
1685	The *Code Noir* is adopted in France to regulate the status of slaves and freemen.
1687	Aniaba (or Aniabi), a young African man, is presented at the court of French King Louis XIV.
1688	Aphra Behn publishes *Oroonoko or, the Royal Slave*.
Late 1600s to 1700s	Enlightenment philosophers develop theories on race and slavery.
1700s	Jacobus Capitein, a former African slave, earns a doctorate from a university in the Netherlands; he becomes famous for his defense of the institution of slavery.
1700s	Francis Barber, a former slave from Jamaica, works in England as an assistant to the famous lexicographer Samuel Johnson.
1701	The Free Soil Principle is recognized in England by Lord Holt.

1707	Tsar Peter the Great of Russia serves as godfather to Abraham Hannibal, a former black African slave who would become a noted Russian general, military engineer, and governor.
1723	Slavery is abolished in Russia.
1736	Anton Wilhelm Amo, a former African slave and first sub-Saharan African to attend any university in Europe, becomes a lecturer at a university in Germany.
1767	The case of Jonathan Strong is heard in England.
1770	James Albert Ukawsaw Gronniosaw publishes his slave narrative in England.
1772	The Somerset Case suggests that slavery is inconsistent with English common law.
1773	African American slave Phillis Wheatley publishes her *Poems on Various Subjects, Religious and Moral* in England.
1773	Bernardin de Saint-Pierre publishes *Journey to Mauritius*, which criticizes slavery.
1777	Bill Richmond, the slave who executed American Revolutionary war hero Nathan Hale, arrives in England, where he becomes a famous boxer.
1777	A French Royal Declaration prohibits the arrival of any new "black, mulatto, or person of color of either sex" into metropolitan France.
1778	A French Council of State *arrêt* prohibits interracial marriages and punishes the offending couples with expulsion to the colonies; all registered blacks are to carry identification cards.
1778	The Royal Pragmatic is issued in Spain to curb unacceptable interracial marriages.
1780	Ignatius Sancho, a former slave, dies; he was the first black African prose writer to publish his work in England and the first black Briton known to have voted in an election.
1786	Jean-Baptiste Lislet-Geoffroy, a French scientist and the son of a former African slave, becomes the first person of African descent elected to the Academy of Science in Paris.
1786	Abolitionist Thomas Clarkson publishes the English version of *An Essay on the Slavery and Commerce of the Human Species, Particularly the African.*

1787	The Society for the Abolition of the Slave Trade is founded in England.
1787	Sierra Leone is founded through English efforts as a home for emancipated slaves.
1787	Quobna Ottobah Cugoano publishes *Thoughts and Sentiments on the Evil and Wicked Traffic of the Slavery and Commerce of the Human Species*.
1788	The Society of the Friends of the Blacks is founded in France.
1789	*The Interesting Narrative of the Life of Olaudah Equiano, or Gustavus Vassa, the African* is published.
1789	Black servant Ignatius Fortuna dies in Germany as a wealthy and respected man.
1790	Vincent Ogé, a biracial merchant from Saint-Domingue, returns to the Caribbean to initiate a doomed rebellion after unsuccessfully petitioning the French National Assembly to give free *gens de couleur* the right to vote.
1790s	Thomas-Alexandre Dumas, the son of a black slave and a French aristocrat, becomes a general in France during the French Revolution.
1790s	Black and biracial deputies from Saint-Domingue arrive in France during the French Revolution.
1791	The Haitian Revolution begins.
1792	During the French Revolution, a legion composed of all black soldiers is created and placed under the command of Chevalier de Saint-Georges, the son of a black African slave and a French aristocrat.
1794	The French Revolutionary government abolishes slavery.
1795	Madame de Staël publishes *Mirza*.
1796	After the death of Angelo Soliman, a former African slave popular at the Habsburg court, the Holy Roman Emperor, Francis II of Austria, claims the former slave's body and has it flayed and stuffed to be put on display in his private museum.
1800s	A series of revolutions for independence in Latin America and the Caribbean against European countries take place; many revolutionary leaders and soldiers are of black African descent.
1800s	Scientific racism is developed in Europe.

1800s to early 1900s	Many African American intellectuals, artists, and writers travel to Europe.
Early 1800s	Joseph Emidy, a former black African slave, becomes a celebrated violinist and composer in Georgian England.
Early 1800s	John Edmonstone, a free black in nineteenth-century England, teaches the young naturalist Charles Darwin the art of taxidermy.
Early 1800s	African American actor Ira Aldridge becomes a success in European theaters, performing many of Shakespeare's plays.
1802	Napoleon reintroduces slavery in the French colonies.
1802	Louis Delgrès leads a group of ex-slaves in Guadeloupe to resist the French forces returning and reintroducing slavery.
1802	George Bridgetower, a biracial musician dubbed "the Abyssinian Prince," becomes an acquaintance of composer Ludwig van Beethoven.
1807	Britain passes the Abolition of the Slave Trade Act.
1808 to 1815	Joachim Murat, a renowned cavalry leader of Moorish descent who was made a grand marshall of France by Napoleon Bonaparte, rules as king of Naples.
1811	The German writer Heinrich von Kleist publishes *The Engagement in San Domingo* about the Haitian Revolution.
1818	Nathaniel Wells, the son of a Welsh merchant and his black slave who inherited his father's Caribbean estates, becomes Britain's first black sheriff.
1820s	Nancy and Nero Prince, both African Americans, move to Russia and work for Tsar Alexander I and Tsar Nicholas I.
1820	William Davidson, a biracial radical activist, is a member of the infamous 1820 Cato Street Conspiracy in England.
1820s	Billy Waters, a black African sailor in the British navy, becomes famous as an eccentric street musician and actor in London.
1820s to 1840s	Cyrille Bissette, a man of biracial descent from Martinique, becomes known for his fiery writings in France that exposed the discrimination against free people of color in the French Caribbean and argues for the abolition of slavery.
1823	The British Anti-Slavery Society is founded.

1823	Madame de Duras publishes *Ourika*, the first full-fledged representation of a black person's interiority in European literature.
1824	Radical biracial abolitionist Robert Wedderborn publishes his autobiography, *The Horrors of Slavery*.
1825 to 1830	*Eugene Onegin*, written by the Russian literary icon Alexander Pushkin, descended from an African slave, is published serially.
1830s	Jean-Louis Michel, a famous swordsman and duelist in Napoleonic France, opens a fencing school in Montpellier.
1830s	Biracial children from well-to-do families in New Orleans are often sent to France to receive a formal education.
1831	The Brown Privilege Bill is passed.
1833	Slavery is outlawed in all British colonies.
1834	French Society for the Abolition of Slavery is founded.
1835 to 1840	Alexis de Tocqueville publishes his *Democracy in America*, which greatly influences European opinion of the United States and its inhabitants, including blacks.
1836	Victor Séjour migrates to Paris, where he writes *Le Mulâtre* (*The Mulatto*, 1837), the first known piece of fiction by an African American writer.
1840s	Abolitionist and former slave Frederick Douglass publishes a *Narrative of the Life of Frederick Douglass, an American Slave* (1845) and tours Europe for the first time.
1840s	Samuel Crowther, a native Nigerian, becomes ordained in England as an Anglican minister.
1844	Alexandre Dumas *père*, the grandson of a black slave, publishes *The Three Musketeers*.
1847	Sweden abolishes slavery after the slaves' freedom was bought by the state.
1848	Denmark and France abolish slavery.
1848	William Cuffay, a black British tailor and leader in the Chartist movement, is arrested in connection with a planned uprising.
1850s	Arthur de Gobineau, a French diplomat and writer, publishes his *Essay on the Inequality of the Races*.

1854	Mary Seacole is refused by British War Offices the right to serve as a nurse because of her ethnicity; she pays her own way to Crimea and becomes an independent nurse for the British army.
1860s	Famous Afro-Brazilian composer and abolitionist Antônio Carlos Gomes studies music in Italy.
1860s	Black British doctor James Africanus Beale Horton becomes an early advocate of African nationalism.
1860s to 1901	Afro-Cuban violinist Claudio Brindis de Sala becomes a sensation in Europe and German Kaiser Wilhelm II's official violinist.
1863	The Netherlands abolishes slavery, including in its colonies.
1869	Portugal abolishes slavery in its colonies.
1870	Spain passes the Moret Law.
1871	The Rio Branco Law of Free Birth takes effect in Brazil.
1870s	The European "Scramble for Africa" begins.
1881	Pierre Loti publishes *Le Roman d'un Saphi.*
1884–1885	Germany and France host the Berlin Conference to discuss European imperialism in Africa.
1887	John Mensah Sarbah becomes the first black barrister in England.
Late 1800s	W.E.B. Du Bois pursues graduate studies in Germany and becomes an advocate of Pan-Africanism.
1896	Josephine Bakhita, a former African slave, becomes a permanent member of the Canossian Sisters in Italy. She is later made a Catholic saint.
1897	After the death of José de Sousa Martins, a revered biracial doctor in Portugal, a quasi-cult forms around him followed by people looking to his spirit to intervene in their recovery of a medical condition.
1898	Black British musician Samuel Coleridge-Taylor composes *Hiawatha's Wedding Feast.*
1900	First Pan-African Congress is held in London.
Early 1900s	Germany bans interracial marriages in its African colonies.

Early 1900s	Blaise Diagne, deputy for Senegal in the French National Assembly, becomes the first black African to serve in the French Chamber of Deputies.
1902	A delegation of Duala chiefs arrives in Germany to attempt to make complaints about the ongoing oppression and mistreatment by the German colonial administration.
1904	Mary Church Terrell is the only black woman to attend the Berlin International Congress of Women in Germany.
1906	John Archer becomes one of the first people of black African descent to hold public office in Britain.
1908	Leopold II transfers control of the Congo to the Belgian government amid protest by white European and black intellectuals over the Congo's administration.
1914	Rudolf Duala Manga, a Duala king and paramount chief educated in Germany, is executed as a resistance leader against the German colonial authorities.
1914–18	Black colonial troops and labor are used in World War I.
1916	Sosthene Mortenol, whose parents were former black slaves, is a French naval captain appointed commander of the Air Defenses of Paris during World War I.
1919	Race disturbances occur in Glasgow.
1920s	Several mixed race children are born to black colonial occupational troops and white German women in the German Rhineland. They are later persecuted by the Nazis.
1920s	African American jazz takes Europe by storm.
1920s	African American Josephine Baker first emerges as a European superstar.
1921	René Maran, a French writer of Guyanese descent, becomes the first black recipient of the prestigious *Prix Goncourt*.
1926	Bakary Diallo writes of his experiences as a *tiralleur* in the French colonial army in World War I.
1929	The German Section of the League for the Defense of the Negro Race is formed.
1930s	Mahjub bin Adam Mohamed, a German colonial soldier in Africa during World War I, becomes a university teacher and actor in Germany before being persecuted by the Nazis.

1930s	Nicolás Guillén Batista, a noted Afro-Cuban poet, goes to Spain during the Spanish Civil War.
1930s	Many African American volunteers fight against Francisco Franco in the Spanish Civil War.
1930 to 1940s	The Nazis persecute blacks in Germany and other parts of Europe, including Josef Nassy and Valaida Snow, performing forced sterilizations and sending them to concentration camps.
1930s to 1940s	Larbi Benbarek becomes an African sports celebrity in Europe.
1931	Harold Moody establishes the League of Coloured Peoples (LCP) in Britain.
1933	Hilarius Gilges, a young Afro-German dancer and communist from Dusseldorf, Germany, is murdered by the Nazis.
1935	The *"L'Etudiant Noir,"* the forerunner of the Negritude Movement, is created in France.
1935	The International African Service Bureau is founded in England by C.L.R. James and George Padmore.
1938	Italy bans marriage between citizens and colonial subjects.
1939–1945	Black colonial troops and labor are used in European military forces in World War II; many African Americans are stationed and fight in Europe.
1940s to 1950s	Several biracial children are born to German mothers and African American servicemen stationed in Europe.
1943	The Imperial Hotel refuses to grant lodgings to the famous black British cricketer, Learie Constantine.
1945	The European decolonization of Africa begins.
1948	The *Empire Windrush* brings 500 Afro-Caribbean migrants to Britain, marking the beginning of an immigration boom.
1948	Jean Genet, a black French writer, is convicted of theft for the tenth time and several French writers successfully petition for a "pardon in advance."
1949	Félix Éboué, the first black French colonial governor and hero of World War II, becomes the first black French citizen to have his remains placed in the Panthéon, a mausoleum reserved for the greatest figures in French history.

1952	Frantz Fanon publishes *Black Skin, White Masks*.
1954	The French government selects African American Eugene Bullard, who served with distinction in the French military during World War I and as a spy during World War II, to light the flame at the Tomb of the Unknown Soldier under the Arc de Triomphe.
1956	First International Congress of Black Writers and Artists is held in France.
1958	Notting Hill Race Riot takes place in London.
1959	Claudia Jones, a Trinidadian activist and journalist, introduces the Notting Hill Carnival.
1959	The Africa Institute is founded in the Soviet Union for research on Africa.
1960s	Lumumba University opens in the Soviet Union to bring students from Africa study to the U.S.S.R.
1960s	African American Civil Rights leaders Martin Luther King, Jr. and Malcolm X travel to Europe to encourage blacks to stand up for social equality.
1960s to 1970s	The Campaign Against Racial Discrimination (CARD) is launched as a protest initiative in Britain to eliminate racism.
1965	Britain passes the Race Relations Act.
1970s	The Notting Hill Carnival in London is transformed into a celebration of Caribbean identity.
1970s to 1980s	Brendon Batson becomes one of the first high-profile black British footballers.
1976	The Notting Hill Carnival Riot occurs in London.
1981	The Brixton race riots occur in England.
1982	Black Briton Val McCalla founds *The Voice*.
1983	David Dabydeen edits *The Black Presence in English Literature*.
1983	Léopold Sédar Senghor is elected a member of the prestigious French Academy.
1985–1986	The Initiative of Blacks in Germany (ISD) and Afro-German Women (ADEFRA) are founded.

1986	*Showing Our Colors: Afro-German Women Speak Out* is published.
1987	Diane Abbott becomes the first black woman to be elected to the House of Commons in the United Kingdom.
1987	Britain adopts the American concept of Black History Month, which in Britain is celebrated in October.
1987 to 2006	Martin Bernal published his three-volume *Black Athena*, a controversial work posing the argument that European classical civilization was primarily rooted in African and Asian cultures, and that previous scholars obscured the influences of these civilizations because of racism and anti-Semitism.
1990s	Afro-German entertainer Cherno Jobatey hosts a morning German television show.
1992	Afro-Caribbean writer Derek Walcott wins the Nobel Prize for Literature.
1993	Lennox Lewis becomes the first British world heavyweight champion in the twentieth century.
1994 to 2004	Arabella Kiesbauer hosts the daily talk-show *Arabella*, modeled on African American Oprah Winfrey's show *Oprah*, on German television.
1995	Scholar Julia Markus published her book arguing that famous English poet Elizabeth Barrett and her future husband, Robert Browning, were of biracial descent.
1996	Calixthe Beyala is awarded the *Grand Prix du Roman de l'Académie Française*.
2001	The French Senate adopts a law recognizing slavery and the slave trade as crimes against humanity.
2002	Penguin Classics publishes a collection of Linton Kwesi Johnson's poetry, *Mi Revalueshanary Fren*, making him the second living poet to receive such an edition.
2002	The remains of Saartjie (Sara) Baartman, derogatorily known as the "Hottentot Venus," who was exhibited and exploited in Europe as an attraction of the grotesque in the nineteenth century, are returned to South Africa by a French museum.
2002	Paul Boateng, a British Labour politician active in the black community for many years, becomes the first black cabinet minister in Britain.

2005	Black and Arab youths riot in the suburbs of Paris.
2005	The Representative Council of Black Associations (CRAN) is established in France.
2006	May 10 is designated a French national holiday to commemorate the abolition of slavery in France and its colonies.
2006	Harry Roselmack becomes the first black lead news anchor on French television.
2007	Adebari Rotimi is elected the first black mayor in Ireland.
2007	Black Briton Patricia Scotland becomes the first woman attorney general.
2007	African and European enforcement agencies increase surveillance of the coastline to reduce illegal African immigration to Europe.
2007	Black European Women's Congress held in Vienna.
2008	Aimé Césaire, one of the founders of the Francophone Negritude movement, dies.
2008	Noah Snow, who founded the first antiracist media watchdog organization in Germany, publishes a book on racism in Germany.

Alphabetical List of Entries

Topical List of Entries

Spain

K

Kiesbauer, Arabella (1969–)

Arabella Cosima-Asereba Kiesbauer is an Austrian television entertainer, model, musician, and writer of black African descent. She was born in Vienna, Austria, in 1969. After the separation of her mother, Hannelore, a German actress, and her father, Sammy Ammissah, an engineer from Ghana, Kiesbauer was raised in Vienna by her grandmother. At school, Kiesbauer studied journalism and dramaturgy.

Kiesbauer entered the entertainment industry as a presenter of the youth magazine *X-Large* on ORF, the Austrian public service television station, from 1989 to 1993, and as presenter of the series *Inter-City* on 3Sat from 1990 to 1991. She emerged as a celebrity after the success of her long-running daily talk show, *Arabella*, which aired on the German television station Pro7 from 1994 to 2004. The German daily talk show was inspired by the American talk show hosted by African American entertainer Oprah Winfrey. In 1995, Kiesbauer's fame made her the target of a letter bomb that injured her assistant.

In 2006, Kiesbauer began hosting a weekly late night talk show on the Berlin television station N24 TV. After only 40 shows, however, Kiesbauer claimed that the stress and fatigue of traveling from Vienna to Berlin regularly was too much for her private life to handle. She has also presented the ORF casting show *Starmania*. Kiesbauer has won numerous German awards for her television work, including the *Bayerischen Fernsehpreis* for Beste Talk-Newcomerin in 1994 and the media award *Das Goldene Kabel* in 1996.

Kiesbauer also works as a model and musician and has published books, including *Nobody Is Perfect!* (2001) and *Mein afrikanisches Herz* (*My African Heart*, 2007). She appeared on the cover and inside pages of the July 1995 issue of the German *Playboy* magazine. Kiesbauer also models and does promotions for Vögele Shoes. She issued a music CD entitled *Number One* in 1994. In 2004, Kiesbauer married Florens Eblinger, a Viennese businessman.

Arabella Kiesbauer, 2003. AP/Wide World Photo.

See also: Central Europe, Blacks in; Germany, Blacks in; Jobatey, Cherno; Music Industry, Blacks in the European; Television, Blacks in European.

Further Reading: The Official Web Page of Arabella Kiesbauer: http://www.arabella-kiesbauer. at/; Wieten, Jan, Graham Murdock, and Peter Dahlgren, eds. *Television Across Europe: A Comparative Introduction.* London: Sage Publications, 2000.

Eric Martone

Kincaid, Jamaica (1949–)

Jamaica Kincaid is a renowned black novelist and journalist from the British Caribbean. Kincaid was born in the former British colony of Antigua in 1949. Her birth name was Elaine Potter Richardson. After her family expressed disapproval of her career choice, she changed her name to Jamaica Kincaid in 1973. When she was young, Kincaid resided with her stepfather and her mother. Because Antigua was a British colony until 1967, Kincaid was educated under the British system. In 1965, she went to Westchester County in New York to work as an au pair.

As a young adult, Kincaid remained in New York and studied photography at the New School for Social Research. She eventually won a full scholarship to Franconia College in New Hampshire. Under the impression that she was too old to be a student, Kincaid dropped out of Franconia after one year and returned to New York to write for *Ingenue* magazine. During this time, she also began writing articles for *The Village Voice.* Her work for these publications attracted the *New Yorker*'s lead editor at the time, William Shawn. In 1978, Kincaid became a staff writer for *The New Yorker* and worked for the magazine until 1995.

Kincaid is most famous for her prolific career as a novelist. *Lucy* (1990) and *Annie John* (1985) are both autobiographical narratives. *Annie John's* success propelled Kincaid to critical acclaim. In 1985, she was among the three finalists for the international Ritz Paris Hemingway Award. A later novel, *Autobiography of My Mother* (1996), explores issues of colonialism as well as her troublesome relationship with her mother. In 1997, Kincaid published *My Brother*, which focused on her experiences with her brother struggling against HIV/AIDS. Her recent novel *Mr. Potter* (2003) explores Kincaid's troubled relationship with her father.

See also: Colonies in the Caribbean, British; Literature, Blacks in British.

Further Reading: Birbalsingh, Frank. *Jamaica Kincaid: From Antigua to America.* New York: St. Martin's Press, 1996; Ferguson, Moira. "A Lot of Memory: An Interview with Jamaica Kincaid." *Kenyon Review* 16:1 (Winter 1994): 163–188; Ferguson, Moira. *Colonialism and Gender Relations from Mary Wollstonecraft to Jamaica Kincaid: East Caribbean Connections.* New York: Columbia University Press, 1994; Ferguson, Moira. *Jamaica Kincaid: Where the Land Meets the Body.* Charlottesville: University Press of Virginia, 1994.

Jennifer Westmoreland Bouchard

King, Martin Luther, Jr.

Martin Luther King Jr. (1929–1968) was an African American Baptist pastor and famous nonviolent Civil Rights Movement leader from 1955 to his assassination in Memphis, Tennessee, in 1968. He won the 1964 Nobel Peace Prize. King's sermons, speeches (such as his 1963 "I Have a Dream" speech), identification with peaceful revolutionary Mahatma Gandhi, and influence on freedom movements around the world have made him a universal messenger for peace. His influence and message were keenly felt in Britain before, during, and after King's two London visits in the 1960s.

In 1961, the London-based Campaign for Nuclear Disarmament (CND), which had adopted King's ideas, rhetoric, and aspects of his nonviolent protest ethos, sponsored his visit to preach from St. Paul's Cathedral's pulpit. King delivered an altered version of his favorite sermon, "The Three Dimensions of a Complete Life," to about 4,000 people. During King's 1964 London visit, on his way to collect the Nobel Prize in Oslo, he spoke against British restrictions on immigration and urged Britain to address racial issues without delay. Both trips also gave King the opportunity to address pressing international issues such as apartheid in South Africa.

King's influence on civil rights struggles in 1960s Britain was substantial. For example, he inspired the creation of the **Campaign against Racial Discrimination (CARD),** Oxford University's SCORE (the Student Campaign for Racial Equality), and the Birmingham Coordinating Committee. To make a self-satisfied British society take notice, these organizations adopted techniques from the American Civil Rights Movement, ranging from sit-ins to boycotts, against color-bar buses and cafes.

Thus King's trips and British civil rights struggles emphasize that his inspiration and influence in London (and Britain) cannot be fully grasped without taking into account both the British and global contexts of decolonization and racial turmoil, in addition to immigration. Indeed, between 1955 and 1968, a considerable number of Caribbean, African, and South Asian immigrants arrived in Britain. Decolonization affected European imperial powers, whereas, to both Britons and King, the problem of race relations seemed a universal, rather than national, phenomenon. Furthermore, when filtered through the British minority struggles prism, King's inspiration and influence played a considerable part in two British antidiscrimination legislations: the Race Relations Acts of 1965 and 1968. These acts made expressions of racial prejudice unlawful in public places (excluding boarding houses and shops) and banned racial discrimination in housing, employment, and all public services.

These laws were largely not enforced, and the combination of police harassment, institutional racism, and visits to Britain by radical African American leaders Malcolm X and Stokely Carmichael (also known as Kwame Ture) gave birth to a more militant black British struggle even before King's death. Similarly, contemporary evaluations of King's influence in London (and Britain) should not overlook the fact that his message might not be effective in tackling the intricacies of Britain's class structure, ethnic, and religious diversities. And yet, 40 years after his assassination, (black) London looks up to King for solutions to youth involvement in gun and knife crimes, and gang cultures.

See also: Black British; Britain, Blacks in; Malcolm X in London; Representative Council of Black Associations (CRAN).

Further Reading: Carson, Clayborne, and Shepard, Kris. A *Call to Conscience: The Landmark Speeches of Dr. Martin Luther King, Jr.* New York: Warner Books, 2001; Lewis, David Levering. *Martin Luther King: A Critical Biography.* London: Allen Lane/Penguin Press, 1970; Sewell, Mike. "British Responses to Martin Luther King Jr. and the Civil Rights Movement, 1954–1968." In Brian Ward and Tony Badger, eds. *The Making of Martin Luther King and the Civil Rights Movement.* New York: New York University Press, 1996.

Saër Maty Bâ

L

Ladinos, Black

Black *ladinos* were persons of African heritage who were familiar with Spanish or Portuguese culture and Spanish or Portuguese languages. Many of them had been born in Spain or Portugal. Blacks born in the Americas were later also referred to as *ladinos*. The full title given them was *negros ladinos*, or "Latinized Blacks." Although mostly slaves, they filled a number of important roles in the Spanish Americas. Besides working as domestic servants and in mines, they also fought against the Amerindians, helped enforce Spanish rule over the Amerindians, and worked as skilled craftsmen or managers for their colonial masters. The importance of the *ladinos* in the colonies was eventually superseded by the large number of Africans unfamiliar with Spanish or Portuguese culture/language brought directly to the New World.

In fifteenth-century Spain, African slaves were not uncommon. Many were purchased by Portuguese merchants in North Africa, then resold in port cities like Valencia, Barcelona, and, especially, Seville. Africans were only one group from which slaves came. Others included Jews, Muslims, whites, and natives of the Canary Islands. Spanish tradition allowed slaves to buy their freedom if they and their owners could agree on a price. Although some free blacks could be found, they still suffered from social and economic discrimination. All blacks were considered to be loyal, but inferior to whites and needing supervision. They were taught Spanish and officially converted to Christianity.

Some of the first Spanish **conquistadors** in the Americas were blacks. For example, Pedro Alonso Niño, a navigator who accompanied Christopher Columbus on his first voyage to America, was a free black born in Spain. The Spanish crown was anxious to prevent disloyal subjects from entering the New World. In 1501, Queen Isabella II of Spain decreed that Jews, Muslims, and newly converted Christians could not immigrate to the Americas. She made an exception for *ladinos*, however, who had been born into Christianity. In 1502, the first Spanish governor on Hispaniola, Nicolas de

Ovando, brought a number of *ladinos* with him as domestic servants. Ovando soon reported that some *ladinos* had escaped slavery and formed their own communities in the mountains of Hispaniola. A temporary ban on the immigration of *ladinos* to the New World was ordered. In 1505, a year after Isabella died, her husband, King Ferdinand, ordered that *ladinos* be sent to the colonies to work in agricultural and mining industries. Ferdinand had learned that the Amerindians were dying in large numbers and a shortage of workers was hampering production. Hundreds of *ladinos* were sent from Spain and, by 1514, the number of *ladinos* on Hispaniola was greater than that of whites.

At first, the Spanish settlers felt safer with *ladino* workers. They knew Spanish customs and seemed loyal. In 1522, however, disgruntled *ladinos* led a revolt in Santo Domingo that threatened the white settlement. Although quickly crushed, *ladinos* were no longer assumed to be loyal. White leaders feared they would make common cause with the Amerindians to expel the Spanish from the Americas. Royal decrees on February 25, 1530, and September 13, 1532 specifically ordered that no white, Jewish, Muslim, or *ladino* slaves be sent to the Americas. Instead, a royal monopoly known as the *asiento* was established to bring black slaves directly from Africa to the Americas. These slaves, known as *bozales*, were believed to be more peaceful and obedient, partly because they did not know Spanish. Ironically, the *ladinos* still brought higher prices when they were sold, thanks to their usually superior skills and knowledge of Spanish.

Although *ladinos* were banned from immigration to the Americas by 1530, they played an important role in the conquest of the New World. Many were skilled craftsmen, such as masons, carpenters, or blacksmiths. Their skills were necessary because many Spanish refused to immigrate. Others participated in the military conquest of the Amerindian peoples. Amerindians reportedly disliked *ladinos* because they were used by Spanish overlords to enforce rules and collect taxes.

See also: Age of Exploration; Colonies in Africa, Portuguese; Colonies in Africa, Spanish; Colonies in the Caribbean, Spanish; Portugal, Blacks in; Slave Trade, Portuguese; Slave Trade, Spanish; Spain, Blacks in; Spanish Army, Blacks in the.

Further Reading: Bennett, Herman L. *Africans in Colonial Mexico: Absolutism, Christianity, and Afro-Creole Consciousness, 1570–1640*. Bloomington: Indiana University Press, 2003; Landers, Jane, and Barry Robinson. *Slaves, Subjects, and Subversives: Blacks in Colonial Latin America*. Albuquerque: University of New Mexico Press, 2006; Rout, Leslie B., Jr. *The African Experience in Spanish America: 1502 to the Present Day*. New York: Cambridge University Press, 1976; Terrell, John Upton. *Estevanico the Black*. Los Angeles: Westernlore Press, 1968.

Tim J. Watts

Laine, Cleo (1927–)

Cleo Laine is recognized as among the best and most versatile all-around vocalists in Europe. Laine was born Clementina Dinah Campbell on October 28, 1927, in Southall, a primarily white, working-class district of London. Her Jamaican father, Alec, fought with the British during World War I. Her English mother, Minnie, was disowned by her parents for marrying a black man. Until the early 1950s, Laine performed occasionally, but did not pursue singing as a career. She married building tradesman George Langridge at age 18, and they bore a son, Stuart, in 1947.

Laine's career took off in 1951 when she successfully auditioned as a vocalist for a well-regarded London jazz group, the Johnny Dankworth Seven. She performed under their banner until 1958, during which time the group rose to popular fame, especially in England. Aficionados praised Laine's original and distinctive vocal style, her improvisation, and her ability to instill freshness into even the most familiar jazz standards.

In 1958, Laine married her bandleader, John Dankworth (having divorced Langridge the previous year) and made her dramatic stage debut as Della, the lead in the Royal Court Theatre's *Flesh to a Tiger*. Although the play received mixed reviews, critics singled out Laine's performance for favorable mention. A steady stream of roles in both musical and "straight" theater followed, including *The Seven Deadly Sins* in the 1961 Edinburgh Film Festival, *Hedda Gabler* in Canterbury in 1970, and the 1985 Broadway musical *The Mystery of Edwin Drood* (for which she received a Tony nomination). She appeared in more than 20 productions, as well as on television and film.

Despite Laine's dramatic achievements, her vocal career never languished. She continued to work with Dankworth in subsequent years while diversifying her repertoire. The 1964 Laine/Dankworth release *Shakespeare and All That Jazz* remains one of their most acclaimed works. They also appeared on BBC programs like the satirical *That Was The Week That Was*. In 1969, they established their first charity, the Wavendon All-Music Plan, which was devoted to musical education and performance in a variety of genres. Later, in 1999, they established a second charity, the Wavendon Foundation. During the 1960s, Laine bore two children, Alexander (in 1960) and Jacqueline (in 1963).

Between 1950 and 2003, Laine released more than 100 recordings in several styles. She is the only woman ever to have been nominated for the prestigious Grammy Award in the categories of jazz, pop, and classical music. She won a Grammy in 1983 for best female jazz vocalist, as well as a Lifetime Achievement distinction at the British Jazz Awards (2002). In 1997, she was made a Dame Commander of the British Empire for her services to music.

See also: Black British; Britain, Blacks in; Colonies in the Caribbean, British; Film, Blacks in European; Jazz, European Reception of; Music Industry, Blacks in the European; Television, Blacks in European; World War I, Black Participation in.

Further Reading: Collier, Graham. *Cleo and John: A Biography of the Dankworths.* London: Quartet Books, 1976; Laine, Cleo. *Cleo.* London: Simon and Schuster, 1994.

Amanda Bidnall

Larsen, Nella (1891–1964)

Nella Larsen was an African American librarian, nurse, and author famous for her 1920s novels published during the Harlem Renaissance. Larsen resisted forms of belonging based on exclusion. Her experiences in Europe during the 1890s to 1930s played an important role in this theme as they helped shape her daring "social consciousness" in a United States that emphasized racial divisions.

Larsen was born Nellie Walker to a working-class, immigrant married couple in Chicago. Her mother, Mary Hansen, was a white Danish seamstress; and her father, Peter Walker, was a black laborer from the Danish West Indies (U.S. Virgin Islands). Larsen had no recollection of her father. Her mother later married a white man, Peter Larsen, who resented the girl's presence. The birth of Larsen's half-sister only exacerbated her feeling of disconnection.

By the late 1920s, Larsen had attended and been expelled from Fisk University in Tennessee after one year for rebellion against strict rules for girls, had lived in Copenhagen, and had studied nursing in New York City. She had also been superintendent of nurses at The Tuskegee Institute in Alabama, but left within one year because she was unable to stand its strict control of women. She then joined New York's Lincoln Hospital and the New York City Department of Health. Larsen helped organize the New York Public Library's "Negro Art" exhibit, and eventually left nursing to train and work as a librarian. She wrote children's games and riddles, the semiautobiographical novels *Quicksand* (1928) and *Passing* (1929), and the short story "Sanctuary" (1930). Larsen returned to nursing in the 1950s, a profession she practiced until her death.

Europe is crucial to a contemporary reassessment of Larsen. Larsen went to Denmark twice: once at the age of 4 with her mother and half-sister to visit her grandparents in the Jutland Peninsula, and again at the age of 16 to live with her relatives in Copenhagen after her expulsion from Fisk. During the first trip (1895–1898), Larsen, seen as different and exotic, spoke Danish and learned the children's games and riddles that she was to translate and publish two decades later. The second trip (1908–1912) made her feel like Helga Crane from *Quicksand:* an oddity. As a culturally and racially mixed woman, Larsen did not belong in Denmark and decided to return to the United States. This latter experience would end in bitter disappointment, with flashes of joy brought about by Larsen's further interactions with Europe.

Larsen read and borrowed themes, narrative, and character development techniques from European writers, a few of whom Larsen met. It is now established that *Quicksand* should be read with Peter Jens Jacobsen, Henrik Ibsen, and Anatole France in mind and that Larsen met Federico García Lorca in New York and introduced him to a "Negro" life in Harlem recorded in *El Poeta en Nueva York*. In the 1930s, Larsen traveled extensively in Europe as a Guggenheim Fellow. Escaping from her crumbling marriage to black physicist Elmer Imes, she went to Barcelona, Madrid, Mallorca, Málaga, Marseille, Lisbon (where she was struck by the lack of curiosity about black people), Nice, Monte Carlo, and Paris, where she lived at the height of singer-entertainer **Josephine Baker**'s stardom.

See also: Authors in Europe, African-American; Du Bois, W.E.B.; Scandinavia, Blacks in.

Further Reading: Hutchinson, George. *In Search of Nella Larsen: The Biography of the Color Line.* Cambridge, MA: Belknap Press, 2006; Larson, Charles, ed. *The Complete Fiction of Nella Larsen: Quicksand, Passing, and the Stories.* New York: Anchor Books, 2001.

Saër Maty Bâ

Las Casas, Bartolomé de (1474/1484?–1566)

Bartolomé de las Casas was a Spanish priest who spent his life living in the New World and in Spain working for the rights of the indigenous people and arguing against slavery using theological reasoning. He is often referred to as the "Father of Liberation Theology," or "Father of the Indians." It was las Casas, however, who suggested the use of black Africans as laborers in America to counter the enslavement of the indigenous people.

Although there is conflicting scholarship of the date of his birth (1474 or 1484), las Casas was born in Seville, Spain. His father was a soldier who sailed with Christopher Columbus in his first voyage from Spain to the New World in 1492. While his father was away amassing wealth from his endeavors with Columbus, las Casas attended schools in Spain. By 1502, he had completed his studies in law and theology. Also in 1502, las Casas took his first trip to the New World with the conquistador Gonzalo Fernández de Oviedo and settled on the island of Hispaniola. While there, las Casas worked as a soldier and was given an *encomienda*, which was a piece of land that included the indigenous people living on it, in reward for his services. It was during this time that las Casas first began to notice the treatment of the native population. Returning to Spain in 1506, las Casas continued his studies for the priesthood, was ordained a deacon and then later a priest.

On his return to Hispaniola, on more than one occasion, las Casas witnessed individual executions or mass slayings of the indigenous people. Such events led him to give up his claim on the lives of the natives on his *encomienda* in 1514. It is at this time that las Casas began preaching what would eventually come to be termed *liberation theology*. The idea behind liberation theology stems from the Christian teachings of Jesus as not only savior, but as a freer of the oppressed. To prevent the enslavement of the native population in the Caribbean, however, las Casas suggested that black Africans be used in America instead. In Christian theology at that time, blacks were believed to be divinely cursed. Although he later changed his mind on this issue after he witnessed the effects on slavery on Africans, Africans were increasingly forced from their homes in Africa to work as slaves in the Spanish Caribbean.

Besides preaching and working among the natives of the New World, las Casas was named Bishop of Chiapas (Guatemala) in 1544 and wrote many works on the subject of liberation theology as well as historical and anthropological works of the New World. He died and was buried at the Convent of Santa Maria de Atocha in Madrid, Spain, in 1566.

See also: Abolition of Slavery, Spanish; Age of Exploration; Cain, Theory of Descent of Blacks from; Colonies in the Caribbean, Spanish; Conquistadors, Black; Hamitic Myth; Slave Trade, Spanish.

Further Reading: Brion, Marcel. *Bartolome de las Casas.* New York: E. P. Dutton, 1929.

Robert Nave

Latin American Colonial Revolutions, Blacks in

The creation and expansion of colonial empires in Latin America were shaped from their onset by the rise and fall of several riots, rebellions, and revolutions, which were either led or supported by blacks in the Caribbean and in South America. During the movements for independence of these colonies in the eighteenth and nineteenth centuries, freed blacks and slaves read the winds of change in the volatile environments of the plantation and the expanding urban colonial settings to advance their own self-determining projects of emancipation within the new ideals of republicanism and national identity.

The participation of blacks in Latin American colonial revolutions can be distinguished in two forms of engagement: first, the one in which black slaves worked from the inside, fighting for the independence of the colony and expecting to eventually win their freedom, and second, all those attempts in which blacks fought against colonial rule for their freedom, regardless of any connections to the shifting conjuncture of the political moment. Regardless of their magnitude, complexity, success, or failure, such as the **Haitian Revolution for Independence** in 1791, or the Muslim revolt in Bahia in 1835, these events show that each of them served as a building block for future action.

This differentiation is important for several reasons. In the case of blacks that engaged in revolutionary movements for independence as members of a white anticolonial army, the integrated black divisions were invariably seen as ways to contain loses of white soldiers. In general, they were given the worst and most dangerous jobs. In returning from these campaigns, their efforts would often be overlooked. As a result, in some cases, blacks would still have to fight against a bureaucratic process in order for promises of freedom to be acknowledged and finally granted. These contingents of emancipated blacks, however, represented a small portion compared to the majority that still remained enslaved. In the case of the blacks that looked for freedom by their own means in association with other enslaved ones, their initiative and tenacity were determining factors that usually led to the establishment of a chain of events demonstrating that blacks had their own resistance movement that could not be encompassed by the colonial desire of emancipation from Europe.

The prime example is the Haitian Revolution. A slave revolt in 1791 on Saint Domingue ultimately resulted in the establishment of Haiti, the first independent black republic. Inspired by the ideals of the French Revolution, this movement was a powerful influence on the end of the slave trade and a benchmark against slavery that shaped abolitionist ideas in the United States, Europe, and Latin America. Centuries before the Haitian Revolution emerged as the most emblematic case of colonial revolution made by the slaves themselves, however, the maroons in Jamaica, Cuba, and other locations in the Caribbean fought several wars against the British, Spanish, and French.

As movements for independence begin to take shape in the colonies in Latin America during the nineteenth century, the participation of blacks in the armed forces of countries such as Argentina and Brazil provided an insight into how they were quick to understand that they could create a platform to demand emancipation and citizenship, which they used afterward to guarantee the freedom of others still in captivity.

The Black Legions of Buenos Aires is one among many examples that could be drawn from Brazil, Cuba, or Venezuela to illustrate several characteristics that are present in the participation of blacks in military institutions in those countries. They served in the army in expectation of three things: freedom, civil equality, and social mobility.

The symbol of a military unit represented for these men the possibility of manumission sponsored by the state, which offered better guarantees than a business agreement with a private party that could be revoked, undone, or not upheld. The continuous need for more men for the anticolonial struggle, and the internal wars within Latin America during the postcolonial period, demonstrates that enlisting in the army became established as a desirable option for free blacks and slaves, especially in urban settings.

Another example is that of the Black Militia Officers of Salvador, in Brazil. These officers struggled to establish a place for themselves in the state apparatus during the changes from a colonial empire in the 1790s, through the independence period in 1822, and the liberal "second" empire in the 1830s under Pedro II. These black officers held great expectations for the independent Brazil that they helped to create. As a result of their efforts, they became the representatives of the freed black Brazilians. The liberal reforms that started in the 1820s proposed, and finally abolished, the militia in 1831, thereby putting an end to the dreams of the participants of the Henriques, as the black militias were then nicknamed.

See also: Biassou, Georges; Colonies in the Caribbean, British; Colonies in the Caribbean, Dutch; Colonies in the Caribbean, French; Colonies in the Caribbean, Spanish; Delgrés, Louis; L'Ouverture, Toussaint; Slave Revolts in the British Caribbean; Spanish Army, Blacks in the.

Further Reading: Andrien, Kenneth J. *The Human Tradition in Colonial Latin America: The Human Tradition around the World.* Wilmington: Scholarly Resources, 2002; Davis, Darién J. *Beyond Slavery: The Multilayered Legacy of Africans in Latin America and the Caribbean.* Lanham, MD: Rowman and Littlefield, 2007; Hart, Richard. *Slaves Who Abolished Slavery.* Kingston, Jamaica: Institute of Social and Economic Research, University of the West Indies, 1980; James, Cyril L. R. *The Black Jacobins: Toussaint L'Ouverture and the San Domingo Revolution.* London: Penguin, 2001; Kraay, Hendrik. *Afro-Brazilian Culture and Politics: Bahia, 1790s to 1990s.* Armonk, NY: M. E. Sharpe, 1998; Landers, Jane, and Barry Robinson. *Slaves, Subjects, and Subversives: Blacks in Colonial Latin America.* Albuquerque: University of New Mexico Press, 2006; Naro, Nancy Priscilla. *Blacks, Coloureds, and National Identity in Nineteenth-Century Latin America.* London: Institute of Latin American Studies, 2003; Reis, João José. *Slave Rebellion in Brazil: The Muslim Uprising of 1835 in Bahia.* Baltimore: Johns Hopkins University Press, 1993; Segal, Ronald. *The Black Diaspora.* London: Faber, 1995.

Augusto Ciuffo

Latino, Juan (1518–1596)

Juan Latino was a black African poet and humanist in Renaissance Spain. He was born in Baena in 1518, the son of a slave belonging to Luis Fernández de Córdoba, the Duke of Sessa. It is possible that the Duke of Sessa was also his father. Along with his master's son, Latino was sent to Grenada to be educated. In his studies, Latino excelled in classical languages and music. In 1545, he received a degree from the University of Granada.

After receiving his freedom, Latino received an academic position in Grenada. Luis Fernández de Córdoba's son, Gonzalo Fernández de Córdoba, became Latino's protector. In 1547 or 1548, Latino married one of his high society students, Ana Carleval. The dramatist Diego Ximénez de Enciso (1585–1633) later wrote a comedy entitled *Juan Latino* relating the events of the interracial love affair between Latino and his wife.

Between 1573 and 1585, Latino published three volumes of poetry in Latin. He contemplated on the condition of being black and rejected a social hierarchy derived from the color of one's skin. An example of this is Latino's poem, *"Asturias Carmen,"* which was dedicated to Juan of Austria following his military victory over Muslim insurrectionists in Grenada known as the War of the Alpujarras (1568–1572). In the poem, Latino raises the position of blacks by connecting them to biblical Ethiopia and rejecting ideas promoting the natural existence of slavery. In a reversal of fate, he imagines an Ethiopia in which whites occupy a subordinate position in society and praises being black.

See also: Cain, Theory of Descent of Blacks from; Colonies in Africa, Spanish; Colonies in the Caribbean, Spanish; Hamitic Myth; Interracial Marriages, Laws Banning; Renaissance, Blacks in the; Slave Trade, Spanish; Spain, Blacks in.

Further Reading: Earle, T. F., and K.J.P. Lowe, eds. *Black Africans in Renaissance Europe.* New York: Cambridge University Press, 2005; Spratlin, V. B. *Juan Latino, Slave and Humanist.* New York: Spinner Press, 1938.

E. Agateno Mosca

Le Bon, Gustave (1841–1931)

Gustave Le Bon was a French psychologist, sociologist, and physicist. He wrote several works in which he explained his theories. He is well known for his work on herd behavior and crowd psychology. He also elaborated theories regarding national traits and racial superiority.

Le Bon was born in France in 1841 and he studied medicine there. From the 1860s to 1880s, Le Bon toured various parts of Europe, Asia, and Africa. During his travels, he wrote on archaeology and anthropology. In 1894, he established his scientific reputation when he published *The Psychology of Peoples.* The next year, Le Bon published *The Crowd: A Study of the Popular Mind.* The book was a bestseller and Le Bon became a fixture in French intellectual circles. He also contributed to debates in physics with his book, *The Evolution of Matter.* In 1898, Le Bon argued that he observed a kind of radiation that he termed "black light."

In 1910, Le Bon published *Political Psychology and Social Defense.* In 1912, he published *The Psychology of Peoples.* Le Bon advocated racial inequality and believed non-Europeans to be inferior. He criticized European colonial expansion under the premise that it would be a fruitless endeavor, for inferior races could never reach the level of superior ones.

See also: Gobineau on Races and Slavery; New Imperialism; Scientific Racism.

Further Reading: Le Bon, Gustave. *The Psychology of Peoples: Its Influence on Their Evolution.* New York: Macmillan, 1898; Widener, Alice, ed. *Gustave Le Bon: The Man and His Works.* Indianapolis: Liberty, 1979.

E. Agateno Mosca

Levy, Andrea (1956–)

Andrea Levy is a **black British** writer best known for her fictional works depicting the life and complexities faced by minorities in Britain. She has four major novels to her credit and was most widely acclaimed for her fourth book, *Small Island* (2004), which has received numerous awards.

Levy's parents have influenced her writing. Although both her parents are native-born Jamaicans who moved to Britain at separate times in 1948, the story of her father is perhaps the most famous. Her father was one of approximately 500 West Indians coming from the Caribbean on the ship *Empire Windrush*. Many of these people, mostly men, were moving to Britain after performing military service in World War II. The arrival of the ship in a homogeneous Britain created some controversy. With the arrival of the *Windrush*, Britain started to become more multicultural, thus making the name of the ship famous.

Levy was born in 1956 in London, where she still resides. She did not start writing until later in life. She describes herself as a "late reader" and states that television had a greater influence on her than did literature in her earlier years. She did not read a book of fiction until she was 23 years old, believing that there was nothing to be learned by reading fiction. When she did begin to write her novels, however, Levy focused on the experience of being black in a predominantly white Britain.

To date, Levy has penned four novels: *Every Light in the House Burnin'* (1994), which is semi-autobiographical; *Never Far from Nowhere* (1996); *Fruit of the Lemon* (1999); and *Small Island*, for which she is most famous. *Small Island* won the Orange Prize in Britain, which is a prestigious literary award given to women authors in Britain.

See also: Britain, Blacks in; Colonies in the Caribbean, British; Literature, Blacks in British; World War II, Black Participation in.

Further Reading: Fleming, Robert. "Clean sweep: Andrea Levy Defines What It Is to Be Black, British and a Literary Lioness." *Black Issues Book Review* 7:4 (July 2005): 16 (2).

Robert Nave

Lewis, Lennox (1965–)

Lennox Claudius Lewis, a black Briton, is a retired professional heavyweight boxer who often referred to himself as "the pugilist specialist." In his boxing career, he was an Olympic gold medalist, one of the greatest heavyweight boxers of the twentieth century, and the first British world heavyweight champion in more than 100 years.

Lewis was born in London in 1965 to Jamaican parents. At the age of 12, Lewis moved to Canada. In high school, he excelled in athletics. He was particularly drawn to boxing and trained under Coach Arnie Boehm. Lewis finished his amateur career with a record of 85 wins, 9 losses. In 1983, Lewis won the gold medal at the World Junior Championship. In his Olympic boxing career, Lewis won a gold medal as part of Team Canada in 1988.

In 1989, Lewis moved to England and made his professional boxing debut. He won the European title in 1990 and the British Commonwealth heavyweight title in 1992. Consequently, Lewis was one of the top boxers in the world. In 1992, World Boxing Council (WBC) world heavyweight champion Riddick Bowe refused to fight Lewis, who was then the number one contender. Consequently, the WBC stripped

Bowe of the title and awarded the WBC world heavyweight championship to Lewis in 1993. Thus Lewis became the first British world heavyweight champion in the twentieth century. In 1994, Lewis suffered his first major defeat when he lost the WBC world heavyweight title to Oliver McCall. Lewis battled through several opponents, including Tommy Morrison, who starred in the fictional boxing film *Rocky V*, and former Olympian Ray Mercer, however, to become a top contender to regain the championship.

In 1997, Lewis gained his revenge for his 1994 defeat, knocking out McCall in the fifth round to become the first British boxer to regain the WBC title. Lewis successfully defended his WBC championship against several opponents.

In March 1999, Lewis boxed one of his most celebrated opponents, World Boxing Association (WBA)/International Boxing Federation (IBF) heavyweight champion Evander Holyfield, to a controversial draw. A rematch was scheduled for November later that year. In the rematch, Lewis won by decision, becoming undisputed world heavyweight champion. After several successful title defenses, Lewis lost the undisputed title to Hasim Rahman in 2001. Unable to accept defeat, Lewis defeated Rahman in a rematch seven months later to reclaim the WBC, WBA, and IBF world titles to become a three-time heavyweight champion.

In 2002, Lewis finally had a boxing match with the infamously wild Mike Tyson, who had been suspended from boxing for biting off his opponent's ear. In the widely publicized spectacle that became the highest grossing event on pay-per-view television at the time, Lewis decisively knocked Tyson out in the eighth round. Lewis then successfully defended his undisputed world heavyweight title against Vitali Klitschko in 2003. With his boxing legacy secured, Lewis announced his retirement from the sport in 2004 as the reigning undisputed world heavyweight champion. At his retirement, Lewis had a professional career record of 41 wins, 2 losses, and 1 draw.

See also: Black British; Britain, Blacks in; Colonies in the Caribbean, British.

Further Reading: Lewis, Lennox. *Lennox.* London: Little, Brown, 2002; Lewis, Lennox, and Joe Steeples. *Lennox Lewis: The Autobiography of the WBC Heavyweight Champion of the World.* London: Faber and Faber, 1994; The Official Web Page of Lennox Lewis: http://www.lennoxlewis.com/lennox/.

Mark Cordery

Lislet-Geoffroy, Jean-Baptiste (1755–1836)

Jean-Baptiste Lislet-Geoffroy was a French scientist and the son of a former African slave, and in 1786, he became the first person of African descent elected to the Academy of Science in Paris. Jean-Baptiste was baptized in August 1755 in Saint-Pierre, Île Bourbon (now Réunion), part of a chain of islands in the Indian Ocean off the southeastern coast of Africa that includes Île de France (now Mauritius) and Madagascar. His baptismal certificate lists only his first name. His mother was Niama, an African slave, who was freed on the day of his baptism by her master, Jean-Baptiste Geoffroy. The granting of freedom to Niama also applied to her son, as an individual's status as free or slave depended on that of his or her mother. Geoffroy was likely Jean-Baptiste's father, and if he had any intentions on marrying his former slave, such an official action was prohibited under French law. Jean-Baptiste lived with his parents on the Islet of Basin Plat and adopted the place name as a surname.

Geoffroy, an engineer and cultivated man, recognized Lislet's intelligence and gave the boy a rudimentary education in reading, writing, Latin, math, and science. During 1771, Lislet became a guide for Philibert Commerson, an explorer and French naturalist, during his expeditions in the area. Lislet went on to become an established engineer, botanist, astronomer, and cartographer in the French overseas territories in the area. In 1780, Lislet, interested in meteorology, began to establish an accurate record of weather data in the Indian Ocean region until 1834. In 1786, while still in his thirties, he was elected as the first black member of the prestigious Academy of Science in Paris.

During the French Revolution, Lislet initially sympathized with the revolutionaries. He became involved with French revolutionary colonial governance. Legal changes brought about during the revolution allow Geoffroy to formally adopt Lislet and make him his heir; however, Geoffroy still did not make any public claims of paternity. Thus Lislet's new surname became Lislet-Geoffroy. In 1810, after the fall of Île de France, Lislet-Geoffroy was charged with making an inventory of the buildings and fortifications for the British. He continued to work as an engineer for the British and eventually became a British citizen.

See also: *Code Noir* (France), Colonies in Africa, French; Enlightenment Philosophers and Race; Enlightenment Philosophers and Slavery; French Revolution, Blacks in the; Interracial Marriage, European Laws Banning.

Further Reading: Fleming, Beatrice, and Marion Pryde. *Distinguished Negroes Abroad.* Washington, DC: Associated Publishers, 1946.

Eric Martone

Literature, Blacks in British

An important shift in the representations of blacks occurred in the Renaissance. For a better understanding of this shift, an awareness of the theoretical and historical conditions that shape the development of a European racial consciousness is important. The literary treatments of blacks in British literature are directly related to this shift. During the sixteenth and seventeenth centuries, Britain began to develop a racial consciousness that coincided with its emergence as a dominant naval power. Britain developed a sense of race as a meaningful and significant way of dividing human beings into distinct groups. In this epoch, race was not always clearly grasped, but the way in which it was understood historically becomes a problem, especially for the cultural and scientific communities. The English, for instance, had already attributed certain types of behavior to people from specific regions, such as the "wild" Irish. The racial differences the English drew between themselves and their neighbors were cultural. Yet, as the English interacted with such ethnic groups as New World natives and Africans through the voyages of discovery, colonialism, and the European slave trade, they began to define race by skin color. Thus some Renaissance writers were in search of new definitions of race based on empirical and inductive principles, refuting conventional interpretations of race handed down to them. Bolstered by geographical explorations and new commercial development, biblical and classical theories of race could no longer satisfy the new demands of the period. This shift in the meaning of race from culture to encompass the physicality of the body is central to an understanding of the representations of blacks in British literature of the Renaissance, and these representations continue to influence and shape literary images of black peoples hundreds of years later.

SIR THOMAS BROWNE.   Influenced by Sir Francis Bacon's scientific method to revaluate traditional knowledge and promote practical learning, the English physician and writer Sir Thomas Browne (1605–1682) questioned many of the superstitions and common beliefs of his age. Book Six of Browne's *Pseudodoxia Epidemica* (1646) is crucial to understanding his use of race and his interrogations of the racial assumptions of his time.

In Book Six, Browne calls into question the climatological and biblical explanations for blackness. In the former explanation, blackness is an effect of climate. In the ancient myth of Phaeton, Ethiopians' black complexion derived from the heat and scorch of the sun. Browne argues that this account was a myth. He raises several problems with this theory, such as if the sun alone was responsible for blackness, then it should follow that the migration of dark-skinned people to more moderate climates and the reverse (the movement of fair people to hotter regions) should result in a corresponding change in skin color. Since peoples' complexions do not alter simply because of migration, Browne dismisses climatology as ever being the source of blackness. The implication is that climate is not a necessary condition for race.

The second theory for blackness is the curse of God. In the Bible, Ham (or in Browne, "Cham") is cursed and this curse was interpreted as blackness. One problem Browne has with this explanation is the difficulty of ascribing the descendants of this curse to a particular region. Although Browne's own prejudice is felt in passages where fairness is described as "a constant and agreeable hue," or when he argues that the peoples of Sicily and parts of Spain "deserve not so low a name as tawny" and "low as blackness," he also writes of blackness that "Whereas men affirm this colour was a curse, I cannot make out the propriety of that name, it neither seeming so to them, nor reasonably unto us." Furthermore, "Thus we that are of contrary complexions accuse the blackness of the **Moors** as ugly." Browne does link race with skin color, but not in a way that we would readily identify it as racist: he does not endow blackness with a pejorative moral meaning. Browne's response to blacks and blackness is ambivalent. On the one hand, he views racial otherness with a considerable amount of cultural relativity; on the other hand, his views of blacks and blackness are not free of value judgment.

RENAISSANCE DRAMA.   As is the case with Browne, the dramatists of the late sixteenth and early seventeenth centuries also reveal a racial consciousness. The first dramatic representation of an African on the English stage is in George Peele's *The Battle of Alcazar* (1594). Blackness can presuppose a diabolical and barbarous nature, such as Peele's Muly Mahamet. In other plays, the correlation between black skin and treachery is more complicated. In William Shakespeare's *Titus Andronicus*, for instance, Aaron's actions are clearly savage. Yet, on the other hand, his defense of his son displays his parental affection. Renaissance dramatists bring Europeans and non-Europeans together in such a way that a conflict ensues between what one might call a principle of virtue and a principle of savagery. The paradox, though, is that because Aaron is capable of exhibiting virtue as well as great cruelty, his blackness cannot explain or define him. Blackness in Renaissance texts signifies more than skin color. Aaron's schemes to destroy the political order in Rome also threatens the entire social and domestic fabric. His adulterous relationship with Tamora, the white queen of the Goths, produces an interracial child. He usurps both the domestic authority and political power of Tamora's husband and Rome's king, Saturninus. As is the case with *Titus Andronicus*, blacks and blackness in Renaissance drama often signal moral corruption as well as introduce sexual pollution and political disorder into the society.

Shakespeare's **Othello** and Elizabeth Cary's *The Tragedy of Mariam* are also deeply racialized dramas. In *Othello*, Iago's use of animal imagery brings out the hideousness of Othello's marriage to Desdemona. In Shakespeare's language, Othello is "an old black ram" who is "tupping" Desdemona, "the white ewe." In addition to bestiality in these texts, blackness is being used to trope femininity. When the Venetian virgin is tainted sexually in Othello's imagination, she is symbolically blackened. Desdemona's presumed infidelity has tarnished Othello's "name, that was as fresh/as Diana's visage, is now begrimed and black/As mine own face." This is not the only representation of Othello's blackness, however. Shakespeare's Othello is a converted Christian; his rejection of Islam might enable Shakespeare to defy the stereotypical identification of blacks with savagery. At the beginning of the play, Shakespeare allows Iago to spew his considerable racial hatred without restraint. When Othello finally enters the stage in the second scene of Act One, however, his temperance and dignified bearing deflates Iago's representation of Othello as sexually intemperate and savage. Othello's conformity and transcendence of the stereotypical attributes associated with blackness remain in tension throughout the play.

Similarly, in Cary's play, Salome is slighted as a "sun-burnt blackamoor" and denigrated as "an ape." Contrastingly, Mariam's whiteness and chasteness are a foil to Salome. This clear divide between blackness and whiteness continues in the play. In addition to Salome, Cleopatra is important to the treatment of blackness in the play. Physically and sexually, Cleopatra is racially marked as black. Cleopatra's race fluctuates in Renaissance texts, especially in relation to her sexual and political temperance. As a point of comparison, in Mary Sidney's *The Tragedy of Antonius*, Cleopatra is a distinctly white heroine. Whereas her blackness denotes her lack of virtue in Cary, her whiteness in Sidney is an external sign of her internal worth and virtue. As Renaissance drama indicates, the racial discourse in this period develops in relation to views of femininity, in particular female sexuality.

In large part, Renaissance dramatists did not heed Browne's caution that it is fallacious to impose any single "property" to an ethnic group based on race. As Browne observed, extrinsic attributes do not bring us any closer to a genuine understanding of blacks. As Shakespeare and other dramatists demonstrate again and again, barbarity and cruelty (as well as virtue) are possible modes of being for blacks and whites, as well as for women and men. Yet the frequency with which representations of non-Europeans and non-Christians draw correlations between their ethnicity and savagery suggests that in the Renaissance, blackness is beginning to define the morality, temperance, and sexuality of large groups of people. The meaning of blackness is historical; this means that a race or an ethnic group is always in the process of thinking of itself in relation to the world in which it finds itself at any given moment with respect to its political, social, religious, cultural, and economic conditions. In the Renaissance, as Britain was beginning to transform itself into a dominant naval power, and by the beginning of the eighteenth century into a slave-trading nation, Britain was in a state of flux, and so too was its discourse of blackness.

EARLY TWENTIETH-CENTURY REPRESENTATIONS OF BLACKS. Three hundred years after the Renaissance, British representations of blacks continued to show signs of a search for new definitions of race. Twentieth-century British literature attempted to throw off and deconstruct more than three centuries of racism. Although such stereotypical associations of blacks with bestiality, savagery, and sexual intemperance are increasingly interrogated and rejected, there is still a sense that British writers are still unable to fully shed the racial assumptions of previous ages.

Joseph Conrad's *Heart of Darkness* (1902) is a case in point. Although Conrad was Polish, his text is a significant piece of English literature. Conrad's novella is often read as an attack on colonialism. The violence of European imperialism is clearly represented in Conrad's text. The images of Africans literally worked to death produce discomfort and outrage in the reader. The images of "moribund shapes" and "black bones" haunt Conrad's text. Representations of young black men chained, beaten and groaning under the burden of European racism, bring into relief the horror and savagery of colonial exploitation and victimization of native African populations.

In contrast, Conrad's text is also read to promote racist assumptions. Chinua Achebe, the Nigerian novelist, has attacked Conrad as a "bloody racist." In spite of his criticisms of European colonialism, Conrad clearly reproduces Victorian racial ideologies. He writes of Africans as "strings of dusty niggers" and of a "lot of people, mostly black and naked, moved about like ants." Whereas Conrad attempts to penetrate the psychology of the European mind when it is confronted with absolute evil, black Africans are merely dehumanized as abstractions. He writes of "the white of their eyeballs glistening. . . . their bodies streamed with perspiration; they had faces like grotesque masks." Although Conrad's narrator reluctantly admits that these howling, leaping, black bodies are human, their link with civilized Europeans is buried in the abyss of the past: "what thrilled you was just the thought of their humanity—like yours—the thought of your remote kinship with this wild and passionate uproar."

Shakespeare's treatment of the black Othello contrasts sharply with such writers as the Romantic poet Samuel Coleridge (1772–1834). Coleridge rejects that Shakespeare intended Othello to be a black-skinned African; Shakespeare, he argues, would never imagine a royal birth for a black barbarous African. A comparison of Shakespeare with Coleridge and Conrad highlights the shifting representations of blacks in British literature. In the 300 years separating Shakespeare's age from Conrad's, blacks in British literature are in general stripped of their dignity and humanity. As Coleridge intimates, in the nineteenth-century discourse of blackness, it was unthinkable to associate black people with regality and nobility. The cultural relativity with which Browne viewed racial otherness belongs to Shakespeare's age, not Conrad's. That being said, the pendulum begins to swing the other way in Conrad's age. Although *Heart of Darkness* reproduces the racial and racist assumptions of the Victorian Age, Conrad's text also discloses the horrors and brutality of European colonialism, and as such, it is a landmark text.

As Shakespeare and Conrad illustrate, representations of blacks in British literature is heterogeneous. What is consistent, however, is the existence of a racial and racist discourse, which attempted to define blacks physically, culturally, and sexually. In the age of Shakespeare, the definition of blackness was in flux, and it was possible for writers to view blackness with a certain amount of cultural relativity. As England entered fully into the slave trade in the eighteenth century, representations of black people changed accordingly.

See also: Black British; Britain, Blacks in; Browning, Elizabeth Barrett; Civil Rights Movement in Twentieth-Century Great Britain; Colonies in Africa, British; Colonies in the Caribbean, British; Dabydeen, David; D'Aguiar, Fred; Gilroy, Beryl; Hamitic Myth; Johnson, Linton Kwesi; Kincaid, Jamaica; Levy, Andrea; Okri, Ben; Palamedes, Sir; Phillips, Caryl; Renaissance, Blacks in the; Riley, Joan; Robin Hood Legend, Blacks in the; Shinebourne, Janice; Slave Trade, British.

Further Reading: Barthelemy, Anthony Gerard. *Black Face, Maligned Race: The Representation of Blacks in English Drama From Shakespeare to Southerne.* Baton Rouge: Louisiana State University Press, 1987; Bates, Jonathan, ed. *The Romantics on Shakespeare.* London: Penguin Books, 1992; Browne, Sir Thomas. *Pseudodoxia Epidemica; or, Enquiries into very Many Received Tenents and Commonly Presumed Truths.* ed. Robin Robbins. Oxford: Clarendon, 1981; Carretta, Vincent. *Unchained Voices: An Anthology of Black Authors in the English-Speaking World of the Eighteenth-Century.* Lexington: University of Kentucky Press, 1996; Cary, Elizabeth. *The Tragedy of Mariam: The Fair Queen of Jewry.* eds. Barry Weller and Margaret W. Ferguson. Berkeley: University of California Press, 1994; Dabydeen, David, ed. *The Black Presence in English Literature.* Manchester: Manchester University Press, 1985; Earle, T. F., and K.J.P. Lowe, eds. *Black Africans in Renaissance Europe.* New York: Cambridge University Press, 2005; Innes, C. L. *History of Black and Asian Writing in Britain, 1700–2000.* Cambridge: Cambridge University Press, 2003; Mark, Peter. *Africans in European Eyes: The Portrayal of Black Africans in Fourteenth and Fifteenth Century Europe.* Syracuse: Maxwell School of Citizenship and Public Affairs, 1974.

Richardine G. Woodall

Literature, Blacks in French

Most of the early contemporary African and Caribbean literatures originated as a form of protest against assimilation and French dominance. The most influential black Francophone literary movement of the twentieth century was undoubtedly **Négritude.** **Léopold Sédar Senghor,** one of this literary movement's guiding figures, later became the first president of the Republic of Senegal in 1960. In Paris during the 1930s, he met many French Caribbean black writers, including **Aimé Césaire** from Martinique and **Léon Damas** of French Guiana. Together, they began an examination of Western colonial values and a reassessment of how African and Caribbean cultures were being represented by European writers. In 1947, they founded *Présence Africaine*, a leading literary journal for black writers in Paris. In addition, Senghor's *Anthologie de la nouvelle poésie nègre et malgache* (*Anthology of New Black and Madagascan Poetry,* 1948) was an important influence in the formation of the idea of Négritude and included poets from all over the Francophone world including Africa, the French Caribbean territories, and Madagascar.

During this time, Martinican writer Suzanne Roussy Césaire was experimenting with surrealist poetics in her expressions of *Négritude* ideology, including essays "*Le grand camouflage*" ("The Great Disguising," 1945) and "*Malaise d'une civilization*" ("Discontent of a Civilization," 1942). In a similar vein, poet and essayist Lucy Thésée was using surrealist techniques to describe a uniquely black, feminine understanding of the world.

In 1947, Birago Diop emerged on the Francophone literary scene with his *Les contes d'Amadou Koumba* (*Stories of Amadou Koumba*, 1947). Diop was a Senegalese poet and storyteller who recorded traditional oral folktales of the Wolof people. His work helped to reestablish global interest in African folktales published in French. During the 1950s and 1960s, Diop became one of the most prominent African Francophone writers. His tales combined realism, humor, and fantasy to express various facets of the human condition.

Two significant Francophone novelists from Cameroon are Mongo Beti (pseudonym of Alexandre Biyidi), who wrote *Le Pauvre Christ de Bomba* (*The Poor Christ of Bomba*, 1956), and Ferdinand Oyono, author of *Une Vie de boy* (*Houseboy*, 1956) and *Le Vieux Nègre et la médaille* (*The Old Black Man and the Medal*, 1956). These novels sought to counter the propaganda of the French government that portrayed educated Africans as simply "black Frenchmen."

Although the Congolese poet Tchicaya U Tam'si wrote of his people's agonies, he did not claim to be the spokesman of his country or race like the Négritude writers. In *Le Mauvais Sang* (*Bad Blood*, 1955), *Feu de brousse* (*Bush Fire*, 1957), *À triche-coeur* (*By Cheating the Heart*, 1960), *Épitomé* (1962), and *Le Ventre* (*The Belly*, 1964), he explored his personal experiences and sufferings through poems in which surrealist, Christian, mythological, and sexual imagery is intertwined.

Guinean author Camara Laye established his reputation with *L'Enfant noir* (*African Child*, 1953), an autobiographical account depicting life in a traditional African town. Another of his important works is the novel *Le Regard du roi* (*Radiance of the King*, 1954), which recounts a white man's journey to gain personal atonement in the jungles of West Africa. In his third novel, *Dramouss* (*A Dream of Africa*, 1966), Laye criticizes life under the ruling party of Guinea. Such views were affected by his status in 1965 as a political refugee in Senegal.

In 1956, Ousmane Sembène wrote and published a novel under the title *Le Docker Noir* (*The Black Docker*, 1956) based on his experiences as a Senegalese man living in France. He has grown to become one of the most prolific African writers of the twentieth century. The majority of Sembene's literary work is a critique of the conflicted relationships between the colonizer and the colonized, the state and the people, the rich and the poor, and the elders and youth. Thus, his novels address the universal issues involving tensions that are created by power relations. Other well-known novels by Sembène include *Les bouts de bois de dieu* (*God's Bits of Wood*, 1960), *L'Harmattan* (1964), and *Xala* (1974).

The1960s brought about the development of the philosophical novel in Francophone Africa, led by Sheikh Hamidou Kane in *L'Aventure ambiguë* (*Ambiguous Adventure*, 1961), and by Yambo Ouologuem in *Le Devoir de violence* (*Bound to Violence*, 1968). Both writers are of Sudanese origin and craft their novels partly as "conversations" between Islam and Christian spirituality, or between traditional autocracy and colonial rule.

Senegalese author Mariama Bâ was the recipient of the first Noma Award for publishing in Africa for *Une Si Longue Lettre* (*So Long a Letter*, 1980), and Aminata Sow Fall, a fellow Senegalese writer, earned recognition for *La Grève des battu ou les déchets humains* (*The Beggar's Strike*, 1979), an ironic novel written with great skill and attention to cultural detail.

In the 1980s, Martinican authors Patrick Chamoiseau, Raphael Confiant, and Jean Bérnabé theorized *la créolité* in their seminal work *Eloge de la créolité* (*In Praise of Creoleness*, 1989). They described this philosophical and literary movement as a departure from the universality and monolinguism that was encouraged by *Négritude*. The *créolité* movement sought to overturn the dominance of French as the language of culture and literature in the French Caribbean. Instead, it championed the use of Antillean Creole in literature.

Today, France is home to hundreds of immigrant authors from the Francophone world. Texts by authors of immigrant origin explore what it means to be French and are often infused with debates about French national and cultural identity. They address themes such as cultural hybridity, linguistic identity, and the theorization of "otherness." Authors at the forefront of this movement are Calixthe Beyala, Bessora, and Alain Mabanckou. Calixthe Beyala left Cameroon at age 17 and arrived in France where she studied and published numerous novels. In 1993, she was awarded the *Grand prix littéraire de l'Afrique Noire* and the *Grand Prix du Roman de l'Académie Française* in 1996. Her extensive bibliography includes *Seul le diable le savait* (*Only the Devil Knows*, 1990), *C'est le soleil qui m'a brûlée* (*The Sun Hath Looked Upon Me*, 1996), and *Tu t'appelleras Tanga* (*Your Name Shall be Tanga*, 1996). Bessora is an author of Swiss-Gabonese descent who uses satire, irony, and intertextuality in her novels to undo stereotypical images of immigrants and to introduce a model of identity based on the image of "transplanting," rather than "rootedness." Her novels include *53 cm* (2000), *Les Tâches d'encre* (*The Ink Stains*, 2000), and *Deux bébés et l'addition* (*Two Babies and the Bill*, 2002). Alain Mabanckou is the author of six volumes of poetry and five novels. In 2006, he recently received the *Prix Renaudot*, one of the highest and most prestigious literary prizes in France, for his novel *Memoires de porc-épic* (*Memoirs of a Porcupine*, 2006). Other novels include *African Psycho* (2003) and *Verre cassé* (*Broken Glass*, 2005).

See Also: African Diaspora; Colonies in Africa, French; Colonies in the Caribbean, French; France, Blacks in; Haitian Revolution in Francophone Literature.

Further Reading: Cazenave, Odile. *Afrique sur Seine. A New Generation of African Writers in Paris*. New York: Lexington Books, 2005; Cazenave, Odile. *Rebellious Women*. New York: Lynne Rienner, 1999; Kesteloot, Lilyan. *Black Writers in French: A Literary History of Negritude*. Washington, DC: Howard University Press, 1991; Lewis, Shireen. *Race, Culture, and Identity: Francophone West African and Caribbean Literature and Theory from Négritude to Créolité*. New York: Lexington Books, 2006; Miller, Christopher. *Theories of Africans: Francophone Literature and Anthropology in Africa*. Chicago: University of Chicago Press, 1990; Thomas, Dominic. *Nation-Building, Propaganda, and Literature in Francophone Africa*. Bloomington: Indiana University Press, 2002.

Jennifer Westmoreland Bouchard

Literature, Blacks in German and Central European

The role of blacks in German and Central European literature has gradually shifted over time from one in which black identity was usually stereotyped and portrayed by white Europeans to one in which blacks in Europe gained their own voice through writing literature. Enlightenment morality plays, which use black characters as a foil, provide early representations. The libretti for operas in Vienna, such as Antonio Salieri's *Die Neger* (1804) and even Wolfgang Amadeus Mozart's *Die Zauberflöte* (*The Magic Flute*, 1791), featured black characters and were immensely popular. In the nineteenth century, works such as **Heinrich Von Kleist**'s *The Engagement in St. Domingo* (1811) focused on issues of race by depicting a love affair between a white man and a black woman in Haiti during the **Haitian Revolution for Independence** in 1803. German colonial literature also explored themes of racism and conflict in the late nineteenth and early twentieth centuries.

Beginning in the late twentieth century, however, Afro-German literature, the literature of German authors of black descent, became visible on the literary scene. Although Afro-Germans had lived in Germany before the 1980s, they began to write as a way to gain their voice and legitimize their existence in German society. When African American poet and feminist Audre Lorde taught a 1984 course at the Freie Universität in Berlin on African American women poets and conducted a workshop in English, she encouraged and inspired black German women to write about their own experiences. As a result of her advice and support, Germans of black descent began to refer to themselves as "Afro-Germans," giving Afro-Germans their own identity instead of having others create one for them.

Audre Lorde's influence also extended into literature, most notably with the groundbreaking work *Farbe Bekennen: Afro-deutsche Frauen auf den Spuren ihrer Geschichte* (*Showing Our Colors: Afro-German Women Speak Out*, 1986), which contained histories of blacks in Germany, personal accounts, interviews, poetry, and prose, edited by May Opitz (**May Ayim**), **Katharina Oguntoye,** and Dagmar Schultz. *Showing Our Colors* was the first visible book written by Afro-Germans and also the first visible book placing Germans of black descent within a German national framework. The book insists that Afro-Germans are individuals "whose self-defined identities are no longer shameful secrets in the countries of our origin, but rather declarations of strength and solidarity." It is arguable that this groundbreaking book gave birth to the Afro-German movement, for, after its release, movements such as the **Initiative of Blacks in Germany (ISD)** and **Afro-German Women (ADEFRA)** sprang up as more Afro-Germans began to meet and organize.

In the wake of *Showing Our Colors*, other works in Afro-German literature appeared. Anthologies focusing on themes and stories of the marginalized were especially prevalent. Anthologies such as *Power of the Night, a Black German Anthology* (1991), *Distant Connections* (1993), and *Talking Home: Frauen of Color in Deutschland* (1999) were strong testaments to the power of language and its ability to validate and celebrate the lives of black Germans. Whereas *Talking Home* discusses the idea of a "homeland" and deals directly with gender, *Distant Connections*, whose title comes from a poem by May Ayim, examines the complicated ways in which racism, anti-Semitism, and classism impact women's lives.

Ayim's work was itself a galvanizing force in Afro-German literature. Born as May Opitz in Hamburg in 1960, she changed her surname to that of her Ghanaian father to more strongly and actively acknowledge her African heritage. Educated at the University of Regensburg, she received attention first for her work in *Showing Our Colors.* Her anthologies of poetry, such as *Blues in Schwarz-Weiss* (*Blues in Black and White*, 1995), set her apart as a great poet and figure in literature. *Blues in Black and White* pays homage to Langston Hughes and his use of the blues as an expression of mourning. Her works often deal with the theme of identity, femininity, dehumanization, and discrimination. Yet her sharp insight and good humor made her poetry accessible to those of all backgrounds in Germany, while still exposing others to the difficulties of being Afro-German in a society unwilling to accept others. Despite her early death in 1996, Ayim's work continues to influence readers and writers alike.

Other figures in Afro-German literature include those who have published their autobiographies, especially **Ika Hügel-Marshall** and **Hans-Jürgen Massaquoi** (b. 1926). Massaquoi's autobiography, *Destined to Witness* (1999), conveys the difficulties of growing up black in Nazi Germany. Born to a white German mother and an elite Liberian father, Massaquoi grew up (like many German children during the 1930) wanting to join the Hitler Youth. Yet he also soon became the target of racist national-socialist ideologies. Although he was not persecuted like the Jews in Germany, he was nonetheless considered a second-class citizen in his own home. Hügel-Marshall's experience as an Afro-German is quite different, although her autobiography also has a tone of alienation and isolation that pervades the work. Born as one of the many *Besatzungskinder,* or "occupation children" after World War II, her father was an African American soldier and her mother a white German. When her mother was encouraged to give her up, Hügel-Marshall was forced to endure the harsh racisms of several institutions. Hügel-Marshall's original subtitle for her work was *"ein afro-deutsches Leben"* or "an afro-German life." The subtitle was eventually changed to "a German life" to demonstrate the universality of the German experience among Germans of different backgrounds.

Although blacks in Germany and Central Europe have only begun to express their views and gain their voice in the mid to late twentieth century, they nevertheless represent a strong minority in German literature. The prolific body of work produced by Afro-Germans continues to grow and reach audiences worldwide.

See also: Afro-Germans; Colonies in Africa, German; Nazis and Blacks in Europe; Pamoja; *Parzival,* Feirefiz in; World War II, Black Participation in.

Further Reading: Blackshire-Belay, Carol, ed. *The African-German Experience: Critical Essays.* Westport, CT: Praeger, 1996; Gilman, Sander. *On Blackness Without Blacks: Essays on the Image of the Black in Germany.* Boston: G. K. Hall, 1982; Grimm, Reinhold, and Jost Hermand, eds. *Blacks and German Culture.* Madison: University of Wisconsin Press, 1986; Mazon, Patricia, and Reinhild Steingrover, eds. *Not So Plain as Black and White: Afro-German Culture and History, 1890–2000.* Rochester: University of Rochester Press, 2005; Oguntoye, Katharina, May Opitz, and Dagmar Schultz. *Showing Our Colors: Afro-German Women Speak Out.* trans. Anne Adams. Amherst: University of Massachusetts Press, 1991; Poikane-Daumke, Aija. *African Diasporas: Afro-German Literature in the Context of the African-American Experience.* London: Lit Verlag, 2007.

Kira Thurman

L'Ouverture, Toussaint (1743–1803)

Toussaint L'Ouverture was an eighteenth-century leader of an anti-French uprising for the abolition of slavery in Saint Domingue (present-day Haiti). He was born Pierre Dominique Toussaint on the Bréda plantation in Haut-du-Cap, in the French colony of Saint-Domingue. He is believed to have descended from a chief of an African tribe, whose son was captured and sold into slavery. Francois Dominique Toussaint Bréda, as L'Ouverture was known before the **Haitian Revolution for Independence,** was born as a slave but was later freed and taught to read and write by an ex-priest. His origins are often traced to an African chieftain of the Arada tribe from Dahomey, but no tangible evidence exists to support this. By 1779, he was a freeman, married to Suzanne Simone Baptiste and growing coffee on rented land that was cultivated by a dozen slaves.

As the French Revolution began in 1789, the revolutionary sentiments also spread in Saint Domingue, where the slaves demanded freedom and rights as promised by the Declaration of the Rights of Man and Citizen. When plantation owners refused to compromise, a slave uprising began in the Cap Français hinterland in the summer of 1791. There is no evidence that Toussaint directly participated in early stages of this uprising, and he is said to have saved the lives of the Bréda plantation manager and his family early in the revolt. The first record of his presence among the rebels is in December 1791, when he took part in negotiations between white and black leaders.

Toussaint later joined the revolt, first working as a doctor, and later serving under rebel leaders Jean-François and **Georges Biassou,** proving his military skills. In 1793, they allied with the Spanish in Santo Domingo on the eastern side of the island, and Toussaint entered the Spanish service fighting the French plantation owners. The Spanish deployed forces to support the rebel slaves in the north of Saint Domingue. Toussaint, who had taken up the Spanish banner in February 1793, came to command his own forces and took control of north-central Saint Domingue. Spain and Britain, meanwhile, had reached an informal arrangement to divide the French colony between them: British forces landed in the southern portions of the island while the Spanish continued their operations in the north.

In September 1793, local French revolutionary authorities decided to abolish slavery to gain slave support and save the colony from Spanish and British encroachment. Confirmation of the National Assembly's decision (February 1794) to abolish slavery had a great influence on Toussaint, now calling himself Toussaint Louverture (L'Ouverture), who decided to change sides in May 1794. He quickly became the leading black general under the French authorities. He achieved notable success against his former allies until a peace agreement was signed between France and Spain in 1795. The treaty required Spain to cede its holdings on Hispaniola to France and deny supplies and funding to the rebel forces fighting under the Spanish colors. The armies of Jean-François and Biassou were soon disbanded, and many flocked to the standard of Toussaint, the remaining black commander of stature.

By 1796, Toussaint emerged, through his military talents, as one of leading figures in Saint Domingue when the French revolutionary authorities appointed him lieutenant governor of Saint Domingue. Distrustful of all parties, Toussaint set out to consolidate his political and military positions. He took advantage of the fact that France was occupied with the Revolutionary Wars in Europe to further secure his authority on the island. He influenced the French commissioners to appoint him commander-in-chief of all French forces on the island and, acting from this position of strength, he moved to establish an autonomous state under black rule. In 1798, without authorization from French authorities, Toussaint negotiated with the British, who had invaded the colony five years before, and concluded a secret treaty providing for withdrawal of British troops, commerce with Jamaica, and the rehabilitation of pro-British colonists. The next year, Toussaint entered into negotiations and signed a commercial agreement with the United States. The same year, Toussaint turned against his main opponent, André Rigaud, who controlled Saint Domingue's southern peninsula. He sought to secure Rigaud's allegiance and incorporate *gens de couleur*, Rigaud's main supporters, into his future state, but his plan was thwarted by the French authorities, who saw in Rigaud their last opportunity to retain dominance over the colony and control Toussaint.

In the bloody "war of the south," Toussaint's predominantly black forces clashed with Rigaud's army. By 1800, Toussaint and his lieutenant, Jean-Jacques Dessalines, defeated Rigaud's troops and captured their center of Les Cayes. Toussaint then expanded his operations to the Spanish-controlled portion of the island where slavery was still practiced. By 1801, he achieved virtual control of the colony by using his troops and influence with ex-slaves, who composed an overwhelming majority of Saint Domingue's population. He consolidated his position as Saint Domingue's ruler with a new colonial constitution, which named him governor-general for life.

After a decade of civil strife, Saint Domingue was devastated and its sugar and coffee exports plummeted. Toussaint realized that the survival of his new state depended on an export-oriented economy. Hoping to generate commercial revenues to revive the colony, he then chose to adopt a policy of forced plantation labor that was similar to slave labor used by previous plantation owners. To implement his policies, he also adopted a more authoritarian style of leadership and established a military dictatorship, which he believed was most effective under the circumstances.

In the meantime, France, under the new leadership of First Consul Napoleon Bonaparte, sought to recover its lucrative colony. Saint Domingue was also essential for future French exploitation of the Louisiana Territory in North America. Toussaint sought to assure Bonaparte of his loyalty to France, but he refused to accept French authority on the island. In early 1802, a French military expedition, led by General Charles-Victor-Emmanuel Leclerc, Bonaparte's brother-in-law, arrived in Saint Domingue and moved against Toussaint and his forces. By May 1802, unable to defeat the French and with some of his lieutenants defecting, Toussaint chose to negotiate a treaty with Leclerc on condition that there would be no return of slavery. After the treaty was signed, he was allowed to retire to his estate, but was soon arrested on charges of plotting an uprising against the French authorities. Toussaint was quickly deported to France, where he arrived in July 1802. A month later, he was sent to the fortress of Fort de Joux in the Jura Mountains in eastern France. Confined to a squalid cell and neglected, Toussaint lived for another year before succumbing to pneumonia in April 1803.

See also: Abolition of Slavery, French; Colonies in the Caribbean, British; Colonies in the Caribbean, French; Colonies in the Caribbean, Spanish; Delgrès, Louis; French Revolution, Blacks in the; Haitian Revolution in Francophone Literature; Lislet-Geoffroy, Jean-Baptiste; Ogé, Vincent; Slave Trade, French; Sonthonax, Léger Félicité.

Further Reading: Bell, Madison. *Toussaint Louverture: A Biography.* New York: Pantheon Books, 2007; Césaire, Aimé. *Toussaint Louverture: La Révolution française et le problème colonial.* Paris: Présence Africaine, 1981; Geggus, David P., and David B. Gaspar, eds; *Turbulent Time: The French Revolution and the Greater Caribbean.* Bloomington: Indiana University Press, 1997; James, C.L.R. *The Black Jacobins: Toussaint L'Ouverture and the San Domingo Revolution.* London: Allison and Busby, 1994; Nicholls, David. *From Dessalines to Duvalier: Race, Colour, and National Independence in Haiti.* Cambridge: Cambridge University Press, 1979.

Alexander Mikaberidze

M

McCalla, Val (1943–2002)

Val Irvine McCalla was a controversial **black British** publisher and the founder of *The Voice*, an influential weekly newspaper that catered to Britain's black community. He was born in 1943 in Jamaica. He studied accounting at Kingston College before moving to Britain in 1959. McCalla hoped to serve in the Royal Air Force as pilot, but ended up performing bookkeeping functions. Afterward, he volunteered at the newspaper *East End News* while maintaining employment as an accountant.

The early 1980s was a period of racial unrest in Britain. Blacks and black issues did not receive much attention in the media, and when they did, it was often negative. McCalla decided to found *The Voice* in 1982 as a vehicle for the British Afro-Caribbean and black British community to express themselves. *The Voice* was meant to appeal to a new generation of black Britons whose parents had been immigrants. The newspaper was not afraid to cause controversy and targeted what it perceived as racism in British society. *The Voice* was launched at the **Notting Hill Carnival** and it became very influential and popular. It established itself as a recognized, if not official, mouthpiece for the black British community and campaigner for black rights.

As a result of *The Voice*'s success, McCalla became an extremely wealthy man. His publications helped launch the career of numerous black journalists. McCalla owned other publications including *Chic* and *Pride*. In 1991, he founded *The Weekly Journal*.

See also: Britain, Blacks in; Civil Rights Movement in Twentieth-Century Britain; Colonies in the Caribbean, British; McDonald, Trevor; Massaquoi, Hans-Jürgen; Media, Blacks in Contemporary European.

Further Reading: Ainley, Beulah. *Black Journalists, White Media*. Stoke-on-Trent, UK: Trentham Books, 1998; Morrison, Lionel. *A Century of Black Journalism in Britain*. London: Truebay, 2007.

E. Agateno Mosca

McDonald, Trevor (1939–)

Trevor McDonald, the first black television news anchor in the United Kingdom, was born in San Fernando, Trinidad. As a young child, he watched the BBC World Service to improve his command of the English language. He started his career in the media through the Blue Circle Network, a university broadcast at Naparima College in San Fernando.

McDonald started his professional career as a producer for the BBC's World Service and the BBC's Caribbean Service in 1962. In 1969, he moved to London to work for the BBC's World Service. He subsequently was a reporter for Independent Television News (ITN) from 1973 to 1978, a sport correspondent from 1978 to 1980, a diplomatic correspondent from 1980 to 1982, and a newscaster for *Channel 4 News* from 1987 to 1989. His presentation of the *News at Ten* bulletin from 1991 to 1999 and from 2001 to 2005 brought him popular recognition. He also hosted Granada Television's *Tonight with Trevor McDonald* from 2001 to 2005. In 2006, he signed a two-year contract with ITN to produce a documentary show and a new series of interviews. In June 2007, McDonald began hosting the new ITV television series *News Knight with Sir Trevor McDonald.*

As evidence of his professionalism, McDonald was awarded the Television and Radio Industries Club's "Newscaster of the Year" and received a National Television Award for Special Achievement in 2003. He was honored with a Royal Television Society Journalism Award for Lifetime Achievement in 2005. McDonald is also an honorary vice president of Optical Charity Vision Aid Overseas (VAO) and Chancellor of London South Bank University. He holds an honorary award from the University of Plymouth and was knighted in 1999.

His books include biographies of cricketers Clive Lloyd (1985) and Viv Richards (1987) and an autobiography, *Fortunate Circumstances*, published in 1993. Although aware of racial problems in the country, McDonald always claimed he had never encountered racism in his professional and personal life. Because of his popularity as one of a few black media professionals, he has been criticized for not using his position to fight racial discrimination.

See also: Black British; Britain, Blacks in; Colonies in the Caribbean, British; Media, Blacks in Contemporary European.

Further Reading: McDonald, Trevor. *Fortunate Circumstances.* London: Weidenfeld and Nicholson, 1993.

Tristan Cabello

McGrath, Paul (1959–)

Paul McGrath, a biracial football (American soccer) defender, played for the Republic of Ireland's national team from 1985 until 1997. He is predominantly known as Ireland's most famous sportsman.

McGrath was born as Paul Nwobilo. His father was Nigerian and his mother, Betty McGrath, was Irish. Afraid of the repercussions of an illegitimate, biracial child, McGrath's mother traveled to London, where she gave birth to him and gave him up for adoption when he was four weeks old. McGrath was raised in a series of orphanages in Dublin, Ireland.

McGrath developed feelings of insecurity and isolation while growing up black in a predominantly white community. Although he felt that could not tell fellow teammates of his troubles, he managed to find some security in youth football leagues. He played for the Pearse Rovers and later for Dalkey United. Eventually, McGrath attracted the attention of football scouts and obtained a position on the professional team, St. Patrick's Athletic in 1981. McGrath excelled in his sport at St. Patrick's and earned the nickname the "Black Pearl of Inchicore."

McGrath's professional career took off rapidly, and in 1982, he transferred to Manchester United under the leadership of Roy Atkinson. Problems with injured knees and alcohol addiction hindered McGrath's relationship with the new owner of Manchester United, Alex Ferguson. In 1989, McGrath transferred to Aston Villa and played for them until 1996. During his stay at Aston Villa, he picked up numerous awards, such as Player of the Year, and helped his team win the Cup in 1994 and 1996. On the international scene, McGrath helped Ireland achieve worldwide acclaim.

McGrath has admitted to alcohol addiction and has told his life story in an autobiography titled *Back from the Brink*. His years of alcohol addiction led to several suicide attempts, which McGrath attributes to his troubled childhood. Yet despite his personal problems, McGrath still managed to attract the acclaim of fans worldwide. He remains celebrated as one of Ireland's best athletes.

See also: Batson, Brendon; Britain, Blacks in; Colonies in Africa, British; Henry, Thierry; Ireland, Blacks in; Wharton, Arthur.

Further Reading: McGrath, Paul, with Cathal Dervan. *Ooh, Aah, Paul McGrath: The Black Pearl of Inchicore.* Edinburgh: Mainstream Publishing, 1994; McGrath, Paul, with Vincent Hogan. *Back from the Brink: The Autobiography.* London: Arrow, 2006.

Dawn P. Hutchins

Machado de Assis, Joaquim María (1839–1908)

Joaquim María Machado de Assis, a Brazilian realist novelist and author, is one of the greatest black writers in Western literature. Machado de Assis's work was heavily influenced by English writers, such as Shakespeare and John Milton, and French realists, such as Gustave Flaubert and Emile Zola. In turn, Machado de Assis has been a great influence on many writers in the nineteenth and twentieth centuries. He also translated many works of Shakespeare into Portuguese, thereby making the English playwright more accessible to Portuguese audiences, and even based his *Dom Casmurro* (1899) on Shakespeare's **Othello.**

Machado de Assis was born in 1839 in Rio de Janeiro. His father was Francisco José de Assis, a black housepainter and descendant of freed slaves, and his mother was María Leopoldina Machado de Assis, a Portuguese washerwoman who died when her son was young. Machado De Assis was said to have taught himself to write, and after gaining skill in Portuguese, he studied French and then English until he was fluent in both.

As a teenager, Machado de Assis worked for newspapers in Rio de Janeiro and published his first works in the early 1860s. In 1869, he married Carolina Xavier de Novaes, the descendant of a Portuguese noble family and soon managed to get a position in public service. He wrote many more books, including *Contos Fluminenses* (*Fluminensis Tales*, 1870); *Ressurreição* (*Resurrection*, 1872); *Histórias da Meia Noite* (*Stories of Midnight*, 1873); *A Mão e a Luva* (*The Hand and the Glove*, 1874); *Americanas* (collection of poetry, 1875); *Helena* (1876); and *Iaiá Garcia* (*Mistress Garcia*, 1878). Many of these books sold well, but in about 1880, Machado de Assis's style of writing changed dramatically. He wrote a novel, *Memórias Póstumas de Brás Cubas* (*The Posthumous Memoirs of Bras Cubas*, 1881), which resembled, to some degree, the works of British writers George Meredith and Laurence Sterne. He then wrote a number of other works, including *Histórias sem data* (*Undated Stories*, 1884) and *Páginas recolhidas* (*Retained Pages*, 1899).

In 1896, Machado de Assis founded the Brazilian Academy of Sciences and served as its president from 1897 until his death. In 1899, he published his most famous novel, *Dom Casmurro* (*Sir Dour*), which deals with the theme of jealousy. Casmurro, meaning "obstinate," is the main character and has obvious similarities to Shakespeare's *Othello*. *Dom Casmurro* is a fictional memoir written from the point of view of Bento (Bentinho), a jealous husband. He believes that his wife, Capitu (a version of Shakespeare's Desdemona), has betrayed him with his best friend and has given birth to an illegitimate son. Bento's evidence to support his suspicions is weak, however, and could be explained by paranoia. Therefore the novel, with its unreliable narrator, never presents a straight answer to the question of whether Capitu has betrayed her husband.

Machado de Assis was involved in translating Shakespeare and other English writers into Portuguese. His later works included *Esaú e Jacó* (*Esau and Jacob*, 1904), *Relíquias da Casa Velha* (*Relics of the Old House*, 1906), and *Counselor Aires's Memorial* (*Memorial de Aires*, 1908).

Further Reading: Caldwell, Helen. *The Brazilian Othello of Machado de Assis*. Berkeley: University of California Press, 1960; Caldwell, Helen. *Machado de Assis: The Brazilian Master and His Novels*. Berkeley: University of California Press, 1970; Lisboa, Maria Miguel. *Machado de Assis and Feminism: Re-reading the Heart of the Companion*. Lewiston, NY: Edwin Mellen Press, 1996.

Justin Corfield

McKay, Claude (1889–1948)

Claude McKay was a Jamaican novelist and communist, who, after living for a time in England as arguably Britain's first black journalist, became a noted figure in the Harlem Renaissance. He was born in September 1889 in Jamaica. His father was a farmer. In 1912, McKay, who started working as a policeman, eventually became noticed by Walter Jekyll. Jekyll assisted McKay in publishing his first poetic collection, *Songs of Jamaica*. The collection was significant as the first set of poems published in Jamaican Creole. McKay's next volume, *Constab Ballads* (1912), recounted his times as a law enforcement official.

In late 1912, McKay went to Booker T. Washington's Tuskegee Institute in Alabama. During McKay's time in the United States, especially during his experiences in South Carolina, he was shocked at the racist attitudes and the restrictions on blacks in public facilities. McKay left to go to Kansas State University and, in 1914, decided against becoming an agronomist and moved to New York. In New York, McKay married Eulalie Lewars, his childhood sweetheart. After six months, McKay and his wife returned to Jamaica, where he continued to write poetry. In 1917, he published *Seven Arts* under the pseudonym "Eli Edwards." McKay then started working as a waiter on the Jamaica railways and then became politically active.

McKay had been unhappy with the nationalist ideals espoused by black leader Marcus Garvey, as well as the National Association for the Advancement of Colored People (NAACP), which he saw as too middle class. This led to his involvement in the new alternative African Blood Brotherhood, a semisecret revolutionary group. Soon afterward, McKay moved to London, England, where he wrote for *Negro World* and became involved in the International Socialist Club in Shoreditch. In Shoreditch, McKay started associating with many leftwing intellectuals and began to write for *Workers' Dreadnought*, which published a large number of his articles. While living in England as a paid journalist, McKay may have been the first black journalist in Britain.

McKay attended the 1920 Communist Unity Conference that established the British Communist Party. Continuing writing, McKay's famous book, *Home to Harlem*, was in 1928. The book, which detailed life on the streets of Harlem in New York, had a profound influence on black intellectuals across the globe, including those in Britain and continental Europe. Furthermore, it won the Harmon Gold Award for Literature. McKay's later books included *Banjo* (1930), *Gingertown* (1932), and *Banana Bottom* (1933). His two-volume autobiography appeared in *A Long Way from Home* (1937) and *Harlem: Negro Metropolis* (1940). His *Selected Poems* (1953) was published posthumously.

Disillusioned with communism, McKay became a Roman Catholic. He died from a heart attack in May 1948.

See also: Authors in Europe, African American; Britain, Blacks in; Colonies in the Caribbean, British; Literature, Blacks in British; Media, Blacks in Contemporary European.

Further Reading: Cooper, Wayne. *Claude McKay: Rebel Sojourner in the Harlem Renaissance.* New York: Schocken, 1987; Hones, Bridget. "With 'Banjo' by My Bed: Black French Writers Reading Claude McKay." *Caribbean Quarterly* 38:1 (1992): 32–39; McKay, Claude. *A Long Way from Home.* New York: Lee Furman, 1937; McKay, Claude. *Harlem: Negro Metropolis.* New York: E. P. Dutton and Co., 1940; Rani, Kandula Nirupa. *Claude McKay: The Literary Identity from Jamaica to Harlem and Beyond.* Jefferson, NC: McFarland and Company, 2006.

Justin Corfield

Magi, Representations of the

The Christian traditions associated with the story of the birth of Jesus of Nazareth celebrated every year at Christmas (December 25) have had a profound impact on the imagination of the West. The retelling of the infancy narrative from the Gospels of Luke and Matthew has served as a powerful vehicle for the communication of the central claims of Christianity about Jesus and the models of human responses toward him. Within the Gospel of Matthew (Matt 2:1–12), magi come to Bethlehem, where Jesus is born, from the East asking to see the newborn king of the Jews because they have seen his star rising and they wish to pay him homage with gifts of gold, frankincense, and myrrh. Warned in a dream not to return to King Herod, who desired the destruction of the child, they return to their own homes after their act of reverent devotion to him. This story served to articulate the twofold reaction toward Jesus: rejection (Herod) and acceptance (the magi). For Matthew, the true king of the Jews was not King Herod, but the baby in Bethlehem. The magi, as Gentiles, or non-Jews, had recognized the revelation from God through the signs of nature, which eluded the learned within the Jewish court of worldly power.

The adoration of the magi depicted in the Gospel of Matthew, rather than the devotion of shepherds in the Gospel of Luke (Lk 2:8–14), first captured the attention of the pious in the early centuries of Christianity. As early as the third century, the visitors from the East make their appearance in a fresco within the Roman catacomb of Priscilla. In the literature of Christianity, the impulse to supplement Matthew's account with specific details proved irresistible. Soon, the European Christian tradition set the number of magi at three, because of the number of gifts, and gave them the status of kings. They were given the names of Melchior, Caspar, and Balthasar, and their veneration was linked with the solemn feast of the Epiphany (January 6). Their saintly remains were believed to repose within the cathedral of Cologne, and a depiction of them formed the centerpiece of many nativity liturgical dramas. Central to their symbolic importance was that they represented the acceptance of Jesus as the Messiah, or Savior, by all humanity; thus they represented the three regions of the earth (Europe, Asia, and Africa). Further, they were thought of as representing the three chronological periods of old age, middle age, and youth, as well as different races.

The emphasis on one of the magi being black can be found as early as the eighth century in Irish commentaries on the Gospel of Matthew (Pseudo-Bede, *In Matthaei Evangelium Exposito*). By the year 1000, a clear magi legend articulated itself within the devotional and religious culture of the emerging Middle Ages. That tradition would become well known through the efforts of Johannes de Hildesheim in his comprehensive summation of the whole magi mythology, the *Historia Trium Regum*, penned toward the end of his life in 1364–1375. An English translation of the *Historia Trium Regum* can be found in *The Early English Text Society* (1886). This work affirms that one of the magi, Caspar, was a black Ethiopian and the tallest of the three. It was he who offered, with tears, the gift of myrrh. This text of Johannes, along with the emerging awareness of black Africans in Europe in the fifteenth century, would give rise to the explosion of devotional pictorial and dramatic representations of Gentile piety through the image of the black magi. Some examples of important works of art that codified the artistic rendering of the black magi tradition would be the Bavarian *Wurzach Altarpiece* of Hans Multscher (1437); Albrecht Dürer's *Adoration* (1504); Hieronymous Bosch's *Adoration* of ca. 1500–1510; and Andrea del Sarto's fresco in the atrium of SS. Annunziata in Florence (1511). This tradition, which continues to the modern period, would reverently depict the black magi in gestures of adoration and, as such, serves as one important positive way of integrating black non-Europeans into the Christianized Western world.

See also: Age of Exploration; Art, Blacks as Represented in European; Benedict the Moor, Saint; Black Madonna Tradition; Cain, Theory of Descent of Blacks from; Hamitic Myth; Maurice, Saint; Popes, African; Renaissance, Blacks in the.

Further Reading: Kaplan, Paul. *The Rise of the Black Magus in Western Art*. Ann Arbor: UMI Research Press, 1985.

Lawrence F. Hundersmarck

Malcolm X in London

Malcolm X (1925–1965), an African American civil rights leader, spent half of the final two weeks of his life in England, primarily London, where he gave two speeches and several interviews that had a substantial impact on the civil rights movement in Britain. Malcolm flew from New York to London on Friday, February 5, where he attended a weekend conference of the Council of African Organizations. He addressed the gathering on February 8, advocating unity between Africans and black Americans, and decrying the negative depiction of both in the United States news media. Malcolm traveled to Paris on February 9 at the invitation of African American students there, but French officials denied him permission to enter the country.

On returning to London, Malcolm was interviewed on February 10 by *Flamingo*, a monthly magazine produced by black Londoners. In the interview, Malcolm returned to several themes that he often emphasized during this period of his life, including the international context of the civil rights struggle in the United States; the inspiring examples of ongoing anticolonial revolutions in Africa and Asia; the necessity of unity in the face of a powerful enemy; and the damage caused by demeaning images of blacks in the American press.

Malcolm was able to develop all those themes at much greater length in his most important talk in London, a February 11 speech at the London School of Economics organized by the university's Africa Society. The transcript indicates that Malcolm was more relaxed than in the previous day's interview, in which most of his answers were curt, and his trademark sense of humor is evident. He warned against any reliance on liberal politicians, applauded the emergence of an "independent Africa," and concluded the speech with a call to blacks in Western countries to see themselves as "part of the oppressed masses all over the world" who "today are crying out for action against the common oppressor." Malcolm commented briefly on his split with the Nation of Islam in the discussion period. It is notable that throughout his week in Europe, he rarely mentioned the Nation, preferring to speak about international developments and the struggle against racism at home and abroad.

While in London, Malcolm was also interviewed by the South African *Sunday Express*, the *Ghanaian Times*, the London *Times*, and the New China News Agency. He told the Chinese journalists that the United States was doomed to failure in their military efforts in Vietnam, where its choice was "to die there or pull out."

The day before leaving England, Malcolm visited Smethwick, a suburb of Birmingham that had recently experienced racial tension. He returned to New York on Saturday, February 13, and maintained a busy schedule over the next week. He was assassinated as he took the podium to address an audience at Harlem's Audubon Ballroom on Sunday, February 21.

See also: Black British; Britain, Blacks in; Civil Rights Movement in Twentieth-Century Great Britain; King Jr., Martin Luther.

Further Reading: Malcolm X. *The Final Speeches: February 1965.* New York: Pathfinder Press, 1992; Malcolm X Project (Columbia University): http://www.columbia.edu/cu/ccbh/mxp/; Marable, Manning. *Malcolm X: A Life of Reinvention.* New York: Viking/Penguin, 2009.

John M. Cox

Man in the Iron Mask

Nabo the **Moor** was an African who became a favorite at the court of Queen Marie-Teresa of France during the seventeenth century. He disappeared mysteriously and was once suggested as being the famous prisoner known as the "Man in the Iron Mask."

From North Africa, Nabo lived at the French Royal Palace of Louis XIV at Versailles. Ten or twelve years old, and two feet three inches tall, he was given to Queen Marie-Teresa as a wedding present when she married Louis XIV at Saint Jean-de-Luz on June 9, 1660. The queen, the daughter of Philip IV of Spain, brought with her a large dowry and was, herself, of short stature. Within four months of the marriage, Nabo had become her favorite. He accompanied her when she made short journeys and appeared with her in at least one painting. Soon, it was realized that Nabo had significant musical talents. As a result, Paul Auget, the director of the King's Music, taught him how to play the guitar. As a result, Nabo took the surname *"d'Auget."*

Louis XIV and Maria Therese had a son, born on November 1, 1661 (Louis "The Grand Dauphin," grandfather of King Louis XV); and on November 18, 1662, they had a daughter, who died on December 30. Soon after, Louis XIV started having an affair with his sister-in-law, and it seems that the queen may have started an affair with Nabo, by then 15 or 16 years old. On November 16, 1664, the queen went into premature labor, and she gave birth to a dark-skinned daughter. Rumors circulated quickly that Nabo was the father. The baby, named Marie-Anne of France, was sickly; and by the end of the year, it was announced that the girl had died on December 26, barely five weeks old. Nothing more was known about Nabo.

There were theories that the girl had survived and, known as the "Mooress of Moret," she became a nun at the Benedictine Convent at Moret. There were also theories that she assumed the name of Sister Louis-Marie-Therese, and that the king had endowed the nunnery with 20,000 crowns, with the Grand Dauphin visiting the place on occasions. This story became part of the play *Las Meninas*, which took its name from the painting by the Spanish artist Velasquez.

Nabo's fate continues to remain a mystery. Certainly, he disappeared from court, and there are theories that he was the infamous man held in the Royal Prison at the Bastille, Paris, as the "Man in the Iron Mask." This story was revived by the writer Pierre-Marie Dijol, suggesting that this is why the name Eustache d'Auger became associated with the mysterious legend of the prisoner known as the "Man in the Iron Mask." When the prisoner died in 1703, he was buried in Paris under the name "Marchiali." Although many historians suggested that this was because the prisoner was the North Italian politician Ercole Antonio Mattioli, Dijol put forward an alternative theory for the name. Nabo, as he was from North Africa, was often known by his slang name "Ali." After he was given an honorific title, "Marquis," it was not long before he became known as "Marquis Ali," or "Marchiali." Given that one of the few identifying features of the prisoner was that he was tall, however, Nabo seems an unlikely candidate.

See also: Courts, Blacks at European Aristocratic; France, Blacks in.

Further Reading: Dijol, Pierre-Marie. *Nabo, ou le Masque de fer.* Paris: Editions France-Empire, 1978; Michael of Greece, Prince. *Louis XIV: The Other Side of the Sun.* London: Orbis, 1983; Noone, John. *The Man Behind the Iron Mask.* Stroud: Alan Sutton, 1988.

Justin Corfield

Maran, René (1887–1960)

René Maran, a French writer of Guyanese descent, was the first black recipient of the prestigious *Prix Goncourt* in French literature. He was born aboard a boat bound to Fort-de-France, Martinique, in 1887. As a boy, his family moved to Gabon, where his father served in the colonial service. Maran attended a boarding school in Bordeaux, France. He later became a member of the French colonial service in French Equatorial Africa. Maran's experiences in the French colonial service served as the inspiration for much of his literary output, including *Batouala*, which won the *Prix Goncourt* in 1921.

To many literary critics, Maran's work marks the beginning of African and Caribbean literature in French. He came to argue for an African identity in terms of the context of a sort of **Pan-Africanism.** In this sense, his work is often considered a precursor to the **Négritude** movement.

Some of Maran's major collections of poetry include *La Maison du Bonheur* (1909) and *La Vie Intérieure* (1912). Some of his major novels include *Batouala* (1921), *Le cœur serré* (1931), *Le Livre de la Brousse* (1933), and *Un Homme pareil aux autres* (1947).

See also: African Diaspora; Colonies in Africa, French; Colonies in the Caribbean, French; Damas, Léon; Du Bois, W.E.B; Fanon, Frantz; France, Blacks in; French Army, Blacks in the; Literature, Blacks in French; Senghor, Léopold Sédar; World War I, Black Participation in.

Further Reading: Cameron, Keith. *René Maran.* Boston: Twayne Publishers, 1985; Maran, René. *Batouala.* trans. Alexandre Mboukou and Barbara Beck. Portsmouth, NH: Heinemann, 2008; Ojo-Ade, Femi. *René Maran: The Black Frenchman: A Bio-critical Study.* Washington, DC: Three Continents, 1984; Peabody, Sue, and Tyler Stovall, eds. *The Color of Liberty: Histories of Race in France.* Durham, NC: Duke University Press, 2003.

Eric Martone

Marché Dejean

The *Marché Dejean,* commonly referred to as the "African Market," is a popular open-air neighborhood market located in the Goutte d'Or quarter in the 18th arrondissement of Paris, France outside of the Château-Rouge subway stop. Men, women, and children in native African clothing are typically found there working tables, trading spots, and places to eat. The area, which includes several specialty shops in the surrounding streets, is usually boisterous and crowded, featuring much mingling, shopping, and bargaining as people from all over the greater Paris area attempt to purchase exotic foodstuffs and ingredients, clothing, hair products, and other items from Europe, Africa, and the Caribbean. Hawkers also line the *Marché Dejean*, peddling cheap watches and perfumes.

The surrounding neighborhood of the *Marché Dejean* is composed of multiethnic diverse inhabitants and has been in recent history a working-class area with its fair share of crime and destitution. The area, one of Paris's most cosmopolitan neighborhoods, is currently home to a number of Africans and North Africans who have immigrated to France. Several different languages are spoken in the area around the *Marché Dejean*, including different Northern and Western African dialects and Arabic, with French serving as a universal language.

During the nineteenth century, provincial workers moved to Paris to help build the improvements to Paris as part of the designs of Baron Georges Haussmann. These workers lived in what became part of the 18th arrondissement. The remains of the Haussmann buildings were used to build inexpensive housing in the area, which caused its growth. At the beginning of the twentieth century, in addition to the steady supply of new inhabitants from the French provinces, there was an influx of immigrants to this area, at first from Belgium and Poland, and then from Italy and Spain. During the 1920s, there was an influx of new Berber inhabitants from Algeria, which at that time was still part of France. More Algerians arrived after World War II to help rebuild Paris, which had been damaged during the war. After the Algerian war, there was a wave of immigration from Africa to France that has continued steadily to the present.

The African inhabitants of the *Marché Dejean* area derive from such sub-Saharan countries as Senegal and Cameroon and from northern African countries such as Morocco, Tunisia, and Algeria. These countries have historically had ties with France as part of the French colonial empire. There are also immigrants from the Caribbean (the Antilles and Jamaica), East Asia (China), and India living in the area to work. Consequently, within the small area of Paris around the *Marché Dejean*, one can see the effects of colonialism on the metropole (or "mother country") and the emerging struggle to find a French identity in a pluralist society.

See also: Colonies in Africa, French; Colonies in the Caribbean, French; France, Blacks in; Immigration to Europe, Illegal African; May 10 Holiday (France); Race Riots in Europe; World War II, Black Participation in.

Further Reading: Winders, James. *Paris Africain: Rhythms of the African Diaspora*. New York: Palgrave Macmillan, 2006.

Eric Martone

Massaquoi, Hans-Jürgen (1926–)

Hans-Jürgen Massaquoi, a German native, grew up in Nazi Germany and came to the United States on a student visa. He eventually become a U.S. citizen and worked for almost 40 years with *Ebony Magazine*, where he eventually became managing editor.

Born in January 1926, Massaquoi grew up in a Germany devoid of many racial minorities. Massaquoi's father, Al-Haj, was the son of the Liberian Counsel General in Hamburg, Germany. While in Hamburg, Al-Haj met Massaquoi's mother, Bertha Baetz, a German nurse. The couple never married. In the early 1930s, Massaquoi's diplomatic grandfather returned to Liberia to run unsuccessfully for the presidency of the country. Al-Haj followed his father, but Bertha refused to go to Liberia and also refused to let her son accompany his father there. It was during this time that Adolph Hitler and the Nazis assumed control in Germany.

Massaquoi was able to advance while living under the Nazi regime despite being without a father, not being affluent, and being a minority. Before his father returned to Liberia, Massaquoi lived in a household with German servants, thus living in an environment where the Africans were superior in social class and rank to their white servants. Furthermore, and especially in 1936, Massaquoi had strong black role models who were from the United States, as news of Jesse Owens in the 1936 **Olympics** and the great fights between Max Schmeling and Joe Louis provided a source of strength and pride for the 10-year-old. Even without a father living at home, Massaquoi was surrounded by many "father figures" in Germany, especially at school, where the idea of a "fatherland" was indoctrinated into every child.

Massaquoi did face some racial challenges during his childhood in Nazi Germany. Being in the nearly all-white city of Hamburg, he stood out because of his dark appearance. At school, he was sometimes taunted by other children who shouted, "*Neger, Neger, Schornsteinfeger!*" ("Negro, Negro, chimney sweep!") Ironically, in recent years, a German producer made a television movie on the life of Massaquoi using the taunt as the title of the movie. Despite these taunts, Massaquoi was never attacked or imprisoned like so many other minorities during the Nazi regime.

There was little opportunity for Massaquoi in Nazi Germany. Consequently, after the war, he took a post with the British military, which was occupying Hamburg. He served as a translator, which ignited his interest in communications. In 1948, Massaquoi went to live in Liberia with his father's family, but he found the country to be too racially charged. Soon after, he applied for a student visa to the United States and became an aviation mechanics student in Chicago. When the Korean War began, Massaquoi volunteered for military service and served with the 82nd Airborn Division. Because he never left the United States, and lived in the pre-Civil Rights era South, Massaquoi was very aware of the racial divide in the United States.

After the Korean War, and now a citizen of the United States, Massaquoi graduated from the University of Illinois in 1957 and immediately began working for *Ebony Magazine*, where he remained for nearly 40 years and eventually became managing editor. During his tenure at the magazine, Massaquoi met with and interviewed many of the great African American figures.

After years of encouragement by his friend Alex Haley, Massaquoi, upon his retirement, decided to write a book on his experiences growing up in Nazi Germany. In *Destined to Witness: Growing Up Black in Nazi Germany* (1999), Massaquoi tells his story and shares his interpretations and views of one of the most volatile times in world history.

See also: Afro-Germans; Germany, Blacks in; Gilges, Lari; Media, Blacks in Contemporary European; Nassy, Josef; Nazis and Blacks in Europe; Snow, Valaida; Television, Blacks in European.

Further Reading: Massaquoi, Hans-Jürgen. *Destined to Witness: Growing Up Black in Nazi Germany.* New York: William Morrow, 1999.

Robert Nave

Matheus, John (1887–1983)

John Frederick Matheus was an African American playwright and academic who completed part of his graduate studies in Paris, France. The settings of many of Matheus's literary pieces focused on the diverse experiences of the **African Diaspora.**

Matheus was born in September 1887 in West Virginia. He attended public schools in Steubenville, Ohio, and Western Reserve, before going to Columbia University, where he graduated in 1921. After completing summer school at the University of Paris (Sorbonne), Matheus proceeded to the University of Chicago. He visited Haiti, Cuba, and Liberia, and later set some of his plays and short stories in these countries.

From 1911 until 1913, Matheus was a teacher of Latin at Florida Agricultural and Mechanical College in Tallahassee. He was later a professor of modern languages at West Virginia State College from 1913 until 1922. There, Matheus became professor of Romance languages from 1922 until 1953, when he then became professor emeritus.

During his career, Matheus won several distinctions and published several works. In May 1925, Matheus won the Opportunity short-story competition with his short story, *Fog,* which was set on the borders of West Virginia and Ohio. The next year, he won first prize in the personal-experience section, second prize in the drama section, and an honorable mention in both the poetry and short story sections. In 1930, Matheus became a member of the commission appointed by the League of Nations to investigate allegations of forced labor in Liberia. In 1936, Matheus jointly edited *A Reader on Alexandre Dumas.* His one-act play, *Cruiter,* set in a log cabin in lower Georgia, was performed in 1940, and in 1945–1946, Matheus taught English in Haiti under the auspices of the Inter-American Educational Foundation. His work influenced many others, including composer Clarence Cameron White (1880–1960), who used one drama by Matheus to put together *Onaga: A Haitian Opera in Three Acts* in 1938.

Retiring from West Virginia State College after a 40-year career there, Matheus was professor of foreign languages at Maryland State College from 1953 until 1954. He worked as professor of Romance languages at Dillard University in New Orleans from 1954 until 1957. Matheus then held a succession of positions as assistant professor of foreign languages and literature at Texas Southern University in Houston from 1959 to 1961, visiting professor of German and French at Hampton Institute from 1961 to 1962, and professor of Romance languages at Kentucky State University in 1962. Matheus died in February 1983.

See also: Authors in Europe, African American; Dumas *père*, Alexandre; Haitian Revolution for Independence.

Further Reading: Andrews, William, Frances Smith Foster, and Trudier Harris, eds. *The Oxford Companion to African American Literature.* New York: Oxford University Press, 1997; Lowney, John. "Haiti and Black Transnationalism: Remapping the Migrant Geography of Home to Harlem." *African American Review* 34: 3 (Autumn 2000): 413–429.

Justin Corfield

Maurice, Saint (?–287 c.e.?)

Saint Maurice, Knight of the Holy Lance, is a saint in the Roman Catholic Church. According to historical accounts that remain incomplete, Maurice was a soldier from Africa who was martyred by the Roman Army to which he belonged when he and his troops refused to worship the Roman gods. In the Catholic Church, Maurice's Feast Day is September 22. He is the patron for soldiers, especially the papal Swiss Guards.

Maurice was a soldier of reported high rank of the Roman Army. He was the commander of a legion called the Theban Legion. This legion comes from the Upper Nile, where Egypt borders the Sudan, and comprised mostly Christians. During the reign of Diocletian and his co-emperor, Maximian Herculius, Maurice and the Theban Legion were ordered into service. Maximian commanded the forces of the Roman Army in Gaul (present day France/Switzerland) to put down a reported rebellion of the citizens of Gaul. On their arrival at Martigny, near the lake of Geneva, Maximian ordered the troops to worship the Roman gods with a ritual sacrifice. Protesting this non-Christian activity, and believing that the people of Gaul did nothing to incur the wrath of the Roman Army, Maurice and the Theban Legion retreated to Agaunum (present-day Saint-Maurice-en-Valais), disobeying Maximian's orders to return and conform to the rituals. Maximian ordered every tenth soldier of the Theban Legion executed, but Maurice did not capitulate. Such actions led to a second round of sacrifice of every tenth man. Without achieving success, Maximian ordered the entire slaughter of the Theban Legion.

Although much of this depiction is viewed as skeptical, Bishop Eucherius of Lyons, in an attempt to authenticate the legend of Maurice, documented this story. The story was substantiated further by other rulers in the area of Saint-Maurice in Switzerland, and, consequently, the story became established history. A cultlike following of Maurice developed through the years and is still active.

The Holy Lance, which came to be associated with Saint Maurice, is an ordinary wing-shaped spearhead without the shaft that has a slit in the middle of the lance-head containing a nail that is supposed to have been used to crucify Jesus of Nazareth. The lance is believed to be the one that was used by the Roman centurion, Longinus, to pierce the side of Jesus while he was on the cross. To believers, this piercing caused blood and water to flow from the inflicted wound on Jesus. There is great significance in the action of the piercing, which symbolizes the birth of the Catholic Church. The water that came from the wound symbolizes baptism, and the blood represents the transubstantiation of blood into the wine as celebrated in the Eucharist within the Catholic Church.

Meeting of Saint Erasmus of Formiae and Saint Maurice by Matthias Grunewald (1517–1523). Alte Pinakothek, Munich, Germany. Bildarchiv Preussischer Kulturbesitz / Art Resource, NY.

The exact point in time when the Holy Lance became associated with Maurice is unclear. The connection possibly dates to the reign of Henry III of France (1039–1056), for an inscription, bearing the name of Maurice was placed on the lance-head at the point where the nail was being held in place. On closer study, and according to weapons experts, however, wing-shaped spearheads were not found until the sixth and seventh centuries, making it highly unlikely that Maurice ever brandished such a weapon.

See also: Germany, Blacks in; Holy Roman Army, Africans in the; Roman Empire, Black Iconography and the.

Further Reading: Suckale-Redlefsen, Gude. *The Black Saint Maurice.* Houston: Menil Foundation, 1987.

Robert Nave

May 10 Holiday

May 10 has been designated a national holiday in France since 2006 to commemorate the abolition of slavery in France and its colonies. The holiday, the first of its kind in Europe, comes as France increasingly debates its colonial past and the role of immigrants from France's former colonies in French society.

French president Jacques Chirac announced the holiday in January 2006 at a reception held in honor of the Committee for the Memory of Slavery. According to a January 30 press release from the French government, Chirac shared his desire that beginning in 2006, "Metropolitan France should honor the memory of the victims of slavery and commemorate its abolition." Furthermore, in his speech, Chirac expressed that, "in human history, slavery is a wound, a tragedy which has caused enormous suffering on every continent." He further presented the idea that democracy is incompatible with slavery and all that it represents, and that "slavery must be given its rightful place in primary and secondary school curricula."

May 10 was chosen as the date for the holiday, for on that day in 2001, the French Senate adopted a law recognizing slavery and the slave trade as crimes against humanity. The law was the first of its kind in Europe; however, France continues to face difficulties charting a course to deal with multiethnic diversity. The bulk of France's immigrants hail from its former colonies, particularly those in the Caribbean and Africa. While Chirac was president, his conservative government had often adopted strict immigration legislation and supported controversial legislation concerning how colonialism should be taught in schools. Further troubles arose as a result of high unemployment rates, particularly among the young, and poor living conditions for immigrants. Race riots in Paris in 2005, orchestrated by many black and Arab youths, also caused concern.

During the first annual celebration of the holiday in 2006, Chirac inaugurated a temporary piece of art in Paris featuring a bamboo arch with photographs of culturally diverse individuals. The Panthéon, which holds the remains of France's greatest citizens, provided free entry to the tombs of those individuals significant to the abolition of slavery. The Louvre Museum and the National Library in Paris gave special tours highlighting pieces of art and manuscripts pertinent to slavery and the slave trade. The city of Nantes, which occupied a prominent role in the French slave trade, held a moment of silence. Other cities throughout France held ceremonies, readings, concerts, and other events to celebrate cultural diversity and commemorate the French abolition of slavery.

See also: Colonies in Africa, French; Colonies in the Caribbean, French; France, Blacks in; Race Riots in Europe; Slave Trade, French.

Further Reading: Chapman, Herrick, and Laura Frader, eds. *Race in France: Interdisciplinary Perspectives on the Politics of Difference*. New York: Berghahn Books, 2004; Dorigny, Marcel, ed. *Abolitions of Slavery: From L. F. Sonthonax to Victor Schoelcher, 1793, 1794, 1848*. trans. New York: Berghahn Books, 2003; Lebovics, Herman. "The Musée du Quai Branly: Art? Artifact? Spectacle!" *French Politics, Culture and Society* 24:3 (Winter 2006): 96–110.

Eric Martone

Media, Blacks in Contemporary European

Contemporary European media differ from U.S. media in several ways, but one of them concerns the representation of blacks. Although seeing black news reporters and news anchormen and anchorwomen is nothing unusual in the United States, blacks in contemporary European media are rare despite the increasing numbers of black Europeans and blacks residing in Europe. They remained virtually invisible in European media until the 1990s, with few exceptions. In European countries, in general, and in contrast to the United States, for instance, blacks are hardly represented in contemporary media such as journalism and broadcast news. Because race does not exist as a census category, no official data exist with regard to how many blacks actually live in Europe. Some were born and raised in European countries, whereas others went to Europe as soldiers, students, or refugees. A number of blacks are the children of these migrants. Some of the black journalists and television news reporters are from the United States, the Caribbean or from African countries; others are Afro-descendants with a white European parent.

FRANCE.   There are some prominent journalists and television news reporters in France of black descent. Some of the most prominent are **Harry Roselmack,** Audrey Pulvar, and Christine Kelly. Despite efforts to increase the representation of minorities in the media, France, similar to most other European countries, still has a long way to go.

In the wake of the 2005 race riots in France, the French government decided that it had to ensure that the media reflected the diversity of the French people. In July

2006, Harry Roselmack, the first black evening news anchorman on the French TV station *TF1*, entered the French TV scene. *Club Averroes*, an organization advocating the increased representation of minorities in the French media, considered his position a sign of progress.

Black journalist Audrey Pulvar, who was born in Martinique, became the first black news anchorwoman, but on a smaller scale than Roselmack. Pulvar studied economics at Rouen and journalism in Paris. She started working for a regional program (*France 3*). A few years afterward, she also started working also for *LCP*.

Christine Kelly, born in Guadalupe, is a black journalist, TV reporter, and TV show host. Similar to Pulvar, Kelly was a TV reporter for *France 3* in different regions, such as Rouen and Tours, starting in 1997. Three years later, *LCI* hired her as a news anchor. She became the first black female to broadcast news nationwide.

GERMANY.   Germany ranks among those European countries that feature some black news broadcasters. Since the 1990s, the appearance of black talk show hosts and journalists has gradually increased. Some of the most prominent are **Cherno Jobatey,** Jeannine Kantara, Nkechi Madubuko, and Noah Sow.

Cherno Jobatey, who was born in Berlin, has worked as a journalist. He has been contributing to newspapers and magazines, such as *taz, Die Welt, Die Zeit, Der Spiegel*, and others. Jobatey has degrees in political science (Free University, Berlin) and music (Musicians' Institute, Hollywood, LA). In addition, he has hosted radio shows and, since 1992, the popular TV morning news show *ZDF-Morgenmagazin.*

Jeannine Kantara is a journalist with a social sciences degree from the Open University in England. Kantara is cofounder of the **Afro-German** organization, **Initiative of Blacks in Germany (ISD)**, and codirector of its Berlin office. Kantara is also editor of the Afro-German magazine, *afro look.*

John A. Kantara, born in Bonn to a white German mother and a Ghanaian father, has degrees in political science (Free University, Berlin, 1991) and international journalism (City University, London, 1992). Kantara, a freelance journalist and filmmaker, has contributed to TV shows produced by TV stations, such as *ZDF*, *3sat*, and *Vox.*

Nkechi Madubuko, who was born in Giessen to Nigerian parents, studied sociology, media, and psychology. Madubuko is currently a doctoral student at Philipps-University, Marburg. Apart from hosting several TV shows, such as the TV music station *VIVA Zwei* (1996–1999), *Premiere World*, and *DSF*, she has worked as an actress and is an accomplished athlete (high jump).

Noah Sow, who was born in Straubing, is a musician, producer and author, who had her own TV shows on German TV stations, such as *WDR* and *HR*. In addition, Sow worked as a radio host on radio stations like *Radio Fritz*. She started the first antiracist media watchdog organization in Germany, *der braune mob*, in 2001 and published a book on racism in Germany in 2008.

UNITED KINGDOM.   As with the other European countries, the United Kingdom has few black journalists and news anchors. In the 1950s, black publications appeared in the United Kingdom such as the *West Indian Gazette*, the *Jamaican Gleaner*, and the *Caribbean Voice*. In the late 1970s to late 1990s, several African-Caribbean newspapers like the *Caribbean Times*, the *Journal*, and the *New Nation* were published and competed with each other.

The United Kingdom is the only European country with an association of minority journalists. This association, *Aspire*, was founded by Mutale Nkonde and Corinne Amoo. Nkonde is a news and current affairs researcher at the BBC, and Amoo is a researcher for a production company. As of 2007, the association lists about one dozen board members and approximately 250 members. The existence of the U.S. organization *National Association of Black Journalists* gave the impetus to the establishment of *Aspire* in 2003.

There are some prominent journalists and television news reporters in the United Kingdom of black descent. Some of the most prominent are **Trevor McDonald** and Esther Armah.

Trevor McDonald, who was born in Trinidad, was the first black news anchor in the United Kingdom. McDonald started working for BBC Radio in London in 1969. In 1973, he joined *ITN (Independent Television News)*. Queen Elizabeth II knighted him in 1999, the same year in which he received several other honors. McDonald published his autobiography in 1993.

Esther Armah is a black British journalist who owns the multimedia company *Centric Productions* and has appeared on the radio. Armah has worked as a journalist in the United Kingdom, the United States, and Ghana. She has written for newspapers and magazines such as *The Guardian* (UK), *Essence* (US) and *New Ghanaian*. In 2006, she published a self-help book.

See also: Afro-German; Black British; Initiative of Blacks in Germany (ISD); Massaquoi, Hans-Jürgen; Race Riots in Europe; Television, Blacks in European.

Further Reading: Ainley, Beulah. *Black Journalists, White Media.* Stoke-on-Trent, UK: Trentham Books, 1998; Armah, Esther. *Can I Be Me?* Bloomington: iUniverse, 2006; Jobatey, Cherno. *Fit wie ein Turnschuh: minimaler Aufwand—maximaler Erfolg.* Munich: Knaur, 2005; Kelly, Christine. *Francois Fillon, le secret et l'ambition.* Paris: Editions du Moment, 2007; Kelly, Christine. *L'Affaire Flactif.* Paris: Calmann-Lévy, 2006; McDonald, Trevor. *Fortunate Circumstances.* London: Weidenfield and Nicholson, 1993; Morrison, Lionel. *A Century of Black Journalism in Britain.* United Kingdom: Truebay, 2007; Sow, Noah. *Deutschland Schwarz Weiß. Der alltägliche Rassismus.* Munich: Bertelsmann, 2008.

S. Marina Jones

Medici, Alessandro de (1510–1537)

Alessandro de Medici, the first duke of Florence, was the last of the senior branch of the Italian Medici family to rule Florence and the first to become a hereditary duke. Known as *"il Moro"* ("the **Moor**"), Alessandro was the first black head of state in modern European history, although his African ancestry is rarely mentioned. He was an influential Renaissance figure and is the ancestor of a number of noble and royal houses in Europe.

Alessandro was born in 1510 to a black servant in the Medici household. After her later marriage to a muleteer, she is referred to as Simonetta da Collavechio. Alessandro was raised by Lorenzo II de Medici, Duke of Urbino, who was the grandson of the famous statesman Lorenzo I de Medici, known as "the Magnificent." The renowned Renaissance politician and writer Niccolò Machiavelli dedicated *The Prince*,

Alessandro de Medici. Scala / Art Resource, NY.

a guide for rulers that extolled the virtues of tyranny that must be used to maintain power, to Lorenzo II. Many historians, however, believe that Alessandro was actually the son of Giulio de Medici (the future Pope Clement VII), himself an illegitimate Medici child raised by his uncle, Lorenzo the Magnificent. Alessandro's physical appearance reflected his black ancestry, which was noted by his contemporaries and became the basis of his nickname.

In 1523, after his election as pope, Giulio relinquished the lordship of Florence to the young Alessandro and his nephew Ippolito de Medici. Although both were illegitimate, they were the last members of the elder branch of the Medici family. Because both were too young to govern effectively, Giulio appointed a regent, Cardinal Silvio Passerini. During the regency, republican sentiment grew in Florence. When Holy Roman Emperor Charles V sacked Rome in 1527, the people of Florence seized the opportunity to reinstall a republic. Alessandro and Ippolito, along with the rest of the Medici family and primary supporters, fled.

Eventually, papal and imperial factions made peace. After such a situation, in 1530, Charles V decided to restore the Medici to power in Florence. With military assistance and endorsement as ruler from Charles V, Alessandro was installed as the Florentine head of state. Around the same time, Clement VII made Ippolito a cardinal and sent him on a temporary mission to Hungary. In an attempt to secure Alessandro's legal and political position as head of Florence, Clement VII made an agreement with Charles V that would bestow on Alessandro the hereditary title of duke of Florence. Previously, the Medici had attempted to avoid such titles to maintain ostensibly Florentine aspirations for a republic. In 1532, a new constitution was adopted and Alessandro became the hereditary duke of Florence and perpetual head of state.

After the death of Clement VII in 1534, Alessandro's political opponents, which included members of junior branches of the Medici family, attempted to remove him from power. In 1535, the Florentines appointed Ippolito their representative to bring grievances against Alessandro to Charles V. Ippolito died on his way to the court, probably from malaria, although some have speculated that he was poisoned on Alessandro's orders. Charles V continued to uphold Alessandro's right as ruler and offered the Italian duke his daughter, Margaret of Austria, in marriage as a sign of support. Shortly after the wedding, however, Alessandro was assassinated by his distant cousin, Lorenzino de Medici, to further republicanism.

Medici officials, in fear of an uprising upon news of Alessandro's death, attempted to hide the corpse and arrange a secret burial to delay a public response; however, the Medici managed to maintain control of Florence after Alessandro's assassination. Rather than establish a regency for Alessandro's four-year-old son, Giulio, the family instead transferred power to Cosimo I de Medici, head of a junior branch of the family, who was older and had a greater chance of restoring order and consolidating power. Cosimo served as the guardian of Alessandro's children. Later, Cosimo made Giulio first admiral of the Knights of San Stephano, which was an order of chivalry developed to counter the Turks. Alessandro's daughter, Giulia, eventually married her distant cousin Bernardino de Medici. She and her husband relocated to Naples, where they gained the principality of Ottaiano. Alessandro was buried in the cemetery of San Lorenzo in a magnificent tomb by Michelangelo, solidifying his status as a Renaissance patron.

See also: Courts, Blacks at European Aristocratic; Italy, Blacks in; Renaissance, Blacks in the.

Further Reading: Brackett, John K. "Alessandro de Medici, first Medici Duke of Florence, 1529–1537." In *Black Africans in Renaissance Europe.* eds. T. F. Earle and K.J.P. Lowe. New York: Cambridge University Press, 2005, pp. 303–325; Hare, Christopher. *The Romance of a Medici Warrior.* New York: Scribner's, 1910; Hibbert, Christopher. *The House of Medici: Its Rise and Fall.* New York: Morrow, 1975; Winspeare, Massimo. *The Medici: The Golden Age of Collecting.* Livorno: Sillabe, 2000.

Eric Martone

Meneses, Cristóbol de

Cristóbol de Meneses was a Dominican monk who lived in Spain during the sixteenth century. His father was a Spanish nobleman and his mother was a black African.

From a young age, Meneses was trained by Spanish Roman Catholics for holy orders and joined the Order of Saint Dominic. Moving to Granada, in southern Spain, from where the **Moors** had ruled until 60 or so years earlier, Meneses was involved in religious pursuits, and for a long time was involved in study.

Along with the traveler **Leo Africanus,** Meneses befriended Don Juan (or Don John) of Austria, brother of King Philip II of Spain, after the battle of Lepanto, in which the combined Christian fleets destroyed that of the Ottoman Empire in 1571. It appears that Meneses spent the rest of his life in the Order of Saint Dominic.

See also: Spain, African Invasions of; Spain, Blacks in.

Further Reading: Allen, Alma. "Literary Relations between Spain and Africa: An Introductory Statement." *The Journal of Negro History* 50:2 (April 1965): 97–105; Schomburg, Arthur. "Two Negro Missionaries to the American Indians: John Marrant and John Stewart." *The Journal of Negro History* 21: 4 (October 1936): 394–405; Spratlin, Valaurez. "Juan Latino, Slave and Humanist." *Crisis* (September 1932): 281.

Justin Corfield

Merida, Juan de

Juan de Merida, known as *El Valiente Negro de Flandes* ("The Valiant Negro of Flanders"), appeared in the play of the same name by Andrés de Claramonte (c.1580–1626), a minor Spanish poet. The story is semilegendary, with little evidence of it being based on the life of an actual soldier. Little is known about the life of Andrés de Claramonte except that he lived in Murcia in southeast Spain, where he became the director of the theater that flourished at the time, and attracted attention from many from the capital, Madrid. It was in Murcia that *El Valiente Negro de Flandes* was first performed.

The basis of *El Valiente Negro de Flandes* is that a black slave named Juan de Merida gained his freedom and then went to Flanders, where he fought in the army of Fernando Álvarez de Toledo, the third duke of Alba, who was governor of the Spanish Netherlands from 1567 until 1573. The Duke spent most of that time fighting against the Dutch Protestant burghers, who were aided by the English. De Merida acquitted himself bravely in combat and managed to gain the attention of the duke himself. The former slave was described as a noble Spanish soldier, but the "color of his skin prevented him from being a true caballero." In the play, de Merida complains about racism in a long monologue, but he does not let this stop him from defending what he sees as right and just. He demonstrates bravery in battle and is promoted to the rank of sergeant. Later still, de Merida gains a commission and becomes a captain.

The high point in the story of the fighting has de Merida entering the Flemish encampment by himself, managing to capture the duke of Orange and turn what would otherwise have been a defeat for the Spanish into a victory. This episode leads to the climax of the play, when de Merida was presented to the Spanish king for bravery. Overawed by this, his only words are *"Soy un negro, un negro soy"* ("I am a negro, a negro am I").

See also: Netherlands, Blacks in the; Spain, Blacks in; Spanish Army, Blacks in the.

Further Reading: Brachfield, F. Oliver. *Inferiority Feelings in the Individual and the Group.* Westport, CT: Greenwood Press, 1972; Spratlin, V. B. "The Negro in Spanish Literature." *The Journal of Negro History* 19:1 (January 1934): 60–71.

Justin Corfield

Michel, Jean-Louis (1785–1865)

Jean-Louis Michel was a famous swordsman and duelist of biracial descent during the Napoleonic era in Europe (1799–1815). Many of his contemporaries praised him as the greatest master of the art of fencing in the nineteenth century.

Little is known about Michel's early life. It seems that he came to France from the French colony of Saint-Domingue (modern Haiti). During the French Revolution (1789–1799), Michel, an orphan, attempted to enlist in the revolutionary French army in the 1790s while he was an adolescent. Even though he was of African descent, it was not a barrier to his enlistment. The new French Republic had even formed a black regiment under the Chevalier de Saint-Georges and had temporarily abolished slavery. Michel had a small physique, making him appear weak, but since members of the French army were impressed by his determination, it was arranged for master swordsman D'Erape to instruct him.

When Michel was 17 years old, he was sent into active service and fought for France in the Napoleonic Wars (1799–1815) throughout Europe. Napoleon Bonaparte had emerged as the French emperor in 1804, and the European powers made repeated alliances to remove Napoleon and prevent the spreading of the French Revolution. During the Peninsular campaign, in which French forces invaded and occupied Spain to prevent Portugal from trading with Britain, leader of the anti-Napoleon forces, Michel was master-of-arms of the Third Division's 32nd Regiment. This division also included the First Regiment, composed of Italians recruited from the sections of Italy under French influence. There was much animosity between Michel's regiment and the Italian regiment.

In 1814, to end the animosity between regiments within the same division, commanding officers decided to hold a tournament in Madrid. They ordered Michel and Giacomo Ferrari of Florence, Italy's most renowned swordsman and the Italian regiment's master-of-arms, to select 15 of their individual regiments' best men. On the day of the tournament, Ferrari arrived with 14 additional men, and Michel arrived alone. Michel first engaged Ferrari, who was defeated and killed. Michel proceeded to take on each of the additional 14 Italians, one at a time, until they, too, were defeated. The whole affair lasted less than an hour. The surviving Italian swordsmen and Michel shook hands as a symbol that the animosity between the two regiments was now past them. As news of Michel's success spread, he became a celebrity in France and participated in subsequent duels. Napoleon even sent Michel the Legion of Honor.

Michel retired from the army in 1830 and settled in Montpellier, where he opened a famous fencing school. Michel developed his own method of fighting, emphasizing the conservation of movement, which came to be taught throughout France. In later years, he argued against dueling to the death and promoted it as a form of competition. Michel enjoyed great wealth and social status, and many of his students hailed from the nobility. He married a local physician's daughter and died after his wife in 1865, blind in both eyes from cataracts.

See also: Abolition of Slavery, French; Colonies in the Caribbean, French; French Army, Blacks in the; French Revolution, Blacks in the; Saint-Georges, Le Chevalier de.

Further Reading: Cross, Thomas, and Ernie Kirkham. *Introduction to Fencing.* 2nd ed. Champaign, IL: Stripes Publishing, 1996.

Eric Martone

Mirsky, D. S. (1890–1939)

D. S. Mirsky was the pseudonym of Dmitry Petrovic Mirsky, a Russian political and literary historian. He was a member of an aristocratic Russian family, although he gave up his princely title. He fought in the Russian army during World War I before the outbreak of the Russian Revolution and the overthrow of the tsar.

From 1920 to 1931, Mirsky lived in exile in Britain. He promoted the knowledge of Russian literature in Britain. In pursuit of this objective, he promoted English translations of many Russian pieces of literature. Mirsky wrote one of the first critical biographies of **Alexander Pushkin** in 1926. The work did much to propel the literary reputation and study of Pushkin, who was of black descent, particularly in the English-speaking world.

In 1931, Mirsky joined the British Communist Party. He asked for a pardon from Soviet authorities and was granted permission to return to Soviet Russia. Shortly thereafter, he was arrested and placed in a labor camp, where he died.

See also: Russia, Blacks in; Soviet Propaganda, Blacks and; World War I, Black Participation in.

Further Reading: Mirsky, D. S. *Pushkin.* London: George Routledge, 1926.

Eric Martone

Mirza (1795)

Mirza is a short story by late eighteenth-century and early nineteenth-century French author Madame de Staël in which she castigated the French slave trade and advocated the abolition of slavery. The story was written in 1786 when Staël was 20 years old. She later published the story in 1795 with a preface.

Staël's preface serves to encourage the French abolition of slavery despite the negative perceptions of blacks that had escalated after the outbreak of the **Haitian Revolution for Independence.** She further encourages readers to adopt a positive response to her fictitious black African characters, despite the present state of violent social upheaval. Consequently, Staël's work differs from other portraits of black Africans in contemporary novels (such as Jean-Francois Saint-Lambert's *Ziméo*) that depicted blacks as prone to violence, ignorance, drunkenness, and sexual acts. Staël's story, which combines melodrama with antislavery polemic, focuses on Mirza, a black African woman, and her tragic love for Ximéo. Within the story, Mirza speaks out against the institution of slavery; and through this long speech, Staël's voice and Mirza's are one.

Mirza takes place in Africa and is told from the point of view of Ximéo, a "noble savage" from the African kingdom of Cayor and a son of a chief. At birth, Ximéo is engaged to **Ourika.** One day while hunting, Ximéo overhears a woman singing. He discovers that the woman, Mirza, also composes the beautiful songs that she sings. Ximéo is enchanted by Mirza and seeks to win her heart by telling her that despite her intellectual pleasures, she needs the pleasures of love to complete her being. Mirza's love for Ximéo becomes very intense, yet Ximéo ultimately rejects her and marries Ourika. After his marriage, Ximéo attempts to return to Mirza to offer her his friendship but is taken prisoner in war. He is then sold as a slave to European traders. Mirza arrives and gives a long heartfelt speech that convinces the European traders to release Ximéo. Unable to live without her lover, however, Mirza stabs an arrow through her heart.

See also: Abolition of Slavery, French; Colonies in Africa, French; France, Blacks in; French Revolution, Blacks in the; Literature, Blacks in French; Slave Trade, French.

Further Reading: Herold, J. Christopher. *Mistress to an Age: A Life of Madame de Stael.* New York: Grove Press, 2002; Kadish, Doris. "The Black Terror: Women's Responses to Slave Revolts in Haiti." *French Review* 68:4 (1995): 668–680; Staël, Germaine de. "Mirza." trans. Francoise Massardier-Kenney. In *Translating Slavery: Gender and Sex in French Women's Writing, 1783–1823.* ed. Doris Kadish and Francoise Massardier-Kenney. Kent: Kent State University Press, 1994.

Eric Martone

Missionaries in Africa, European

European missionaries made substantial efforts to spread Christianity in sub-Saharan Africa beginning in the fifteenth century. Such efforts intensified during the **New Imperialism** in the nineteenth century. The first European missionaries were Catholic, but Protestant missionaries also became active in Africa. The conversion to Catholicism connected those Africans to the universal Catholic Church under the supreme guidance of the popes in Rome. Many of the Protestant congregations set up in Africa by European missionaries retained significant identification with European churches. In both cases, some Africans were sent to Europe to receive training in becoming priests or reverends.

The Portuguese were the first Europeans to make considerable efforts to convert sub-Saharan Africans to Christianity. During the fifteenth century, Catholic missionaries often accompanied Portuguese explorers as they attempted to examine Africa. Although some attempts were unsuccessful, one of the Portuguese missionaries' greatest successes came when the Kingdom of Kongo converted to Christianity in the 1490s. Despite such efforts, Catholic missionary activity declined in the sixteenth and seventeenth centuries.

The first Protestant missionaries to sub-Saharan Africa were former slaves. In the eighteenth century, many former slaves, who had supported the British in the American Revolutionary War and had moved to Nova Scotia in Canada, left to settle in **Sierra Leone** in Africa. They established several Christian communities.

In the early nineteenth century, European missionaries started to arrive in Africa to establish mission villages and mission stations. As the European powers began to carve up Africa among themselves, the nature of African missionary work underwent a change. Missionaries became more closely associated to the different European powers. African rulers no longer exercised primary political power. Missionaries became subject to the colonizing European powers. The European powers used missionaries and their work to help control Africa. Thus missionaries ultimately became an informal component of the colonial structure that maintained European control through cultural and political domination.

In the nineteenth century, during the height of European imperialism, one of the justifications for colonialism was the need to "civilize" Africans. One of the means of achieving this goal was to make them Christian. African religions were viewed as inferior, barbaric, and evil. Some missionaries set up schools, which in varying degrees served the interest of the European colonizers. A European education became one of the means to spread European ideas among Africans and for Africans to gain higher status.

See also: Afonso, King of Kongo; Age of Exploration; Colonies in Africa, British; Colonies in Africa, French; Colonies in Africa, Portuguese; Crowther, Samuel Adjai.

Further Reading: Ballard, Martin. *White Man's Gold: The Extraordinary Story of Missionaries in Africa.* Westport, CT: Greenwood Press, 2008.

E. Agateno Mosca

Moody, Harold (1882–1947)

Harold Arundel Moody was one of a renowned circle of expatriate black intellectuals who were politically active in Britain during the 1930s and 1940s. His greatest public achievement was founding the League of Coloured Peoples (LCP), an organization devoted to protecting the welfare of blacks in Britain and the world.

Moody was born on October 8, 1882 in Kingston, Jamaica, the eldest of six children, to Charles and Christina (née Ellis) Moody. He received his education in Jamaica and then moved to London in 1904 to study medicine at King's College. He received his M.B., B.S. in 1912 and his M.D. in 1919. During these years, he started a successful private practice and worked as medical superintendent of the Marylebone Medical Mission, but was refused a post at King's College Hospital on account of his race. In 1913, he married Olive Tranter, an English nurse with whom he had worked at Marylebone; they had six children together.

Moody was a devout Congregationalist and in England became increasingly involved in Christian organizations with local and international scope. These included the Colonial Missionary Society (he became chairman in 1921), the London Missionary Society (chairman in 1943), and the Christian Endeavour Federation (president in 1931).

In 1931, Moody established the LCP as an interracial organization formed to educate and press for black civil rights through legal and governmental channels. It aimed to aid black people in distress, spur public interest in colonial welfare, and improve race relations in general. Under Moody's direction, the LCP cultivated an image of moral uprightness and middle-class respectability. Moody used his own influence to draw prominent individuals (both black and white) into association with the league. At times, these tendencies caused tensions with more radical and black organizations.

The LCP was one of the most visible and effective pressure groups for black civil rights before 1945. Within Britain, it protested the color bar and lobbied particular cases of discrimination, such as the "alien" treatment of black British seamen in port towns like Cardiff and Liverpool. In 1933, Moody founded the LCP paper, *The Keys*, which remained in circulation until 1939, in addition to publishing several pamphlets. Internationally, the LCP evolved into an articulate proponent of colonial issues: it denounced Italy's invasion of Abyssinia in 1935, and later (in 1944) advocated full colonial self-government and the official prohibition of racial discrimination in Britain. Moody often used the language of common imperial membership to argue the equality of all British subjects, regardless of race. He remained politically active until his death from influenza on April 24, 1947.

See also: Black British; Britain, Blacks in; Colonies in Africa, British; Colonies in the Caribbean, British.

Further Reading: Kilingray, David. *Race, Faith and Politics: Harold Moody and the League of Coloured Peoples.* London: Goldsmiths' College, 1999; MacDonald, Roderick J. "Dr. Harold Arundel Moody and the League of Coloured Peoples, 1931–1947: A Retrospective View." *Race* 14:3 (1973): 291–310; Rush, Anne Spry. "Imperial Identity in Colonial Minds: Harold Moody and the League of Coloured Peoples, 1931–50." *Twentieth Century British History* 13 (2002): 356–383.

Amanda Bidnall

Moors

In Europe during the Middle Ages and early modern period, the term *Moor* was used broadly in reference to black African, Berber, and Arab Muslims from the region of northwest Africa who settled in parts of Spain and Portugal and certain Mediterranean islands, such as Sicily. In its modern usage, the term refers to those who speak the Hassaniya Arabic dialect in parts of Mauritania, Morocco, Algeria, Western Sahara, Niger, and Mali. Furthermore, particularly in the Spanish usage, the term can be used in general reference to all Muslims. Many European languages' words for all things dark derive from the term *Moor* (such as *moreno*), and many surnames also derive from Moor, such as Moore, Muir, Morello, and Mauros.

The term *Moor* derives from the Greek word "*mauros*," which means "black" or "very dark." In Latin, the word became "*mauro*" (plural "*mauri*"). In the Middle Ages, European descriptions of Moors ranged from black, dark skinned, to swarthy in complexion. Such terms are subjective and reflect the diverse ethnicities of Africa, which through conquest and intermarriage became even more ambiguous. For example, Berbers, the original inhabitants of northwest Africa, became a mixture of a variety of peoples from East Africa, North Africa, West Africa, and sub-Saharan Africa.

The Romans controlled western North Africa, what they called Mauritania (from "*mauri*"), but what is today Morocco and Algeria. Moors figured prominently as an ally of Carthage against Rome in the **Punic Wars** and accompanied Carthaginian general Hannibal in his campaigns. Moorish conversion to Islam in the late seventh century formed a formidable force with Arab allies. In 711, Taarik ibn Ziyad led an African invasion of Spain. His army crossed the Pyrenees into the kingdom of the Franks, where their advance was stopped at the Battle of Tours in 732 by Charles Martel. Withdrawing back into Spain, in 756, Adb-al-Rahman founded the Umayyad dynasty, establishing a long period of Moorish, Islamic rule.

The Moors had a profound impact on the cultures of the areas that they conquered, particularly Spain. The Moors brought silk and crops, such as rice, cane sugar, dates, lemon, ginger, and cotton. They are thought to have brought the lute and an early version of the guitar, the *Kithara*, and are further credited with understanding the curvilinear nature of light rays, eventually leading to the development of corrective lenses. They understood astronomy, documenting the spherical nature of the Earth and its gravitational pull. By the tenth century, Moorish Spain was well in advance of its European counterparts. Its public baths, through which hot water was conveyed through pipes in the walls, were well known. The city of Cordoba's streets were cleaner, paved, and well lit much earlier than the streets of London or Paris. Watermills were reintroduced, numbering more than 5,000 at a time when Europe had none. The Moors in Spain and Africa could also boast having the most literate populations. Education was universal, as women became doctors, and Jews attended university and had freedom to practice religion (although all nonbelievers paid a tax). Paper was used widely at a time when it was still unknown in the rest of Europe, giving rise to a plethora of bookshops. Cordoba became the intellectual center of Europe, drawing scholars to make use of more than 70 libraries.

Internal divisions allowed for the advance of Christian armies. The city of Toledo fell in 1105, but as it did, one of the world's greatest libraries was revealed to Christian Europe. Greek, Roman, and Arab manuscripts on philosophy, astronomy, and mathematics were then disseminated throughout the Christian world. The books on navigation alone would serve as the foundation of European exploration in the fifteenth and sixteenth centuries. Southern Spain remained Moorish until the unification of Spain in the fifteenth century. The last stronghold at Granada gave way in 1492. Thereafter, Moors were exiled, forced to convert, or killed, thus ending arguably Europe's most cosmopolitan, tolerant, and heterogeneous society of the Middle Ages.

See also: Frederick II and the Moors of Sicily; Heraldry, Blacks in European; Italy, African Invasions of; Moor's Head Symbol; Spain, African Invasions of.

Further Reading: Fletcher, Richard. *Moorish Spain.* 2nd ed. Berkeley: University of California Press, 2006; Nicolle, David, and Angus McBride. *The Moors: The Islamic West, 7th-15th Centuries AD.* Sterling Heights, MI: Osprey, 2001; Seminario, Lee Anne Durham. *The History of the Blacks, Jews, and Moors in Spain.* Madrid: Playor, 1975.

Thomas Martin

Moor's Head Symbol

The heraldic symbol of the Moor's head (or blackamoor's head), which depicts the profile of a black African **Moor,** appears on the traditional flags of Aragon (Spain), Corsica (France), and Sardinia (Italy), and the coat of arms of the Algarve (Portugal).

As a heraldic sign, the Moor's head, generally facing to the viewer's left (in heraldic terms, facing right), depicts black African features and usually has a ribbon around the head. This was generally fitting the traditional descriptions of the Islamic Moors from modern-day Morocco and Algeria, some of whom were taken as slaves in Spain, Portugal, and other parts of the Western Mediterranean. Why the Moor's head has the ribbon, or headband, is not known for certain, although some Moors wore it as a sign that they were chieftains.

The use of the Moor's head in the coat of arms of Aragon in northern Spain was first recorded in 1281 during the reign of Peter III. Four Moors' heads around a red cross were used within the Aragonese coat of arms during an early stage in the *Reconquista,* during which Catholic Spanish forces eventually united to expel the Muslims from the Iberian Peninsula. At this time, Catholic Aragon served as a base for attacks on Moors elsewhere in Spain. The coat of arms depicting four Moor's heads around a red cross appears to have been used until 1387, when the original Aragonese coat of arms (without the Moors' heads) was restored. Their use seems to have returned after the battle of Alcoras in 1046, during which Ramiro I, king of Aragon, defeated the Moors. Consequently, such use of the Moor's heads are intended to represent the conquest of Moorish kings during combat.

With Aragon's close connections with the islands of Sardinia and Corsica (at times, exercising political control over the islands), this may also explain the subsequent

Flag of Corsica. Courtesy of keyboardsamurai, http://www.flickr.com/photos/keyboardsamurai/ 416681617.

appearance of the Moor's head there, especially on the arms of Cagliari, the capital city of Sardinia. There have also been suggestions that the head might be that of **Saint Maurice**, the black patron saint of the Holy Roman Empire, which exerted control over parts of Italy. This theory extends a more positive origin to the use of the Moor's head. The Moors on the current flag of Aragon are small and have long headbands, far more prominent than those used in Corsica.

The Moor's head seems to have been used in Corsica when Arrigo della Rocca, the leader of the pro-Aragonese party in Corsica, introduced his coat of arms and that of Aragon in 1376, which may have included the Moor's head, although this is not known for certain. In 1547, Colonel Sampiero of the Corsican Regiment in the army of Charles V, king of France, may have used a Moor's head in the center of his flag, which had a black field and a white cross. Some historians, however, doubt that the French would allow an Aragonese symbol to appear on banners of their soldiers, although mercenary bands from Corsica and Sardinia may have used them. In a painting dating from before 1466 in the Church of St. Francis in Arezzo, in central Italy, a banner showing a Moor's head is visible.

During the sixteenth and seventeenth centuries, the Moor's head had become a recognized symbol of Corsica. For examples, the symbol appeared on an atlas by Italian geographer Mainaldo Galerati in 1573, and one by Dutch map maker Johann Blaeu in 1662. Gradually, many other atlases came to use the Moor's head as a popular symbol for Corsica and the tradition continues in later atlases. In 1760, nationalist leader Pasquale Paoli (1725–1807) proposed a flag for Corsica, then under the control of France, that included a Moor's head along with the fleur-de-lis. After the French Revolution, the fleur-de-lis were removed. From 1794 to 1796, Paoli, attempting to create a Corsican kingdom under British control, again used a Moor's head, this time with the English Royal Arms. More recently, Corsican nationalist protestors have brandished white flags with a Moor's head, for example during the Aléria protest in the 1970s.

The Moor's head used on the Sardinian flag is quite different in some respects from its counterpart in Corsica, but there are some similarities. Again, the face is black, with visible white eyes, and a headband. This time, however, the heads (there are four on the Sardinian flag, with a red cross in the middle) face to the viewer's right. This flag was used in Sardinia from about the fourteenth century and appears in the *Encyclopedia Britannica* from 1771. Sardinia formally adopted the traditional flag with the Moor's heads as its symbol in 1999.

Although the Moor's heads appear on the coat of arms of the Algarve, Portugal, they are radically different from those of Aragon, Sardinia, and Corsica. The Moor's heads on the arms of the Algarve are facing forward and shown wearing turbans, with two Moors' heads and two heads of kings, transposed. The transposed heads depict the Islamic kings of Africa and the Christian kings of Portugal.

See also: France, Blacks in; Heraldry, Blacks in European; Holy Roman Empire, Black Iconography and the; Italy, Blacks in; Portugal, Blacks in; Spain, African Invasions of; Spain, Blacks in.

Further Reading: Woodcock, Thomas, and John Robinson. *The Oxford Guide to Heraldry.* 2nd ed. New York: Oxford University Press, 2001.

Justin Corfield

Moret Law, Spanish

The Moret Law (1870) was a milestone in the history of emancipation of the slaves in the colonies of Spanish Empire. It contributed to a certain degree in ameliorating the condition of slaves in the Spanish colonies in the Caribbean, particularly Cuba and Puerto Rico. The emancipation movement in Cuba was gradual, as slavery was intertwined with the sugar economy of Cuba. The main element of the Cuban economic system was the *ingenio* (sugar plantation). In 1867, the last recorded slave ship had arrived in Cuba. Any sudden and far-reaching move would deteriorate relations between whites and Africans in Cuba. Although the pressure from Britain and the Civil War in the United States accelerated the process of ending slavery in the Spanish Empire, the process was not rapid. The law was the work of the minister for colonial affairs and member of the Spanish Abolitionist Society, Segismundo Moret y Prendergast (1838–1913). The twice-elected liberal parliamentarian from the town of Almadén and a future premier, Moret was an advocate of the Spanish abolition of slavery throughout the Spanish Empire and expressed his views in the parliament. There was opposition from a lobby representing the colonial slave owners. The idealists, reformers, and individuals desiring better methods of production argued vehemently for emancipation.

The Moret Law was approved in Spain on July 4, 1870. It was to take effect in Cuba and Puerto Rico and gave freedom to slaves born after September 17, 1868, as well as individuals over 60 years old. The slaves helping the Spanish government in the *Guerra de los Diez Años* or Ten Years' War in Cuba (1868–1878) were to be liberated. The government of Spain freed the slaves that it owned. Individuals owning slaves received 125 paestas for each slave as compensation. The paesta was a new currency for Spain introduced in 1869 and was equal to 0.29 grams of gold or 4.5 grams of silver. The state could not provide money to the slave owners making the law ineffective in many cases. Moret also came under criticism from radical groups, as the law was not enough to satisfy them. The gradual strategy envisioned in the Moret Law, however, worked as the supply of labor was not discontinued, and the slaves not coming under the law worked as wage earners in plantations. The Moret Law also did not permit the sudden, mass freeing slaves. In October 1868, slavery was finally abolished in Cuba, freeing 30,000 people.

Two Puerto Ricans, Román Baldorioty de Castro (1822–1889), who was a teacher, politician, and political activist, and Brigadier General Luis Padial (1832–1879) helped Moret in legislation of the Moret Law. In 1867, individuals of black descent numbered about 310,000, and whites numbered about 346,000. The Moret Law initiated a *Registro Central de Esclavos* (Central Slave Registrar) in 1872 that collected detailed data about slaves for a genealogical chart. Their country of origin, sex, names of parents, as well as masters were taken into account. In 1873, slavery was finally abolished in Puerto Rico.

See also: Abolition of Slavery, Spanish; Colonies in the Caribbean, Spanish; Rio Branco Law of Free Birth; Slave Trade, Spanish.

Further Reading: Aimes, Hubert. *A History of Slavery in Cuba, 1511 to 1868.* New York: Octagon Books, 1967; Bergad, Laird. *The Comparative Histories of Slavery in Brazil, Cuba, and the United States.* New York: Cambridge University Press, 2007; Corwin, Arthur. *Spain and the Abolition of Slavery in Cuba, 1817–1886.* Austin: University of Texas Press, 1967; Knight, Franklin. *Slave Society in Cuba during the Nineteenth Century.* Madison: University of Wisconsin Press, 1970; Scott, Rebecca. *Slave Emancipation in Cuba: The Transition to Free Labor, 1860–1899;* Pittsburgh: University of Pittsburgh Press, 2000.

Patit Paban Mishra

Morien, Romance of (1200s)

Sir Morien, a black Moorish knight, is the subject of a romantic epic poem written in medieval Dutch during the thirteenth century set in the mythical era of King Arthur of England and the Knights of the Round Table. *The Romance of Morien,* which nears 5,000 lines, is preserved as a component of the *Lancelot-Compilatie.* The epic relates the tale of Morien, the son of an African Moorish princess and Agloval, one of Arthur's knights, who arrives in Britain on a quest to find his vanished father. The epic is notable for its positive portrayals of an African knight and the inclusion of such a character in the Arthurian legend, an evolving narrative within Western literature that has emerged as a central component of British and European folklore.

Statue of the Black Knight, Cathedral of Magdeburg, Germany, c. 1250. Courtesy of Carija Ihus.

The epic story tells of the adventures of Sir Agloval, who went searching for Sir Lancelot, a Knight of the Round Table. In his search, Agloval traveled through the lands of the **Moors** and encountered a beautiful African princess. Although pledged to marry, Agloval abandoned the princess, who now bore his child, to continue his search for Lancelot. The princess bore a son, Morien, who grew into a handsome and strong young man. Now grown, Morien embarks on a quest to find his lost father after he and his mother are disinherited from their lands. In his quest, Morien encounters and eventually wins the admiration of Sir Lancelot and Sir Gawain, another prominent Knight of the Round Table, who are searching for Perceval, a new knight and the brother of Agloval. They assist Morien in his efforts. After a series of adventures, Morien is reunited with his father. Father and son return to the land of the Moors, where Agloval marries his lost love, Morien's mother, and wins back her lands.

The poem describes Morien as black, including his face, body, and limbs, and as a great warrior dressed in black Moorish armor. In the poem, Morien is loyal, articulate, skilled in the art of war, and brave. Consequently, Morien, despite his black African origins, is depicted as a paragon of the virtues of European knighthood.

The Romance of Morien is likely a verse translation of an original French prose version, which is now lost, although a German origin has been suggested. The Dutch compiler presents a mixture of earlier and later elements of the Arthurian legend. None of the adventures related in *The Romance of Morien* are preserved in any English texts. Morien is presented as kin to Perceval, who is associated with the quest for the Christian Holy Grail, or the cup of Jesus of Nazareth used at the Last Supper before his crucifixion, in the Arthurian legend. In earlier versions, Perceval emerges as the Grail hero, but later versions make Galahad, Lancelot's son, the hero. The anonymous compiler of *The Romance of Morien* indicates that, in some versions, Perceval is Morien's father; however, he decided to maintain convention that Perceval died a virgin, and was hence suitable for the Holy Grail. The action within the epic occurs before the Knights of the Round Table's quest for the Holy Grail. The compiler attempts to connect events within *The Romance of Morien* to the episodes within twelfth-century French poet Chrétien de Troyes's unfinished *Perceval, the Story of the Grail*, and the Vulgate Cycle, which is a series of eight medieval French volumes dating from the thirteenth century detailing tales of Arthur, his knights, and the quest for the Holy Grail. Both works are among the most significant and influential of the medieval versions of the Arthurian legend. The character of Morien and his birth parallels that of Wolfram von Eschenbach's character Feirefiz in *Parzival*, which is a medieval German version of the Arthurian legend.

See also: Palamedes, Sir; *Parzival*, Feirefiz in.

Further Reading: Ashley, Mike. *The Mammoth Book of King Arthur: Reality and Legend, the Beginning and the End.* London: Robinson, 2005; Kooper, Erik, ed. *Medieval Dutch Literature in its European Context.* Cambridge: Cambridge University Press, 1994; *Morien: Arthurian Romance Unrepresented in Malory's "Morte d'Arthur."* Trans. Jessie L. Weston. Bournemouth, Hants: Nutt, 1901.

Eric Martone

Morris, Bill (1938–)

William Manuel Morris, better known as Bill Morris, was the first person of black descent to head a British trade union. He was born on October 19, 1938 in Bombay, Manchester, Jamaica, and came to Britain to join his widowed mother, who was living in Handsworth, Birmingham. She had left Jamaica after the death of her husband, a part-time police officer. Morris worked in an engineering company and also enrolled in the Handsworth Technical College. In 1958, Morris joined the Transport and General Workers' Union (TGWU) and began to hold a succession of increasingly influential posts in the union. He was elected as a shop steward at Hardy Spicers, an automobile part manufacture concern, in 1963, and showed keen interest in union activities. There was dispute over trade union recognitions and Morris was deeply involved in attempts to resolve the dispute.

From the 1970s, Morris's influence began to grow in the TGWU. He was a full-time official from 1973. He worked as district officer and later as secretary of the Northampton District from 1973 to 1979. As the national secretary for the Passenger Services Trade Group from 1979, Morris emerged in the national spotlight. The Trade Group was looking after interest of employees working in bus and coach. He had become knowledgeable about labor history, industrial relations, health programs, housing, and safety measures. In 1986, Morris was the deputy general secretary of the TGWU. His responsibilities included education programs, better service conditions, and equal opportunities. Morris had to look after TGWU's white-collar workers as well as transport sectors.

In 1991, Morris was elected general secretary of the TGWU and again reelected after four years. He was the first black person to hold such an important position. As a moderate trade union activist, his relationship with the radical elements was not always good. Morris never hesitated to defend the rights of workers. On many occasions, he criticized the ruling establishment and industrial organizations over racial policies. He challenged the blatant racial discrimination practiced in the Dagenham factory of the

Ford Motor Company. Under the stewardship of Morris, the TGWU strived hard with the successive Labour governments for minimum wage and better pension benefits. The sound financial judgment of Morris resulted in the union's surplus asset. When he took charge, it had a deficit of £12 million. When he gave charge to Tony Woodley upon retirement in October 2003, however, the TGWU had property worth £240 million.

Morris occupied various positions on several boards in his long career, including the BBC advisory committee, the Commission for Racial Equality, the Employment Appeals Tribunal, and the TUC General Council. He was a board member of the International Transport Workers' Federation, a director of Unity Trust Bank, and a nonexecutive director of the Bank of England. Morris was the recipient of the Order of Jamaica (2002) and a knighthood (2003). He was made a life peer in April 2006.

See also: Black British; Britain, Blacks in; Colonies in the Caribbean, British.

Further Reading: Brivati, Brian, and Richard Heffernan. *The Labour Party: A Centenary History.* New York: St. Martin's Press, 2000; Coates, Ken, and Tony Topham. *The History of the Transport and General Workers' Union.* Cambridge: Blackwell, 1991; Fisher, John. *Bread on the Waters: A History of TGWU Education, 1922–2000.* London: Lawrence and Wishart, 2005.

Patit Paban Mishra

Mortenol, Sosthene (1859–1930)

Sosthene Mortenol, whose parents were former black slaves, was a French naval captain appointed commander of the Air Defenses of Paris during World War I. He was born in November 1859 in Guadeloupe, an island in the West Indies (Caribbean), and went to school in France. He was the first nonwhite person to attend the Polytechnic School in Paris in October 1880. He began his military service in 1882 when he joined the French Navy. He served on many campaigns, seeing action in the battle for Madagascar in 1894. He also traveled to the Congo and China before World War I. Mortenol was one of more than 500,000 Africans serving in the French military during World War I (1914–1918). Most were from North and West Africa, but 30,000, like Mortenol, came from the West Indies.

In 1916, General Joseph Galliéni (1849–1916) appointed Mortenol as commander of the Air Defenses of Paris, a position he held with great distinction and dedication until the end of World War I. He was rewarded for his service by being appointed in 1921 commander to the French Legion of Honor, the highest honor that can be bestowed on a citizen of France in recognition of a person's service to the country.

See also: Abolition of Slavery, French; Colonies in the Caribbean, French; France, Blacks in; French Army, Blacks in the; World War I, Black Participation in.

Further Reading: Rogers, J. A. *World's Great Men of Color.* vol. II. Reprint. New York: Touchstone, 1996.

Robert Nave

Mpundu Akwa (1879–1914)

Ludwig Paul Heinrich Dika Mpundo Niasam Akwa (Mpundu Akwa) was an African colonial delegate to Germany who won a legal battle to prove his innocence after false accusations were brought against him because of his opposition to the German colonial administration.

Mpundu Akwa was born on July 4, 1879. He was the son of King Dika Akwa, who became one of the signatories of the so-called *Schutzvertrag* (protectorate treaty) with the German representative Gustav Nachtigal that started German colonial rule in Cameroon. In 1888, Mpundu Akwa was sent to Germany and went to school in Paderborn. Four years later, he moved to Kiel to work as a trainee at a trading company, but he returned to Cameroon in 1893. During his stay in Germany, the little "Prince from Cameroon" was often invited to stay at the homes of the upper class and gentry for whom the "exotic" stranger was a "decorative" addition as well as a symbol of their cosmopolitanism. When Mpundu Akwa returned to Cameroon, he worked as an interpreter for the colonial government, but he soon antagonized the infamous governor Jesco von Puttkamer when he complained about the mistreatment of Africans.

In 1902, Mpundu Akwa returned to Germany as a member of a delegation of Duala chiefs that tried to make complaints about the ongoing oppression and mistreatment by the colonial administration. After the departure of the delegation, he stayed in Germany. He hoped to establish himself as a businessman and to serve as a representative of the Akwas. The colonial administration in Cameroon tried to enforce his return, and Mpundo Akwa was expelled from the territory of Hamburg. Instead of returning to Cameroon, however, he settled in Altona, a nearby town.

Shortly thereafter, Mpundu Akwa fell into financial trouble because the colonial authorities in Cameroon under Governor von Puttkamer prevented the collection of money for his support by the Akwas. In April 1904, he was accused of fraud. He was charged with having purchased goods on credit intending to defraud on several occasions and fraudulently using the title of "prince" to deceive his business partners. The trial took place more than a year after his arrest, but he was successfully defended by his lawyer, Moses Levi. Levi was convinced that the reasons behind Mpundo Akwa's arrest and accusation were found in his position as a resolute opponent of German colonial administration, which by charging him, would be able to enforce his extradition to Cameroon. With a conclusive defense and final speech, Levi brought about a verdict of not guilty for Mpundu Akwa. In spite of being constantly under attack by colonial circles in Germany, he continued his political activities and published the bilingual journal *Elolombe ya Kamerun* ("Sun of Kamerun") in 1908.

Mpundo Akwa's attempts to gain an economic foothold in Germany failed. In 1911, he finally returned to Cameroon to try his luck as a tradesman in his home country. A rumor was circulated either by the colonial authorities or by the Cameroonians that he planned to liberate Cameroon from German colonial rule. Consequently, he was arrested. In the summer of 1912, Mpundo Akwa was sentenced to prison and exiled to Banyo in Northern Cameroon. After he attempted break out, he was enchained and sentenced to 25 lashings. During his imprisonment, Mpundo Akwa wrote a history of Duala in the form of a letter to the governor. He died mysteriously, presumably in 1914, during his internment in northern Cameroon.

See also: Colonies in Africa, German; Germany, Blacks in.

Further Reading: Joeden-Forgey, Elisa von. "Defending Mpundu: Dr. Moses Levi of Altona and the Prince from Kamerun." In Leonard Harding, ed. *Mpundu Akwa. Der Fall des Prinzen von Kmaerun. Das neuentdeckte Plädoyer von Dr. M. Levi.* Münster: LIT, 2000, pp. 84–114.

Marianne Bechhaus-Gerst

Murat, Joachim (1767–1815)

Joachim Murat was a renowned cavalry leader of Moorish descent who was made a grand marshall of France by Napoleon Bonaparte. Murat married Napoleon's sister and later became king of Naples from 1808 to 1815.

Murat was born in 1767 to an innkeeper in the Auvergne region of France. Many of the inhabitants of the Auvergne, including Murat, were descendants of the **Moors** that had settled in the region, driven from Spain as part of the *Reconquista*, which was the movement to drive the Muslims out of the Iberian Peninsula and unify the country. Murat maintained that he descended from Moorish kings and many of his contemporaries, particularly Laura, Duchess d'Abrantés, who was a famous chronicler of the era and wife of French Marshall Junot, commented on Murat's biracial features.

Murat enlisted in the French cavalry, later joining the King's Constitutional Guard and then the regular army. During the French Revolution (1789–1799), Murat attained the favor of rising general Napoleon Bonaparte, who assisted the French Republic by containing counterrevolutionary factions. Napoleon made Murat one of his aides-de-camp during the campaign into northern Italy as part of the French Revolutionary Wars against the European coalition against the French Republic. Murat rose to become commander of the cavalry. During Napoleon's 1798 Egyptian campaign, meant to weaken Britain by threatening its holdings in India, Murat served under General **Thomas-Alexandre Dumas.** Murat's valor won him a promotion to division general.

After Napoleon returned to France, he plotted the coup of the Eighteenth of Burmaire in 1799, in which he seized control of the government. Murat assisted Napoleon in seizing power and commanded the forces that dissolved the National Convention. Such loyalty won Murat the gratitude of Napoleon, who made Murat governor of Paris and gave him his sister, Marie Caroline, in marriage in 1800. Napoleon later became emperor of France in 1804. After Murat's victories in subsequent campaigns, he became a marshal of the French Empire (1804) and later grand duke of Berg and Cleves (1806).

When the Bourbon dynasty was overthrown in Naples, Napoleon made his brother Joseph king. After Napoleon transferred Joseph to rule Spain, Murat and Caroline became rulers of Naples in 1808. During Napoleon's disastrous Russian campaign in 1812, Murat abandoned his military post to return to Naples. As Napoleon's final defeat to a European coalition seemed imminent in 1814, Murat attempted to negotiate a deal with the Austrian Empire to retain the throne of Naples.

In 1815, Murat, realizing that the European powers intended to restore the Bourbon dynasty in Naples, deserted his new allies and prepared to strengthen his rule in Italy by military strength. The Austrians defeated Murat in the Battle of Tolentino in 1815. He plotted an attempt to regain Naples through an insurrection in the southern

Italian region of Calabria. During the attempt, Murat was arrested by the forces of the Bourbon dynasty and executed by firing squad.

See also: Spain, African Invasions of; French Revolution, Blacks in the.

Further Reading: Boers, Michael. *Europe under Napoleon.* New York: Oxford University Press, 1996; Cole, Humbert. *The Betrayers: Joachim and Caroline Murat.* New York: Saturday Review, 1972.

Eric Martone

Music, African Influences on European

African influences on European music were various during the twentieth century, given the colonial experience and many diverse exchanges. Many European audiences were open to jazz from the 1920s and 1930s and celebrated the African American performer **Josephine Baker.** That same openness was also made toward Africa. Some famous European singers were born in Africa, including Georges Moustaki (born Giuseppe Mustacchi, in 1934, in Alexandria, Egypt); Dalida (born Yolanda Gigliotti, in 1933, in Cairo, Egypt); and Enrico Macias (born Gaston Ghrenassia, in 1938, in Algeria), who grew in the French colonial era of the "*Algérie française,*" when Algeria occupied a status similar to a province of France.

Although born in southern France, singer and composer Charles Trenet wrote a few songs that referred to Africa and even included some lyrics that were sung in African Creole, including "*Béguine à Bango*" (1938) and "*Gala Poté*" (1956). The latter was supposedly recorded on the island of Mauritius in Africa.

The cross-cultural exchanges between Africa and Europe appeared in various situations and settings. Some European tours of "traditional" African shows were made in the 1950s in a mixture of intense songs and shaking dances, with flamboyant costumes and fake rituals that gave the impression of catching the essence of the obscure African soul. With an all-black cast, the show entitled "*Ballets africains de la République de Guinée*" was even recorded and released as an LP with the cover description "*Orgie de rythme, de couleurs*" ("Orgy of rhythm and colors").

The musical and traditional art from the colonies (or former colonies) enabled a wonderful cross-cultural spectacle that included simultaneously blacks and a few whites. For example, in Belgium, the Choir from King Baudoin ("*Les Troubadours du Roi Baudoin*") recorded a sacred mass based on African rhythms, with drums and a black choir, entitled *Missa Luba,* that was quite influential in the early 1950s. Its main theme ("Gloria") even became the musical leitmotiv for the soundtrack of Pier Paolo Pasolini's feature film *The Gospel according to St. Matthew* (1964). The origins of this project lie in the Catholic tradition: a Belgian missionary, Father Guido Haazen, went to the Congo in 1953 and created a choir made of 45 young boys plus their 15 professors. This choir later toured in 1958 in Holland, West Germany, and even joined another choir from Vienna for a special concert. *Missa Luba* was released on LP by Philips Records around 1960 in two original versions, which were spontaneous and exuberant. Many commercial "remakes" of *Missa Luba* were produced from the 1970s, for instance in Kenya, but without the original choir, and without the magic of the authentic, vintage version.

Although jazz was a constant influence in Europe, French artists were in some cases inspired by African music. Early in his career, French songwriter Serge Gainsbourg (born Lucien Ginsburg, 1928–1991) wrote a few pop songs in French based on African rhythms and drums on an overlooked album entitled *Gainsbourg Percussions* (1964). In fact, on this album, Gainsbourg also copied a previously released song by Harry Belafonte called "The Jack-Ass Song" (from his famous *Calypso* LP from 1956). Gainsbourg gave the song new French lyrics (but without the mention of the true songwriters Lord Burgess and Bill Attaway) under the new title *"Tatoué Jérémie."*

In 1967, French songwriter Jacques Dutronc introduced a song entitled *"La Compapade,"* which is like a parody tribal jam with incantations that are repeated in an obsessive and funny mood. The parody preceded by two decades the ethnic fashion that would invade France in the 1990s. In *"La Compapade,"* Dutronc sings nonexistent words (in any language) that imitate primitive talking. When Dutronc reintroduced this odd song in his 1990s concerts during the World Music wave, audiences in France seemed to adore it and often sang along.

In 1972, French songwriter Michel Fugain created a mainstream musical with African and French singers and dancers entitled "Big Bazar." The songs *"Là-bas dans les îles"* and *"La Fête"* were inspired by African roots and had a tremendous success on the French airwaves.

African artists like Ali Farka Touré (from Mali) had greater presence in Europe from the 1980s. Some signed contracts with multinational record companies and therefore had more exposure in Western Europe, but less in communist countries like East Germany, Hungary, and Poland. Still, in those days, many Europeans could think of only one artist from South Africa: the white South African Johnny Clegg.

A compilation CD entitled *Le Beau Temps Des Colonies* ("The Glory Colonial Days') gathered 19 vintage French songs from the colonial period, with humorous titles mainly recorded in the 1950s by French artists about everyday life in Africa. Songs in the collection included *"Les Africains"* ("Africans"), *"On A Fait La Nouba"* ("We Ball Tonight"), *"Timicminé La Pou Pou"* ("The Little Chick"), and *"Le Petit Négro"* ("The Little Negro"). This odd, confusing, long-forgotten heritage is also part of the history of the African presence in European culture during the French colonial days in Africa and elsewhere. Some lyrics depicting the African characters would likely be deemed racist by modern standards, but they were accepted as normal a century ago. All these songs were a mixture of popular French song writing from the 1930s and later, with an "exotic" instrumental atmosphere, or rhythms, borrowed from Africa.

See also: Jazz, European Reception of; Music Industry, Blacks in the European; Musicians in Europe, African-American Classical; Pop Music, Blacks in Contemporary European.

Further Reading and Listening: Dutronc, Jacques. *Jacques Dutronc au Casino de Paris.* CD. Paris, Tristar, 1992; Fugain, Michel. *Michel Fugain et le Big Bazar 1972,* LP, Able, ABL-7011; Gainsbourg, Serge. *Gainsbourg percussions.* CD. Polygram France, 1999 [1964]; Haazen, Guido, with the Choir of King Baudoin. *Missa Luba.* LP, Philips Records, B 14.723 L; La Troupe Nationale. *Ballets africains de la République de Guinée.* LP. Conakry, Éditions Syliphone, SLP 14. Distribution Sono Disc, Paris; *Le Beau Temps Des Colonies.* CD. Paris, Milan Music, 2006; Marshall, Bill, ed. *France and the Americas: Culture, Politics, and History.* Santa Barbara, CA: ABC-CLIO, 2005.

Yves Laberge

Music Industry, Blacks in the European

In most cases during the twentieth century, the preservation of the African traditions, material culture, and musical heritage was made by European institutions ("International Music Council," "International Institute for Comparative Music Studies and Documentation"), ethnographic museums, and by UNESCO from the 1950s. Recordings of African traditional music were made by anthropologists for decades, but few were released commercially. Paul Collaer, among the pioneers, created the series "UNESCO—Collection" on the Musicaphon label in 1965 with field recordings of songs by "primitive" African tribes like the Ba-Benzélé Pygmies. Other field recordings in this series included music from Rwanda, Ethiopia, and the Central Africa Republic. These LPs were available only in specialized record stores in France, West Germany, Switzerland, or through UNESCO offices.

In France, the label *Le Chant du Monde* was somewhat similar to Folkways in the United States, which produced ethnic music. *Le Chant du Monde* ranks among the first labels to include traditional African music in its catalogue, beginning in 1950. Two decades later, also in Paris, Pierre Toureille produced many LPs of traditional African music on the label OCORA, affiliated with Radio-France, ORSTOM, and Musidisc (the latter replaced by distributor Harmunia Mundi). They released recordings (chants, rituals) made in Gabon, Burundi, and Zaïre in the early 1970s. Their 1987 CD *Musiques urbaines à Kinshasa* was so popular that it went out of print and was reissued only two years later, which is unusual in world music.

During the same decade in Boulogne (near Paris), Frédy Bonnaud and Jean-Pierre Calvel created the label *Playa Sound*, dedicated to traditional African and Asian music and focusing on rhythm. They released instrumental LPs (and later CDs) of field recordings from Senegal, Mauritania, and two LPs with pygmies. In Switzerland, the precious recordings made in 1973 and 1974 with the "Aïzo" and "Gun" tribes in Bénin were released on a CD co-produced by the Musée d'Ethnographie in Geneva with the help of the collections of the *Archives sonores du Musée d'Ethnographie*" in Neuchatel.

NEW NETWORKS FOR BLACK ARTISTS.   With the advent of the LP in the late 1950s, many independent record companies dedicated to jazz, blues, soul, and even traditional African music appeared in various European countries. Before 1970, few recording companies had the opportunity to distribute their LPs in both America and Europe, for many independent labels had to license their products for distribution abroad.

In England, the *Liberty* recording label had agreements with independent companies like Fantasy in California, but they also recorded some original LPs in their "Groundhog Series" with a few African American artists who stayed near the Spot Studios in London. An example is *Hand Me Down My Old Walking Stick* by Big Joe Williams in 1968. Other British labels dedicated to U.S. blues singers included Joy Records (distributed by President Records) and Ember Records, both in London, which released albums by Lightnin' Hopkins in the 1960s, and Indigo Records (part of Sanctuary Records) for CDs, for instance the Ivory Joe Hunter catalogue from the 1950s. These European reissues of previous U.S. recordings were sometimes the only way to get rare recordings originally made during the 1950s on 78 RPM on independent labels (such as Baton, King, Ivory) and never released elsewhere. This is the case for New York singer Ann Cole, whose recordings were reissued only once, in England during the 1980s.

Still active in England, JSP Records specializes in releases in the 4CD Box Set format, with re-releases of collections of about 100 songs by African American artists who recorded from the 1920s to the early 1940s to avoid legal issues regarding copyright material of less than 60 years. Selected artists are not always jazzmen and bluesmen, as proven by the inclusion of gospel singer Blind Willie Johnson, but also the jazz vocal quartet the Mills Brothers.

Among other British companies operating in the 1980s and 1990s, Charly Records (also known as "Charly R&B") and ACE Records specialized in the licensing and the re-release of albums made by African American singers who had recorded on U.S. labels owned by blacks, such as Vee Jay, or on the famous Chess label, mainly in the 1950s: Jimmy Reed, John Lee Hooker, Elmore James, and many more. Charly Records began issuing a compilation double LP with all the blues songs covered by the Rolling Stones presented in their obscure versions by the original artists (from Chuck Berry to Bo Diddley and Amos Milburn). The Charly label even released the CD of the famous blues reunion concert from 1963 with Muddy Waters, Willie Dixon, Howlin' Wolf, Sonny Boy Williamson, and Buddy Guy under the misguided title *Live Action* in 1992.

In Italy, a similar record company, *Blues Encore*, also carried out the same catalogue as Charly and ACE, with African American artists such as Big Joe Turner, T-Bone Walker, J. B. Lenoir, and Jimmy Reed. A French record company, *Disques Vogue*, already known for its releases of French artists (like Françoise Hardy and Jacques Dutronc), included English singers such as Petula Clark. They also had a series of LPs with numerous African American artists, including Fats Waller, Louis Armstrong, **Duke Ellington,** Count Basie, Erroll Garner, Thelonious Monk, Charlie Parker, Dizzie Gillespie, Johnny Hodges, Teddy Wilson, and Sarah Vaughan.

In Denmark, Storyville recorded African American musicians in jazz and blues from 1952, producing original albums of black musicians Big Joe Williams, Otis Spann, and Big Bill Broonzy that were sometimes re-released in the United States through licensing with labels such as Everest Records (in Los Angeles, California), in their "Archive of Folk Music" series. Meanwhile, in Amsterdam, Diving Duck Records also specialized in African American music, with reissued albums by black musician Lightnin' Hopkins released in the 1980s (from recordings made in the early 1950s).

In France, new labels dedicated to blues and jazz emerged in the 1970s, such as Black and Blue and, later, Evidence. This label did not release a European version of albums made in the United States; they recorded original sessions of African American artists in their studio in Paris and then released exclusive records. For instance, legendary U.S. bluesman Robert Jr. Lockwood recorded a tribute to Robert Johnson entitled *Robert Jr. Lockwood plays Robert and Robert*, a CD with 13 songs recorded at the Sysmo Studio in Paris in 1982. Another African American bluesman, Eddy Clearwater, recorded an album entitled *Blues Hang Out* in the same Paris studio in 1989. The French labels ZETA and Blues Collection, part of EPM in Paris, specialized in re-released recordings from the 1930s and 1940s. They produced countless compilations, including *Big Bill Broonzy in Chicago 1932/1937, Sonny Boy Williamson Vol. 1*, and *Blues with Girls*.

In Germany, the music series "Quadromania" released more than 200 low-priced box sets of African American artists between 2001 and 2008, mainly jazz and some blues, from Cab Calloway to Teddy Wilson, Big Bill Broonzy, and B.B. King. These box sets usually include four CDs with a total of about 80 songs, mostly early recordings that are more than 50 years old to avoid paying copyrights according to European legislation. In Austria, the label Document Records specialized in reissues of vintage blues music taken from original 78 RPM from the 1920s to the 1940s. Meanwhile, in Spain, the label Fresh Sound Records re-released some classic jazz LPs on CD, for instance Art Blakey's Jazz Messengers groundbreaking album titled *Cu-Bop* (originally issued in the United States in 1958).

WORLD MUSIC AND POP IN EUROPE.   With world music becoming more popular in record stores and on the airwaves during the 1980s, some new record companies served as relays for African music in Europe, as CDs manufactured in African countries were almost impossible to find in European record stores. A label like World Circuit Records produced CDs (presented as "Music from Hot Countries") with African artists like Ali Farka Touré and Oumou Sangare (both from Mali), Alex Konadu (from Ghana), Abdel Asis El Mubarak and Abdel Gadir Salim (both from Sudan), the Orchestra Baobab (from Senegal), Dimi Mint Abba (from Mauritania), and the group Black Umfolosi (from Zimbabwe).

In the 1980s, some African producers based in Paris launched their own label sponsored by Nubia, the *Association africaine d'auteurs-éditeurs* (African Association of Authors and Publishers). Moustapha Cissé released an LP entitled *Cissé/Danses rituelles d'Afrique* in 1989 with ritual music from Sierra Leone, Mali, and Sénégal.

On the pop scene, the British New Wave group Culture Club, cofounded by singer Boy George (George O'Dowd) and a black bass player, Mickey Craig, emerged in 1981. Some of their hits, such as "Church of the Poison Mind," included a powerful black backup singer, Helen Terry. From the 1980s, other pop groups in Britain, such as The Specials, The Selecter, and The Beat, included black and white members who had lived most of their lives in Europe, or were dedicated to reworking black music (like Ska and Reggae) into a new sound. In the mid-1990s, the British pop group The Spice Girls included a black member who was born in northern England: the singer Melanie Janine Brown, or simply "Mel B" (aka Scary Spice).

See also: Music, African Influences on European; Musicians in Europe, African American Classical; Pop Music, Blacks in Contemporary European.

Further Reading and Listening: Borel, François, ed. *Bénin, Rythmes et chants pour les Vodun / Rhythms and Songs for the Vodun.* 1990. Neuchatel (Switzerland), Musée d'Ethnographie. Disques VDE- GALLO, VDE, CD-612; Lane, Jeremy. "Jazz." In *France and the Americas: Culture, Politics, and History.* ed. Bill Marshall. Santa Barbara, CA: ABC-CLIO, 2005; Muddy Waters, Buddy Guy, Howlin' Wolf, Sonny Boy Williamson, and Willie Dixon. *Live Action.* CD. Charly Blues Masterworks, Vol. 15. BM 15, 1992 [1963]; Zaïre. *Musiques urbaines à Kinshasa.* OCORA, C 559007 HM 65. 1989 [1987].

Yves Laberge

Musicians in Europe, African American Classical

African American classical musicians, whether performing in concert halls or singing in opera houses, have had a strong presence in Europe since the nineteenth century. Receiving support from both Europe and the United States, musicians studied and performed throughout Europe in the nineteenth and twentieth centuries, often participating in major performances in its most prestigious concert halls.

In the early nineteenth century, African American performers traveled to Europe to play for a more accepting audience than could be found in the United States, as well as to gain notoriety. William Henry Lane (ca. 1825–1852), for example, performed with a minstrel group in England in 1849, causing writer Charles Dickens to call him "the greatest dancer known." Singers such as Elizabeth Taylor Greenfield (ca. 1824–1876), however, typify the kind of African American musician visiting Europe. Adopted by a Quaker at infancy, "The Black Swan," as she was often called, received a strong education in Pennsylvania before studying in London in 1853, giving a command performance for the queen. Several other African American opera singers in the nineteenth century performed in Europe for royalty and the pope, including Marie Selika (1849–1937), heralded as the "Queen of Staccato"; Flora Batson Bergen (1864–1906); and Matilda Sissieretta Jones (1869–1933), also known as the "Black Patti," in reference to the reigning prima donna of the time, Adelina Patti. Jones, who made her 1895 debut at the Wintergarden Theatre in Berlin, Germany, received high acclaim and praise from music critics and enthusiastic audiences alike for her vocal range and abilities.

The nineteenth century also featured a rise in African American concert instrumentalists, including Francis "Frank" Johnson, who won wide acclaim in England in 1837. Thomas Green Bethune, also known as "Blind Tom" because of his visual impairment, was a pianist whose debut in England led to much praise in both Europe and the United States. Victor Eugene McCarty was one of the first African American musicians to study abroad by enrolling himself in the elite Paris Conservatory in 1840. String players, such as Will Marion Cook and Felix Weir, also benefited from an education in Europe. Cook, who lived in Berlin from 1887 to 1889, studied with the great violinist, Josef Joachim, and Weir studied at the Conservatory of Leipzig, Germany.

African American classical musicians increasingly found more opportunities to study and perform in Europe in the twentieth century. African American composers, conductors, singers, and instrumentalists experienced an open-door policy in regard to professional engagements often lacking in the United States. African American opera singers dominated opera houses in Europe during the nineteenth century. The twentieth century continued to see a rise of African American instrumentalists performing and studying in Europe, including Raymond Lawson (1875–1959), a pianist who studied in Europe with Ossip Gabrilowitsch in 1911. Carl Diton (1886–1962), like many other students, received a scholarship to study in Europe and studied in Germany from 1910 to 1911, as did Helen Hagan (1896–1964), who studied in France with the famous composer Vincent D'Indy. Violinist Louia Vaughn Jones (1895–1965) also took the opportunity to study music in Europe.

It was Hazel Harrison (1883–1969), however, who brought about much praise and a wide audience, as the first African American musician to have studied exclusively in the United States and perform with a European orchestra. The career of Harrison, born in La Porte, Indiana, took off in 1904 when she performed both the Grieg and Chopin (Opus 11) piano concertos with the Berlin Philharmonic Orchestra. Her performance was so outstanding that it caused one newspaper to question whether the alleged "caucasian blood in her veins" was responsible for her talent, an argument that demonstrates the overt racism many musicians still struggled to overcome. As time passed, more African American instrumentalists traveled to Europe to study with great teachers and perform with top orchestras. Pianists like Andre Watts (b. 1946) are excellent examples of instrumentalists who, in the post–World War II era, appeared with leading symphony orchestras in Europe.

Opportunities for African American conductors to study and conduct music especially grew in the twentieth century, as conservatories and orchestras in Europe were more willing to accept African American conductors than their American counterparts. Dean Dixon (1915–1976), for example, was one of the first to become a successful conductor, having studied at Julliard and debuted with the New York Philharmonic. As he could not find a position in the United States, he moved to Europe and resided there from 1949 to 1970, serving as the musical director of the Göteborg Symphony in Sweden and the Hesse Radio Symphony in Frankfurt, Germany. Everett Lee (b. 1919) studied at the Saint Cecilia Academy in Rome and privately with Max Rudolph, yet was also unable to find a position in the United States as a conductor. Eventually, he moved to Europe (1953–1973), conducting the Munich Traveling Orchestra in Germany and the Norrkoping Symphony in Sweden, as well as other orchestras. Orchestra conductors were eventually able to land positions in American orchestras; for example, Paul Freeman (b. 1936) studied at the Hochschule für Musik in Berlin and conducted the Helsinki Symphony in Finland.

African American composers also studied in Europe, often working with some of the most famous teachers in both Europe and America. Howard Swanson (1907–1978), whose works have been recorded by the Vienna Staatsoper Orchestra and the Vienna Orchestra, studied with Nadia Boulanger at the American Academy in Fontainebleau, France in 1938. He remained in Europe until World War II, when he was forced to return to the United States. Ulysses Kay (1917–1995), who would eventually win the prestigious Prix de Rome, studied in Rome as an associate of the American Academy.

The role of the opera singer dominated the musical world in the twentieth century. From the 1920s until the 1980s, African American opera singers rose into the highest musical circles in Europe, causing sensations among European presses and audiences alike. Beginning in the 1920s, the idea that African American singers were expected to first receive critical acclaim in Europe before they could perform in American opera houses drove many to Europe. Also, opportunities for singers to perform in opera houses, in addition to concert halls, increased in the twentieth century. Before this time, those who traveled to Europe to perform usually toured as concert singers and did not receive professional engagements with opera companies.

Making his debut in April 1920 at London's Aeolian Hall, Roland Hayes (1887–1976) was the first successful black male singer to achieve high praise from both European and American audiences alike. African American singer Marian Anderson (1921–1993), arguably one of the greatest figures in music history in the twentieth century, toured Europe in the 1930s under a professional European management, making her debut in Paris. As a result of her success in Europe, she would eventually break many barriers in the United States, including her performance in 1955 with the Metropolitan Opera Company (she was the first black artist to sing with the company). Singers such as Lillian Evanti (1890–1967), **Paul Robeson** (1898–1976), Caterina Jarboro (1903–1986), and Jules Blesdoe (1898–1943) were successful in the post–World War II era and performed throughout Europe.

The wave of African American musical migration to perform in prestigious opera halls in Europe continued, and opera companies such as La Scala in Milan and Covent Garden in London welcomed the presence of "exotic" and glamorous African American singers to their stages. African American singers also benefited from the attention: Leontyne Price (b. 1927) made her European debut at the Staatsoper in Vienna, Grace Bumbry (b. 1937) caused a storm in 1961 as the first black singer to appear at the famous Bayreuth Festival in Germany, Simon Estes (b. 1938) received numerous professional contracts with German opera companies (and also sang at Bayreuth in 1978), and Jessye Norman's (b. 1945) professional career in the United States and Europe took flight as a result of sher professional engagement with the Deutsche Opera in Berlin. Thanks to the postwar boom in Europe and the United States, opera singers truly became superstars, performing for audiences on the radio, on recordings, and even being seen and heard on television.

The relationship between African American classical musicians and the European continent is an older one, albeit occasionally troublesome. Although the idea persisted (and continues to endure) that African American musicians went to Europe to escape the racially charged and turbulent atmosphere in the United States, there were still certain racial stereotypes that affected musicians abroad. African American opera singers, for example, were ironically able to gain acceptance in European opera companies in the late nineteenth and twentieth centuries by performing roles in operas that featured black characters, such as *Aida.* As Grace Bumbry's performance in Bayreuth indicated, however, the ability to transcend such roles and play nonblack characters was often met with conflict and tension. Like Hazel Harrison, instrumentalists faced the challenge of finding audiences who were willing to accept their inherent and natural talent and musical abilities in an age in which blacks were still deemed racially inferior. Nonetheless, opportunities still presented themselves to African Americans who, full of talent yet with very few outlets in the United States to perform, gladly welcomed an opportunity to share their gifts and musical ideas with the world.

See also: Artists in Europe, African-American; Authors in Europe, African-American; Jazz, European Reception of; Music, African Influences on European; Music Industry, Blacks in the European.

Further Reading: Southern, Eileen. *The Music of Black Americans: A History.* 2nd ed. New York: W. W. Norton, 1983.

Kira Thurman

The Mysterious Island (1874)

Neb, depicted as an African American servant, is a character in French literary icon Jules Verne's *The Mysterious Island* (1874), which is a sequel to both *20,000 Leagues Under the Sea* (1870) and *Captain Grant's Children* (1868).

The Mysterious Island, which takes place during the American Civil War, details the adventures of five Union prisoners who escape from a Confederate camp in a hot air balloon. Those five escapees are Captain Cyrus Smith, a railroad engineer; Neb (short for Nebuchadnezzar), Smith's African American servant; Pencroff, a sailor; Harbert, the young son of Pencroff's captain, who has died; and Gideon Spilett, a journalist. The group ends up on an uncharted island in the South Pacific, which they name Lincoln Island in honor of President Abraham Lincoln, who freed American slaves through his Emancipation Proclamation. Under the leadership of Cyrus Smith, the group develops a sustainable community on the island and overcomes many hardships for survival. The mystery of the island is the seemingly inexplicable occurrences and items on the island as characters, devices, and events suddenly appear to resolve situations or conclude plots.

Eventually, the group discovers a message in a bottle that leads them to search for and discover Ayrton, a character from *Captain Grant's Children*. The group returns to Lincoln Island through a tempest by following a fire beacon, which seemingly no one in the group had lit. The band of pirates, which Ayrton formerly associated with, decide to use the island as a hideout. Later, their ship is mysteriously destroyed and the crew killed with no visible wounds. Finally, the mystery of the island is revealed to be Captain Nemo, the lead character of *20,000 Leagues Under the Sea.* He and his fantastic submarine, the Nautilus, were not destroyed and ultimately escaped to Lincoln Island. Volcanic eruptions destroy the island and the characters escape through the help of Nemo, who dies.

Verne repeatedly tells the reader that Neb (who is called Nab in the original French after Nabuchodonosor) is not a slave, but rather a servant. Neb, the son of former slaves, had been freed by Smith, a native of Massachusetts, but Neb has refused to leave his former master's side. There is a seeming contradiction in Verne's depiction of Neb, at one hand praising the character and attempting to depict him as an equal, while simultaneously depicting him as naïve and under the paternalistic guidance of his former white master. Verne describes Neb as loyal, vigorous, agile, graceful, intelligent (although sometimes naïve), amiable, and kind. Consequently, although Verne's novel presents a positive series of characteristics in its image of blacks in the character of Neb, he is still a servant to his white master. In addition, Smith demonstrates a paternalistic attitude toward Neb, although he is treated with respect by the other castaways. Furthermore, Neb equally uses his native ingenuity, along with the other castaways, to transform the island into a thriving haven of civilization. Consequently, through the character of Neb, Verne, at least in part, acknowledges the contributions of blacks to European and Western civilization.

See also: Abolition of Slavery, French; France, Blacks in; Literature, Blacks in French.

Further Reading: Verne, Jules. *The Mysterious Island.* trans. Jordan Stump. New York: Modern Library Classics, 2004.

Eric Martone

N

Nassy, Josef (1904–1976)

Josef Nassy was an artist of Jewish and black African descent who was interned in a Nazi German concentration camp during World War II (1939–1945). Nassy, who was living in Belgium at the time of the war's outbreak, was one of the 2,000 holders of U.S. passports seized by the Nazis.

Nassy was born in Surinam (Dutch Guiana) in 1904. His father, a successful businessman, descended from Jews who had fled Spain during the Inquisition, which sought to eliminate all dissenters from the Catholic faith. Nassy's family, however, no longer practiced Judaism. In 1919, Nassy moved to New York, where he completed high school. In 1926, he received a certificate in electrical engineering.

In 1929, Nassy left the United States to go to England for employment. Before his departure, Nassy acquired a U.S. passport by fraudulently claiming to have been born in San Francisco in 1899. In 1906, much of San Francisco's public records had been lost during a devastating earthquake. Consequently, the U.S. government issued the passport because it could not refute the claim. Nassy acquired a position installing sound systems for a film company in England, later performing the same work in France and Belgium.

In the 1930s, Nassy decided to become an artist and to study at the fine arts academy in Brussels, Belgium. He married a Belgian woman in 1939. At this time, Nassy attempted to gain money working as a portrait artist. The next year, Nazi Germany invaded Belgium. The United States remained out of World War II until Germany's ally, Japan, attacked Pearl Harbor in December 1941. Consequently, in 1942, Germany and the United States were at war. The Germans seized Nassy, who had decided earlier against fleeing Belgium, on April 14, 1942, on the grounds that he was now an enemy national residing in territory under German occupation.

Nassy was sent to the Beverloo transit camp in Leopoldsburg, Belgium. He remained there for seven months, when he was then transferred to Germany. In Germany, Nassy was imprisoned at the Laufen internment camp and Tittmoning in Bavaria. He remained a prisoner until the end of the war. During Nassy's captivity, he created a visual diary composed of more than 200 illustrations, many of which document daily life in internment camps.

At Laufen and Tittmoning, the Germans followed the rules of the Geneva Convention for prisoners. Consequently, Nassy, although under several restrictions, was not detailed for forced labor and usually received proper food rations from the Germans and from Red Cross packages. The international YMCA supplied Nassy with sketch pads and other materials to maintain his visual diary. By 1945, Nassy's fellow inmates included about 850 other holders of American or British passports, about a dozen of whom were also of black descent.

In May 1945, the U.S. Army liberated Nassy's internment camp at Laufen. He was repatriated to Belgium and in the following years participated in several exhibitions showcasing Holocaust art. In 1984, art collector Severin Wunderman purchased Nassy's entire collection of work and, in 1992, donated it to the United States Holocaust Memorial Museum.

See also: Artists in Europe, African American; Gilges, Lari; Nazis and Black POWs; Snow, Valaida; World War II, Black Participation in.

Further Reading: Rothschild-Boros, Monica. *In the Shadow of the Tower: The Works of Josef Nassy, 1942–1945.* Irvine, CA: Severin Wunderman, 1989.

Eric Martone

Nazis and Black POWs

During World War II (1939–1945), thousands of black soldiers from Allied armed forces became prisoners of war (POWs) of Nazi Germany. The French contingent of black POWs, mostly soldiers from French West Africa (*tirailleurs sénégalais*), was by far the largest. Many black POWs suffered massacres and abuses from members of the German army and, occasionally, civilians.

During the German campaign in France in the spring of 1940, Nazi propaganda depicted the black African soldiers of the French army as savages who had mutilated German prisoners. In a perceived act of revenge, German army and SS units murdered several thousand black French prisoners after having captured them. According to a cautious estimate, at least 3,000 blacks were murdered after having surrendered, and a probably much larger number were killed in battles where no prisoners were taken. The massacres often occurred after prolonged close combat and wherever the *tirailleurs sénégalais* mounted determined resistance toward the end of the campaign. No general order to kill black prisoners existed, and the behavior of German units was inconsistent. Some German officers and soldiers, assisted by French medical personnel, actively prevented massacres. Still, on the way to prisoner-of-war camps, black soldiers continued to experience abuses from rearguard troops. Many blacks received no water or food, and daily murders and beatings were common.

A few black POWs were used for research in tropical medicine and pseudoscientific racial studies throughout the war, but the situation for most of them improved in the late summer of 1940, and remained stable until the evacuation of France in the summer and fall of 1944. Black prisoners from the French army (approximately 16,000 in mid-1941) were generally kept in German camps in occupied France and treated fairly, as camp inspections by the French government and the Red Cross report. The prisoners were working on farms, in forestry, and on public work projects. Many black prisoners suffered from pulmonary disease, but the German army was willing to liberate sick prisoners. Conditions deteriorated again in the summer and fall of 1944, as some prisoners became victims of Allied bombings as the remaining prisoners were moved from France to mainland Germany. There, they suffered from food shortages and intense bombings. Most French black prisoners were liberated by advancing Allied armies in France or Germany, whereas a significant number of them escaped and joined the French resistance shortly before the liberation. A few of these ex-prisoners were caught by the Germans and sent to concentration camps.

A small number of African American soldiers also fell into German hands, particularly in the last months of the war. During the Battle of the Bulge, 11 black soldiers were murdered by a Waffen-SS unit in Wereth (Belgium) on December 17, 1944. German civilians and police occasionally mistreated or murdered black airmen belonging to downed bomber crews. In many cases, local Nazi leaders had called on the population to take revenge on downed allied aircrews. A small number of blacks from Britain and the British colonies also became prisoners of war in Nazi Germany. Some of them were held in separate barracks belonging to the German camps in France that housed French African prisoners.

See also: British Army, Blacks in the; French Army, Blacks in the; Germany, Blacks in; Gilges, Lari; Gobineau on Races and Slavery; Massaquoi, Hans-Jürgen; Nassy, Josef; Nazis and Blacks in Europe; Olympics (1936); Rhineland Blacks; Scientific Racism; Snow, Valaida; World War I, Black Participation in; World War II, Black Participation in.

Further Reading: Echenberg, Myron. *Colonial Conscripts: The Tirailleurs Sénégalais in French West Africa, 1857–1960.* Portsmouth, NH, and London: Heinemann and James Currey, 1991; Fargettas, Julien. "Les massacres de mai-juin 1940." In *La campagne de 1940.* ed. Christine Levisse-Touzé. Paris: Tallandier, 2001, pp. 448–464; Kesting, Robert. "Blacks Under the Swastika: A Research Note." *Journal of Negro History* 83 (1998): 84–99; Killingray, David. "Africans and African Americans in Enemy Hands." In *Prisoners of War and Their Captors in World War II.* eds. Bob Moore and Kent Fedorowich. Washington, DC: Berg, 1996, pp. 181–204; Koller, Christian. *"Von Wilden aller Rassen niedergemetzelt." Die Diskussion um die Verwendung von Kolonialtruppen in Europa zwischen Rassismus, Kolonial- und Militärpolitik (1914–1930).* Stuttgart: Franz Steiner, 2001; Mabon, Armelle. "La singulière captivité des prisonniers de guerre coloniaux durant la Seconde Guerre mondiale." *French Colonial History* 7 (2006): 181–197; Scheck, Raffael. *Hitler's African Victims: The German Army Massacres of Black French Soldiers in 1940.* New York: Cambridge University Press, 2006; Thomas, Martin. "The Vichy Government and French Colonial Prisoners of War, 1940–1944." *French Historical Studies* 25:4 (2002): 657–692.

Raffael Scheck

Nazis and Blacks in Europe

Nazi ideology, based on racist and supremacist doctrines of the nineteenth century, assigned a very low value to black people. Given that Nazism believed that the mixing of races created degeneracy, people of mixed background were viewed with special contempt and were considered a danger to the health of the allegedly superior German race. Although blacks were not subjected to a bureaucratically organized genocidal program, as were the Jews, and, to some extent, the Sinti and Roma, blacks and mixed-race people suffered discrimination, abuse, and murder, both in Nazi Germany and, later, in the Nazi-occupied parts of Europe.

Nazi doctrine with respect to blacks was influenced heavily by the crude Darwinist tenets of racist philosophers, such as Josephe-Arthur de **Gobineau** (1816–1882) and Houston Stewart Chamberlain (1855–1927), which stressed a value-based hierarchy of races. These prejudices received scientific legitimation by the dubious, but influential, studies of anthropologists Fritz Lenz (1887–1976) and Eugen Fischer (1874–1967), who had written a book on mixed-race children in the colony German Southwest Africa (modern Namibia). Although some Nazi ideologists argued that Jews and blacks were related genetically, the Nazis always considered the threat emanating from Jews much more serious than the threat represented by blacks. Nevertheless, they made several public pronouncements against blacks. During the occupation of the German Rhineland by French troops in the years after World War I, the newly founded Nazi party latched on to the international propaganda campaign designed to discredit, in particular, the black soldiers in France's occupation army, which culminated in 1921–1923. In his programmatic writing *Mein Kampf*, future German dictator Adolf Hitler made contemptuous remarks about black soldiers from the Allied armies in World War I and during the occupation of the Rhineland. Echoing a widespread anti-Semitic belief, he argued that Jews had masterminded the stationing of black troops on German soil in order to "contaminate" the pure German race. Once in power, the Nazis passed laws that declared marriages between white Germans and blacks illegal (October 1933) and organized a program for the sterilization of biracial children. From 1937 onward, German authorities tracked down and forcibly sterilized approximately 500 biracial children from the Rhineland. The infamous Nuremberg Laws (1935), although directed primarily against Jews, reiterated the principle that German citizenship could be based only on "blood," and that mixed marriages between Germans and "non-Aryans" were illegal.

There were about 3,000 blacks and biracial people in Nazi Germany, among them immigrants from the former German colonies in Africa, musicians and dancers, acrobats, a few diplomats and businessmen with their families, and some students from various African countries. During World War II, thousands of black civilians, particularly in France and Belgium, also fell under German control, and the German army took close to 16,000 black Africans as prisoners of war from the French army. Blacks did not experience the massive and pitiless persecution suffered by Jews in the Nazi empire, but they did suffer daily discrimination and intimidation. Those blacks who had German passports before 1933 lost their German citizenship. Deprived of citizenship and most forms of legal protection, blacks and biracial people in Germany were treated as outlaws and experienced many insults and attacks from white Germans. Black men and women might be ineligible for the ration cards distributed to the white population, and employers often refused to hire anybody but "Aryans." Because unemployment insurance covered only citizens, jobless blacks were left without any state support. In school, any denunciation from a white child, or his or her parents, could induce the school administration to ban a black or biracial child from school. The memoirs of **Hans-Jürgen Massaquoi,** son of the Liberian Consul General in Hamburg and a German woman, paint a vivid picture of a biracial child wanting to fit in, yet being confronted with a multitude of racist-discriminatory acts, while being protected by some friendship networks, but also threatened because these networks themselves were suspect to the Nazis.

Although Nazi propaganda created a public mood for racism, many of these acts of aggression and discrimination started from civilians without specific guidance from the authorities. Older prejudices against blacks seem to have motivated such outbursts of racism, and the Nazi state made sure that they could happen with impunity. The popular hostility toward blacks, however, proved to be an embarrassment to the German Foreign Office and to some circles of the Nazi party who wanted to recreate a German colonial empire in sub-Saharan Africa including, but not limited to, the former German colonies. News of blatant acts of racism in Nazi Germany spread in African countries and damaged Germany's prestige. Still, for much of the Third Reich, the Nazi interest in African colonies mitigated at least the official persecution of blacks and biracial people.

Given Nazi ideas about "cleansing" German culture of foreign and "degenerate" influences, the Nazis tried to eradicate black influence in the arts, fashion, and music. Jazz, in particular, was condemned by Nazi propagandists. During the war, however, Propaganda Minister Joseph Goebbels found it imperative to develop and broadcast a German form of jazz because the popularity of American music, including jazz, induced many Germans to break the law by listening to foreign radio programs that offered jazz music.

Given the Nazis' emphasis on sports and their claim that "Aryans" were physically superior to other peoples, athletic competitions involving blacks assumed special importance for the Nazi press. When German boxer Max Schmeling defeated the African American boxer Joe Louis in 1936, the Nazi press celebrated Schmeling's victory as proof of Aryan superiority over black "sub-humans." This confidence was shaken, however, when African American athletes, foremost Jesse Owens, won a large share of medals at the **Olympics** (1936) in Berlin. Hitler was so upset that he refused to shake hands with the black athletes. In 1938, moreover, Joe Louis defeated Schmeling in a rematch after only one round.

The realm of film and the circus seem to have presented something of a safe haven for many blacks in Nazi Europe. Films with colonial content such as *Germanin,* showing the development of a revolutionary German medicine against tropical illnesses, and *Carl Peters,* focusing on the life of a German colonial pioneer, required large numbers of blacks for crowd scenes; consequently, prisoners of war, women from the Paris underworld, and Afro-German circus artists were drafted to play in such films. Film and the circus, traditionally associated with "exotic" artists, allowed some blacks to continue their careers in Nazi Germany in relative security. Actor Ludwig Mbebe Mpessa (alias Louis Brody, 1892–1951), who was famous before the Nazi rise to power, played in at least 23 films in the Third Reich. Nevertheless, blacks in the film and circus realm generally had to pay a humiliating price for their continued toleration by strictly adhering to the stereotypes and roles defined for them by German society and Nazi lawmakers. Denunciation and Nazi laws could rapidly become a mortal threat even for these blacks, as was experienced by the actor Bayume Mohamed Husen (1904–1944). Husen, who had played in the film *Carl Peters*, was arrested during the work for a new film because he had allegedly committed "racial shame," meaning an amorous liaison with an "Aryan" woman, in 1941. He was sent to the concentration camp of Sachsenhausen near Berlin, where he perished on November 24, 1944.

Husen belonged to an unknown number of black and biracial people who were sent to concentration camps. In most cases, skin color was not decisive for their deportation, but it appears to have exacerbated their experience in the camps by making them a special target for scorn and abuse from the guards, and sometimes even from fellow prisoners. Some blacks detained or killed by the Nazis were involved in anti-Nazi organizations. **Lari Gilges,** a 24-year-old communist from Düsseldorf, was arrested and murdered in the summer of 1933. Several black political activists and members of the resistance from France were also sent to concentration camps. The American jazz musician **Valaida Snow** was arrested by the Nazis in 1940 and badly mistreated during her captivity.

During the German campaign against France in 1940, Nazi propaganda conjured up images of savage black French soldiers who would mutilate German prisoners, eat raw cows, and behave like "beasts." These propaganda images, inspired directly by Hitler and Goebbels, created an intense hostility toward blacks and helped trigger massacres of black French prisoners of war. Hitler ordered that the surviving prisoners be held in German-occupied France, so that they would not spread tropical diseases to Germany and "contaminate" the German race by mingling with German women. Occasional German abuses of black prisoners from the French army and, in 1944–1945, the American army, did happen, but they were the exception rather than the rule.

Altogether, the Nazi images of blacks and policies toward them were never consistent. One of many problems was the delineation between North Africans and black Africans: although North Africans, particularly the Arabs and Berbers, were considered of much higher racial stock than sub-Saharan (black) Africans, Nazi policies and popular racism did not always distinguish between them. It mattered little, for example, whether a biracial child from the Rhineland had an Algerian (North African) or black father. Moreover, the Nazi authorities themselves often acted at cross-purposes, with some institutions and organizations urging moderation toward blacks to avoid endangering Germany's colonial claims, and others pushing for racial "purity" at all cost.

See also: Afro-Germans; Central Europe, Blacks in; Colonies in Africa, German; Film, Blacks in European; French Army, Blacks in the; Gall, Franz Josef; Germany, Blacks in; Jazz, European Reception of; Nassy, Josef; Rhineland Blacks; Scientific Racism; World War I, Black Participation in; World War II, Black Participation in.

Further Reading: Campt, Tina. *Other Germans: Black Germans and the Politics of Race, Gender, and Memory in the Third Reich.* Ann Arbor: University of Michigan Press, 2004; Coquery-Vidrovitch, Catherine. *Des victimes oubliées du Nazisme: Les Noirs et l'Allemagne dans la pre-*

mière moitié du xxe siècle. Paris: Le Cherche-Midi, 2007; Kesting, Robert. "The Black Experience During the Holocaust." In *The Holocaust and History: The Known, the Unknown, the Disputed, and the Reexamined.* eds. Michael Berenbaum and Abraham Peck. Bloomington: Indiana University Press, 1998, pp. 358–365; Kesting, Robert. "Blacks Under the Swastika: A Research Note." *Journal of Negro History* 83 (1998): 84–99; Kesting, Robert. "Forgotten Victims: Blacks in the Holocaust." *Journal of Negro History* 77 (1992): 30–36; Lusane, Clarence. *Hitler's Black Victims: The Historical Experiences of Afro-Germans, European Blacks, Africans, and African Americans in the Nazi Era*. New York: Routledge, 2002; Martin, Peter, and Christine Alonzo, eds. *Zwischen Charleston und Stechschritt: Schwarze im Nationalsozialismus*. Hamburg: Dölling und Galitz, 2004; Massaquoi, Hans J. *Destined to Witness: Growing up Black in Nazi Germany*. New York: W. Morrow, 1999; Mazón, Patricia, and Reinhild Steingröver, eds. *Not so Plain as Black and White: Afro- German Culture and History, 1890–2000*. Rochester: University of Rochester Press, 2005.

Raffael Scheck

Négritude

Négritude is a literary, ideological, and political movement developed in the 1930s by a group of young Caribbean and African intellectuals in Paris, France. The founders of Négritude, known as *"les trois pères"* ("the three fathers"), were author and politician **Léopold Sédar Senghor,** Martinican poet **Aimé Césaire,** and the Guianian poet **Léon Damas**. Négritude was premised on the notion that solidarity in a common African diasporic identity was necessary to overcome the social and political rhetoric of French colonial racism and domination. The movement can be characterized by its Marxist ideals, denunciation of Europe's lack of humanity, and valorization of African history, traditions, and beliefs.

The term *négritude* was first used in 1935 by Césaire in *L'Étudiant noir*, the journal he started in Paris with fellow students, Senghor, Damas, Gilbert Gratient, Leonard Sainville, and Paulette Nardal. *L'Étudiant noir* also published Césaire's *"Négreries,"* which is recognized not only for its disavowal of cultural assimilation as a strategy for resistance, but also for returning to the word *nègre* a positive meaning. Previously, especially during colonization, the word *nègre* had been used in an offensive, pejorative sense.

The Négritude movement was highly influenced by African American authors of the Harlem Renaissance, particularly Langston Hughes and **Richard Wright**. The Harlem influence was shared by the Negrismo movement in the Spanish-speaking Caribbean, which, of course, differed in language, but was in many ways united with the goals of Négritude.

Another source of inspiration for Négritude came from Haiti, where there had been a burgeoning of black culture in the early twentieth century. Haitian history is also significant to the **African Diaspora** thanks to the **Haitian Revolution for Independence** led by **Toussaint L'Ouverture** in the 1790s. Césaire wrote of Haiti as the place where Négritude appeared for the first time.

European and other forms of surrealism provided aesthetic influence and political support to the Négritude movement. In particular, Martinican Négritude writers including Césaire, Suzanne Césaire, and René Ménil took up surrealism as a revolutionary method and a means of criticizing rational, European culture. In 1940, they formed a journal entitled *Tropiques*, featuring their work, along with that of André Breton, Lucie Thésée, and Aristide Maugée, that was largely informed by this revolutionary surrealist aesthetic.

In 1948, existentialist philosopher Jean-Paul Sartre analyzed Négritude in his essay, *"Orphée Noir"* ("Black Orpheus"), which served as the introduction to a volume of Francophone poetry called *Anthologie de la nouvelle poésie nègre et malgasy de langue française* (*Anthology of New Black and Malgasy Poetry in the French Language*), compiled by Senghor. Sartre characterizes Négritude as the opposite of colonial racism in a Hegelian dialectic. According to him, Négritude was an "anti-racist racism" that was essential for the ultimate goal of racial unity.

In the 1960s, Négritude philosophy was criticized by certain black writers as being insufficiently militant and essentialist. South African poet and political activist Keorapetse Kgositsile argued that the movement was based too much on celebrating blackness in terms of a white aesthetic and was unable to put forth a new kind of black perception that would free black intellectuals and artists from white conceptual paradigms. Despite criticism, however, Négritude ideals have continued to inspire racial and cultural movements of liberation and justice throughout the twentieth and early twenty-first centuries.

See also: Colonies in the Caribbean, French; Colonies in the Caribbean, Spanish; Haitian Revolution in Francophone Literature; Literature, Blacks in French.

Further Reading: Arnold, James A. *Modernism and Negritude: The Poetry and Politics of Aimé Césaire.* Lincoln, NE: iUniverse Press, 2000; Bâ, Sylvia Washington. *The Concept of Negritude in the Poetry of Léopold Sédar Senghor.* Princeton, NJ: Princeton University Press, 1973; Chidi, Ikonne. *Links and Bridges: A Comparative Study of the Writings of the New Negro and Negritude Movements.* Ibadan, Nigeria: University Press PLC, 2006; Jones, Edward Allen. *Voices of Négritude: The Expression of Black Experience in the Poetry of Senghor, Césaire, and Damas.* Valley Forge, PA: Judson Press, 1971; Kesteloot, Lilyan. *Black Writers in French: A Literary History of Negritude.* Washington, DC: Howard University Press, 1991; Markovitz, Irving Leonard. *Léopold Sédar Senghor and the Politics of Negritude.* New York: Heinemann Educational Press, 1969; Popeau, Jean Baptiste. *Dialogues of Negritude: An Analysis of the Cultural Context of Black Writing.* Durham, NC: Carolina Academic Press, 2003; Sharpley-Whiting, T. Denean. *Negritude Women.* Minneapolis: University of Minnesota Press, 2002.

Jennifer Westmoreland Bouchard

Netherlands, Blacks in the

Blacks have existed in the Netherlands in substantial numbers since the fifteenth century. Many Dutch were involved in the slave trade and in obtaining colonies in Africa and the Americas in the early modern period. Some former slaves managed to attain high status in early modern Dutch society. A notable example was **Jacobus Capitein**, a former African slave who earned a doctorate degree in the Netherlands during the eighteenth century.

A sizable portion of the population of the contemporary Netherlands is from sub-Saharan Africa or is of black African descent. The majority of the sub-Saharan Africans in the Netherlands originate from Somalia, Cape Verde, Ghana, Angola, Ethiopia, Eritrea, Congo, Nigeria, and Sudan. Many of those of black African descent come from the former Dutch colonies of Suriname and the Netherlands Antilles. The Netherlands Antilles, which are five islands in the Caribbean Sea, are an autonomous component of the Kingdom of the Netherlands. Beginning in the postwar era, many Afro-Caribbeans migrated to the Netherlands for employment.

Many immigrants in the Netherlands of sub-Saharan Africa are of recent origin. There are a variety of reasons for such a migration, including asylum, employment, family formation, family reunion, and education. Although sub-Saharan African immigrants and their children are dispersed throughout the Netherlands, many tend to congregate in areas between the major cities of Amsterdam, Rotterdam, and Utrecht. A portion of sub-Saharan African immigrants either return to their countries of origin or migrate to a third country after a few years.

Sub-Saharan African immigrants in the Netherlands often have difficulty immediately entering the Dutch labor market. African immigrants have varying levels of education. Many need to adjust to the Dutch environment, such as learning to speak Dutch. African immigrants from English-speaking African countries can fall back on English. African immigrants from Francophone and Lusophone African states, however, have greater difficulty adjusting. Black immigrants often face discrimination in attempts to find employment and housing. The government has sought to cooperate with unions and employers' groups to reduce minority unemployment rates to make them comparable to the national average. As a result, the rate of the increase of minority positions has been much higher than among the general population. The 1998 Act on the Stimulation of Labor Participation by Ethnic Minorities, for example, was established to increase job opportunities for minorities.

The influx of sub-Saharan African immigrants has led to new cultural differences in the Netherlands. For example, many of the immigrants and their children are Muslims. The harsh social and political environment toward immigrants in general and Muslims in particular has made it hard for African immigrants to adjust to the Netherlands. The Dutch education system places African children in low-level courses because of their poor Dutch. Such children are often left behind in the Dutch educational system. Facing social ostracism, some Africans youths resort to crime.

Many black immigrants from Africa and the Caribbean suffer from racially motivated incidents ranging from racist pamphlets to harassment, physical assaults, and the destruction of property. The National Bureau to Fight Racial Discrimination was established to collect nationwide statistics in incidents of discrimination. Collected data indicate an increase in the amount of reported acts of discrimination. The Equal Opportunities Committee has also reported the same trend. The increase in the amount of reported acts of discrimination has been attributed to greater awareness of the complaints process and changing societal attitudes.

The Dutch government has pursued efforts to increase public awareness of racism and discrimination. In 1997, prosecution norms for discrimination were strengthened. Penalties were raised for discrimination committed by groups (political parties, corporations, etc.) because organizational discrimination was perceived as more dangerous than that of individuals. Police were mandated to report thoroughly complaints of discrimination. Police officers found guilty of discrimination face disciplinary measures and criminal charges.

To give each other support, black residents in the Netherlands have formed various aid organizations. Some of these organizations are religious in nature, and some, such as those that united in 2004 as the Sudan Civil Society Forum in the Netherlands, are of a more political nature. The Sudan Forum was established to create a contact point for Dutch nongovernmental organizations.

See also: Abolition of Slavery, European; Amo, Anton Wilhelm; Boer War; Colonies in the Caribbean, Dutch; Illegal African Immigration to Europe; Piet, Zwarte; Prostitution in Europe, Blacks and; Race Riots in Europe; Slave Trade, Dutch; Xenophobia and Blacks in Europe.

Further Reading: Blakely, Allison. *Blacks in the Dutch World: The Evolution of Racial Imagery in a Modern Society.* Bloomington: Indiana University Press, 1994; Cross, Malcolm, and Hans Entzinger, eds. *Lost Illusions: Caribbean Minorities in Britain and the Netherlands.* London: Routledge, 1988; Van Heelsum, A., and T. Hessels. *Afrikanen in Nederland, een profile.* Den Haag: Ministerie van Justitie, 2005.

E. Agateno Mosca

New Imperialism

During the late nineteenth to early twentieth centuries, the major European powers used various forms of political control over weaker powers to dominate much of the world. The European expansion abroad was fueled by desires for raw materials and new markets to further European industrial and commercial expansion, as well as for prestige and strategic purposes. One of the primary areas targeted by European imperial expansion was Africa, resulting in a "scramble" that would devour most of the continent. During the era of the New Imperialism, conservatives in Europe often used colonialism as an occasion for national cohesion. Some European powers viewed overseas empires as outlets for a surplus home population.

The imperial expansions that composed the New Imperialism occurred amid increasing competition between the industrialized countries (the major European powers, United States, and Japan) over raw materials, strategic power, prestige, and commercial markets. Such competition emerged after the breakdown of the general European peace and cooperation established by the Congress of Vienna in 1815, which reconfigured Europe after the defeat of Napoleon to restore a balance of power. Until 1871, when Prussia defeated France and subsequently unified Germany, Britain had prospered from its position as the supreme industrial and naval power in the world, which enabled it to act as a dominating force in world trade. As British dominance began to wane, changes occurred in the European and global economies, and in the internal composition of Europe. The unifications of Italy (1866) and Germany (1871) removed internal rivalries in Central and Southern Europe that had kept these areas out of external affairs. Newly industrializing powers, such as Germany, sought external commercial markets and sought to break Britain's dominance in world trade. Furthermore, competition was intensified as a result of a depression (1873–1896) in Europe and a period of price deflation that ultimately put pressure on European governments to promote home industry and the adoption of protectionist policies, rather than those of free trade. Therefore new colonies were perceived as sources of both cheap raw materials and new commercial export markets devoid of foreign competition.

The New Imperialism led to new social views concerning colonialism. Social Darwinism became common during the late nineteenth century and European powers, particularly France and Britain, took on self-appointed civilizing missions to parts of the world. British writer Rudyard Kipling, for example, wrote his famous poem on the "White Man's Burden" to encourage Europeans to bring their form of civilization, which they perceived as superior, to the world.

In the late nineteenth century, European powers began to occupy Africa in greater proportions. In 1875, the major European possessions in Africa were French Algeria and the British Cape Colony. By the early twentieth century, however, only Ethiopia and Liberia were free of European control. An informal empire of dominance was replaced by formal empires of occupation. In the 1870s, explorers David Livingston and H. M. Stanley opened the way for European penetration of the African interior. In the late 1870s, King Leopold II of Belgium organized a corporation under his control to negotiate treaties with African chiefs to gain occupation of the Congo after the Belgian government refused to get involved in the colonial scramble. France in particular, but also Germany, soon began to expand their presence in Africa and began to make dubious territorial claims. Increased European competition in Africa led to the **Berlin Conference** (1884–1885), which sought to regulate European actions in Africa to maintain peace and mutual profit. At the Conference, Leopold II was granted control over the **Congo Free State** developed from land in Central Africa. He was supported in his claims by both Germany and Britain at the expense of territorial claims by the French and Portuguese. The Congo, however, became infamous for the atrocities committed against the local population and led to an international scandal that forced him to turn over the colony to the Belgian government in 1908.

In 1882, Britain dissolved the dual control of Egypt between itself and France. Britain subsequently proceeded to launch initiatives, including the occupation of the Sudan, to control the Nile River Valley and the Suez Canal. Such actions increased tensions with France and its territories in Africa and almost led to conflict between the two powers at Fashoda in 1898. In 1899, Britain sought to complete its occupation of South Africa. British expansion in East Africa prompted British attempts to build a "Cape to Cairo" railroad linking the empire from north to south. German occupation of territory in East Africa, however, thwarted British efforts until after World War I. Meanwhile, France continued to establish its empire in northern and western Africa. By the time of World War I (1914–1918), Britain controlled more of Africa than any other European country, followed by France and then Germany.

See also: Boer War; Colonies in Africa, British; Colonies in Africa, Dutch; Colonies in Africa, French; Colonies in Africa, German; Colonies in Africa, Italian; Colonies in Africa, Portuguese; Colonies in Africa, Spain; Scientific Racism; World War I, Black Participation in; Zulu War.

Further Reading: Anstey, Roger. *Britain and the Congo in the Nineteenth Century.* Oxford: Clarendon Press, 1962; Ascherson, Neal. *The King Incorporated.* New York: Doubleday and Company, 1964; Bauer, Ludwig. *Leopold the Unloved: King of the Belgians and of Wealth.* trans.

Eden Paul and Cedar Paul. Boston: Little, Brown and Company, 1935; Collins, Robert O., ed. *The Partition of Africa: Illusion or Necessity.* New York: John Wiley, 1969; Crowe, Sybil E. *The Berlin West Africa Conference 1884–1885.* New York: Longmans, Green and Company, 1942; Emerson, Barbara. *Leopold II of the Belgians: King of Colonialism.* New York: St. Martin's Press, 1979; Forster, Stig and Wolfgang J. Mommsen and Ronald Robinson, eds. *Bismarck, Europe, and Africa: The Berlin Conference 1884–1885 and the Onset of Partition.* New York: Oxford University Press, 1988; Gavin, R. J., and J. A. Betley, eds. *The Scramble for Africa: Documents on the West Berlin Conference and Related Subjects 1884/85.* Ibadan, Nigeria: Ibadan University Press, 1973; Hochschild, Adam. *King Leopold's Ghost: A Story of Greed, Terror, and Heroism in Colonial Africa.* New York: Houghton Mifflin, 1998; Pakenham, Thomas. *The Scramble for Africa.* London: Weidenfeld and Nicolson, 1991; Power, Thomas Francis. *Jules Ferry and the Renaissance of French Imperialism.* Morningside Heights, New York: King's Crown Press, 1944; Sesay, Amadu, ed. *Africa and Europe: From Partition to Interdependence or Dependence?* London: Croom Helm, 1986; Taylor, A.J.P. *Germany's First Bid for Colonies 1884–1885: A Move in Bismarck's European Policy.* London: Macmillan, 1938.

Eric Martone

Notting Hill Carnival

The Notting Hill Carnival, also known as the African-Caribbean fair, is the largest street fair in Europe and regularly attracts crowds of more than two million revelers. It is held in the Notting Hill area in London, England, over two days during the August Bank Holiday weekend, with a children's day on Sunday, focusing specifically on the costumes, and the adult carnival on Monday. It takes its inspiration from pre-Lenten Catholic festivities, which in the Caribbean were transformed into carnivals, as freed slaves injected the celebrations with their own cultural metaphors, hybrid music, and dance. The first Notting Hill carnival, however, was more a street party than an expression of African-Caribbean heritage. Indeed, there is some debate about its origins. Guyanese activist Rhaune Laslett has long been credited with creating the Notting Hill carnival, as indeed has the journalist and community activist, **Claudia Jones**. Whomever its originator, the Notting Hill carnival is today a symbol of the endurance and continued vitality of African-Caribbean culture in Great Britain.

Most West Indian (Caribbean) immigrants to the United Kingdom in the postwar period settled in London, although significant numbers also went to Midlands cities, like Nottingham and Birmingham. Widespread and pervasive housing discrimination meant that black people tended to congregate in areas where, for various reasons, landlords were more amenable. In West London, Ladbroke Grove and Notting Hill became the primary sites of black settlement, although tensions were evident between West Indian immigrants and the white working-class community from the outset. In the 1950s, working-class British youth culture was influenced greatly by the nationalist rhetoric of groups such as Oswald Mosley's British Union of Fascists, which promoted open hostility toward black immigration. Among the youth groups influenced by this ideology were the "teddy boys," who were associated with American rock and roll music and a distinctive style of dress that was a parody of Edwardian attire.

In August 1958, a "teddy boy" gang attacked a Swedish woman who was married to a Jamaican as she walked to her home in Notting Hill. Rioting ensued, and over a two-week period, gangs of white youth combed the area attacking black people on the streets and in their homes. Such violence culminated in the murder of West Indian carpenter Kelso Cochrane. The violence continued until the beginning of September, when the police arrested the gang leaders. It was in this context that Jones organized the fair in January 1959 in Saint Pancras Town Hall to bring together the different communities. In 1965, lingering tensions between whites and West Indian immigrants led Laslett, also a community leader, to organize an outdoor event intended to build bridges within the community by celebrating its ethnic and cultural diversity. Many ethnic associations participated in the event, which was held over the August bank holiday weekend, including the Asian, Caribbean, African, Irish, and Scottish. It was a cultural festival that featured poetry, international song and dance, a folk concert, and darts matches in local pubs. The focus, therefore, was not exclusively on the West Indian community.

Under the direction of Trinidadian schoolteacher Lesley Palmer, the carnival was transformed during the 1970s, acquiring a distinctly Caribbean identity. Palmer introduced Caribbean-style masquerade costumes, as well as the steel and costume, or "mas" bands, to Notting Hill. To attract black youth, he also introduced the "sound-system" (mobile disco), and reggae music, which had a positive impact on attendance. By the mid-1970s, the carnival was attracting crowds of up to half a million people, although as it grew to a national scale, problems arose over policing of the event.

Notting Hill Carnival, 2006. Courtesy of Damian Rafferty, Flyglobalmusic.com.

Police perceptions of black youth criminality encouraged the adoption of aggressive policing methods in urban areas during the 1970s that seemed intended to antagonize black youth. As a result, aside from the public safety issue of uncontrolled crowds at the carnival, there was also, in terms of policing, the problem of large numbers of black youth congregated in one place. On the last day of carnival in 1976, violence erupted as black youth rioted in reaction to continual harassment and arbitrary arrests by the police, whose numbers amounted to between 3,000 and 1,600 officers on that day. The Notting Hill carnival riot of 1976 left 300 police injured, 65 police vehicles damaged, and several shops looted and is credited with having influenced the passage of the Race Relations Act of 1976, which prohibited racial discrimination. Nonetheless, tensions between the police and black youth continued to mar the carnival for at least another decade, and for some time there were fears that it would be banned. By the late 1990s, however, it had become a firmly established part of London's cultural calendar, with the number of participants and attendees rising.

In 2002, concerns about the size of the carnival, and its financing and management, led to the mayor of London appointing the Carnival Review Group to look at ways of managing the event, which by then contributed approximately £93 million to the British economy. Upon the review group's recommendation, changes were implemented to the carnival route in 2002. Community organizers who want the route to remain close to its geographical roots, however, have staunchly rejected proposals that it be moved to Hyde Park. As far as financing, the carnival now attracts corporate and government sponsorship and the Carnival Arts Committee receives funding from the Arts Council UK. In addition, the Notting Hill Carnival Enterprise Committee has encouraged an increase in the number of food stalls and vendors selling merchandise along the carnival route as a way of further raising the commercial value of the event. In 2002, a public limited company, The Notting Hill Carnival Trust Ltd., was brought in to run the carnival, but community organizers became disgruntled at the way in which the Trust managed financial resources and the lack of accountability. Consequently, in 2003, it was replaced by The London Notting Hill Carnival Ltd.

See also: Black British; Britain, Blacks in; Civil Rights Movement in Twentieth-Century Great Britain; Colonies in Africa, British; Colonies in the Caribbean, British; Race Riots in Europe.

Further Reading: Drain, E. *Twentieth Century Theatre: A Sourcebook of Radical Thinking.* London: Routledge, 1995; Picard, D., and M. Robinson, eds. *Festivals, Tourism and Social Change: Remaking Worlds.* Clevendon, United Kingdom: Channel View, 2006.

Joyce A. Kannan

O

Ogé, Vincent (?–1791)

Vincent Ogé was a biracial merchant from Saint Domingue (Haiti) who tried to convince the French National Assembly to give free *gens de couleur* (people of color) the right to vote. Meeting no success, Ogé returned to Saint Domingue to enact his plan, by force if necessary; however, he was captured and tortured to death. Ogé's failure to secure rights for individuals of biracial descent while leaving slavery untouched proved that emancipation was an all or nothing proposition: men of biracial descent and black Africans must overcome racial divisions and cooperate to make all free, or none would be free.

Ogé was born into a well-to-do family in France's most valuable colony, Saint-Domingue, in the mid-eighteenth century. Ogé was well educated and wealthy. He ran a profitable trading business and held valuable property on Saint-Domingue. Even though his father was white, however, Ogé was still part black, so he was still considered a free "person of color." Despite his wealth, Ogé was not allowed to vote because of his biracial status. Free *gens de couleur*, some of quite respectable wealth, were tolerated by white planters, but their rights were upheld by custom, tradition, and tacit white acceptance alone; there was no legal recourse or support otherwise for their freedoms.

The French Revolution in 1789 represented the dawning of a new era. Ogé was encouraged by the possibilities that this moment seemed to represent. Accordingly, he appeared in October 1789 before the National Assembly to argue his case for the expansion of the right to vote to *gens de couleur*. Ogé contended that as free citizens born into the French empire, *gens de couleur* deserved equality under the law. His proposal was fairly conservative, and not all free *gens de couleur* were included; too much black African blood or a lineage only recently emancipated would exclude many from the law. Ogé had no intent to end slavery itself, but merely to grant legal rights to free *gens de couleur.* Despite Ogé's best efforts, however, the political power of French slave masters triumphed.

Although rebuffed by the National Assembly, Ogé returned home in the summer of 1790 all the more committed. He now saw coercion and violence as acceptable means to achieve his desired end. In October 1790, Ogé sent an ultimatum to the local assembly of Saint-Domingue, located at Le Cap François. He demanded suffrage for *gens de couleur* and claimed that pacifying the biracial population would ensure the continuance of slavery on the island. This was a covert threat, for Ogé was suggesting that if his demands were not met, he would unleash a slave revolt.

Ogé received no response and began raising an army, perhaps a few hundred men strong. His force was mostly *gens de couleur,* and in keeping with his defense of slavery, he was unwilling to support slaves or let them join his rebellion. While leading his force toward La Cap François, Ogé met an army detachment of 600 men that was sent to quell the uprising. The rebels emerged victorious, but fear recruited a much larger colonial force, which soon met Ogé and destroyed his army. Ogé barely escaped with his life and fled to Spanish Santo Domingo. The Spanish returned him to Saint-Domingue. On February 26, 1791, Ogé spent his last hours being broken on the wheel. His death, however, inspired others to rebel. In August 1791, a massive slave uprising rocked Saint Domingue, forcing the French National Assembly to give freedom to those of biracial descent and African alike.

See also: Abolition of Slavery, French; Belley, Jean-Baptiste; Colonies in the Caribbean, French; French Revolution, Blacks in the; Haitian Revolution for Independence; Haitian Revolution in Francophone Literature; Slave Trade, French.

Further Reading: Dubois, Laurent. *Avengers of the New World: The Story of the Haitian Revolution.* Cambridge, MA: Belknap Press, 2004; Ott, Thomas O. *The Haitian Revolution, 1789–1804.* Knoxville: University of Tennessee Press, 1973.

Joshua M. Rice

Oguntoye, Katharina (1959–)

Katharina Oguntoye is a leading Afro-German feminist writer and historian. Oguntoye was born in 1959 in the former East Germany. Her father was Nigerian and her mother was German. Oguntoye spent her childhood in West Germany and, for a few years, lived in Nigeria. In West Germany, she suffered from racial abuse, and as a teenager in search of her identity, found a distinct lack of work on the Afro-German experience. At university, she met African American writer Audre Lorde, who helped her greatly, and May Opitz (**May Ayim**), with whom she traveled in Nigeria. In Nigeria, Oguntoye experienced blending into crowds easily and began to identify strongly with West Africa.

In 1986, Oguntoye, along with Opitz and Dagmar Schultz, wrote *Farbe Bekennen: Afro-Deutsche Frauen auf den Spuren ihrer Geschichte* (published in English as *Showing our Colors: Afro-German Women Speak Out*). The book details the lives of 14 Afro-German women in both West Germany and East Germany. The book received much critical acclaim and was the first work to detail the Afro-German identity, tracing it back to early German involvement in Africa, the establishment of the German colonies in Africa, and then recent developments in Afro-German cultural heritage. Many people in Africa, as well as in Britain and the United States, wanted an English-language edition of the book. Finally, in November 1991, the book was published in English with an introduction by Audre Lorde.

The original publication of *Farbe Bekennen* led to the **Initiative of Blacks in Germany (ISD),** which was formed to bring Afro-Germans together, and the beginnings of an assertion of the Afro-German identity. Oguntoye has continued to write books that address the Afro-German female experience, focusing on both gender and racial issues.

See also: Afro-German Women (ADEFRA); Afro-Germans; Colonies in Africa, German; Germany, Blacks in; Literature, Blacks in German and Central European.

Further Reading: Hodges, Carolyn. "The Private/Plural Selves of Afro-German Women and the Search for a Public Voice." *Journal of Black Studies* 23: 2 (December 1992): 219–234; McCarroll, Margaret. *May Ayim: A Woman in the Margin of German Society.* Master of Arts Thesis, Florida State University, 2005; Oguntoye, Katharina, May Opitz, and Dagmar Schultz. *Showing our Colors: Afro-German Women Speak Out.* trans. Anne Adams. Amherst: University of Massachusetts Press, 1991.

Justin Corfield

Okri, Ben (1959–)

Ben Okri is an internationally acclaimed **black British** poet, short story writer, and novelist from Nigeria. He has succeeded in projecting African history and culture (particularly that of Nigeria) in his literary works. His works comprise a variety of literary genres, including realism, modernism, and oral forms with African flavor.

Okri was born in Minna, in north central Nigeria. After his birth, his father moved to England to study law. Consequently, Okri received his early education in London. In 1968, he and his family returned to Nigeria, where he continued his education. After high school, Okri worked as a clerk at a paint store. During this time, he started writing articles on social and political issues. By 1980, Okri had published his first novel, *Flowers and Shadows.*

Okri later returned to England, where he attended the University of Essex to study comparative literature. During this period, he published a second novel, *The Landscapes Within* (1982). He became poetry editor of *West Africa Magazine,* a position he held until 1987. Between 1983 and 1985, Okri worked as a broadcaster for the BBC World Service on a program entitled "Network Africa." In 1987, he published a short story collection, *Incidents at the Shrine.* That same year, the work won several prestigious awards, including the Commonwealth Writers Prize for Africa and the Paris Review/Aga Khan Prize for Fiction. *Stars of the New Curfew* was another short story collection published in 1988. It won the Guardian Fiction Prize later that year.

In 1991, Okri published *The Famished Road,* the first volume of a new trilogy. The novel garnered international recognition and won the Booker Prize for Fiction. The trilogy continued in the novels *Songs of Enchantment* (1993) and *Infinite Riches* (1998). Other fictional novels by Okri include *Astonishing the Gods* (1995); *Dangerous Love* (1996), which won the Italian Premio Palmi (2000); *In Arcadia* (2002); and *Starbook* (2007). Okri has also published a collected volume of poetry, *An African Elegy* (1992); an epic poem, *Mental Flight* (1999); and an essay collection, *A Way of Being Free* (1997).

In his career, Okri has won many distinctions. He became a Fellow of the Royal Society of Literature in 1987. In 1995, he won the Crystal Award (World Economic Forum). Okri has also received honorary doctorates from the University of Westminster (1997) and the University of Essex (2002). He was also awarded an OBE (Order of the British Empire) in 2001.

See also: Britain, Blacks in; Colonies in Africa, British; Literature, Blacks in British.

Further Reading: Lim, David C. L. *The Infinite Longing for Home: Desire and the Nation in Selected Writings of Ben Okri and K. S. Maniam.* New York: Rodopi, 2005; Moh, Felicia Oka. *Ben Okri: An Introduction to His Early Fiction.* Enugu, Nigeria: Fourth Dimension, 2002; Nnolim, Charles E. *Approaches to the African Novel: Essays in Analysis.* London: Saros, 1992. Quayson, Ato. *Strategic Transformations in Nigerian Writing: Caality and History in the Work of Rev. Samuel Johnson, Amos Tutuola, Wole Soyinka and Ben Okri.* Bloomington: Indiana University Press, 1997; Wilkinson, Jane, ed. *Talking with African Writers.* London: Heinemann, 1991.

Mary Afolabi Adeolu

Oldfield, Bruce (1950–)

Bruce Oldfield is a **black British** fashion designer. Oldfield was born in 1950 to an Irish woman and a Jamaican boxer. He was entrusted to a Barnado's home when he was six months old after his mother's placement into a psychiatric hospital. Oldfield became the foster child of Violet Masters, a seamstress who lived in County Durham. Although living close to poverty, she had adopted three other biracial children and taught them how to sew at an early age. At eight years old, Oldfield was already designing dresses for his sister's dolls.

Oldfield was a student at the Ripon Grammar School in Yorkshire. He also attended Sheffield City Polytechnic in Yorkshire from 1961 to 1967. He then began to study fashion design at Ravensbourne College of Art in Kent from 1968 to 1971. Determined to be a star in the fashion industry, he applied to art school. Oldfield graduated from St. Martin's School of Art in 1973. Thanks to his outstanding student shows, he was chosen to design a collection for Henri Bendel, the New York department store.

After living in New York City for a couple of months, Oldfield moved back to London in 1975. He created his own company with a bank loan and a Barnardo's grant. Starting as a ready-to-wear operation with chains of stores in Europe and America, his business developed into a couture store in 1978 for individual clients. In 1980, noticed for his work with actress Charlotte Rampling, Oldfield was asked to dress Lady Diana Spencer, who was then about to marry Prince Charles.

Oldfield still dresses European and American actresses and international royalty. His most famous clients have included Sienna Miller, Jemima Khan, Anjelica Huston, Faye Dunaway, Melanie Griffith, Jerry Hall, Queen Noor of Jordan, and Queen Rania of Jordan.

Oldfield was awarded the OBE (Order of the British Empire) for services to fashion and industry in 1990. He holds Honorary Fellowships to the Royal College of Art, the University of Durham, and the University of Sheffield. He was governor of The London Institute in 1999 to 2001 and Trustee of the Royal Academy of Arts in 2000 to 2002. In 2001, Oldfield received an honorary doctorate in civil law from the University of Northumbria at Newcastle. In 2005, he received an honorary doctorate from the University of Central England. He is also a vice president of Barnardo's. Oldfield published his autobiography, *Rootless*, in 2004.

See also: Boateng, Ozwald; Britain, Blacks in; Campbell, Naomi.

Further Reading: Oldfield, Bruce. *Bruce Oldfield's Season*. London: Pan Books, 1987; Oldfield, Bruce. *Rootless*. London: Arrow, 2004.

Tristan Cabello

Olympics of 1936

The 1936 Summer Olympics remain a highly contested event. The International Olympic Committee (IOC) had awarded the games to Berlin in 1931, two years before the Nazis came to power. After 1933, countries both east and west debated whether to participate in games hosted by Germany's Nazi government. Was it possible to participate in 1936 and not condone the regime, which as early as 1933, had already begun to euthanize its mentally disabled and persecute its Jews? Many argued that two-week games might become a massive publicity spectacle for Nazi Germany and therefore sought to boycott the 1936 Olympics or to change the location.

Half a century after the end of World War II, observers continue to debate the moral outcome of having participated in the 1936 Olympics in Berlin now knowing how the Nazis sterilized Germany's black population, and sent Jews, gypsies, homosexuals and other political "undesirables" to their deaths. Many observers refer to the 1936 Olympics as the "Nazi Olympics," as public events that promoted the Nazi regime, or Third Reich. Others refuse this appellation, saying that the events at the Olympics, namely the triumph of African American athletes, disproved Nazi ideology itself. For people of black African descent, the games produced greatly ambivalent results: The 1936 Olympics proved a cultural breakthrough for African Americans in that they gained worldwide recognition as athletes, but the Olympics also became an opportunity for racism and the advancement of faulty racial theories.

Sports have always been used as occasions to rally national and local pride, and, as such, sports are innately political. This was especially clear to the Nazis, who viewed athletics not merely as paramilitary training, but as a cultural practice with great powers of public persuasion. The Nazi government imagined the nation as a "total work of art," in which the whole of cultural life had been reinvented according to Nazi racist and fascist aesthetics. Nazism infiltrated every aspect of daily life from the fonts used in newspapers, the handwriting taught in school, to laws regarding interracial marriages. Among the key concepts of Nazi Germany was a "healthy" Aryan aesthetic, which survived to strengthen the national character. Sports offered abundant images of "strength and beauty" according to the Nazi worldview. Joseph Goebbels, Minister of

Propaganda of the Nazi government, proclaimed in 1933, "German sport has only one task: to strengthen the character of the German people, imbuing it with the fighting spirit and steadfast camaraderie necessary in the struggle for its existence."

After 1933, "non-Aryans" (e.g., people of Jewish descent, gypsies, and Europeans not of Germanic descent) were refused entry to athletic clubs and public facilities. American newspapers published critical editorials about Germany and entreated the president of the American Olympic Committee, former American athlete Avery Brundage, to withdraw American participation. Brundage and the rest of the committee traveled to Berlin to evaluate the political climate, but were unable to access the political situation based on their findings. Ultimately, Brundage argued for attendance and insisted on the apolitical nature of the games.

Yet, nothing was apolitical in Third Reich. Since Nazi Germany was a society in which every aspect of life was administered by the government, separating culture from politics was impossible. Indeed, the great success of the Nazis was their ability to politicize seemingly nonpolitical experiences. The 1936 Olympics was a perfect example of Nazi cultural politics and political subterfuge. Propaganda Minister Goebbels hired filmmaker Leni Riefenstahl to film the Olympics, but set up a front organization so that her *Olympia* would not appear to be funded by the government when it was, in fact, supposed to be a vehicle for Germanic "strength and beauty." Riefenstahl leant her talents to the Third Reich to glorify "Aryan" beauty, and her film of the Olympics frames itself with many references to the ancient Greeks. Yet it is Riefenstahl who captured on celluloid the famous 100-meter gold medal race of African American athlete Jesse Owens.

Jesse Owens, a collegiate sprinter and high jumper, was the son of a sharecropper and the grandson of American slaves. He won four gold medals in the 1936 Olympics, making history not only for the world and the Germans, but also for African Americans. African Americans had been ambivalent about attending the Olympics. They disdained the fascists and were concerned about the safety of blacks in a regime that was violently racist against Africans from anywhere in the **African Diaspora;** however, they also recognized an opportunity for public recognition. Once the IOC promised protection, most African American newspapers argued in favor of participation in the Olympics and took the position that seeing blacks succeed would persuade the world of the falsehood of Nazi racial ideology.

After the campaign for an Olympic boycott was abandoned, 18 African Americans (16 men and 2 women) made the American teams and headed for Berlin. This was the greatest number of blacks to participate by that time, and was three times as many as had taken part in the previous 1932 Los Angeles Games. They were also the only blacks representing any country in the world (the only Africans were white South Africans). Three of the top American black athletes were returning Olympians. The African Americans participating in the 1936 Olympics included Thomas "Eddie" Tolan Jr., the first black athlete to win two Olympic gold medals; Ralph Harold Metcalfe, a sprinter who was known as the world's fastest human; John Youie Woodruff, who had a come-from-behind victory in the 800-meter run and was the first to win a gold medal; Matthew "Mack" Robinson, the older brother of Baseball Hall of Famer Jackie Robinson who won the silver medal in the men's 200 meters; Cornelius Cooper

Johnson, a high jumper whose winning height of 2.03 meters was an Olympic record; and Jackie Wilson, who won a silver medal in boxing for the United States.

Most spectacular among these famous victories was Owens, whose four gold medals are said to have thoroughly scandalized the Nazis, who were still reeling from the initial shock of seeing Woodruff steal the first gold medal in his surprise win. There are greatly varying accounts of whether Hitler snubbed Owens after his first gold medal win. Hitler is said to have refused to shake Owens's hand, but records also show that Hitler had decided to avoid Nazi embarrassment by refusing to shake the hand of any non-German winner. Owens's triumph at the Olympics was a great moment for Americans, for it disproved Nazi ideas of Aryan superiority. Whatever the Nazi propaganda had hoped to show about white superiority, it had failed with Owens's four gold medals and also with the popularity of Owens, for whom the German crowd went wild, shouting "Jesse" with a Teutonic accent. Such public adulation of an African American galled many Nazi leaders. The Nazi newspaper founded by Goebbels, *Der Angriff,* complained that the Americans had humiliated themselves by allowing their black "auxiliaries" to win gold medals for them.

Ironically, Owens's triumph had an unexpected racist outcome as well, in that it seemed to prove the Nazi biology of race, rather than the hard work that black athletes had devoted to their training. Attempting to regain their false sense of racial superiority, Nazis adopted a new tact and falsely asserted that the blacks won at the Olympics only because they were biologically different (closer to animals), with their big thighs and longer feet, and, therefore, it was unfair to let them compete at all.

In the end, the African American athletes won 14 medals in total, and, for a moment, enjoyed public recognition. Yet, the return to America, with its "Jim Crow" laws intact, proved a dark reality for the African American athletes. For example, Owens was denied amateur status for having so many financial offers despite the fact that they never materialized.

See also: Germany, Blacks in; Interracial Marriages, European Laws Banning; Scientific Racism; World War II, Black Participation in.

Further Reading: Bachrach, Susan D. *The Nazi Olympics: Berlin, 1936.* Boston: Little, Brown and Company, 2000; Cohen, Stan. *The Games of '36: A Pictorial History of the 1936 Olympic Games in Germany.* Missoula: Pictorial Histories Publishing Company, 1996; Hilton, Christopher. *Hitler's Olympics: The 1936 Berlin Olympic Games.* Stroud: Sutton Publishing, 2006; Large, David Clay. *Nazi Games: The Olympics of 1936.* New York: W. W. Norton, 2007.

Ruth Starkman

Oroonoko (1688)

Oroonoko, or the Royal Slave, is a seventeenth-century novella by Aphra Behn (1640–1689), often claimed to be the first woman in English literature to make a living as an author, detailing the tragic story of an African slave in Suriname in the 1660s. Behn worked as a spy for King Charles II of England during the Second Dutch War; however, she did not receive all the money owed her for her ser services. On her return to England, Behn, who was also a widow, was desperately in need of money. Her poetry sold well and she began to write plays. After becoming a successful playwright, Behn turned toward extended narrative prose. Her last work participated in the amatory genre of British literature, which predated the invention of the novel and was an early predecessor of the romance novel.

Oroonoko (1688) focuses on the heroic title character, who is the grandson of an African king. Oroonoko falls in love with Imoinda, who is the daughter of the king's chief general. The king, however, also falls in love with Imoinda and gives her the sacred veil, which means that she is commanded to become his wife. After a short time in the king's harem, Imoinda and Oroonoko plan a secret rendezvous; however, the two lovers are discovered. The king has Imoinda sold as a slave to punish her. Meanwhile, Oroonoko is captured by an English slaver captain. Imoinda and Oroonoko are both taken to Suriname, which at that time was an English colony in the Caribbean. In Suriname, the two African lovers are reunited under their new Christian names (Caesar and Clemene). The English deputy-governor, William Byam, becomes attracted to Imoinda's beauty. Oroonoko organizes an unsuccessful slave revolt. The slaves surrender after obtaining Byam's promise of amnesty. Oroonoko, however, is whipped as punishment. To prove his natural worth and to avenge his honor, Oroonoko plots to assassinate Byam. To protect Imoinda from being violated and sexually abused, Oroonoko murders her too after discussing the matter with her. Imoinda dies with a smile on her face. As Oroonoko is mourning the loss of his true love, he is found before he can commit suicide and is sentenced to be publicly executed by dismemberment. During his execution, Oroonoko bravely bares the pain without crying out and with the utmost dignity.

Oroonoko is written in both the first and third person. The narrator related the events in Africa, but then portrays herself as a witness to the events in Suriname. The narrator is the daughter of a man sent to Suriname from England to serve as the new deputy-general of Suriname; however, her father dies during the voyage. The narrator and her family are welcomed into the settlement and she describes her interactions with the people of Suriname interspersed with the main plot of the love story between Imoinda and Oroonoko. After the love story's conclusion, the narrator returns to England.

Behn most likely did not intend for the novella to serve as a protest against slavery per se, although the institution of slavery is not depicted in a positive light and the English slaver captain is one of the most despicable characters. The novel depicts Behn's strong sense of monarchism. To Behn, without a true and natural leader, a king, Suriname could not prosper. Furthermore, the true measure of one's worth was their ability to keep his word. Behn's novel was written amid the political turmoil that culminated in the English Glorious Revolution of 1688, during which the Catholic English King, James II (bother of Charles II) was overthrown and replaced by his Protestant daughter, Mary, and her husband, the Dutch William of Orange, in the view that a Catholic could not be the head of the Protestant Church of England. In *Oroonoko*, written before the Glorious Revolution took place, Behn's work was meant to criticize those elites in England who had sworn loyalty to James II, yet plotted to overthrow him, the true king. The novel is very anti-Dutch (Holland assumed control of Suriname in the late 1660s, shortly after the events of the novella), in part because of Behn's experiences as a spy in the Second Dutch War and because the nobles were seeking to replace James II with William of Orange, who was also Dutch.

Oroonoko is the first English novel to depict a black African in a sympathetic manner; however, the novella is more concerned with the nature of kingship than with race. Oroonoko is a king (regardless of his race) and therefore his execution is an act of regicide and detrimental to the entire colony. Oroonoko possesses a character that is more noble than any other in the novella. Yet, he is described as having European features, and is therefore naturalized as a European aristocrat. He is not described as having an African appearance and therefore his greatness is connected to his European characteristics. Later criticism called *Oroonoko* a work of humanitarianism and Behn a precursor to Harriet Beecher Stowe, who wrote *Uncle Tom's Cabin*.

Thomas Southerne adapted Behn's novella as a play, which was staged in 1695 and published in 1696. The play was hugely popular and did much to increase the popularity of Behn's novella, which had disappointing initial sales. The play made a major change in the story of the novella, however, by making the character of Imoinda white instead of black, thereby adding the element of interracial love to the tragedy.

See also: Abolition of Slavery, British; Colonies in the Caribbean, British; Colonies in the Caribbean, Dutch; Interracial Marriages, European Laws Banning; *Mirza* (1795); *Othello* (1603); *Ourika* (1823); Slave Trade, British.

Further Reading: Behn, Aphra. *Oroonoko and Other Writings.* ed. Paul Salzman. New ed. New York: Oxford World's Classics, 1998; Southerne, Thomas. *Oroonoko.* eds. Maximillian Novak and David Rhodes. Lincoln: University of Nebraska Press, 2003; Todd, Janet, ed. *Aphra Behn Studies.* New York: Cambridge University Press, 1996; Todd, Janet, ed. *The Secret Life of Aphra Behn.* New Brunswick, NJ: Rutgers University Press, 1997.

Eric Martone

Ortíz, Leonardo (Dates Unknown)

Leonardo Ortíz was an Afro-Spanish lawyer of the Royal Court in sixteenth-century Spain. The exact dates of Ortiz's birth and death are unknown. The location of his birth is also unknown. As the interracial child of a black African mother and a white Spanish knight of a military order, it seems likely that he was born in Grenada, where he also spent most of his life. He probably studied law at the University of Grenada, earning the *licenciado*, which was the license needed to teach and practice law. In early modern Spain, where most blacks were either enslaved or struggling as poor freed people or runaways, Ortíz's high social status was exceptional. The life of Ortíz thus represents a remarkable addition to the historical picture of black Africans living in Renaissance Europe.

Ortíz was first mentioned by Francisco Bermúdez de Pedraza in his *Antiguedades y Excelencias de Granada* from 1608. Before turning to **Juan Latino,** the better-known Afro-Spanish professor of Latin at the University of Grenada, Bermúdez de Pedraza included a chapter entitled "On Three Famous Blacks of This City." After briefly mentioning the black embroideress Catalina de Soto, Bermúdez de Pedraza also portrayed two other male contemporaries of Latino: the Dominican priest **Cristóbol de Meneses** and the Licenciado Ortíz; however, the biographical information provided is scarce. According to Bermúdez de Pedraza's church history of Grenada, published in 1638, Ortíz lived with his black mother and took care of her. The relationship with Ortíz's white father, however, seems to have been broken. When asked about the reasons Ortíz hated his father, he offered a paradoxical response recorded in Bermúdez de Pedraza's account that provides a glimpse into the complex dynamics in his interracial family: "I owe more to my mother who gave me such a good father than to my father who gave me such a despicable mother."

See also: Renaissance, Blacks in the; Spain, Blacks in.

Further Reading: Bermúdez de Pedraza, Francisco. *Antiguedades y Excelencias de Granada.* Madrid: Por Luis Sanchez, 1608; Bermúdez de Pedraza, Francisco. *Historia eclesiástica de Granada.* Granada: Por Andrés de Santiago, 1638; Casares, Aurelia Martín. "Free and Freed Black Africans in Granada in the Time of the Spanish Renaissance." In Thomas F. Earle and Kate J. P. Lowe, eds. *Black Africans in Renaissance Europe.* Cambridge: Cambridge University Press, 2005, pp. 247–260; Queija, Berta Ares, and Alessandro Stella. *Negros, Mulattos, Zambaigos: Derroteros Africanos en los Mundos Ibericos.* Sevilla: Escuela de Estudios Hispano-Americanos/Consejo Superior de Investigaciones Scientificas, 2000.

Holger Drössler

Othello (1603)

The Tragedy of Othello, The Moor of Venice (1603), a masterpiece in British literature, is a dramatic tragedy by Renaissance literary icon William Shakespeare. The psychological drama focuses on the character of Othello, a Moorish general in Italy, who is betrayed by his companion, Iago. The drama, which explores themes such as racism and religious conflict, has remained popular for more than 400 years.

Othello has gained critical acclaim through its portrayal of racial and religious themes, as it has a Muslim **Moor** in the lead role. Shakespeare knew much about history and literature and frequently used such knowledge as sources for his dramas. He would have been exposed to such writers as the Italian novelist and poet, Giovanni Battista Giraldi (also know as Cinthio), whose story, *Hecatommithi* (1565), likely inspired Shakespeare's *Othello.* Shakespeare reinvented Cinthio's text, not only by making it a play, but also by giving the characters deeper meaning and adding new plot developments.

Cinthio's plot unravels as the Ensign (Shakespeare's Iago) accuses Disdemona (Shakespeare's Desdemona) of having an affair with the Captain (Shakespeare's Cassio). Some critics point to the fact that Iago's desire to wrong Othello in Shakespeare's plot is fueled not only by evilness, but also by jealously. In Cinthio's version, the Ensign falls in love with Disdemona, but he feels that she does not choose him because she is in love with the Captain, rather than the Moor. The Moor and the Ensign conspire to murder both Disdemona and the Captain, provided that the Ensign can provide proof that the two are having an affair. The Ensign subsequently has his daughter steal a handkerchief given by the Moor to Disdemona. The Ensign then places the handkerchief on the Captain's bed. The Moor encourages the Ensign to murder the Captain; however, the assassination attempt only results in the loss of the Captain's leg. The Ensign then kills Disdemona with the support of her husband. After the Captain recovers, the Ensign conspires with him against the Moor by convincing the Captain that it was the Moor who was responsible for both the attempt on his life and the murder of Disdemona. The Moor is arrested and imprisoned and later killed by Disdemona's family. The Ensign is later arrested following a dispute in Italy and tortured.

Some major differences in the plot are apparent in Shakespeare's adaptation. First and foremost, the Moor has a name: Othello. Othello elopes with Desdemona right before the Venetians gather to discuss the Turkish attack on Cyprus. Othello is summoned as an advisor. In front of the Senate, Desdemona's father accuses Othello of witchcraft, seducing his daughter to marry him. Othello defends himself successfully before the Senate and he leaves Venice to command its army against the Turks. Meanwhile, Othello's companion, Iago, harbors bitterness against him for promoting Cassio above him. Iago takes advantage of being away at war to make Othello jealous of Desdemona. Iago manages to get Cassia drunk and involved in a fight; as a result of his behavior, Othello demotes Cassio and promotes Iago. After Cassio sobers up, Iago encourages him to entreat Desdemona to plead to Othello on his behalf.

Othello and Desdemona in Venice by Théodore Chassériau (1819–1856). Erich Lessing / Art Resource, NY.

Meanwhile, Iago works on Othello, attempting to make him suspicious of Desdemona and Cassio. Desdemona drops her first gift from Othello, a handkerchief, which is stolen by Emilia, Iago's wife, for Iago. The handkerchief is planted in Cassio's quarters. Iago then goads Cassio to describe his affair with his mistress, Bianca, while Othello listens in secret. Bianca's name is never mentioned, so Othello assumes that Cassio is describing an affair with Desdemona. Enraged, Othello begins to plan the murder his wife and orders Iago to murder Cassio. Iago convinces another soldier, Roderigo, to murder Cassio. The attempt fails and Iago murders Roderigo to prevent him from revealing Iago's role. During the night, Othello smothers Desdemona in their bed in a rage of jealousy. Emilia arrives, and as Othello tries to explain his actions, she reveals to him that the affair was the invention of Iago. Emilia calls for the guard, hoping to get Iago arrested. Instead of facing his guilt, Iago rids himself of his wife, adding to the pervasive evilness portrayed by this character throughout Shakespeare's plot. The guard attempts to arrest both Iago and Othello, but Othello commits suicide.

In Shakespeare's play, the figure of Othello is characterized as a well-respected noble Moor. In Europe at the time, the terms *Moor* and *black* were used interchangeably and in reference to Muslims from North or West Africa residing in the Mediterranean area. Consequently, there has been argument as to whether Othello was a black character of sub-Saharan decent or an Arab from North Africa. Many have concluded with some controversy that Shakespeare intended for Othello to be black. Such a conclusion has been based on Othello's physical description and the taunts concerning his origins used in the play's dialogue as per its publication in the First Folio in 1623. For example, some scholars have argued that Othello's description as having "thick lips" suggests a subjective characteristic common to black Africans. In addition, the play on language throughout the tragedy (such as black and white, as well as light and dark) may imply that Othello was of black African decent. Nonetheless, it is unclear to some whether Othello should be a black man. Certainly, in an era of globalization and increasing cultural diversity, many modern scholars and productions support the idea of portraying Othello as black man.

Othello was a noble, heroic, and well-respected leader, as well as a warrior who won the heart of Desdemona, a Venetian. Such traits tended not to be recognized by the Elizabethans as Moorish qualities. Unlike the stigma attached to many brutish Moors, Othello was capable of establishing relationships such as his with Desdemona. Desdemona's choice of Othello as her husband was something not easily accepted in European society and Othello knew this, which left him vulnerable to love her. The thought of Desdemona being unfaithful was something that Othello may have envisioned as possible, for he felt undeserving to have such a beautiful and virtuous woman; this, in turn, reflected his feelings of low self-esteem. When Othello falsely discovered that Desdemona betrayed him, his barbaric "ram"-like nature pervaded, enabling him to murder his wife. Although Othello murdered her by being deceived by Iago, thereby, in essence, also making him a victim, the Elizabethans would not have expected anything less from a Moor. Upon the revelation of Iago's evil plot against Othello, Othello's guilt overcame him and he committed suicide, once again making him seem a strong hero, while creating feelings of pity from the audience for his misfortune.

The theme of racism has a presence in the play as well. For instance, the lead character, a Moor, eloped with Desdemona, a white Venetian woman, who was also a senator's daughter. Such an act was something unheard of to many Elizabethans. In fact, many European countries even passed laws banning interracial marriage (and Elizabeth I tried to expel blacks from England, as she thought there were too many). In addition, the Elizabethans attributed the color black to death and evil, and the interracial marriage between Desdemona and Othello was, according to Brabantio, Desdemona's father, "against all rules of nature," (1.3.102). In addition, he accused Othello of casting a spell on her and using witchcraft, because to him, there was no other explanation: "[T]hou hast enchanted her/. . . .Thou has practic'd on her with foul charms/Abus'd her delicate youth with drugs or minerals (1.2.62–75)." These accusations must have been difficult for Othello to endure, especially from his father-in-law; yet, at the same time, they were inevitable. The character of Othello felt ostracized by a white, European community, which may be thought-provoking for viewers who connect their understanding of racism to their own experiences and culture.

In terms of a political and historical context, the play also raises issues about the religious conflict between Christians and Muslims that pervaded Europe. At the time of the play, Muslims had invaded and at times occupied parts of Spain and Italy. Furthermore, opposition between these two religious groups had escalated in the Middle Ages during the Crusades. Ironically, Othello, a Muslim Moor, had been sent to settle the religious conflict between the Turks and Christians on Cyprus. His treatment by the Venetians exemplifies the religious unrest present. The irony was that Othello did not fit the stereotype of a warrior Moor and Muslim. His political promotion and treatment as a soldier in European society did not fit the attitudes of the time. He was sent predominantly by a Christian society to end unrest because he did not behave as a Moorish brute, but as someone who proved that he could demonstrate civility, which was how he remained until the climax of the tragedy unfolded. Some argue that he held it together until the breaking point.

Othello has been a timeless piece, and the lead role has been played by many popular actors. Several famous black actors who have played Othello on film or television include **Ira Aldridge, Paul Robeson,** Gordon Heath, James Earl Jones, Willard White, and Laurence Fishburne. Some famous white actors who have played Othello on film or television include Orson Welles, Lawrence Olivier, and Anthony Hopkins. Olivier played the role in blackface in the 1960s, which was controversial at the time. Some unique stage adaptations of Shakespeare's *Othello* have included the depiction of Othello as a white man while using black actors for the rest of the cast. Such an idea toys with society's conception of racial power and politics, emphasizing the play's depiction of alienation through racial prejudice to make it a universal injustice.

In addition, in the nineteenth century, Shakespeare's play was also turned into an Italian opera, *Otello,* by Verdi. The role has been performed by such great tenors as Luciano Pavarotti and Placido Domingo.

See also: Britain, Blacks in; Cain, Theory of Descent of Blacks from; Hamitic Myth; Italy, African Invasions of; Italy, Blacks in; Literature, Blacks in British; Spain, African Invasions of.

Further Reading: *Black Presence: Asian and Black History in Britain, 1500–1850* (Online Exhibit from the British National Archives). http://www.nationalarchives.gov.uk/Pathways/black history/; Kaul, Mythili, ed. *Othello: New Essays by Black Writers.* Washington, DC: Howard University Press, 1997.

Nicole Martone

Ourika (1823)

The best-selling novella *Ourika* (1823), the first full-fledged representation of a black person's interiority in European literature, was published by the aristocratic Frenchwoman Claire Louise Lechat de Duras, née de Coëtnempren de Kersaint (1777–1828). It is also the first novella in French to focus on interracial love, the first novella set in Europe to have a black female protagonist, and the first French literary text narrated by a black heroine.

Set around the time of the French Revolution, Duras's *Ourika* relates the story of its eponymous Senegalese hero, rescued from slavery and placed under the protection of a French aristocratic family. A conversation she overhears awakens her sense of racial difference and of social exclusion. When Ourika later becomes aware that her sisterly affinity for the grandson of her benefactress has turned into love, she realizes her precarious position as an ineligible other because of prejudice against her skin color, and, feeling severed from humankind, she becomes a nun (a role in which she is often cast in visual portrayals). After she tells her story to a male doctor, whose first-person account makes up the narrative frame, he informs the reader eventually that Ourika has died.

Based on a true story, Duras's novella, with its embedded narrative on the impossibility of interracial love, written in the tone of *larmoyance* (tearjerker), started an international cult. *Ourika* appeared in four editions in 1824 alone and was translated into Italian, German, English, and Spanish. Furthermore, the novel inspired not only royal comment by French King Louis XVIII and artistic endorsement by German author Goethe, but also the writing of a sequel, a parody, several elegies, theatrical adaptations, and the creation of a famous 1825 painting by François Gérard.

Duras's *Ourika* is part of the second wave of the movement for the French abolition of slavery, a reaction to the 1802 reinstatement of slavery under Napoleon Bonaparte and the 1805 reaffirmation of the ever stricter **Code Noir.** The code, in turn, was mainly sparked by the violent slave revolt on Saint Domingue begun in 1791 that had largely wiped out the fledgling abolitionist momentum of the French Revolution. French colonists' response to *Ourika* (resentment for the novella's antislavery impetus) was in tune with escalating ideologies of the perceived black menace to French racial purity. It is against this problematic political context that readers must measure Duras's phenomenal success, as well as her achievement in bringing *Ourika* to France, and in imagining, with her black protagonist, the equality of black and white.

See also: Abolition of Slavery, French; Colonies in Africa, French; Colonies in the Caribbean, French; France, Blacks in; French Revolution, Blacks in the; Haitian Revolution for Independence; Haitian Revolution in Francophone Literature; Literature, Blacks in French; Ourika, Charlotte.

Further Reading: De Jean, Joan, and Margaret Waller. "Introduction." In Claire de Duras. *Ourika: An English Translation.* trans. John Fowles. New York: Modern Language Association of America, 1994. O'Connell, David. "*Ourika*: Black Face, White Mask." *French Review* 47 (1974): 47–56; Sollors, Werner. "Endings." *Neither Black Nor White Yet Both: Thematic Explorations of Interracial Literature.* Cambridge: Harvard University Press, 1997, pp. 336–359.

Charlotte Szilágyi

Ourika, Charlotte (1783?–1798)

The 1823 French novella **Ourika,** written by Claire de Duras, was based on the life of an actual Senegalese girl, Charlotte Catherine Benezet Ourika, who was captured as an infant and brought to France as a slave during the eighteenth century. She became a domestic servant before being raised in "high society" and living in the home of the Marshal-Prince of Beauveau under the protection of his wife.

Ourika was separated from her family in Africa and brought to France by Stanislas Jean Boufflers, Chevalier de Boufflers, at the end of his term as governor of Senegal

(February 1786 to December 1787). Although the Chevalier de Boufflers was regarded often as one of the more enlightened administrators in the French Empire at the time, he exhibited little concern for slaves. A surviving 1788 letter from him to Madame de Sabran records that he had a number of gifts, including a parakeet for Queen Marie Antoinette, a horse for the Marshal de Castries, and a "little captive" for Madame de Beauvau. Chevalier de Boufflers was the nephew of Charles Juste de Beauvau-Craon (1720–1793), a powerful French nobleman who had been the governor of Languedoc and then governor-general of Provence. When de Boufflers returned to France, he became a regular at Madame de Beauvau's salon.

Although the salon was an interesting place for men like Bouflers, Ourika, adopted by Madame de Beauvau, was isolated. Although she was well cared for in terms of food, comforts, and luxuries, Ourika's was lonely and her exotic appearance was meant to entertain guests and make a visit to the salon a more "interesting" experience. Madame de Beauvau's grandson, however, did make friends with Ourika. When Ourika was small, she was treated deferentially, but as she grew up, she realized that she was in a difficult predicament.

Ourika was kept isolated from everyday society, being solely a way of entertaining visitors by her presence. At one ball, in particular, she was dressed in exotic African clothes, but began to suffer from racist remarks, and realized that she would obviously have little chance of meeting any possible husband. This led to extreme depression, and Ourika likely suffered from self-hatred. Little is known for certain about Ourika's thoughts, although there is a brief record of some of them (including her acquired Christian values) in Madame de Beauveau's memoirs. Ourika survived the Reign of Terror during the French Revolution, and died in 1798, at the age of 15 or 16.

See also: Abolition of Slavery, French; Courts, Blacks at European Aristocratic; Enlightenment Philosophers and Race; Enlightenment Philosophers and Slavery; France, Blacks in; French Revolution, Blacks in the; Slave Trade, French.

Further Reading: Kadish, Doris, and Françoise Massardier-Kenney, eds. *Translating Slavery: Gender and Race in French Women's Writing, 1783–1823*. Kent, OH: Kent State University Press, 1994.

Justin Corfield

P

Padmore, George (1902–1959)

George Padmore (born Malcolm Ivan Nurse) was a Trinidadian devoted to the emancipation and unification of Africans and those of African descent. He can be considered the "Father of **Pan-Africanism**," even if African-American intellectual **W.E.B. Du Bois** (1868–1963) is generally given the title.

Nurse was born in Arouca (the British colony of Trinidad) on July 28, 1902. He went to school in Trinidad, where he was a friend of **C.L.R. James** (1901–1989). Nurse was probably introduced to politics and Pan-Africanism by his father. After being an apprentice pharmacist, Nurse left Trinidad with his pregnant wife, Julia Semper, in 1924 for Fisk University in Tennessee. After enrolling at Fisk in medicine in 1925, he moved to Howard University in Washington, D.C. to study law.

In 1927, during his political activism within the Communist Party, Nurse changed his name to George Padmore. Within the International Trade Union Committee of Negro Workers (ITUCNW), and as head of the new Negro Bureau, Padmore traveled to Moscow, Russia; Hamburg, Germany; and West Africa. He wrote pamphlets for the ITUCNW, including *The Life and Struggles of Negro Toilers* (1931).

Padmore resigned from the Comintern in 1934 and settled in London in 1935. That same year, along with C.L.R. James, he formed the International African Service Bureau, which fought for Africans and colonial peoples for democratic rights and self-determination. The International African Service Bureau also created the Pan-African Federation, of which Padmore soon became the international secretary.

Padmore established the Pan-African News Agency and became a founding member of the Asiatic-African United Front Committee and the Movement Against Imperialism. He opposed the British government with *Africa: Britain's Third Empire* (1949). *Pan-Africanism or Communism* (1956) discredited the imperialists' propaganda inferring that all political activism in Africa and the demands for independence were inspired by communism.

Probably before his move to Ghana, Padmore married Dorothy Pizer and became Kwame Nkrumah's (1909–1972) personal representative and advisor. Padmore organized the Conference of Independent States, which was held in April 1958 in independent Ghana. He was soon elected secretary-general of the All African People's Conference, which used the motto "Independence and Unity."

Padmore worked all his life for various newspapers, linking readers to the black world. By organizing conferences (including the Pan-African Congress held in Manchester, England in 1945), he tried to promote freedom for all colonized peoples. Padmore died in London in 1959. He was given a state funeral in Accra and his ashes were interred in Christianborg Castle in October 1959.

Padmore's many other books include *How Britain Rules Africa* (1936); *African and World Peace* (1937); with Nancy Cunard, *The White Man's Duty* (1942); with Dorothy Pizer, *How Russia Transformed Her Colonial Empire* (1946); and *The Gold Coast Revolution* (1953).

See also: African Diaspora; Britain, Blacks in; Colonies in Africa, British; Colonies in the Caribbean, British.

Further Reading: Adi, Hakim, and Marika Sherwood. *The 1945 Pan-African Congress Revisited.* London: New Beacon Books, 1995; Friedland, William H., and Carl G. Rosberg. *African Socialism.* Stanford: Stanford University Press, 1964; Hooker, James. *Black Revolutionary: George Padmore's Path from Communism to Pan- Africanism.* Westport, CT: Praeger, 1967.

Laëtitia Baltz

Palamedes, Sir

Palamedes, a Moorish knight, is a member of the Knights of the Round Table in Arthurian legend and a prominent character in the tale of Tristan and Isolde. In some tales, Palamedes also ventures on a hunt of the Questing Beast, a strange monster from Arthurian legend that had the head and neck of a snake, the body of a leopard, the haunches of a lion, and the feet of a stag.

Palamedes is portrayed in literature as the son of King Esclabor, a lord of Babylon, who converts to Christianity. Palamedes and his two brothers, Safir and Segwarides, join King Arthur's Knights of the Round Table in Britain. Palamedes appears in the Post-Vulgate Cycle, which is a collection of the major old French prose cycles in Arthurian literature; Thomas Malory's *Le Morte d'Arthur* (*The Death of Arthur*), which is one of the most famous and significant versions of the Arthurian legend in early modern English; and the *Romance of Palamedes*, which exists in fragments and as a component of late thirteenth-century Italian writer Rustichello da Pisa's *Roman de Roi Artus* (*Romance of King Arthur*). In the Post-Vulgate Cycle, Palamedes converts to Christianity during the quest for the Holy Grail, the cup used by Jesus of Nazareth at the Last Supper. Such an act releases Palamedes from earthly desires, and Percival and Galahad, both fellow Knights of the Round Table, assist Palamedes in slaying the Questing Beast. Both the Post-Vulgate Cycle and *Le Morte d'Arthur* depict Palamedes, along with his brother and fellow knight, Safir, siding with Lancelot, King Arthur's closest friend, after his affair with Queen Guinevere, Arthur's wife, is exposed. Palamedes and Safir eventually travel with Lancelot to France, where Palamedes becomes duke of Provence.

Palamedes also plays a significant role in the tale of Tristan and Isolde, an influential tragic romance retold in numerous sources and with many variations dating from the medieval period. The tale, whose earliest versions hail from twelfth-century Norman poets, details the adulterous and doomed romance between a Cornish knight, Tristan, who becomes a member of the Round Table, and an Irish princess, Isolde, who is destined to marry Mark, the Cornish king and Tristan's uncle. Palamedes initially appeared in the *Prose Tristan*, an expansion of the Tristan and Isolde legend dating from the thirteenth century that fully connects the tale to the arc of the Arthurian legend. In the tale, Palamedes is one of the knights competing to marry Isolde in a tournament in Ireland. Palamedes ultimately loses to the handsome Tristan, a fact that delights the beautiful Isolde; however, Tristan fought as a representative of his uncle. In combat, Tristan spares Palamedes's life on the condition that he refrain from bearing arms for one year or to pursue Isolde romantically. After Isolde marries King Mark, Palamedes saves Isolde's servant, Brangaine, and eventually joins the Round Table. Palamedes's unrequited love for Isolde leads to much animosity between him and Tristan, leading to a number of undecided or postponed duels. Tristan and Palamedes eventually reconcile, but they maintain a tempestuous relationship.

See also: Moors; *Morien, Romance of* (1200s); *Parzival*, Feirefiz in.

Further Reading: Grimbert, Joan. *Tristan and Isolde: A Casebook.* New York: Routledge, 2002; Lacy, Norris. Th*e Arthurian Handbook.* 2nd ed. New York: Routledge, 1997; Malory, Thomas. *La Morte d'Arthur.* ed. Stephen Shepherd. New York. W. W. Norton, 2003; *The Romance of Tristan.* trans. Renee L. Curtis. New York: Oxford University Press, 1994.

Eric Martone

Pamoja

Pamoja (Movement of the Young **African Diaspora** in Austria) is an organization composed of young individuals of black African descent living in Austria founded in 1996. Austria has a small black population, prompting many black Austrians to feel isolated or ostracized from mainstream society. Furthermore, black Austrians face prejudice and discrimination, as well as negative stereotypes within Austrian society.

Pamoja promotes black interests in Austria and attempts to unite the black community into a cohesive force to implement positive change. Consequently, Pamoja means "together" in Swahili, an African language, and its logo is an Adinkra symbol from Ghana called Pempamsie, which means "unity is strength." In pursuit of this objective, Pamoja holds meetings, seminars, and other community activities. The organization attempts to promote positive aspects of black culture and identity to create better race relations through education and understanding. As part of this objective, in 1997, the organization introduced **Black History Month** celebrations in Vienna.

See also: Afro-German Women (ADEFRA); Campaign Against Racial Discrimination (CARD); Central Europe, Blacks in; Initiative of Blacks in Germany (ISD); Literature, Blacks in German and Central European; Representative Council of Black Associations (CRAN).

Further Reading: Karner, Christian. "Austrian Counter-Hegemony: Critiquing Ethnic Exclusion and Globalization." *Ethnicities* 7:1 (2007): 82–115; Wodak, R., and M. Reisigl. "Discourse and Racism: European Perspectives." *Annual Review of Anthropology* 28 (1999): 175–199.

Eric Martone

Pan-Africanism

Pan-Africanism refers to a range of ideologies and practices that are by no means always in accord. There are two aspects to Pan-Africanism: its political focus with pragmatic objectives and its philosophical focus, founded on the idea that there is an African cultural essence possessed by Africans and their descendants, wherever they may be. Sometimes these two aspects are united in a single movement or ideology, sometimes not. Pan-Africanism arose as a response to European actions, such as the claims of African inferiority, lumping Africans into a single category, and racial discrimination.

The trans-Atlantic slave trade is critical to the development of Pan-Africanism for two reasons. First, huge numbers of Africans from all over the continent were taken to the Americas, where they forged a new, common identity. Second, the trans-Atlantic slave trade ultimately led to the European colonization of Africa, giving peoples from all over the continent the shared experience of European imperialism. Both these processes led to the emergence of a consciousness as "black" or "African." The development of a Pan-African consciousness began first in the Americas.

Some African-identifying Americans argued that that descendants of Africa could never be free in the Americas and that they would achieve full freedom only in Africa. These were the sentiments that spurred the various "Back to Africa" movements that emerged in the Americas. Jamaica-born and longtime U.S. resident, Marcus Garvey, was the most famous proponent of this view. Most descendants of Africa in the Americas remained in the continent of their birth, but some migrated to Africa. Modern Liberia dates from the colonization efforts of African Americans in the first half of the nineteenth century; and **Sierra Leone,** which was founded in the late eighteenth century, also received a small, but notable, number of colonists from different parts of the Americas. The Virgin Islands-born polymath Edward Wilmot Blyden, who migrated to Liberia and spent the rest of his life in Africa, is considered by some to be "the father of Pan-Africanism."

In 1900, the Trinidadian lawyer Henry Sylvester Williams convened the first Pan-African Conference in London. The conference was attended by Africans as well as people of African descent from the Americas. Subsequently, United States scholar **W.E.B. Du Bois** convened a series of Pan-African Congresses. The first was held in 1919 in Paris to run concurrently with the Versailles Peace Conference that ended World War I. The Second Pan-African Congress was held in 1921 in successive sessions in several European cities, including London, where the "London Manifesto" was passed. The Fifth Pan-African Congress met in Manchester, England in 1945 and was a turning point in the history of Pan-Africanism and the Congresses. For the first time, Africans, many of whom would later lead their respective countries after independence, took center stage. Like previous meetings, this Congress passed resolutions condemning racial discrimination around the world.

In 1957, Ghana (formerly the Gold Coast) became the first sub-Saharan African country to gain its independence. Kwame Nkrumah, Ghana's leader, was one of the organizers of the 1945 Pan-African Congress and had been involved in a variety of Pan-Africanist movements in the United States and United Kingdom, where he had studied. Nkrumah called for a United States of Africa. He had a Pan-Africanist vision that was staunchly continental. This view was reflected in the First Conference of Independent African States in Ghana in 1958. The only independent African countries at the time were Ghana, Liberia, Sudan, and the countries of North Africa. Some Pan-Africanists rejected the inclusion of North African states on the basis that they were culturally different from sub-Saharan Africa.

Pan-Africanism is often seen as belonging to the Anglophone world, but many prominent Francophone activists and intellectuals, such as the politician **Blaise Diagne** of Senegal, participated in the Pan-African Congresses. **Négritude,** a movement that developed in the Francophone world, is often regarded as the Francophone equivalent. As with Pan-Africanism, the views of the proponents of Négritude range over a wide spectrum. Some theorists of Négritude subscribe to the view that there is an African cultural essence, whereas others focus on the need for unified political action. Whatever their position, all promote black pride.

In 1963, the Organization of African Unity (OAU) was founded in Addis Ababa, Ethiopia, to promote greater continental integration and cooperation. By this time, most African countries were independent, with the exception of the settler colonies of South Africa. The OAU maintained a position in support of black majority rule in these countries. The Pan-Africanist objective of greater African cooperation was taken up by the African Union, which was founded in 2002.

See also: African Diaspora; Alcindor, John; Césaire, Aimé; Colonies in Africa, British; Colonies in Africa, Dutch; Colonies in Africa, French; Colonies in Africa, German; Colonies in Africa, Italian; Colonies in Africa, Portuguese; Colonies in Africa, Spanish; Colonies in the Caribbean, British; Colonies in the Caribbean, Dutch; Colonies in the Caribbean, French; Colonies in the Caribbean, Spanish; Fanon, Frantz; Horton, James; James, C.L.R.

Further Reading: Adi, Hakim. *West Africans in Britain, 1900–1960: Nationalism, Pan-Africanism and Communism.* London: Lawrence and Wishart, 1998; Esedebe, Peter O. *Pan Africanism: The Idea and Movement, 1776–1963.* Washington, DC: Howard University Press, 1982.

Anene Ejikeme

Pareja, Juan de (1610?–1670)

Juan de Pareja was a slave of African descent who worked in the household of Spanish painter Diego Velázquez of Seville, Spain. Pareja eventually earned his freedom and went on to become a noted painter of his time.

Although there is conflicting scholarship on the date and circumstances of his birth, Pareja was born to Zulema, who was either a **Moor** or a West Indian slave. His father is unknown and speculation is that he was also either a Moorish slave, or a white Spaniard. When Pareja was five years old, his mother died and he became the property of the famous painter Diego Velázquez. Research suggests several different versions of Velázquez's acquisition of Pareja.

Juan de Pareja. Portrait by Diego de Velázquez, c. 1650 © The Metropolitan Museum of Art/Art Resource, NY.

Although not employed to be a painter, Pareja watched Velázquez carefully. Velázquez would not allow Pareja to paint, but they developed a close bond as Pareja began working with Velázquez, serving as a color grinder and assistant. How Pareja became a free man is not certain, but there are two versions of note. The first is rather simple. It is suggested that on the death of his wife and recognizing their close bond of friendship, Velázquez freed Pareja. The other version is more complex. As the story goes, Velázquez was awaiting a visit from the king of Spain, Philip IV. Unknown to Velázquez, Pareja had begun painting in secrecy. Velázquez had many of his works of art on display for the king to view and, according to this story, Pareja put one of his paintings among the others. The king noticed Pareja's painting and liked it, which was, in essence, the start of his own career as an artist.

There are two well-known paintings involving Pareja. One of the paintings is a portrait of Pareja by Velázquez. Research suggests that Velázquez made the portrait of Pareja in preparation for another painting that he was going to paint under difficult circumstances. The second painting, named the "Calling of St. Matthew," is Pareja's best-known work and currently hangs in the Prado in Madrid.

See also: Art, Blacks as Represented in European; Colonies in the Caribbean, Spanish; Gomez, Sebastian; Latino, Juan; Spain, Blacks in.

Further Reading: De Treviño, Elizabeth Borton. *I, Juan de Pareja*. New York: Bell Books, 1965.

Robert Nave

Parzival, Feirefiz in

Feirefiz Angevin is a courtly knight and the biracial half-brother of the main character Parzival in the Middle High German epic poem *Parzival* (c. 1200–1210) by Wolfram von Eschenbach (1170?–1220?). Feirefiz, the son of the white knight Gahmuret of Anjou and the Queen Belakane, a **Moor,** has the checkered appearance of a magpie, with face and hair both black and white. As one of Wolfram's creative additions to earlier romances of the quest for the Holy Grail, or the cup used by Jesus of Nazareth at the Last Supper, the story of Feirefiz is memorable, not only for its unusual representation of blackness, or its exploration of the moral coding of the black/white contrast, but also for the questions it raises about the relation between modern perceptions of race and religious color symbolism.

The presence of Feirefiz in the narrative of Parzival's moral growth from birth to becoming Grail King is significant. On a quest after his father, the heathen Feirefiz challenges Parzival in a climactic duel and, through his knightly prowess and noble character, proves to be the only opponent equal to Parzival: Gaining strength by thinking of his wife Sekundille, Feirefiz recovers from a blow to his helmet, sees his opponent without a sword, and after flinging his own sword, even circumvents the chivalric code by revealing his identity first. Recognizing each other, the two embrace and go to the British King Arthur. Subsequently, Feirefiz is admitted to the legendary Knights of the Round Table and Parzival becomes Grail King. Feirefiz is baptized and later establishes Christianity in India, and **Prester John,** the son Feirefiz has with his second wife Repanse de Schoye, becomes the legendary Christian priest and king.

Because of his appearance, Feirefiz is often regarded as a foil for Parzival, embodying and visually representing the flawed nature his half-brother must overcome in his journey to triumph, as well as symbolizing the black and white appearance of writing the text of the romance itself. The hierarchic contrast of black and white, however, introduced early in the poem as the metaphorical opposition between the darkness of hell and heaven's brightness, and rooted in Christian symbolism, does not apply to racial difference; the representations of Belakane's purity and virtue, and of Feirefiz's heathen nobility as tantamount to its Christian counterpart in Parzival, are often regarded as examples of attitudes toward blackness that are unmarked by color prejudice. Some scholars, however, diverge from this interpretation of race, often citing the problematic act of conversion.

Yet the character of Feirefiz raises issues not only of hierarchy, but also of heredity. Set in a text that emphasizes lineage, Feirefiz has also been regarded an early literary manifestation of the interest in questions of interracial genealogy, and of human origins in general.

See also: *Morien, Romance of;* Palamedes, Sir.

Further Reading: Lampert, Lisa. "Race, Periodicity, and the (Neo-) Middle Ages." *Modern Language Quarterly* 65 (September 2004): 391–421; Sollors, Werner. "Origins." In *Neither Black Nor White Yet Both: Thematic Explorations of Interracial Literature.* Cambridge: Harvard University Press, 1997, pp. 31–47; Swinburne, Hilda. "Gahmuret and Feirefiz in Wolfram's 'Parzival.'" *Modern Language Review* 51 (1956): 195–202.

Charlotte Szilágyi

Phillips, Caryl (1958–)

Caryl Phillips is a **black British** novelist, essayist, and playwright. Much of his work is characterized by a concern with the themes and repercussions of the Atlantic slave trade, and the resulting ambiguity of black identity.

Phillips was born in the village of St. Pauls, St. Kitts, in the West Indies (Caribbean), and moved with his family to England when he was 12 weeks old. After growing up in mostly white, working-class neighborhoods in Birmingham and Leeds, Phillips attended Queen's College, Oxford, where he graduated with an honors degree in English language and literature in 1979.

Phillips began his career as a playwright. His first play, *Strange Fruit*, was produced in Sheffield in 1980, and was followed by a number of plays for stage and radio. In 1985, Phillips published his first novel, *The Final Passage*. Like much of Phillips's early work, *The Final Passage* examines the cultural dislocation of West Indian immigrants in Britain.

After the publication of *The Final Passage*, Phillips continued working in multiple genres. He published a second novel, *A State of Independence*, in 1986, and a screenplay, *Playing Away*, that same year. A travelogue, *The European Tribe*, was published in 1987, and a third novel, *Higher Ground*, in 1989. *Higher Ground* marked a shift in the complexity and scope of Phillips's writing. It featured a global setting and multiple narratives, both of which would become hallmarks of the author's later work.

In 1991, Phillips won the London *Sunday Times* Young Writer of the Year award for his novel *Cambridge*, which he followed three years later by *Crossing the River* (1994). An epic, multithreaded story of 250 years of **African Diaspora,** *Crossing the River* was one of the most critically celebrated novels of the year, winning the James Tait Black Memorial Prize, and being short-listed for the Booker prize.

In recent years, Phillips has confronted the subject of the African Diaspora most explicitly in his nonfiction. An anthology, *Extravagant Strangers* (1997), a second travelogue, *The Atlantic Sound* (2000), and a book of essays, *A New World Order* (2001) all directly address this theme. At the same time, the scope of Phillips's fiction continues to widen. *The Nature of Blood* (1997) centers around a Holocaust survivor, and *A Distant Shore* (2003) concentrates on the relationship between a retired British schoolteacher and an African immigrant. Phillips's recent novel, *Dancing in the Dark* (2005)—a fictionalization of the life of vaudevillian Bert Williams—is his first book set entirely in the United States.

In addition to his writing, Phillips has taught at colleges and universities throughout the world. Along with full professorships at Amherst College and Barnard College, he has held visiting teaching positions in many countries, including Ghana, Poland, Canada, Singapore, and Barbados. In 2005, Phillips became a professor of literature and creative writing in the Yale University English Department.

See also: Britain, Blacks in; Civil Rights Movement in Twentieth-Century Great Britain; Colonies in the Caribbean, British; Literature, Blacks in British.

Further Reading: Ledent, Bénédicte. *Caryl Phillips.* Manchester: Manchester University Press, 2002

Kristen Roupenian

Piar, Manuel Carlos (1774–1817)

Manuel Carlos Piar was the biracial general-in-chief of the revolutionary army that fought the Spanish during the Venezuelan War of Independence. Piar was born in 1774 in Willemstad, Curacao. His father was a Spanish sailor and his mother was a Dutch woman of black African descent. Piar grew up facing racial discrimination, and when he was 10 years old, he and his mother moved to La Guaira in Venezuela, then a Spanish colony. Although Piar did not attend school, he was able to read and write, establish basic general knowledge, and learn to speak several languages. In 1797, Piar took part in the unsuccessful Gual and Espana Conspiracy to try to achieve independence from

Spain. In 1804, Piar was serving in the Spanish militia against the British, who were trying to take Curacao. Three years later, he was supporting the revolutionaries in Haiti against the French.

Piar's early military adventures inculcated in him a desire to achieve Venezuelan independence from the Spanish. He joined the revolutionary forces and served in the navy at Puerto Cabello, where he was put in command of a ship involved in fighting the Spanish at the 1812 Battle of Sorondo on the Orinoco River. The Spanish were soon able to gain the upper hand in the fighting, and Piar sought refuge on the island of Trinidad, which was controlled by the British. In 1813, he returned to Venezuela, where he was appointed a colonel in the army. Piar successfully led his men against the Spanish and enabling the eastern part of Venezuela to claim independence. In 1814, promoted to brigadier general, Piar led his troops in attacks on Spanish garrisons in Barcelona, Caracas, and Cumana, but he was defeated by José Tomás Boves near El Salado. In spite of Piar's defeat, he was appointed major general and participated in the Los Cayes expedition. In 1816, Piar defeated the Spanish under Francisco Tomás Morales at El Juncál. He then led his soldiers in an attack on Guayana, and in early 1817, lay siege to Angostura. In April 1817, Piar defeated the forces of the Spanish general, Miguel de la Torre y Pando, at San Félix and was appointed general-in-chief of the revolutionary army.

In spite of his success, Piar gained some important enemies in the independence movement, noticeably Simón Bolívar. Bolivar stripped Piar of his field command and gave him leave in June 1817. Part of the friction between Piar and Bolívar concerned the rights of the diverse racial groups in Venezuela. Piar wanted not only to end Spanish control of Venezuela, but also to create an independent country where all the citizens, including those of African (or Indian) descent would have equal rights. Piar started to conspire against Bolívar and joined with his opponents José Felix Ribas, Santiago Marino, and José Francisco Bermúdez. Bolívar, however, seemed to have feared Piar more than his other opponents, who were not interested in rights for Africans. In September 1817, Bolívar had Piar arrested and charged at a court martial with desertion, insubordination, and conspiring against the government. In October, Piar was sentenced to death, and Bolívar confirmed the sentence on the same day. Piar was executed by firing squad against the wall of the Angostura Cathedral. According to tradition, Bolívar, who chose not to observe the actual execution, is said to have heard the firing from within his office and tearfully remarked, "I have shed my blood."

See also: Haitian Revolution for Independence; Latin American Revolutions, Blacks in; Spanish Army, Blacks in the.

Further Reading: Trend, J. B. *Bolivar and the Independence of Spanish America.* London: Hodder and Stoughton, 1946.

Justin Corfield

Pirates, Blacks and Atlantic

Piracy and the slave trade had become intimately related since the beginning of European expansion west into the Atlantic. Some of the first Elizabethan "seadogs," like Sir John Hawkins, began their careers attempting to engage in the potentially lucrative trade of African slaves to Spanish America. Before the *Assiento* of 1713, in which England was contracted by Spain to supply its American colonies with slaves, pirates who preyed on the Spanish Main or off the Eastern and Western coasts of Africa were a major source of slave labor in fledgling Atlantic World communities from Port Royal, Jamaica to Boston, Massachusetts. Not only did most pirate crews before 1713 consider black peoples a valuable commodity for sale in maritime communities known as "pirate nests," on a number of occasions when pirates were brought to trial, black and Amerindian men who worked alongside their white compatriots were found innocent because their racial status deemed them without free will.

There have been numerous cases of individual black pirates before the *Assiento* who clearly fought with equal or greater status than their white cohort. Diego de los Reyes commanded a pirate vessel in league with the Dutch in the 1630s and 1640s, and runaway slaves held positions of authority under the buccaneer Sir Henry Morgan and the notorious William Kidd. One explanation for this break in racial expectations stems from the unusual nature of the maritime world where skill trumped all. Runaway slaves also provided pirates with valuable information about potential targets. There is greater evidence of multiracial crews during the two decades after the *Assiento* among the crews of infamous pirates like Blackbeard, Bartholomew Roberts, and Stede Bonnet. Some even speculate that Blackbeard himself was biracial. The specter of "interracial" pirate crews off their coasts made many colonial officials in slave societies fear that the presence of pirates might inspire slave revolts.

Many historians believe that the existence of multiracial crews proves that pirates presented a radical protest against the socioeconomic and racial oppression of the early eighteenth century. Most of the colorful speeches used to support such interpretations can be found only in sources that have proven to be largely fiction and quite often satiric. For example, the French pirate Captain Misson, in the wildly popular *The General History of the Pyrates* (1724), described a pirate utopia that he allegedly established on Madagascar, where he espoused interracial harmony and challenged the very ideological basis of chattel slavery. Misson, however, was a fictional character likely imagined by Daniel Defoe, whose other work generally posed little challenge to the slave trade. British author John Gay dramatized the "Black Pirate" by turning his lovable rogue from *The Beggar's Opera*, Macheath, into the black-faced pirate Murano in his sequel, *Polly and the Pirates* (1729). Although there were few black pirates in the Atlantic after the 1730s, excluding the Barbary pirates from Africa, they lived on as a literary device during the nineteenth century in popular works like *The Florida Pirate*.

See also: Pirates, Blacks and Mediterranean.

Further Reading: Cordingly, David. *Under the Black Flag: The Romance and the Reality of Life Amongst the Pirates.* New York: Harvest Books, 1997.

Mark Hanna

Pirates, Blacks and Mediterranean

The Barbary pirates, also known as Ottoman Corsairs, were groups of African pirates that operated in the Mediterranean off the coast of North Africa (the "Barbary

Coast," which comprises modern Morocco, Algeria, Tunisia, and Libya), preying on Christian and non-Muslim ships and European cities along the Mediterranean. Many Christian European captives were sold as slaves in the Muslim world. It is estimated that between 1 and 1.25 million Europeans were captured and sold as slaves from the sixteenth to nineteenth centuries in North Africa and West Asia.

As a result of frequent pirate attacks, many Europeans refused to live too close to the Mediterranean coast and many European naval powers lost thousands of ships. There are many recorded incidents of attacks in such European countries as Italy, France, Portugal, Malta, Spain, and as far north as England, Scotland, Ireland, and even Iceland. In 1544, Kahir as Din captured about 9,000 inhabitants of Lipari and sold them into slavery. In 1551, Turgut Reis enslaved the entire population of Gozo, one of the islands comprising Malta, and, in 1555, took about 6,000 prisoners from Corsica as slaves. In 1563, Turgot Reis captured 4,000 Europeans in southern Spain and enslaved them. In 1554, Barbary pirates attacked the Italian city of Vieste, enslaving about 7,000 inhabitants. In 1558, Barbary pirates attacked Ciutadella in Minorca, destroying the town and slaughtering many of its inhabitants; the 3,000 survivors were enslaved. Between 1609 and 1616, Barbary pirates attacked more than 450 merchant ships; the survivors of such attacks were enslaved or ransomed. Those Europeans captured as slaves were sold along with slaves from the trans-Saharan trade routes within the Ottoman Empire, which spanned North Africa, West Asia, and parts of Eastern Europe. Slaves were used for hard labor, for work in the galleys, or in harems.

The North African coast increased in its influence during the fifteenth century, when Ottoman rulers expanded their control over the area. Barbary revolts in the 1600s, however, reduced the Ottomans to little more than nominal rulers of the area. The coast received an influx of **Moors,** many of which had been expelled from Spain. The coast, with an expanding numbers of destitute immigrants, became a place known for piracy and criminal activity under the protection of the Ottoman Empire. The Barbary pirates came to be composed of black and Arab members. The most infamous Barbary pirates included the Ottoman Barbarossa brothers, who took control of Algiers in the early 1500s, and Turgut Reis (also known as Drugot).

The Barbary pirates continued enslaving Europeans well into the nineteenth century. Ships from the Unites States also began to be attacked, prompting the Americans, along with some European countries, to take action against the pirates in the early 1800s. After a successful Anglo-Dutch raid of Algiers in 1816, which immobilized most of the pirate fleet, the pirates were forced to agree to stop enslaving Christians; but the pirates did not adhere to these agreements, prompting a British raid in 1824. Most of the remaining pirate communities along the Barbary Coast were eliminated during the French conquest of Algiers and Tunis in 1830 and 1831. The slave trade officially ended in the Barbary Coast when the European governments granted emancipation.

See also: Italy, African Invasions of; Pirates, Blacks and Atlantic; Spain, African Invasions of.

Further Reading: Davis, Robert C. *Christian Slaves, Muslim Masters: White Slavery in the Mediterranean, the Barbary Coast and Italy, 1500–1800.* New York: Palgrave Macmillan, 2003; Gordon, Murray. *Slavery in the Arab World.* New York: New Amsterdam Books, 1990; Lewis, Berbard. *Race and Slavery in the Middle East: An Historical Inquiry.* New York: Oxford University Press, 1992.

E. Agateno Mosca

Polish Legions in the Haitian Revolution

During the Napoleonic period in Europe (1790s to 1810s), several Polish units served as a component of the French army. After the Third Partition of Poland by Prussia, Austria, and Russia in 1795, which temporarily erased Poland from the map of Europe, many Poles believed that the French Revolutionary government would support the Polish cause. The French Revolutionary government found itself at war with most of royal Europe.

Consequently, Polish soldiers emigrated from Poland to other countries (such as Italy and France) to join local military forces and support the cause of the French Revolution. The number of Polish recruits soon numbered in the thousands, and Polish military units were created under Polish commanders. Such units became known as the Polish Legions and were considered a Polish army in exile under French command. The Polish Legions fought alongside the French army during the Napoleonic wars and took part in most of Napoleon Bonaparte's major military campaigns. Despite Polish support, however, the French government did little to advocate the resurrection of a Polish state.

In 1802, the French government under Napoleon Bonaparte sent the Polish Legions (then numbering about 5,280 men) to Haiti to reinforce the French army there in its attempt to regain the French colony of Saint Domingue. Napoleon sent the Polish Legion to avoid the loss of the units that comprised his main French army. Accompanying the Poles were German and Swiss contingents and other less favored units in the French army. A significant figure in the Polish Legion was General Jablonowski, who was of partial black descent and a prominent member of the Legion. He died of yellow fever on September 29, 1802 in Jérémie, the first Pole to die in Haiti. Many more Poles similarly fell victim to yellow fever and other tropical diseases.

Many Poles became sympathetic to the cause of the natives in the **Haitian Revolution for Independence;** however, only 120 to 150 Poles defected in support of Haitian leader Jean-Jacques Dessalines. Most of the Poles followed their duty and supported the French. In general, the Haitians liked the Poles, whom they felt were less racist than the French. Dessalines had a brigade jokingly nicknamed *Les Polonais*, which was composed of newly arrived Africans. To the Haitians, these Africans, like the Poles, spoke poor Creole. There is some debate on whether the Poles participated in the massacre of 400 black French soldiers in Saint Marc. In 1803, the British declared war on France and the French forces faced increasing difficulties to maintain fighting on Haiti. In the defense of Jérémie, a group of Poles were allowed to sneak away safely to Cuba because their commander let it be known to the British commander that they were both Freemasons, a secret fraternal order. Many of the French and Haitian elites were members of the order of Freemasonry.

By the 1803 French evacuation of Haiti, 4,000 Poles were dead (either from battle or from disease). Only about 700 members of the Polish legion returned to France. About 400 Poles decided to remain in Haiti; some others decided to migrate to nearby islands or the United States. Some of the Poles who immigrated to Cuba worked as privateers against the British. Those who remained in Haiti married Haitian women and had families. These Poles later received special status when the 1805 Haitian constitution barred white ownership of property (Poles, Germans, and Swiss married to

Haitians were exempted). Nevertheless, about 160 Poles received special permission to leave Haiti with their biracial families in 1805.

The loss of thousands of patriotic and loyal Poles in the Haitian Revolution was a blow to the cause of Polish independence. Furthermore, the Haitian experience undermined Polish confidence in the good intentions of France toward resurrecting Poland. Consequently, the black revolutionaries of Haiti emerged as a warning among nineteenth-century Polish nationalists.

See also: Colonies in the Caribbean, French; Russia, Blacks in.

Further Reading: Pachonski, Jan, and Reuel Wilson. *Poland's Caribbean Tragedy: A Study of Polish Legions in the Haitian War of Independence, 1802–1803.* New York: Columbia University Press, 1986.

Eric Martone

Pop Music, Blacks in Contemporary European

Most black artists in contemporary European popular music emerged from the early 1980s hip-hop and rhythm-and-blues movements, especially popular in the United Kingdom, France, and Germany. These movements offered a music that blended elements from the **African Diaspora.**

In the United Kingdom, Music of Life, the first British record label to specialize in the production of hip-hop and rhythm and blues, was founded by Simon Harris in 1982. Derek B, Hijack, the Demon Boys, Hardnoise, and MC Duke were their first artists to obtain critical and commercial success. Originally from Jamaica, Usher D. became Music of Life's most recognizable artist. His style, a blend of reggae and hip-hop, became instantly popular.

Other labels, such as Mango Records and Kool Sweat, produced solo acts and groups that mixed different music styles of the African Diaspora. Caveman and Outlaw Posse created a jazzy hip-hop style. London Posse and Black Radical Mk II were influenced by reggae music. The Wee Papa Girl Rappers, Cookie Crew, and Movie Love created a radio-oriented hip-hop. MC Mell'O mixed jazz and hardcore. A new style of electronic music developed called "grime" (sometimes called "eskibeat" or "sublow"). Musical artists that are representative of this style in the early 2000s include Dizzee Rascal, J-Dawg, Wiley, Sway DaSafo, Lady Sovereign, Ghetto, AC, and Terra and Kano.

In the late 1990s, the United Kingdom offered several regional hip-hop and rhythm-and-blues scenes. Several rappers, such as Blade, Black Radical Mk II, and Overlord X, were located in London. Bristol was also the home to a rise of black musicians, including Massive Attack, the Scratch Perverts, and Smith and Mighty. Bristol later emerged as home to trip hop, which was the name given to a new type of downtempo electronic music. Nottingham gave birth to the Stereo MCs. Leeds launched Braintax and Nightmares on Wax. Manchester was also home to many innovative black musicians including Ruthless Rap Assassins, Krispy 3, the Kaliphz, and MC Tunes.

In France, the descendants from Berber, Arab, African, and West Indian immigrants in European popular music are influential in the rhythm and blues, hip-hop, rai, rap, or *zouk* scenes. The first major hip-hop black French star, MC Solaar, was born in Dakar, Senegal. His 1991 hit *"Qui sème le vent récolte le tempo"* made him the first French hip-hop artist to go platinum.

In the late 1990s, two different styles of hip-hop emerged on the French popular music scene. MC Solaar, Dee Nasty, and Alliance Ethnik represented a more mellow and commercial hip-hop style. Assassin and Suprême NTM were the leaders of the second trend, which was more aggressive and hardcore. Very controversial, these artists often glorified the murder of police officers and other crimes.

Black artists from the 1980s and 1990s were restrained in their references to the African continent, as obvious Afrocentrism would have provided the French anti-Arab extreme right with racist arguments. Some black French artists addressed issues that caused poverty in African states. For example, Bisso Na Bisso's song *"Dans la peau d'un chef"* refers to the corruption of African heads of state. IAM also included many African-related themes in its music. For instance, their 1991 song *"Les tam-tam de l'Afrique"* was one of the first French rap hits to deal explicitly with slavery. The group incorporated images associated with ancient Egypt as several of its members used names reflective of this influence.

In Germany, a community of Turkish artists, including DJ Derezone, TCA, Eko Fresh, and the Microphone Mafia, created a style of "Oriental hip hop." Eko Fresh, in its 1993 *Konig von Deutschland* album, describes the story of a Turkish boy growing up in Germany, torn between Turkish and German cultures and languages, illustrating the issues encountered by many Turkish immigrants in Germany.

In Scandinavia, several black artists became popular in the early 1990s. In Sweden, for example, Neneh Cherry's album *Raw Like Sushi* led the Swedish media to take a closer look at Sweden's native artists. Some Danish English-language rappers, such as Static and NATiLL, Funk Flush, and Delireeus, are well known all around Scandinavia. Popular Danish-language artists include the members of Full Impact Productions (FIP), such as Orgi-E, Bai-D, TrooLS, LOC, Rune Rask, and U$O.

In Ireland, several black artists became popular in the early 1990s. Marxman, for example, two Dubliners (Byrne, Lunny) and two British Jamaicans (Phrase, DJ KI) released the album 33 *Revolutions Per Minute*, which mixed Irish traditional music with hip-hop. Another group, Scary Éire, toured with U2, Gang Starr, Beastie Boys, House of Pain, and Public Enemy.

See also: Afro-Caribbean Music in Britain; Jazz, European Reception of; Music, African Influences on European; Music Industry, Blacks in the European; Musicians in Europe, African American Classical.

Further Reading: Mitchell, Tony. *Global Noise: Rap and Hip Hop Outside of the USA.* London: Ebury Press, 2004.

Tristan Cabello

Popes, African

Three popes of the Roman Catholic Church, specifically Victor I (pope 189–199), Miltiades (or Melchiades) (pope 311–314), and Gelasius I (pope 492–496), have come from Africa. All three were later canonized by the Catholic Church. They originated from the ancient Roman province of Africa (now Tunisia and Libya). The race of the African popes has been debated because of limited evidence, although it is conceivably possible that one or all of them were black African.

Victor I, born in Africa, was pope from 189 to 199 during the reign of Roman Emperor Septimus Severus, who was also from Africa. Before his tenure as pope, the celebration of Easter, which celebrates the believed resurrection of Jesus of Nazareth, was celebrated on different dates in the Roman and Eastern Orthodox Churches. The Eastern Orthodox Church celebrated the feast day on the 14th day of the Jewish month of Nisan (the day before the Jewish holiday of Passover) regardless of what day of the week the 14th fell on since, for they believed that Jesus was crucified on the Friday preceding Passover. The Roman Catholic Church celebrated Easter on the Sunday after the 14th of Nisan. Victor I did not believe in maintaining the tolerance that had allowed two separate dates for the celebration of Easter. He consequently severed ties with those bishops, such as Polycratus, bishop of Ephesus, who opposed his views on Easter and Theodotus of Byzantium. In addition, Victor I changed the language of masses in the Catholic Church from Greek to Latin.

Miltiades, African by birth, was pope from 311 to 314. Little is known about him or his life. During his tenure as pope, the Edict of Constantine, promulgated in Milan in 313, allowed the Christian religion to be practiced freely along with other religions in the empire. Without the persecution that had existed earlier, Christianity began to spread throughout the empire and eventually became the state religion. Constantine, who converted to Christianity, granted Miltiades a grotto in the Lateran Palace.

Gelasius I, an African, had previously served as secretary to Pope Felix III. He unsuccessfully attempted to breach the division between the Roman Catholic and Eastern Orthodox Churches. Part of his failure was in part due to his opposition to the views of the Eastern Roman emperor, Anastasius I, and the patriarch of Constantinople. Gelasius wrote a letter to the emperor arguing that spiritual power is higher than temporal power and that thus even emperors must bow to it. Gelasius also furthered the supremacy of the pope as the head of the entire Church. He worked to eliminate the remaining vestiges of pagan rites and festival in Europe and to suppress the Manicheans, a heretical Christian sect in Rome. Gelasius became known as "the pope of the poor people" because of his generosity, using the Church's riches to ease the common people's suffering during periods of disaster or famine.

See also: Bakhita, Josephine; Benedict the Moor, Saint; Black Madonna Tradition; Cain, Theory of Descent of Blacks from; Hamitic Myth; Heraldry, Blacks in European; Italy, Blacks in; Magi, Representations of the; Maurice, Saint; Roman Emperors, African; Roman Empire in Africa.

Further Reading: Lopes, Antonio. *The Popes: The Lives of the Pontiffs Through 2000 Years of History.* trans. Charles Nopar. Rome: Futura Edizioni, 2005.

E. Agateno Mosca

Portugal, Blacks in

The earliest inhabitants of Portugal were Lusitanian, believed by some to have been descendants of the southwest Asian Phoenicians. The region was under Castilian domination until it was given to Henry of Burgundy as a reward for his service against the

Muslim Afro-Arab **Moors.** In 1143, under Afonso I, Portugal became fully independent. Lisbon was named the capital in the thirteenth century. Except for a brief period of Spanish colonization (1580–1640), Portugal has remained an independent kingdom. Because Portugal was declared the sovereign over Africa by Pope Nicholas V and produced the navigation that initiated the trans-Atlantic slave trade, relations between Luso-Portuguese and Africans are central to the black experience in Europe.

Although parts of Iberia are only five miles from the northernmost tip of Africa, the Mediterranean Sea and Straits of Gibraltar provided historical barriers to African migration to Europe. Portugal was cut off from the major Mediterranean slave routes. Italy and Spain regularly imported Slavs and sub-Saharan Africans through Arab and Turkish merchants, but Portugal relied on the prisoners of the unending wars between the Moors and Christians. By the end of the thirteenth century, the Christians had reconquered Algarve, and all of the parts of Iberian Peninsula that would become Portugal were under Castilian sway. The Castilian sovereigns continued to conduct sporadic border raids but had no other reliable means of acquiring slaves.

Although Portugal captured a few Canary Islanders, it remained focused on the kingdoms of its Muslim enemies. In 1317, Portugal hired the Italian Manuel Pesagno to raid Morocco for slaves. Portugal conquered Ceuta in 1415 and then was soundly defeated 20 years later at Algiers. The first Portuguese explorers to attempt the West African Coast were Anton Gonçalves and Nuno Trist. They went only as far as the coast of Mauritania, but captured 11 Berbers of the Idzzigen. Gonçalves and Nuno's success encouraged Portuguese explorers to attack the Idzzigen; however, they met with the same organized states that had conducted the Moorish slave trade. In 1443, the Idzzigen negotiated the return of two of their nobles for 10 slaves and gold. Through negotiations and raids, the Portuguese were able to procure more than 200 Africans from the region, which they named Guinea in 1444.

Relations between Africans and Portuguese took a dramatic turn during the early fifteenth century under the reign of Prince Henry the Navigator. Henry's curiosity and determination to circumvent the Muslims led him to found a nautical college at Sagres. His explorers commenced voyaging down the coast of Africa, and eventually around the continent. In 1445, Prince Henry founded a slave market at Arguin Bay, Mauritania. This action formalized Portuguese relations with some West African sovereigns and led to the annual deportation of hundreds of persons to Portugal. Horses were used as a medium of exchange. As the demand for slaves increased, West African sovereigns, faced with the death of horses from the tse tse fly, drove up the price.

Two legal victories were crucial to the ability of Portugal to expand southward along the African coast without confrontation with other European naval states. The first was the *Romanus pontifix* issued by the Catholic Church in 1455. The second was the Treaty of Alcáçovas signed between Portugal and neighboring Castile in 1479. Uninhabited Cape Verde was colonized in 1450; Sao Tome by 1500. The Africans deported to and enslaved on these islands were used as plantation workers. Their experiences preceded those of the Brazilians, but like Brazil, the sugar they produced was shipped directly to Portugal. The Portuguese settled at Santiago, Cape Verde to trade with Upper Guinea, as the region from Senegal to Cape Palmas was called. Their contacts were the Mandinga Muslim rulers, from whom they procured Djola, Papel, Balanta,

Beafada, and Nalu ethnics. Most of the peoples delivered to the Portuguese by the Mandinga were destined for Brazil, but others stayed in Cape Verde or were sent north to Portugal. By 1482, the Portuguese had sailed to the kingdom of Kongo, where they opened friendly relations with the Manikongo. They also established a northern fort called St. Jorge da Mina. The Portuguese were familiar with the skill set of the African ethnic groups they were enslaving. Africans in the western Sahara and savannah mined gold and salt, and cultivated crops.

Within two decades, Lisbon had become the hub of Portugal's slave market. In the first seven years of Portuguese slave trade, about 1,000 African people were sold to Iberia. Within a century, about 12,000 individuals passed through Lisbon. Senegal alone provided 400 people annually. That number was insignificant compared to more than 3,000 who were deported annually from Upper Guinea. Enslaved Africans were sold to Spain and Italy. The majority were retained in Portugal as domestic servants. The goods that the Africans produced were sold by individuals and taxed by the crown. Africans worked in drainage, cleared land, and worked the Iberian fields. African women were often employed as water-brokers, coal vendors, and midwives. They might also have done domestic duties such as wet-nursing and hairdressing. One domestic duty that was limited to African women was waste disposal. African women, known as *regateiras,* also sold food from corner eateries.

From Lisbon, the African population was concentrated in Algarve and Evora. As the locales diversified, so did the tasks to which people were placed. By the mid-fifteenth century, Africans were employed in hospitals and homes, often to the detriment of the enslaved individual because they were the first deployed to the sick when plague struck. Some Africans worked in the Portuguese courts as pages, retainers, and ladies-in-waiting.

Within Portugal, the African and European populations regularly intermixed and intermarried. Iberia had been under Moorish domination for seven centuries, and intermixture between Africans, Arabs, Berbers, and Iberians was by no means unusual. Most Iberian slaves had been of mixed-race, whether reflecting millennia of Afro-Euro-Asian mixture in North Africa, or having become Afro-Vandal on Iberian soil. Mixed-race Portuguese, such as the great orator **António Vieira,** brought international honor to Portugal. Don Sesnado, Count of Combra, was an Afro-Lusitanian Christian who had fought the Moors. Both King João IV and João VI were possibly of Afro-Lusitanian background. Sephardic Jews, who voluntarily or forcibly converted to Christianity, brought Afro-Iberian mixture to the islands of Cape Verde, where they mixed with full-blooded Africans. Jews had been royal advisers before the *Reconquista,* and even as "New Christians," some bore the surname "Negro" or "Preto."

After the early sixteenth century, Afro-Portuguese, Africans, and Brazilians of varying origin were often sold by Portuguese merchants in Antwerp. Some Afro-Portuguese intermarried with the indigenous American slaves deported from Brazil and Newfoundland. Portuguese ships often carried African, Afro-Lusitanian, and Afro-Brazilian crews. These sailors contributed to Portugal's successful colonization of Madagascar and even represented Portugal in Macao and Japan. Antonio de Albuquerque de Coelho, who was born in Brazil, sailed Portuguese ships, and served successively as Portugal's governor in Macao, Goa, and East Africa, was descended from black Africans and Amerindians.

Despite frequent ethnic intermixture, the Portuguese did not regard Africans as spiritual equals. First, the incident of religious difference was magnified by the fact that the Muslim Moors had been largely black or "tawny," whereas Iberian Christians were usually white. Some lighter-skinned Muslims also regarded black Africans as "infidels," no matter what religion the latter professed. The antiblack Hamitic doctrine was used by some white Christians, Asian and mixed-African Muslims, and Jews to denigrate the Malians, Ghanaians, and Ethiopians. The "tawny" and "black" Moors had also denigrated white Christians. Thus the Luso-Portuguese fixation with "purity" was in part an attempt to reclaim their heritage from the color prejudice of the Moors.

James H. Sweet states that Alfonso X (king of Castile, Leon, and Galicia) can be largely credited with setting the environment for Luso-Portuguese antiblack rancor. Writing in the thirteenth century, Alfonso's *Cantigas de Santa Maria* declared war on the Spanish Moors and their African allies. By the fifteenth century, the definition of a "true" Portuguese was "whiteness," "Catholicism," and "descent from Lusitanian stock." The 11 Idzzigen kidnapped by Gonçalves were described as deserving bondage by evoking the theory that blacks were the cursed descendants of the biblical Cain.

Baptism was an important way in which Africans were integrated into Portuguese society. The Portuguese monarchy insisted that Africans be baptized while in Africa or once they reached Portuguese shores. Part of the insistence on baptism was because the justification for enslavement was defeat of Muslims, but also spread of the Christian faith. Afonso V received a papal bull entitled *Dum Diversas* (1452) authorizing Portugal to claim all pagan lands for the Christian faith. The unfortunate inhabitants, according to Pope Nicholas V, were subject to eternal servitude whether or not they converted. The *Romanus pontifex* (1455) and *Inter caetera* (1456) defined the lands of "disbelief" as stretching as far away as the Indies.

The lives of both free and enslaved Afro-Portuguese were regulated by slave codes. The major law was developed by King Manuel in the sixteenth century. This law made no distinction between free and enslaved Afro-Portuguese. This meant that free Africans were in danger of deportation to the Americas. It also meant that free African women were in constant danger of sexual assault without recourse to redress. The children of enslaved African women were slaves; thus the offspring of rape or concubinage could be, and were, sold by the fathers. Enslaved Africans could not testify, nor could they own property. Although murder of a slave carried the death penalty, in practice most killers simply paid a debt to the crown. Enslaved Africans were treated so poorly and subject to such harsh conditions that part of King Manuel's motivation for drafting the slave codes was to decree lime-filled burial sites for the numerous corpses that were being "eaten by dogs." In reaction to the draconian laws, Afro-Portuguese founded religious mutual aid societies, fraternities, and knighthoods. Free Afro-Portuguese oversaw the welfare of enslaved Africans. Sometimes free Africans petitioned the crown or sheltered runaways.

Afro-Portuguese contributed to the musical heritage of the world by modifying the kora. The result was the guitar, a new form of Afro-Iberian music, and numerous dances. Some of the dances that can be linguistically tied to Africa are the *mangana*, *arromba*, *guine*, *ye ye*, *caozinho*, *cubanco*, *gandu*, *sarambeque*, *cumbe* and *paracumbe*.

The Afro-Portuguese language was known as *fala de Guine*. Elements of the *fala de Guine* indicate that many Bini and Kongo-speakers formed a large portion of the enslaved Afro-Portuguese communities.

Afro-Portuguese continued the architectural tradition started by the Afro-Arab Moors by designing the *Praca De Toiros* bullfighting ring of Lisbon. They also designed the fishing boats, called *rabelos*, which Edward Scobie claims reflect a Nigerian origin. Even the city of Lisbon bears an Afro-Arabo-Lusitanian name; it was initially called Lashbuna by the Moors.

See also: Abolition of Slavery, Portuguese; Afonso, King of Kongo; Age of Exploration; Berlin Conference (1884–1885); Colonies in Africa, Portuguese; Congolese Nobility, Portuguese Education of; Hamitic Myth; Moor's Head Symbol; Slave Trade, Portuguese; Spain, African Invasions of.

Further Reading: Birmingham, David. *Portugal and Africa*. New York: Palgrave Macmillan, 1999; Forbes, Jack D. *Africans and Native Americans: The Language of Race and the Evolution of Red-Black Peoples*. 2nd ed. Urbana: University of Illinois Press, 1993; Metcalf, Alida C. "Millenarian Slaves? The Santidade de Jaguaripe and Slave Resistance in the Americas." *The American Historical Review* 104:5. (1999): 1531–1559; Nowell, Charles E. "Portugal and the Partition of Africa." *The Journal of Modern History* 19:1 (March 1947): 1–17; Obenga, Theophile, ed. *Readings in Precolonial Central Africa: Texts and Documents*. London: Karnak, 1995; Rodney, Walter. "Upper Guinea and the Significance of the Origins of Africans Enslaved in the New World." *The Journal of Negro History* 54:4 (1969): 327–345; Rogers, J. A. *Nature Knows No Color Line*. St. Petersburg, FL: Helga M. Rogers, 1952; Sweet, James H. "The Iberian Roots of American Racist Thought." *The William and Mary Quarterly* 54:1 (1997): 143–166.

Maryam Sharron Muhammad Shabazz

Prester John

Prester John was a mythical figure who, from the twelfth to seventeenth centuries, was thought by Europeans to be a real personage, ruling over a distant Christian empire beyond the Islamic world, originally located in Asia, but from 1300 onward increasingly associated with Ethiopia. Europeans wanted to believe in the universality of Christianity and in a potential ally in their struggle against the Muslim powers.

The first written reference to Prester John appeared in the *Chronica* of Otto van Freisingen (1145), which reports that he had set out with an army to help the Christian Crusaders in Jerusalem, but was unable to cross the Tigris. In 1165, a letter addressed to the Byzantine Emperor Manuel Comnenus (1143–1180) from the "supreme ruler of the three Indies," Prester John, circulated around Europe. In 1177, Pope Alexander III sent a reply, but no response was received.

The mythical emperor was, most important, a Christian: "Prester" signified "priest." It was thought that he was descended from one of the Three Magi and from the queen of Sheba, and that his empire was vast, with 72 dependent kingdoms. Thus he had massive military power and untold wealth. The sultan of Cairo was said to pay him tribute, owing to his power to change the course of the Nile, which had its source in his kingdom.

The oldest surviving map that portrays Prester John is a portolan chart made by Angelino Dulcert (Mallorca, 1339). Increasingly, Ethiopia was marked on maps as the kingdom of Prester John, probably because of the arrival of regular Ethiopian embassies in Europe from 1329. These delegations visited Venice, Rome, Aragon, Naples, and Milan and established a permanent home in Rome at St. Stephen of the Ethiopians, where from 1537 to 1552, Tasfa Seyon, or "Peter the Ethiopian," edited a New Testament in Ge'ez, the Ethiopian liturgical language. Geographers, however, were not entirely sure where Ethiopia was. The name appears in seven different locations on a Genoese world map of 1457.

The Portuguese voyages to Africa from the late fifteenth century led to the modification and ultimately the dispelling of the myth that had partly inspired them. In 1484, the king of Benin told the Portuguese of a ruler named Ogàmé, a lord of lords, who lived 250 leagues east of Benin and gave his dependents a little cross to cement their friendship. This gave the Portuguese hope that they were close to finding the legendary ruler. In 1521, King Manuel of Portugal wrote to Pope Leo X to tell him that Portuguese captains had found Prester John in Ethiopia. Francisco Alvarez, who spent six years (1520–1526) at the Ethiopian court of Lebna Dengel (David II) and Queen Helena, wrote an account that exploded many of the myths. Europeans began to realize that the Prester's territory was not so vast, his people so Christian, nor his treasury as bottomless as they had dreamed. Although it gradually became clear that even the name "Prester John" was a European invention rather than an Ethiopian reality, the myth lived on, inspiring writers from Shakespeare and Samuel Johnson to John Buchan and Umberto Eco.

See also: Age of Exploration; Colonies in Africa, Portuguese; Italy, Blacks in.

Further Reading: Gumilev, Lev Nikolaevich. *Searches for an Imaginary Kingdom: The Legend of the Kingdom of Prester John.* Trans. R.E.F. Smith. Cambridge: Cambridge University Press, 1988; Silverberg, Robert. *The Realm of Prester John.* New ed. London: Weidenfeld and Nicolson, 2001.

Miranda Kaufmann

Prince, Mary (1788–1833?)

Mary Prince was an African slave from Bermuda who later moved to London, England, where she wrote an account of her life. Her book was the first slave narrative published in England by a black woman.

Prince was born in Brackish Pond, Bermuda. She was the daughter of slaves; her father was a sawyer owned by David Trimmingham, a shipbuilder, and her mother was a household servant for Charles Myners. Myners died in 1788 and Prince and her mother were sold to Captain Darrell, who used them as household servants. Darrell gave Prince to his daughter, who in turn gave her to her own daughter, Betsey Williams. Betsey was the same age as Prince, and the two became playmates and friends. When Betsey's father returned from his regular sea voyages, however, Prince's treatment became worse. When Prince was 12 years old, she was "lent" to the Pruden family and then sold to Captain John Ingham of Spanish Point, where she was regularly in trouble and flogged. Prince was then sold to another slave owner, probably Robert Darrell, who, in 1806, sent her to Grand Turks, where she was put to work in the salt-pans working on gathering salt.

Returning to Bermuda in 1810, Prince was sold to John Wood in 1818. Prince was then taken to the island of Antigua, where she became a domestic servant. On Antigua, Prince joined the Moravian Church and, in December 1826, married Daniel James, a widower and former slave who had already bought his freedom. James worked on the island as a carpenter and cooper. Prince's owner, Wood, however, was angered by the marriage, which had occurred without his permission, and beat her severely.

Wood then moved to London and took Prince with him to work as a servant. Slavery was illegal in Britain at the time, but Prince was unable to leave the family and fend for herself. Furthermore, if she returned to Antigua, she could be enslaved again. Eventually, the Woods threw her out of their household and Prince sought refuge with the Moravian Church in Hatton Garden. Soon afterward, she started working for Thomas Pringle, an abolitionist and secretary of the Anti-Slavery Society. Pringle had Prince dictate the story of her life, which was written down by Susanna Strickland and published in 1831 as *The History of Mary Prince: A West Indian Slave*. The book had an immediate effect, with Prince's former owner, Wood, unsuccessfully suing the publishers for libel. James MacQueen and James Curtin, however, who were prominent supporters of slavery, started denigrating Prince's account of her life. Prince and her publisher then sued the pair and won their case.

Prince was living in England until 1833, but nothing is known of her later life or when she died.

See also: Abolition of Slavery, British; British Anti-Slavery Society; Diallo, Ayuba Suleiman; Equiano, Olaudah; Gronniosaw, Ukawsaw; Slave Trade, British.

Further Reading: Prince, Mary. *The History of Mary Prince: A West Indian Slave*. Mineola, NY: Dover, 2004.

Justin Corfield

Prince, Nancy (1799–1856?) and Nero (?–1833)

Most of what is known about the life of Nancy Gardener Prince, born free in New-buryport, Massachusetts, comes from her self-published *Narrative of the Life and Travels of Mrs. Nancy Prince, Written by Herself* (1850). A deeply religious woman, she contributed to the genres of spiritual autobiography and travelogue, chronicling her life in Russia, which she introduced with a description of the economic hardships that her family experienced in nineteenth-century America. As a child, she was forced to hire herself out as a servant to help supplement the family income. Having resolved to flee a life fraught with financial difficulties, on February 15, 1824, she married Nero Prince and sailed to Russia to enjoy the advantages of a life with this former seaman, who had become a servant in the royal court of Russian Tsars Alexander I and Nicholas I. Little is known about her husband, whom she refers to as Mr. Prince in her *Narrative*. Some believe that her formal address indicated that he was considerably older than she. Others speculate that she called him by his surname because she imitated the manners of her former white women employers or because their marriage was a loveless one. Before migrating to Russia, Nero was a skilled cook who was one of the founders of the Prince Hall Masonic Lodge in Boston, later assuming the position of Grand Master of the Lodge, when Prince Hall died in 1807.

Nancy's *Narrative* details the life of upper-class society grounded in domestic politics, as well as a few of the customs and rituals of the working class that she observed during her nine-year stay in Russia. Having acquired the rudiments of literacy through religious education, she continued educating herself by learning the language of the educated classes. She also learned the art of sewing, specializing in making children's garments.

Descended from a lineage of enslaved ancestors who fought for freedom, Nancy proudly details the history of their accounts of the journey from slavery to freedom. Her story reveals the dramatic escape of her stepfather, Money Vose, who jumped from a slave ship, as well as the heroism of her African grandfather, who fought in the American Revolutionary War at Bunker Hill. Heir to a tradition underscoring emancipation, she took up the mantle in social institutions, including the church, the family, and the school. While in St. Petersburg in Russia, she undertook the task of establishing an orphanage for children in need of food and shelter.

When the cold climate in Russia became unbearable, she returned to Boston in 1833. Her husband promised to join her in two years, after he had acquired some property; however, Nero never made the journey and died soon after her departure.

After a failed attempt at opening an orphanage in Boston in 1839, Nancy used her talents as a teacher and missionary in the newly emancipated Jamaica. Her experiences with sexism and her efforts to educate free blacks in Jamaica were initially published as a separate pamphlet, now part of her *Narrative*.

See also: Colonies in the Caribbean, British; Courts, Blacks at European Aristocratic; Hannibal, Abraham; Russia, Blacks in.

Further Reading: Braxton, Joanne M. *Black Women Writing Autobiography: A Tradition within a Tradition.* Philadelphia: Temple University Press, 1989; Peterson, Carla. *Doers of the Word: African-American Women Speakers and Writers in the North.* New York: Oxford University Press, 1995; Shockley, Anne Allen. "Nancy Gardener Prince." In Anne Allen Shockley, ed. *Afro-American Women Writers, 1746–1933.* Boston: G. K. Hall, 1993, pp. 48–55.

Lena Ampadu

Prostitution in the Caribbean and Latin America Colonies, Blacks and

Prostitution, one of the oldest professions of women in history, was prevalent in the European-controlled colonies in the Caribbean and Latin America. The exact beginning of prostitution in the Caribbean is unclear. The local governments had a difficult time curbing and controlling it. Female slaves were used at times as "money-making instruments" by trading them for sex in exchange for money or other material gains. Female slaves were sexually exploited as concubines and slave breeders.

Prostitution also became widespread as a means of livelihood for black women. In the European colonies in the Caribbean and Latin America, many black or biracial slaves obtained their freedom and turned to prostitution. Such a choice was made in the face of difficulties in supporting themselves, the strict colonial social hierarchies based on race, and the common experience of previous sexual exploitation. Prostitution, combined with slave concubinage, led to the increase of biracial inhabitants in the colonies and the greater efforts of colonial governments to impose a complex social hierarchy based on degradations of blackness.

See also: Colonies in the Caribbean, British; Colonies in the Caribbean, Dutch; Colonies in the Caribbean, French; Colonies in the Caribbean, Spanish; Prostitution in Europe, Blacks and.

Further Reading: Kempadoo, Kamala, ed. *Sun, Sex, and Gold: Tourism and Sex Work in the Caribbean.* Lanham, MD: Rowman and Littlefield, 1999.

Ayotunde Titilayo

Prostitution in Europe, Blacks and

Prostitution is often described as the oldest profession. It can be defined technically as either extreme promiscuity or the act or practice of engaging in sexual acts for financial compensation. Because prostitution has been dominated by teenage females, adult women, and young boys, the business is linked to various forms of slavery, pornography, and domestic servitude. There are multiple forms of prostitution and a hierarchy of legitimacy within the profession. The streetwalker is the most visible face of prostitution and usually looked down on by other sex professionals. The indoor sex worker receives the most prestige. For example, in Nairobi, Kenya, Muslim prostitutes may work indoors (*malaya*), but non-Muslims may serve as streetwalkers (*watembezi* or *wazi-wazi*). Some prostitutes are well paid and the United Nations has reported that the current Western European sex trade is a multibillion dollar industry.

Contemporary Europe has a large number of prostitutes, better known as "sex workers." During the medieval era, some lawyers imaginatively defined a prostitute as a woman who had sexual intercourse with between 40 and 23,000 men. The demographics of prostitution in Europe are shifting. In Turkey, increasing numbers of female prostitutes from Africa and Arab lands are displacing the transvestite sex workers. Young male prostitutes, known as "beachcombers," sell to a female clientele, replacing the better known gigolo. African and Asian prostitutes are replacing Latina American sex workers.

African prostitutes originate from multiple countries. There are large numbers of prostitutes from Nigeria, Ghana, Equatorial Guinea, Cameroon, Algeria, Democratic Republic of Congo, Central African Republic, Morocco, Mali, Tunisia, Ivory Coast, and Senegal. Continental Africans join Afro-Latinas from Brazil, Colombia, Ecuador, Peru, Guadeloupe, Martinique, and Guiana. The majority of African prostitutes are trafficked (a term implying coercion) from Africa or are lured under false pretenses. Groups of traffickers, led by *mesdames* and madams, offer to arrange marriages for potential prostitutes. *Mesdames* or madams are often former prostitutes. Women receive legal permits to work in Mediterranean countries, especially Italy and Spain, and then are taken north illegally. Ghanaian prostitutes often enter the sex trade to cover the debts of arriving in Europe, or are presented with high debts by the traffickers. Many are coerced into drug addiction to keep them in the trade. There is also a wide use of vodun (voodoo) to frighten young women into staying in prostitution. African prostitutes tend to be long-term sex workers because of the difficulties of getting into Europe, the cost of travel overseas, and the distance from their homes of origin. Long-term sex workers usually move in groups, are usually under the control of pimps or madams, have little or no control over their hours, and may work for more than 10 years to repay the usurious costs of getting into Europe.

Because African prostitutes are often in situations of acknowledged debt, with no access to their passports, they are often subject to dangerous situations. Long-term sex workers need to make a large amount of money and therefore often take the clients with the riskiest behaviors. For example, European clients pay extra for sex without a condom, exposing the prostitute to sexually transmitted diseases, including HIV, and pregnancy. Long-term sex work has exploded in recent years, as communication has become easier, while the economies of Africa have deteriorated. The support network Solidarity With Women in Distress reports that 30 percent of sex workers are aware that they will be prostitutes before they leave their home countries. Prostitution is an investment for the sex worker, pimp and/or madam; therefore, the worker takes care of her or his health and seeks prophylactics in the form of regular antibiotics. At the same time, rates of gonorrhea, hepatitis B, and tuberculosis are increasing, and social planners link this phenomenon to the increase in long-term international prostitution. The misuse of medication may also lead to resistant forms of disease.

Europe has long looked at prostitutes as potential sources of disease and has thus attempted to regulate the trade. Alexandre Jean-Baptiste Parent-Duchalet was the founder of the French *maison de tolerance*, a system of legal brothels linked to the penal systems. Europe has also historically blamed prostitution on immigration. At various times, the sex trade has been blamed on Jews, Romany, and **Moors.** Colonialism and the rise of market theories also changed the traditional relationships between prostitutes and their clients. For example, where much of the "indoor" prostitute's work was to provide comfort, seduction, and a boost of the client's morale, the nineteenth century saw what has been referred to as the "popularization of commercial sex." Prostitutes began to focus strictly on debauched "sexual services" that were unavailable to married men. Prostitutes also began to work in assembly line fashion, with the introduction of "conveyor-belt sex" that was strictly for profit.

European laws regarding prostitution vary from country to country, although the European Union regards the migratory sex trade to be a "crime against physical integrity and against freedom." In an attempt to control prostitution and mitigate some of its worst effects, some countries, such as Germany and the Netherlands, legalized the trade. Others, such as France, legalize the trade, but with several limitations. In some European countries, such as Sweden, it is illegal to purchase sexual favors, but the act of selling them is legal.

Increasing African prostitution has had a devastating effect on the image of African immigrants and native-born Afro-Europeans. Coupled with centuries-old European myths and racist fears of hypersexual Africans, the inequities in the global economy have contributed to a view of African women as fundamentally potential prostitutes.

See also: Immigration to Europe, Illegal African; Prostitution in Caribbean and Latin American Colonies, Blacks and.

Further Reading: Carling, Jorgen. *Trafficking in Women from Nigeria to Europe.* International Peace Research Institute, Oslo (PRIO); Edlund, Lena, and Evelyn Korn. "A Theory of Prostitution." *The Journal of Political Economy* 110:1 (Feb. 2002): 181–214; Roberts, Mary Louise. "Gender, Consumption, and Commodity Culture." *The American Historical Review* 103:3 (June 1998): 817–844; Sharp, Lesley A. "The Commodification of the Body and Its Parts." *Annual Review of Anthropology* 29 (2000): 287–328; Skilbrei, May-Len, Marianne Tveir, and Annette Brunovskis. "African Dreams on European Streets: Nigerian Women in Prostitution in Norway." *Jenda: A Journal of Culture and African Women Studies* 8 (2006). Available at: http://www.jendajournal.com.

Maryam Sharron Muhammad Shabazz

Punic Wars

The Punic Wars were a series of three wars fought between the ancient Roman Republic and the Carthaginian Empire based in North Africa for control of the Mediterranean. The First Punic War, fought from 264 until 241 B.C.E., saw the Carthaginians and their allies being defeated in Sicily, with Rome taking control of the island and being able to seize Sardinia three years after the war's end. The Second Punic War, fought from 219 to 202 B.C.E., involved Hannibal, the famous Carthaginian general, who brought the war to Italy with his invasion of the Italian peninsula. The Romans eventually won by landing a force near Carthage, causing Hannibal to return to North Africa, where he was defeated at the Battle of Zama. The Third Punic War resulted in the Romans attacking Carthage in 149 B.C.E., and the city's destruction in 146 B.C.E.

During the first two Punic Wars, the Carthaginians provided generals and fielded a small citizens' army, using their wealth to hire large numbers of mercenaries, while also persuading many allied rulers to provide soldiers. As a result, although the Carthaginian command was almost exclusively drawn from the city of Carthage in North Africa, there were always many African soldiers, especially from Libya, which the Carthaginians had conquered, and from Numidia, which was traditionally allied to Carthage, although its kings did turn against their former allies at the end of the Second Punic War.

The Carthaginians had established their capital city in what had been Libyan land, and many of the Libyans were forced into slavery. Gradually, they were raised to the level of tributary free cultivators, paying high taxes while having to provide soldiers for the Carthaginian army. During the First Punic War, the Libyans made up a large percentage of the Carthaginian army and the expeditionary force sent to Sicily in late 252 B.C.E. The Romans described this force as consisting largely of Libyans, suggesting that they were visibly darker and easily differentiated from those from Carthage.

The Libyan soldiers were generally armed with javelins or spears, and they formed the central core of the Carthaginian army in a number of battles, especially in the First Punic War and at the Battle of Lake Trasimene during the Second Punic War. Many of the spearmen carried a large shield, whereas those with the javelin used a small hide shield. For clothing, they often wore a short-sleeved tunic made of soft red leather that later became known as Morocco leather, and many had their heads shaved except for a scalplock, making them look more ferocious on the battlefield. As well as the Libyans, the Carthaginians also used Moorish javelin soldiers, who mostly fought on foot, recruited from Mauretania (modern-day Morocco). Other **Moors** served as mahouts for the war elephants used by the Carthaginians.

Throughout the First Punic War, it was common for the Carthaginians to use cavalry from Numidia (modern-day Algeria). The Carthaginians tended not to have large troops of cavalry, except for the Battle of Zama in 202 B.C.E., during which the Numidian mercenaries abandoned Carthage and fought on the Roman side. Most of the Carthaginian cavalry were Numidians who operated as skirmishers, riding without a bridle, and possibly using a rawhide noose over the lower jaw of their ponies. Some Numidian leaders wore skins from leopards or other wild cats that they specialized in hunting, with most tribesmen wearing a short, sleeveless tunic, armed with javelins and light spears, as well as knives and daggers, and protecting themselves with a small round shield.

The Numidians were an effective cavalry and much feared by the Romans during their attacks on North Africa in 256 B.C.E. during the First Punic War, and also when Hannibal and his army invaded Italy in the Second Punic War. At the end of the latter conflict, the Romans attempted to persuade Syphax, prince of the Masaesyles tribe in Numidia, to support them. The defection of King Masinissa of Numidia before the Battle of Zama was a major factor in the eventual Carthaginian defeat. King Masinissa sided with the Romans again during the Third Punic War, although 6,000 Numidians fought for Carthage. The Romans later decided to use the Numidians on a more regular basis, and Julius Caesar mentions using Numidian horse archers in his fighting against the Belgae in 57 B.C.E. Furthermore, Numidian horsemen are depicted on Trajan's Column dating from 106–113 C.E.

Hannibal's invasion of Italy during the Second Punic War, and his deployment of Libyans, Moors, and Numidians against the Romans, was the first time that large numbers of Africans fought in Italy. Hannibal used them extensively at the battles of Ticinius in November 218 B.C.E., at Trebbia in December 218 B.C.E., and at Lake Trasimene in April 217 B.C.E., they no longer formed the bulk of the Carthaginian forces at the battle of Cannae on August 2, 216 B.C.E., when Hannibal destroyed the largest army the Romans ever sent against him. This seems possible because the Africans had been depleted by battle and disease and had to be replaced by Spanish and Celtic tribesmen. The Africans had withstood the worst of the fighting at Trebbia, where they were used by Hannibal to outflank the Romans. Consequently, Hannibal made less use of them at Trasimene and held the African heavy infantry in reserve at Cannae.

With the arrival of thousands of Africans in Italy with Hannibal in 218 B.C.E., and Hannibal not leaving until 203 B.C.E., it seems likely that significant numbers of Africans would have settled in the Italian peninsula, including those who were taken prisoner and enslaved. The account by the Roman historian Diodorus that Hannibal massacred the mercenaries whom he could not ship back to Africa seems unlikely, with some settling in southern Italy, and many others being enslaved or killed by the Romans. Certainly, the southern Italian city of Capua, which was Hannibal's base during much of his time in Italy, became a popular center for African gladiators soon afterward.

See also: Italy, Blacks in; Roman Army, Africans in the; Roman Empire in Africa.

Further Reading: De Beer, Sir Gavin. *Hannibal: The Struggle for Power in the Mediter-ranean.* London: Thames and Hudson, 1969; Goldsworthy, Adrian. *The Punic Wars.* London: Cassell, 2000; Healy, Mark. *Cannae, 216 BC: Hannibal Smashes Rome's Army.* Oxford: Osprey, 1998; Wise, Terence. *Armies of the Carthaginian Wars, 265–146 BC.* Oxford: Osprey, 1999.

Justin Corfield

Pushkin, Alexander (1799–1837)

Alexander Sergeyevich Pushkin, one of the greatest writers in all of Russian literature, was a famous nineteenth-century Romantic poet, novelist, and playwright descended from a black African slave. Pushkin popularized the use of vernacular speech in his works, leading to a style of writing that combined romance, drama, and satire that has continued to influence Russian literature ever since. The Russian city of Tsarskoe Selo was renamed Pushkin in his honor in 1937.

Pushkin was born in Moscow in 1799 to a distinguished Russian aristocratic family that traced its nobility to the twelfth century. One of Pushkin's famous ancestors, however, was his great-grandfather **Abraham Hannibal,** a former slave from Africa who became a Russian general and favorite of Tsar Peter the Great. One of Hannibal's sons, Joseph, was a naval commander and a navigator whose daughter, Nadejda, married Count Pushkin, whose grandfather had been privy counselor to Peter the Great and whose father had borne the scepter at the coronation of Catherine the Great.

Pushkin published his first poem while still a teenager. By the time he graduated from the prestigious Imperial Lyceum in Tsarskoe Selo, he had already gained a reputation within the intellectual circles in Russia. After his graduation, Pushkin relocated to Saint Petersburg. During the course of his life, Pushkin became a committed social reformer and advocate of literary radicals. Such a position put him at odds with the Imperial Russian court. Consequently, in the 1820s, he was exiled temporarily (until he petitioned Tsar Nicholas I to release him from exile) and later placed under strict surveillance and censorship. During the 1820s, Pushkin also became a member of the freemasons and the secret society

Alexander Pushkin by Orest Adamovich Kiprensky. Scala / Art Resource, NY.

Filiki Eteria ("Friendly Society"), which supported Greek independence from Ottoman Turkish control.

Pushkin married Natalia Nikolaevna Pushkina-Lanskaya in 1831. The couple later became regular fixtures at the Imperial Russian court. The tsar bestowed on Pushkin the lowest court title, which angered the author who thought that the act was intended to humiliate him. Amidst rumors of his wife's infidelity and increasing debts, Pushkin died in 1837 from wounds sustained in a duel against his wife's alleged lover, Georges-Charles de Heeckeren d'Anthès.

Pushkin had four children with his wife, including a daughter, Natalia, who married into the Dutch royal house of Orange-Nassau. Fearing a political demonstration, the Imperial Russian government gave Pushkin a hurried and small funeral. Later, during the twentieth century, Pushkin, because of his influence on subsequent generations of Russian radicals, became a hero within the new Soviet Union as an opponent of bourgeois culture and the founder of Soviet literature.

Pushkin's most famous works include the poem, *Ruslan and Ludmila* (1820); the narrative poem, *The Gypsies* (1827); the drama, *Boris Godunov* (written in 1825, published in 1831); the poetic drama, *The Stone Guest* (1830); the poem, *The Tale of Tsar Saltan* (1831); the poetic drama, *Mozart and Salieri* (1831); the novel in verse, *Eugene Onegin* (published serially from 1825 to 1832); the short story, *The Queen of Spades* (1833); the poem, *The Bronze Horseman* (1833); the novel, *The Captain's Daughter* (1836); and the unfinished novel based on the life of his ancestor, *The Moor of Peter the Great* (begun in 1827).

See also: Dumas *père*, Alexandre; Mirsky, D. S.; Russia, Blacks in; Soviet Propaganda, Blacks and.

Further Reading: Bethea, David, ed. *The Pushkin Handbook.* Madison: University of Wisconsin Press, 2006; Binyon, T. J. *Pushkin: A Biography.* New York: Alfred A. Knopf, 2003; Briggs, A.D.P. *Alexander Pushkin: A Critical Study.* Lantham, MD: Barnes and Noble, 1982; Nepomnyashchy, Catharine, Nicole Svobodny, and Ludmilla Trigos, eds. *Under the Sky of My Africa: Alexander Pushkin and Blackness.* Evanston, IL: Northwestern University Press, 2006.

Eric Martone

Q

Quassia

Quassia amara is a shrub or small tree generally growing three meters tall in South America. It is used to make a bitter tasting, exotic stomach tonic that became popular in Europe and the Caribbean during the eighteenth century as a cure for vomiting and fever. The plant was named after a former slave from Suriname named "Graman" (Greatman) Quassi.

Quassi was a healer or medical man, who also sold amulets to free African soldiers in Suriname. It seems that the European colonists used Quassi as an informant, seeking him out for information pertaining to such matters as the location of slaves accused of poisoning their masters. He was likely not the discoverer of the plant named after him or its medicinal use, but he was possibly the one who introduced the tonic to European scientists in the colonies. The Amerindians of Suriname were likely the first to discover the medicinal use of the plant. Quassi somehow learned of this use and then sold this information to Daniel Rolander, a student of the Swedish scientist Carl Linnaeus, known as "the father of modern taxonomy." Rolander subsequently brought this information to Europe in 1756. Linnaeus received a specimen of the plant in 1761.

Linnaeus then wrote a dissertation on the plant, which named, described, and categorized it in the field of European botany. Linnaeus's naming system emerged as the natural sciences were becoming more professionalized. Historians such as Londa Schiebinger have argued that through the renaming of plants located in the non-European areas under its domination, European powers reinforced hegemony. Plants were usually named after an illustrious scientist or patron of science associated with the plant's discovery. Therefore the recognition of a former slave whose connection with science was dubious as the "discoverer" of the Quassia was an anomaly within Linnaeus's naming system. Quassi was the only former slave to receive such recognition in the European scientific community.

The naming of the Quassia met with the disapproval of many European scientists. Other botanists of the period, however, sought to praise the former slave and present him as a heroic figure. Such actions were connected to the rise of antislavery movements in Europe at the end of the eighteenth century. Celebrating Quassi as a great discoverer helped the abolitionists' cause by providing an intelligent, reasoning, and heroic former slave to present to the European community.

See also: Abolition of Slavery, European; Scientific Racism.

Further Reading: Schiebinger, Londa. *Plants and Empire: Colonial Bioprospecting in the Atlantic World.* Cambridge: Harvard University Press, 2004.

E. Agateno Mosca

Race Riots in Europe

Since the end of World War II in 1945, Europe has been undergoing an increased demographic shift. The European colonial empires of the nineteenth century finally collapsed and colonies achieved independence. Yet the European labor shortage led to the mass immigration of immigrants from the former colonies to Europe. Immigrant laborers continue to be a significant component of the new European economy. Many of the immigrant laborers who came or are coming to Europe are from sub-Saharan African or of black African descent.

In most European countries, immigrant communities are often located in urban centers and are relegated to slums and poverty-stricken areas. Many immigrants think that they are treated inferior to white Europeans. In the decline of the European nation-state and periods of economic recession, many white Europeans have reacted negatively to immigrants and minorities. Yet in general, racial tensions are rarely addressed constructively in Europe; the trend is to ignore them. In many urban immigrant communities, the police force, which is usually white, has emerged as a symbol of the perceived injustices from the white majority. The police have often been accused of using excessive force on minorities. The combination of these conditions established the setting in which European race riots have occurred.

Britain has had several race riots in the postwar era. The worst race riots in British history occurred in 1958. A group of white men attacked an interracial couple in Notting Hill, a suburb of London. The attack sparked several nights of violence between blacks and whites.

A heavy police presence was blamed for escalating the tensions that erupted into the riots in the Brixton area of London in 1981. Police were attacked, shops were vandalized, and hundreds of people were injured. Police arrested more than 200 people and recorded more than 700 serious crimes. A reporter also died from injuries sustained in the riots. A few days after the Brixton riots, violence erupted in the rundown Toxteth area of Liverpool, in which more than 100 buildings were burned.

Throughout 1985, British police clashed with youths, many of whom were black, in London and Birmingham. Although different incidents sparked these riots, they arose from similar conditions, such as perceptions of racial discrimination, unemployment, poverty, poor living conditions, and hostile relations with the police. The violence in Birmingham spread to Coventry and Wolverhampton in the West Midlands and the St. Paul's district of Bristol. The worst race riot in 1985 occurred at the Broadwater Farm Housing estate, where most of the residents were minority Britons, in the mostly white Tottenham district of London. Residents claimed that the police had set up a heavy police presence in Broadwater without justification. Tension brewed as many black youths felt harassed and treated unfairly. British police had to use plastic bullets to stop the rioting, which culminated in the machete murder of a police officer.

Asians rioted in the Manningham district of Bradford in 1995, vandalizing shops and cars and fighting police. Britain's 2001 race riots occurred initially in April in Bradford. The riots, which escalated, were the result of rising tensions between white and Asian Britons. The most serious outbreak took place in Oldham in May. A fight between a white teenager and an Asian teenager escalated into three nights of pitched battles and street riots. In June, rioting spread to Leeds and then Burnley, after a gang of white men attacked an Asian taxi driver. In July, violence raged for two nights in Bradford as gangs of white and Asian youths fought police.

Other European countries, such as Spain, have experienced recent race riots. In 2000, days of rioting broke out against African immigrants to Spain. Violence erupted after a Moroccan man was arrested on accusations that he stabbed and killed a Spanish woman. The death came two weeks after the prior arrest of a Moroccan man in connection with the deaths of two people. Hundreds of Spaniards marched through towns, shouted racist slogans, and destroyed property. The minority communities under attack requested government protection.

France, too, has been rocked by racial violence in the twenty-first century. In 2005, riots broke out in the suburbs outside of Paris after two minority youths were electrocuted while hiding from police in a power substation. The riots, which lasted for three weeks, exposed the issue of racial conflict in France. Blacks and Arabs, many of whom are Muslim and from immigrant backgrounds, have been forced to remain in the most disadvantaged neighborhoods. In 2007, riots broke out in Villiers-le-Bel, located north of Paris, after two minority youths whose families hailed from Morocco and Senegal were killed in a motorbike crash with a police car. Gangs attacked police and burned cars and buildings. The French government attributed the riots to several causes, including poverty, unemployment, and crime, yet failed to address the issue of racial tensions.

Such incidents are not confined to Britain, Spain, or France. Similar incidents of racial violence, often directed against immigrants, have occurred across Europe, including Italy, Belgium, Luxembourg, Germany, Sweden, Denmark, and Russia. Increasing incidents of urban violence along racial lines is forcing Europe to confront the issue of racism and redefine its own identity.

See also: Britain, Blacks in; Civil Rights Movement in Twentieth-Century Britain; France, Blacks in; Illegal African Immigration to Europe; May 10 Holiday; Notting Hill Carnival.

Further Reading: Hargreaves, Alec. *Immigration, Race, and Ethnicity in Contemporary France.* New York: Routledge, 1995; Rowe, Michael. *The Racialisation of Disorder in Twentieth Century Britain.* Aldershot, UK: Ashgate, 1998.

Eric Martone

Rastafarianism

Rastafarianism is a comprehensive term for a set of discursive principles that has laid the foundation of the Rastafari movement, a religiopolitico movement, which emerged in Jamaica among working-class and peasant blacks in the early 1930s.

The central belief that unites the professed, or those who identify themselves as Rastafarians (also known as "Rastas" or "Rasta wo/man"), is that Haile Selassie I, the former emperor of Ethiopia, is God incarnate. Rastafarians refer to him as *Jah* and consider him the Messiah promised in the Bible. Rastafarianism was named after his precoronation name, Tafari Makonen, with a prefix "Ras" (which can be translated as "head" or "duke"). Upon his accession to the throne in 1930, the Ethiopian Orthodox Church conferred on him the name Haile Selassie, meaning "Power of the Trinity," and the biblical titles "King of Kings, Lords of Lords" and "Conquering Lion of the Tribe of Judah." Selassie was considered to have personified these scriptural statuses and the indicated prophecies.

Why Rastafarianism emerged within the **African Diaspora** among British-ruled Jamaicans remains open to interpretation. Ethiopianism had been common among working-class blacks through the denomination's missionary work, which, like Baptist sects, actively recruited members from current and former slaves. Ethiopianism is a theological tradition in Christianity and is based on biblical references to Ethiopia and the assumption that Ethiopia is the "promised land" for Africans and members of the African Diaspora. Selassie appeared before the deprived African Diaspora in Jamaica as the sovereign of Ethiopia, the only fully independent African nation, as well as the "savior" leading them to "Ethiopia," a home, or Zion, to which they could return.

In Jamaica, the introduction of Ethiopianism did not cause, but rather gave momentum to, the ongoing idealization of Africa. This idealization began within secluded Maroon communities and provided the ideological basis for recurring slave revolts. Before the emergence of Rastafarianism, Marcus Garvey, a Jamaican-born publisher and entrepreneur, had already begun equating enslaved blacks with an African Diaspora and the "promised land" with Africa as part of a mass repatriation movement in Jamaica and the United States.

Many Rastafarians refuse to use the term *Rastafarianism*, and instead use *livity*, which is derived from "divinity" and "living." The term indicates their belief that a way of life is more important than doctrine. Livity consists of, but is not limited to, several components: living on a diet of *ital* food approved of according to laws of the Old Testament (basically vegan or vegetarian diet, characterized by the exclusion of "scavenger" meats, such as pork and shellfish); smoking cannabis, popularly known as *ganja* or "herb," which they consider a sacrament that cleans the body and mind; wearing dreadlocks (often simply called "locks" or "dreads") out of their belief that it is legitimized by the Bible; and symbolic use of the three colors of the Ethiopian flag (red, gold, and green) to sanctify the body and space. Rastafarianism, both as an ideology and as a lifestyle, has already spread throughout much of the world, largely through Jamaican migration and interest generated by Jamaican-born reggae music.

See also: Afro-Caribbean Music in Britain; Black British; Britain, Blacks in; Colonies in the Caribbean, British.

Further Reading: Edmonds, Ennis Barrington. *Rastafari: From Outcasts to Culture Bearers.* New York: Oxford University Press, 2002.

Teruyuki Tsuji

Remond, Sarah Parker (1826–1894)

Sarah Parker Remond was an African American abolitionist and antislavery campaigner in Europe during the nineteenth century. An upholder of human values and a lifelong messenger against segregation, she impressed people on both sides of the Atlantic.

Remond was born on June 6, 1826, in Salem, Massachusetts, to John and Nancy Remond, who were both free. Remond faced racial discrimination along with her family, and they left for Newport, Rhode Island. In 1841, the Salem schools were desegregated and the family returned.

Like her family members, Remond joined the crusade against slavery. Her reading habits and listening to speeches helped her become an antislavery lecturer. She worked for the American Anti-slavery Society and in 1856 toured New York as a speaker against slavery. Her eloquence drew crowds in Massachusetts, Michigan, Ohio, and Pennsylvania. Remond showed concern for blacks, not only in her own country, but also abroad. She wrote in the *Daily News* in 1856 criticizing attacks on blacks in Britain after the rising in Jamaica. Her oratory, determination, dedication, and ability to raise funds resulted in an invitation to Britain.

Remond sailed from Boston on the steamer *Arabia* on December 28, 1858, and reached Liverpool on January 12, 1859. Her first meeting was in the Tuckerman Institute on January 21, 1859, where she spoke forcefully about racial prejudice and brutal treatment of black women. Remond received a rousing welcome from the white women and the abolitionists present. In her tour, she drew crowds and raised funds for the cause of antislavery. Between 1859 and 1861, she addressed 45 meetings in 18 cities in England, 3 in Scotland, and 4 in Ireland. Remond attended the Bedford College for Ladies in London from 1859 to 1861, studying English literature, French, Latin, and history.

During the American Civil War, Remond lectured on behalf of the Unionists. She again undertook tours raising funds to help freed African Americans. She took active part in the deliberations of organizations such as the Emancipation Society and the Freedman's Aid Association of London. The Ladies' London Emancipation Society published her work, *The Negroes and Anglo-Africans as Freedmen and Soldiers* (1864).

Remond left Britain in 1866 and lived in Florence, Italy, for the rest of her life. She enrolled in the Santa Maria Nuova Hospital of Florence as a student at the age of 42. She became a physician and, in 1877, she married Lazzaro Pinto. The later years of her life is shrouded in mystery, except that she met her old friend **Frederick Douglass** (1817–1895), a fellow African-American antislavery crusader, in 1887. Remond died on December 13, 1894 and was buried in Rome.

See also: Abolition of Slavery, British; Britain, Blacks in; Italy, Blacks in.

Further Reading: Bogin, Ruth. *Sarah Parker Remond: Black Abolitionist from Salem*. Salem, MA: Essex Institute, 1974; Loewenberg, Bert, and Ruth Bogin. *Black Women in Nineteenth-Century American Life*. University Park: Pennsylvania State University Press, 1976; Lyman, Darryl. *Great African-American Women*. New York: Gramercy, 2000; Peterson, Carla. *Doers of the Word: African-American Women Speakers and Writers in the North (1830–1880)*. New York: Oxford University Press, 1995; Remond, Sarah Parker. *The Negroes and Anglo-Africans as Freedmen and Soldiers*. London: Emily Faithfull, 1864; Yellin, Jean, and John van Horne. *The Abolitionist Sisterhood: Women's Political Culture in Antebellum America*. Ithaca: Cornell University Press, 1994.

Patit Paban Mishra

Renaissance, Blacks in the

Blacks were in England for more than 1,000 years before the Renaissance, possibly as early as 235 C.E., as slaves, soldiers, and officers. The engravings on an altar excavated in 1934 documents that a division of African soldiers stationed near Carlisle defended Hadrian's Wall. These African soldiers came to England with the ancient Roman army. This division of soldiers is not the only evidence of an early black presence in England. Skeletal remains of a young African girl that dates from 1000 C.E. has been found and archeological excavations during the 1950s unearthed 350 human remains at York, several of which are believed to be those of black Africans. There is no evidentiary trace of blacks in England after the first millennium for several centuries, and when they reappear in the early sixteenth century, they are commodities of the modern slave trade.

During the Renaissance, blacks were brought to many European countries, either directly from Africa or by way of the Caribbean, as musicians, court performers, servants, and slaves. They are found in such European countries as Scotland, England, Portugal, Spain, and Italy. It is not until the eighteenth century that blacks began to record their own histories in Europe; therefore an examination of blacks in the Renaissance relies largely on royal proclamations, court documents, parish records, diaries, advertisements for the sale of slaves, and notices to recuperate those who had fled. The commodification of those of black African descent as slaves suggests that the Renaissance was not a renaissance for blacks in Europe.

The Renaissance is the humanistic revival of classical art, architecture, literature, and learning. It originated in Italy in the fourteenth century and later spread throughout Europe, arriving in England by the sixteenth century. The Renaissance was the age of Copernicus (1473–1543) and Galileo (1564–1642), who advanced the theory that Earth and the other planets revolve around the sun, disrupting the Ptolemaic system of astronomy. The Renaissance was also the age of Shakespeare (1564–1616). This was also the era not only of the new science and incredible literary output, but also of geographical explorations. In 1492, Christopher Columbus sailed west to find a new commercial route to the East and, in the process, "discovered" a new continent. The discovery opened the floodgates for European's unprecedented economic exploitation of this new world and Africa, often cruel and devastating to the native peoples. Europe was breathlessly transforming itself from a system of feudal states into dominant naval and mercantile nations. While innovative art and architecture, and new learning and science, spread light on old superstitions, the influx of immense wealth and new products, such as coffee, tea, and chocolate, fueled the ever-increasing demand for slave labor.

The earliest evidence of a black presence in Britain during the Renaissance is found in Scotland. Early in the sixteenth century, Scottish records document a small group of Africans at the court of King James IV of Scotland. These Africans were probably stolen Portuguese slaves. James authorized the seizure of Portuguese ships to recoup the loss of a Scottish ship to the Portuguese; these slaves were taken along with other booty. Although slavery had not ceased during the Middle Ages, only a small number of Africans were scattered across Europe. At the beginning of the fourteenth century, however, the demand for black slaves increased substantially. The Bubonic Plague, which devastated the labor force in such countries as Italy in 1348, fueled the demand for slaves in many European countries. These slaves came from such diverse areas as Africa, Spain, the Balkans, Constantinople, and Cyprus. Portugal and Spain dominated the traffic in African slaves. Among this group of slaves attached to James's court, one was employed as a drummer and choreographer. Court records indicate that James was especially fond of this drummer for whom he purchased clothes, paid his doctor's bills, and even gave money to his wife and child. James reportedly took this drummer with him on a pilgrimage.

The Scottish poet William Dunbar recorded the presence of several black women attached to King James's court. On December 11, 1504, one of these women was baptized. Two women are referred to as "Blak [sic] Elene" and another as "blak [sic] Margaret." Among Queen Anne's attendants was an unnamed black woman. James loved to be entertained and sometimes even took an active role in the festivities. Dunbar writes of a tournament in 1507 featuring a black knight and a black lady. James himself played the part of the knight. The role of the lady was played by an African woman. The tournament was so successful that it was repeated in 1508. The winner of the tournament was rewarded with a kiss and embrace from the black lady. She was regally dressed in a damask dress and was carried in a chair especially made for the tournament. Although this black lady was dressed in an expensive gown and had the king and other aristocratic men competing for her, her status in this event should not be forgotten. As a slave/courtesan, she could not refuse who kissed and embraced her, or indeed presumably with whom she had sexual relations.

During the Renaissance, blacks in Europe were often stripped of their real names. They were also denuded of their dignity and humanity. The unnamed black lady is a case in point. Often they were compelled to perform for the amusement of aristocratic audiences. Such is the case of four unnamed black men who danced naked in the snow as part of James's court entertainment to celebrate his marriage to Anne. The four young men died later of pneumonia.

In England, blacks also played a part in court entertainment. At the aristocratic courts of King Henry VII (1457–1509) and his son King Henry VIII (1491–1547), records document the presence of a black musician. Although his real name has not survived, he was called John Blanke. Another popular form of aristocratic entertainment was the court masque. James VI of Scotland succeeded Elizabeth I to the throne of England where he became James I. During his reign, the masque became popular at the English court. Written at the request of Queen Anne, *The Masque of Blackness* and *The Masque of Beauty* featured the queen herself and other aristocratic ladies performing with their faces and arms disguised with black paint. Other actual black performers also participated. These masques celebrated the supremacy of whiteness.

The conditions that brought blacks to England as slaves were economics and avarice. During the reign of Queen Mary I (1516–1558), England barely participated in the slave trade. This practice was to change during the monarchy of her half-sister Elizabeth I (1533–1603). The first English man to profit from the slave trade was John Lok, who, in 1552, sold some slaves he captured in Guinea. Three years later, five Africans arrived in England. Although England was not involved officially in the slave trade, it wanted a share of the profitable trade in African gold and ivory. John Lok desired access to this market, and for this purpose, he brought the Africans to England to learn English. On their return to Shama (now part of present-day Ghana), they were to act as interpreters. John Hawkins, however, has the dubious distinction of being the first Englishman to fully traffic in African slaves. Although Elizabeth publicly denounced Hawkins's abduction of Africans and their transportation to other countries without their consent, she nevertheless financed his second voyage in 1564–1565 to secure slaves. Through such voyages, England's black slave population steadily increased from the 1570s. They were engaged in English households primarily as servants, but some were prostitutes and the sexual partners of wealthy Englishmen, as well as court entertainers.

In 1596, and again in 1601, Elizabeth responded to the growing number of "divers [sic] blackmoores [sic]" with deportation orders; however, neither of these orders was successful. It was fashionable among England's wealthiest citizens to have a black slave or two. They simply refused to give up their status symbols. Of course, not all Englishmen of the Renaissance approved of the exploitation of Africans for profit, and there are documented cases of their resistance. Also important is the extant evidence of black resistance to their ill treatment. The first documented court case involving a black slave is recorded in 1677. There is also the interesting case of a black woman who protested against her mistress's intention to ship her off to a plantation. The case ended up before the courts in 1687. In 1691, an unidentified Englishman wrote that as soon as a foreign slave sets foot in England, he or she was no longer a slave. This did not free the slave from servitude; it was not until the early eighteenth century that Lord Chief Justice Holt confirmed this idea.

The experiences of blacks in the Renaissance varied. Some were entertainers for royalty, whereas others were employed as menials in English and Scottish households. Many blacks in this period were deprived of their freedom as well as of their birth names. In some cases, black women contended not only with economic exploitation, but also with sexual victimization. Although some blacks resisted their conditions and took their fight to the courts, the conditions of blacks in the Renaissance could differ in direct relation to their geographical location. The case of a black woman protesting her impending exportation to a plantation suggests that the condition of blacks in the Caribbean and in Europe differed. In many ways, the fourteenth through seventeenth centuries was a period of economic, social, and cultural flowering; but for many others, such as nonwhites and non-Christians, this period was not a renaissance.

See also: Britain, Blacks in; Colonies in Africa, British; Colonies in the Caribbean, British; Common Law, Slavery and English; Free Soil Principle; Literature, Blacks in British; *Othello*; Prostitution in Europe, Blacks and; Roman Army, Africans in the; Slave Trade, British; Slave Trade, Portuguese; Slave Trade, Spanish.

Further Reading: Earle, T. F., and K.J.P. Lowe, eds. *Black Africans in Renaissance Europe.* New York: Cambridge University Press, 2005; Fryer, Peter. *Staying Power: The History of Black People in Britain.* London: Pluto Press, 1984; Hall, Kim F. *Things of Darkness: Economies of Race and Gender in Early Modern England.* Ithaca: Cornell University Press, 1995.

Richardine G. Woodall

Representative Council of Black Associations (CRAN)

In the wake of the Paris race riots in 2005, in which youths, many of whom were black or Arab, protested against social and economic inequalities, blacks in France established the *Conseil Représentative des Associations Noires* ("Representative Council of Black Associations," CRAN). The council, which had been in the planning stages before the riots, united about 60 organizations to form a common front against perceived racism and the lack of (positive) representation in the public sphere. Some of its leading members include Patrick Lozes, politician Christiane Taubira, human rights activist Fodé Sylla, and scholars Pap Ndiaye and Francoise Vergès.

In the early twentieth century, France was perceived by African American intellectuals as a haven from the racism that they encountered in the United States. Indeed, the topic of race emerged as a frequent topic of French intellectual debate. The French debate on racism, however, revolved around French conduct toward its Arab and black African colonies as well as the status of its Pacific territories. After the independence of France's colonies, the topic of race receded from the public arena.

CRAN argues that contemporary France does not adhere to the principles of "liberty, equality, and fraternity" that are the foundations of French republicanism. Many members of CRAN challenge the French model of assimilation, arguing that they can be both black and French. CRAN draws its inspiration from 1960s African American Civil Rights leader **Martin Luther King Jr.** and advocates an American-like policy of affirmative action to support black employment.

Leaders of CRAN have been developing a strategy to realize its goals. The group hopes to mobilize France's black population into a cohesive pressure group or voting bloc. More than 130 local black civic associations make up its membership across France. The group regularly protests perceived racist images or descriptions in the media such as television. It has also protested the way standard French dictionaries define "colonialism" and laws prohibiting the collection of racial and ethnic statistics.

See also: Artists in Europe, African American; Authors in Europe, African American; Colonies in Africa, French; Colonies in the Caribbean, French; France, Blacks in; May 10 Holiday; Race Riots in Europe; Slave Trade, French.

Further Reading: Thomas, Dominic. *Black France: Colonialism, Immigration, and Transnationalism.* Bloomington: Indiana University Press, 2006; Winders, James. *Paris Africain: Rhythms of the African Diaspora.* New York: Palgrave Macmillan, 2006.

Eric Martone

Rhineland Blacks

The armistice after World War I and the Treaty of Versailles gave France and other victorious powers the right to occupy some western provinces of Germany for a limited number of years. The French army of occupation stationed in the Rhineland included soldiers from North Africa and some black soldiers from West Africa (*tirailleurs sénégalais*). These soldiers became the focus of a slander campaign aiming to discredit the use of black troops by the French army and, to some extent, the French occupation of German lands in general. This campaign triggered a strong response, not only in Germany itself, but also in Britain, the United States, Italy, and the Vatican. Not the least a result of this international pressure, the French army agreed to withdraw its black army units from Germany by 1923, although a few black soldiers remained in North African units. The public campaign against the black soldiers depicted the blacks as uncontrollable rapists and perverts. That most accusations remained unproven did nothing to dent the credibility of the campaign. Children from liaisons between black soldiers and German women, called *Rheinlandbastarde* ("Rhineland Bastards"), were later sterilized by the Nazis. The term *Rhineland blacks* refers to the children of African soldiers and German women, regardless of whether the fathers were from black Africa or from North Africa.

Of the 95,000 French soldiers stationed in Germany's westernmost provinces after World War I, there were approximately 20,000 people of color. Most of these soldiers came from North Africa, and only a minority were black *tirailleurs sénégalais*. The French army, which itself did not recognize African soldiers as equal to white French soldiers, at first attempted to establish bordellos with women drafted from Africa; but this program failed miserably because not enough volunteers from Africa could be found, and because African soldiers preferred to use the same German bordellos as white French soldiers. Soldiers of color and German women began relationships, some of which led to marriage. The contacts between Africans and German women triggered much outrage, inspired partly by British journalist E. D. Morel (1873–1924), whose pamphlet *The Horror on the Rhine* claimed that the black troops stationed in Germany were committing outrages and should be withdrawn. The allegations of rape soon became the centerpiece of a massive German press campaign against the "black horror on the Rhine" that enjoyed widespread public support and received funding from the German government. This campaign reflected the German fear of racial miscegenation and the spread of tropical diseases, and it also aimed at discrediting the French army and its occupation of German lands. The smear campaign against the African soldiers usually implied that sexual contacts between Africans and German women were involuntary and emphatically denied that most of these relations were consensual. In fact, the German press campaign notoriously failed to report that almost all of the alleged outrages could not be proven, and that the African soldiers perpetrated proportionally far fewer crimes than those by white French or prewar German units stationed in the Rhineland.

The number of biracial children from the Rhineland occupation was never established with precision, but estimates range from 380 to 800. Already during the Weimar Republic in post-World War I Germany, government officials talked about the alleged dangers these children presented for the "purity" of the German race once they reached puberty. Believing that biracial people were of lesser genetic value, but more likely to have more children than "pure" Germans, some government officials saw the Rhineland blacks as the start of a racial epidemic that would weaken the German nation. One influential proposal was to sterilize these children, but it proved impossible to do this legally. The radical right-wing press suggested that Jews in France had deliberately sent Africans to the Rhine to cause a racial "epidemic" in Germany.

Having come to power, the Nazis decided to do something about the threat allegedly emanating from the Rhineland blacks. In 1933, Prussian Interior Minister Hermann Goering ordered the official registration of all mixed-race children from the Rhineland. On the basis of these data, racial hygienists began their dubious research into the believed racial inferiority of the children. If the biracial children showed severe hereditary illnesses, they could be forcefully sterilized on the basis of a Nazi law passed in July 1933. The experts did their utmost to have their prejudices about the racial "inferiority" of these children confirmed, but they could not classify them as hereditarily ill. Legal sterilization therefore was not possible. An alternative measure was expulsion to another country, but it was dismissed as impractical because it was likely to trigger negative foreign reactions. Finally, a special commission of the German Secret State Police was formed with the purpose of sterilizing the Rhineland blacks illegally. It is possible, although not proven, that Nazi dictator Adolf Hitler had the decisive say in this matter. From 1937 onward, the biracial children from the Rhineland that the German administration had tracked down were sterilized. The mothers often opposed this measure, but the threat of deportation to a concentration camp usually overcame their resistance. German physicians, although probably aware of the illegality of the program, collaborated. Some of the "Rhineland blacks" were later drafted into the German army. The sterilization of the "Rhineland blacks," although affecting only a small number of people, is generally recognized as an important aspect of Nazi Germany's effort to "purify" the race through a broad range of policies from expulsion to sterilization, euthanasia, and genocide. A concise and influential book by German historian Rainer Pommerin (*Sterilisierung der Rheinlandbastarde*), published in 1979, brought this Nazi policy to public attention.

See also: French Army, Blacks in the; Germany, Blacks in; Nazis and Blacks in Europe; Scientific Racism; World War I, Black Participation in.

Further Reading: Campt, Tina. *Other Germans: Black Germans and the Politics of Race, Gender, and Memory in the Third Reich.* Ann Arbor: University of Michigan Press, 2004; Le Naour, Jean-Yves. *La honte noire. L'Allemagne et les troupes coloniales françaises 1914–1945.* Paris: Hachette Littérature, 2003; Marks, Sally. "Black Watch on the Rhine: A Study in Propaganda,

Prejudice and Prurience." *European Studies Review* 13 (1983): 297–334; Maß, Sandra. "Das Trauma des weißen Mannes. Afrikanische Kolonialsoldaten in propagandistischen Texten, 1914–1923." *L'Homme. Zeitschrift für feministische Geschichtswissenschaft* 12:1 (2001): 11–33; Nelson, Keith. "'The Black Horror on the Rhine': Race as a Factor in Post-World War I Diplomacy." *Journal of Modern History* 42:4 (1970): 606–627; Pommerin, Rainer. *Sterilisierung der Rheinlandbastarde. Das Schicksal einer farbigen deutschen Minderheit 1918–1937*. Düsseldorf: Droste, 1979; Reinders, Robert C. "Racialism on the Left: E. D. Morel and the 'Black Horror' on the Rhine." *International Review of Social History* 13 (1968): 1–28.

Raffael Scheck

Richmond, Bill (1763–1829)

Bill Richmond was a former African slave in America who executed Revolutionary War hero Nathan Hale. He was born a slave in New York in 1763. His parents were slaves from Georgia. Richmond became a servant of Lord Percy, the Duke of Richmond (later Duke of Northumberland), from whom he gained his name. Lord Percy was then commanding general of the British forces in New York during the American Revolution. Richmond came to Lord Percy's attention after a tavern brawl involving Richmond and some British soldiers. Lord Percy arranged contests for Richmond against British soldiers in New York as entertainment for guests. Richmond was in Manhattan when Nathan Hale, the American revolutionary agent regarded as the first spy for the United States, was captured by the British in September 1776. The British declared Hale a spy, and Richmond, at the age of 13, was chosen to be the hangman at the execution at the Park of Artillery (modern-day 66th Street and Third Avenue). Richmond presided at the execution on September 22.

In 1777, Richmond went to England with Lord Percy and attended a school in Yorkshire before being apprenticed to a tradesman in York. Although Richmond was small in stature, he became a professional boxer in England. He developed his own style, which involved side stepping his opponents' bull rushes. During the late 1770s, his most notable victories were against boxers George Moore, Paddy Green, and Frank Mayers.

Richmond won numerous bouts in the early 1800s despite suffering a key loss to George Maddox at Wimbledon Commons in 1804. Richmond's loss to Tom Cribb, later the British and then world champion, at Hailsham, Sussex slowed his career. Richmond boxed less frequently after his loss to Cribb, although he did have several more matches. In 1809, Richmond won 100 guineas for defeating George Maddox in a match. During his boxing days, Richmond was a friend of, and later a coach for, Tom Molineaux, another freed slave from America who became a boxer.

After marrying a wealthy woman, Richmond retired from boxing and bought the Horse and Dolphin public house in Leicester Square. He also set up a boxing academy. He died in his home in London in December 1829.

See also: Britain, Blacks in.

Further Reading: Ashe, Arthur. *A Hard Road to Glory: A History of the African American Athlete in Boxing*. New York: Amistad, 1988; Rose, Alexander. *Washington's Spies: The Story of America's First Spy Ring*. New York: Random House, 2006.

Justin Corfield

Riley, Joan (1958–)

Joan Riley is a Jamaican-born writer who has become a major figure in **black British** literature since the publication of her first novel, *The Unbelonging* (1985). Her work often reflects the influence of her experience moving from the Caribbean to Britain.

Born in 1958 in Jamaica, Riley was the youngest of eight children and grew up in a working-class family. At school, she studied the major works of British literature and moved to England, studying at the University of Sussex. She graduated in 1979, and five years later, completed a graduate degree at the University of London. Riley's move from the Caribbean to England influenced her dramatically, and most of her writing deals with the experiences of West Indian (Caribbean) women moving from the West Indies to England.

Riley's first novel, *The Unbelonging* (1985), was about Hyacinth, an 11-year-old girl, who grew up in Jamaica, living with her aunt, and then left the Caribbean to join her father in Britain. There she found the life in inner-city Britain gloomy, and the title refers to her own view of herself. Hyacinth experiences isolation and racial hostility at school and violence from her father; she spends some of her time in daydreams of Jamaica or success in school in England. The story was based partly on the life of a girl that Riley had met while being a social worker, and the book became controversial because some writers perceived it as portraying a negative view of the West Indian community in Britain.

Riley's next novel, *Waiting in the Twilight* (1987), follows the life of an older migrant, Adela. A seamstress in the West Indies, Adela later tries to make a living in Britain. The title of the novel comes from Adela's reflections on her life after she has become a grandmother and has been crippled by a stroke. She has been let down by her husband and lover, but her desire to maintain her dignity at all times never fades. Riley's third novel, *Romance* (1988), is set in the London suburb of Croydon and is about two sisters who contrast their real lives with the fictional imagery associated with romance.

Riley's fourth novel, *A Kindness to the Children* (1992) details the lives of three women, one a Jamaican housewife, the second a first-generation migrant, and the third a second-generation migrant. Between them, they have a range of differing and contrasting views of postcolonial society; the failure of one of them is compared graphically to the relative success of the other two.

Riley teaches black history and culture in Britain and is involved in work for a drugs advisory service, as well as being active in campaigning for single parents. She regularly campaigns on behalf of Afro-Caribbean women in both Jamaica and Britain.

See also: Britain, Blacks in; Civil Rights Movement in Twentieth-Century Great Britain; Colonies in the Caribbean, British.

Further Reading: Riley, Joan, and Briar Wood, eds. *Leave to Stay: Stories of Exile and Belonging.* London: Virago, 1996; Stringer, Jenny, ed. The *Oxford Companion to Twentieth-Century Literature in English.* New York: Oxford University Press, 1996.

Justin Corfield

Rio Branco Law of Free Birth

The Rio Branco Law of Free Birth (also known as the Law of the Free Womb and the September 28 Law), which was passed on September 28, 1871, aimed to reform the institution of slavery in Brazil by mandating a process of gradual emancipation. The law's main provision granted freedom to the newborn children of slaves.

Although Brazil had long faced pressure from England on the slavery question, the violence surrounding the ending of slavery in the United States, together with the abolition of slavery throughout Latin America and the European colonies, brought a renewed urgency to the issue. Responding to an 1866 letter from the French *Comité pour l'Abolition de l'Esclavage* ("Committee for the Abolition of Slavery") that had urged the freeing of all Brazilian slaves, the government relayed the Brazilian emperor Pedro II's commitment to emancipation and his plans to enact changes as soon as Brazil had ended its participation in the Paraguayan War. The war itself had prompted new questions about the morality of the system, as many slaves had been granted freedom in exchange for their service in battle. Eventually, after several changes in ministry leadership after the war, the Viscount of Rio Branco, a conservative politician from the northeastern state of Bahia, pushed through a proposal for reform.

The Rio Branco Law stipulated that children born to slaves would continue to work for their mother's master until reaching the age of 21. Masters had the option of turning slave children over to the state at the age of eight and receiving indemnification for the expense of raising them. The law also granted slaves the right to a *peculio*, or personal savings, that could be used for buying freedom; established the creation of an emancipation fund to free a select number of slaves; freed all slaves belonging to the imperial government; mandated an official national slave registry; and created provisions for young slaves abandoned or turned over to the government by their owners.

The Rio Branco Law set off a heated debate in the Chamber of Deputies and galvanized public debate on the issue of slavery. Slave owners believed the law failed to compensate them sufficiently for substantial loss of property and feared it would usher in a rapid end to slavery. Supporters of abolition described the proposal as "Herod's Law," arguing that it would result in widespread infanticide, as slave owners would have little financial incentive to care for the newborn children. They also criticized the law for its failure to grant freedom to those who had already spent their lives in bondage. Much debated was the status and fate of the newborn children, who became know as *ingênuos* and how they might be affected by the experience of living their early lives under slavery. The law and its failures would later become a focus of the renewed abolitionist struggle of the 1880s. Brazil finally abolished slavery in 1888.

See also: Abolition of Slavery, Portuguese; Moret Law, Spanish; Slave Trade, Portuguese.

Further Reading: Chalhoub, Sidney. "The Politics of Silence: Race and Citizenship in Nineteenth-Century Brazil." *Slavery and Abolition* 27:1 (2006): 73–87; Conrad, Robert. *The Destruction of Brazilian Slavery 1850–1888*. Berkeley: University of California Press, 1972; Nabuco, Joaquim. *Abolitionism: The Brazilian Antislavery Struggle*. trans. and ed. Robert Conrad. Urbana: University of Illinois Press, 1977.

Jessica Callaway Smolin

Roar

Roar was an internationally syndicated television series developed by Shaun Cassidy and Ron Koslow comprised of 13 episodes that aired on the Fox network in the United States in 1997. The television series detailed the adventures of a Celtic prince named Conor in ancient Ireland circa 400 c.e. and his band of followers in their attempts to unite the clans to defeat the invading Roman army. The show was significant for featuring a black African character named Tully (played by African American actor Alonzo Greer) as a member of Conor's band, thereby depicting blacks in Ireland during ancient times.

Tully was introduced to Conor as part of a group of displaced slaves and outcasts under the protection of Galen, a wise man who possessed the secrets of magic and power. Galen serves as a mentor to Conor after the young prince is orphaned and helps him hear the "roar" of the land and of the people, a voice that echoes through every living creature and is the power of life. After Galen's disappearance, several of those under his protection, including Tully, join Conor in his efforts against the Romans. Tully, an apprentice to Galen, is depicted as headstrong and arrogant, but such characteristics are attributed to his youth. Tully served as an equal within the band and experienced no form of racism within ancient Ireland. The inclusion of the character was to appeal to a multicultural society and reflect modern Western civilization. Historically, the presence of Africans in ancient Ireland was minimal at best. Most of those of African descent in the ancient British Isles arrived with the Romans, either as slaves or from dispatched units of soldiers from their provinces in North Africa. Furthermore, although the Romans interacted with Ireland, they never launched a proper invasion.

The series launched the career of film star Heath Ledger (who played the role of Conor) and won a Golden Reel Award (1998) for Best Sound Editing, an Award of Distinction (1999) from the Australian Cinematographers Society, and an Emmy Award nomination (1998) for Outstanding Music Composition for a Series.

See also: Britain, Blacks in; Ireland, Blacks in.

Further Viewing: *Roar—The Complete Series* (DVD). 3 disc set. Universal Studios, 2006.

Eric Martone

Robeson, Paul (1898–1976)

Paul Robeson was an African American concert singer and theater and film actor whose career spanned more than 50 years. Renowned for his activism in the United States and abroad, Robeson was a controversial figure throughout his life and remains the subject of critical interest for both his artistic achievements and social investments.

Robeson was born in Princeton, New Jersey, in 1898. He graduated Phi Beta Kappa from Rutgers University in 1919, the valedictorian of his class, and the first African American man to be named all-American in college football. In 1921, he married Eslanda Cardozo Goode, known as "Essie," a pathology laboratory technician at

Presbyterian Hospital. Robeson played professional football while enrolled at Columbia Law School, from which he graduated in 1923.

After a brief time in a law firm, Robeson embarked on an acting career, starring most notably in Eugene O'Neill's *The Emperor Jones* and *All God's Chillun Got Wings* with the Provincetown Players in New York City in 1924, the latter of which received considerable media attention because of its portrayal of interracial marriage. In 1925, Robeson starred in the London production of *The Emperor Jones* and returned to Europe for a concert tour in 1927. He settled in London until 1939. The son of an escaped slave who became a minister, Robeson achieved wider fame through his critically acclaimed performances of African American spirituals and secular traditionals before a global public. He immortalized the song "Ol' Man River" with the London company of *Show Boat* in the late 1920s and again on Broadway in 1932 and in Los Angeles in 1940. His success in London led to his legendary portrayal of Othello in 1930, a role that he revisited in the United States from 1942 to 1945 with great acclaim.

Robeson's film career began with the 1925 Oscar Micheaux film, *Body and Soul*, followed by the European *Close-Up* group's avant-garde film, *Borderline*, filmed in Switzerland in 1930. In 1933, he filmed *The Emperor Jones*, his first role in a sound film. This was followed by the 1934 *Sanders of the River*, of which Robeson was deeply critical because of its ultimate procolonial stance. He appeared in the film version of *Show Boat* in 1935 and *Song of Freedom* in 1936. In 1937, he was featured in *King Solomon's Mines*, *Big Fella*, and *Jericho*, which was filmed in Cairo. In *The Proud Valley*, released in 1940, Robeson championed the cause of Welsh miners.

At the completion of *The Proud Valley*, Robeson left London and returned to New York at the onset of World War II in Europe. He filmed *Tales of Manhattan* in 1941, attempting to call attention to the difficulties faced by black sharecroppers. Frustrated with Hollywood stereotyping, Robeson served as narrator for the film *Native Land*, a 1942 documentary championing civil liberties. In 1945, the NAACP awarded him the prestigious Springarn Medal.

A gifted linguist, Robeson mastered Russian and German, and in the early 1930s, he began to study African languages and developed an interest in African cultures and societies. He was committed to using his fame in the service of social change, championing the causes of labor, the lower classes, and oppressed peoples worldwide. In 1934, the Russian filmmaker Sergei Eisenstein invited Robeson to the Soviet Union. In 1935, he performed in *Stevedore*, a political play featuring working-class oppression and championing interracial worker solidarity. He appeared in **C.L.R. James**'s play about **Toussaint L'Ouverture**, *Black Majesty*, in London in 1936. In 1937, he publicly supported the Republican government of Spain and spoke out against the spread of fascism and the Japanese aggression toward China, and continued to speak out for workers' causes. In 1938, Robeson visited Spain and sang for soldiers he met, a trip that would mark the intensification of his political activism. He subsequently performed in the left-sympathizing play *Plant in the Sun* at London's Unity Theatre.

Although Robeson never officially joined the Communist Party, his antifascist activism caught the critical attention of American FBI director J. Edgar Hoover, ultimately leading to his appearance before the Tenney Committee in 1946 and leading to the lifting of his passport by the State Department in 1950. The right to travel was not restored to him until 1958. He appeared before the House Un-American Activities Committee on June 12, 1956, and defiantly told the committee, "I am not being tried for whether I am a Communist, I am being tried for fighting for the rights of my people, who are still second class citizens in this U.S. of America." After the return of his passport, he performed *Othello* in Stratford in 1959. In the early 1960s, he was plagued with depression and poor health from which he never fully recovered. He died in New York in 1976.

See also: Britain, Blacks in; Film, Blacks in European; Soviet Propaganda, Blacks and; Spanish Civil War, African Americans in the.

Further Reading: Duberman, Martin. *Paul Robeson.* New York: Alfred A. Knopf, 1988; Robeson, Eslanda Goode. *Paul Robeson, Negro.* New York: Harper, 1930; Robeson, Paul. *Here I Stand.* New York: Othello Associates, 1958.

Allyson Nadia Field

Robin Hood Legend, Blacks in the

The Robin Hood legend, which details the adventures of a band of outlaws who steal from the rich to assist the poor in medieval England, is an evolving narrative within American and British literature, and characters have been added over the centuries to Robin Hood's band. For example, the characters of Maid Marian and Friar Tuck, both modern fixtures within the outlaw band, were not components of the original ballads, which are the oldest versions of the Robin Hood tales. During the twentieth century, an additional character was added to the Robin Hood legend in the form of a Muslim. This character has no standardized name, but has quickly become a fixture within the Robin Hood legend. Azeem, a character from the 1991 Warner Brothers blockbuster film *Robin Hood: Prince of Thieves*, is the most famous version of this character and is also significant for being portrayed as a black Muslim from Africa.

The first mainstream depiction of a Muslim character in Robin Hood's band emerged in the British television series *Robin of Sherwood*, which aired from 1984 to 1986 on the British station ITV. The series was developed by Richard Carpenter. The Muslim character, Nasir, was depicted as an Arab, rather than an African **Moor,** and was portrayed by British actor Mark Ryan. In the series, Nasir worked as a professional assassin in Palestine before his capture by a European crusader and practitioner of black magic named Baron Simon de Belleme. Belleme placed a spell over Nasir that forced him to do his bidding on their arrival in England. In the pilot episode, Nasir is freed from the spell when Robin Hood kills Belleme. Nasir, grateful at being set free and having great respect for Robin's prowess in battle, decides to join Robin's band of outlaws in Sherwood Forest. Nasir appeared in all 26 episodes of the series, remaining a mysterious and quiet character, distinguishable by always battling with two swords at the same time.

According to Carpenter, the character of Nasir was supposed to die in the pilot episode, but the popularity of actor Mark Ryan among the cast and crew inspired Carpenter to retain the character and have him join Robin's band. The series's developers were wary of the audience's and ITV regulator's reaction to a Muslim within Robin's band, as no character had existed previously in any of the original tales or screen adaptations.

The inclusion of the character, however, reflected the changing multicultural society within Britain, resulting in the revamping of a literary tradition to meet the needs of and reflect modern society. The series was a ratings success and almost every major popular depiction of Robin Hood on television or film since this production has included a Muslim character in the outlaw band, making *Robin of Sherwood* one of the most influential depictions of the Robin Hood legends in recent history.

Robin Hood: Prince of Thieves, which starred American actor Kevin Costner in the title role, drew much of its influence from *Robin of Sherwood*. In the film, Azeem, played by African American actor Morgan Freeman, is rescued by Robin Hood, who left England to fight in the Crusades, when they break free from a prison in the Middle East. Azeem believes that he owes his life to Robin; consequently, he devotes his life to Robin's service. The two return to England, where Robin discovers that his father has been murdered over false accusations of practicing black magic. In his attempt to reclaim his lands, Robin is outlawed and Azeem joins Robin's band as his primary confidant. The sheriff of Nottingham, the villain, has an evil sorceress who seems to have a connection to Azeem, who vanquishes her in the film's finale. Since the production of *Robin Hood: Prince of Thieves*, the Muslim character in Robin's band has often been depicted as black.

A unique take on the Robin Hood legend drawing inspiration from *Robin of Sherwood* and later from *Robin Hood: Prince of Thieves* was *Maid Marian and her Merry Men*, a children's television series that aired on the BBC from 1989 to 1994. The show was a comic retelling of the legend, delegating Marian as the head of the band while depicting Robin as an incompetent former tailor. The series, written by British comic Tony Robinson, was a popular family show. Like many British television programs, there was substantial social and pop cultural commentary interwoven within the episodes. Many of the plots spoofed popular films of the era, including *Jurassic Park*. The variation of the black character in the series, named Barrington, was played by British actor Danny John-Jules. The character, known as the "Rasta" merry man from the British Caribbean, would often rap during the episode's songs. Much of the humor was anachronistic. Barington also served as a semi-omniscient narrator in several episodes, similar to the character of Alan-a-Dale in previous versions of the legend.

The BBC launched a series entitled *Robin Hood* in 2006. The British television series includes, yet modifies, the Muslim member of Robin Hood's band. The character Djaq is a dark-skinned Muslim slave brought to England by the villainous Sheriff of Nottingham to work in a mine. Djaq is unique for being a woman and is portrayed by British actress Anjali Jay, who is of South Asian descent. Djaq helps Robin free her fellow slaves and destroy the sheriff's mine using her knowledge of alchemy before joining his band of outlaws. During the series, both Allan-a-Dale and Will Scarlett, two members of Robin's band, develop romantic feelings toward her. The character of Djaq again reveals the changing society of modern British society, in which a character of another race and gender is depicted as an equal and suitable romantic interest for her medieval English (and white) companions. Such a depiction reflects a modern Britain coming to terms with its colonial past and increasingly diverse society.

The adoption of a black Muslim character in British adaptations of Robin Hood has also spread to America. The success of *Robin Hood: Prince of Thieves* inspired a parody from director Mel Brooks entitled *Robin Hood: Men in Tights*. The 1993 film emphasized the role of the black characters, Asneeze, portrayed by African American actor Isaac Hayes, and his son, Achoo, played by African American comedian Dave Chappelle. Asneeze and Achoo are parodies of Azeem. When Asneeze arrives in England, he seeks out his son, Achoo, who is in England as an African exchange student. Much of the humor revolving around the two characters was anachronistic and focuses on stereotypes of African American men. In one scene, Achoo parodies American civil rights figure **Malcolm X** in a speech to rally Robin's outlaw band. The film also depicts Robin's men rapping and indulging in behavior stereotypical of the modern African American archetype in popular culture.

The New Adventures of Robin Hood, an American television series that aired from 1997 to 1999 on the Turner Network (TNT), also incorporated a black Muslim character in Robin Hood's band. The character, Kemal, debuted during the series's second season and was portrayed by African American actor and martial arts expert Hakim Alston. The character of Kemal, both African and a master warrior, clearly derived its inspiration from the earlier characters if Azeem and Nasir. The inclusion of a black Muslim character in the popular American series further solidified the role as a fixture in the Robin Hood legend. Such adaptations for modern audiences reveal the versatility of the Robin Hood legend and its ability to transcend time.

See also: Black British; Britain, Blacks in; Civil Rights Movement in Twentieth-Century Great Britain; Colonies in Africa, British; Colonies in the Caribbean, British; Rastafarianism.

Further Reading: Carpenter, Richard. *Robin of Sherwood*. New York: Penguin, 1985; Knight, Stephen. *Robin Hood: A Mythic Biography*. Ithaca: Cornell University Press, 2003; Pearce, Garth. *Robin Hood: Prince of Thieves—The Official Movie Book*. New York: Mallard Press, 1991.

Eric Martone

Roman Army, Africans in the

Africans played a significant role in the expansion of ancient Rome beyond Italy. The success of the Carthaginian army from North Africa on Roman soil and in other theaters of the **Punic Wars** led to changes in the Roman army. Ultimately, the incorporation of African fighters in Roman forces strengthened the Roman army, as the army provided a pathway for social advancement for Africans.

Until the wars against Carthage, Roman warfare was conducted on land in Italy. Rome relied on superior numbers and in its ability to sustain casualties because of those numbers. The high numbers came from a pool of those who were citizens of Rome throughout the Italian regions, as well as aid from other groups who were allied to Rome and thus obligated to contribute troops.

The Carthaginians were primarily a naval power located in modern Tunisia. Their seamanship allowed them to exploit markets and natural resources lying beyond the Mediterranean into the Atlantic coasts of Africa and Europe. Citizenship was restricted to the city of Carthage. Armies were thus composed of mercenaries with Punic generals.

Among these forces were the Numidians, who lived to the south and west of Carthage (modern Tunisia and Algeria). This collection of tribal groups was best known for their ability as cavalrymen, especially their precision in hurling javelins while riding. Mauretanians from farther west (modern Morocco and western Algeria) were employed as light (without armor) infantry.

The inferiority of the Roman cavalry was evident during Hannibal's invasion of Italy at the end of the third century B.C.E. Hannibal's mounted forces composed of Numidians, Spanish tribal groups, and Celtic groups from modern France, were decisive elements in his victories.

According to Roman historian Livy (first century B.C.E.–first century C.E.), the Numidians did not have infantry. They were trained on horseback from youth. The Numidian tribal chief Syphax considered switching sides to support the Romans during the Second Punic War (221–202 B.C.E.). One of the members of the Roman delegation sent to discuss the alliance remained behind to train Numidians in Roman heavy infantry tactics and formations. Syphax was pleased enough with the results that he was credited as saying that he trusted this new infantry now as much as he trusted his cavalry. He would remain loyal to Carthage, however.

The Romans were able to buy off the leader of another of the dominant Numidian tribes, Masinissa, with the promise of being left in control of the bulk of Numidian lands and the ability to encroach on Carthaginian land at will. His cavalry played a decisive role at the Battle of Zama in 202 B.C.E., which left the Carthaginian general, Hannibal, outflanked and unable to defeat the Roman force. This battle marked the end of the Second Punic War.

The first appearance of Africans in the Roman ranks was earlier in the Second Punic War. Numidian cavalry switched from Carthaginian to Roman sides after the Roman victory near Nola in Spain in 215 B.C.E. These riders were faithful and effective fighters for the Romans throughout the war. Livy notes that "African" deserters aided the Roman siege of Iliturgi in Spain in 206 B.C.E.

Despite the success of employing these fighters, it would be nearly a century before the use of the Numidian cavalry would become commonplace. Numidians and Mauretanians also were used as light troops during the first century B.C.E. Even then, the use of all auxiliaries (units comprising non-Italian persons) was usually limited to particular campaigns in which Roman armies would negotiate with local peoples for troops and horsemen. Numidian cavalry were an exception, as they were used all over the empire. At the very earliest, it was not until the reign of the Roman Emperor Augustus (21 B.C.E.–14 C.E.) that auxiliaries became permanent components of standing armies. Under Augustus and those who followed, auxiliary troops would be rewarded with citizenship and land after 25 years of service. This was the primary path to citizenship for Africans of indigenous birth (those who were not descendents of Italian colonists or lived in cities that were granted citizenship privileges for service to Rome). Mauretanian and Numidian auxiliaries were recorded in areas of Europe ranging from Britain to Greece.

This path was necessary until the Roman emperor Caracalla, who was from Africa, issued a proclamation that made all freeborn males citizens of Rome. Most prejudice in Roman society against Africans was rooted either in cultural differences or lesser economic status, rather than genetic or physical differences. The Romans understood that any person could assimilate into Roman culture. Tolerance of any person was proportionate to economic power. There was no hindrance to social mobility for Africans in the Roman army or in society, although the military generally provided a quicker path to status elevation.

As African provinces were annexed into Rome, Roman civil wars were fought in Africa as well, and African auxiliary forces swelled the Roman ranks for these campaigns. Pompey's Numidian cavalry nearly destroyed Julius Caesar's forces repeatedly. It was not until Caesar's infantry charged the cavalry at Pharsalus in Greece (48 B.C.E.) that Pompey's African cavalry was checked. The charge was successful because the Numidians typically did not wear armor and avoided direct contact with troops, especially with Roman troops who were skilled swordsmen.

A Numidian rebellion by Tacfarinas (17–24 C.E.) required the Roman army to learn and adopt the guerilla tactics used by the Numidians in order to defeat them. Curiously, it was his training in Roman tactics that led to early successes against the Romans. Numidian cavalry tactics were also adopted by the Romans, and African horses became prized as well.

The African-born Roman emperor Septimius Severus made a number of noticeable changes in the Roman army. Severus became emperor after a civil war. To bring stability and create loyalty, Severus increased the soldiers' pay by half. Another enormously popular move was allowing soldiers to marry local women while in service in frontier regions. Further, promotion from within the ranks was made easier, both for military posts and civil positions. After Severus's son, Caracalla, extended citizenship to all freeborn males in the empire, it became increasingly difficult to trace Africans in the ranks, as they were no longer distinct from Roman contingents.

See also: Italy, Blacks in; Moors; Popes, African; *Roar*; Roman Emperors, African; Roman Empire in Africa; Terentius Afer.

Further Reading: Dixon, Karen and Pat Southern. *The Roman Cavalry*. New York: Routledge, 1992; Goldsworth, Adrian. *Roman Warfare*. London: Cassell, 2000; Thompson, Lloyd. *Romans and Blacks*. Norman: Oklahoma University Press, 1989.

Mark Anthony Phelps

Roman Emperors of African Origin

Five ancient Roman emperors were of African origin: Septimius Severus, Geta, Caracalla, Marcus Opellius Macrinus, and Marcus Aemilius Aemilianus. The exact race of each of these emperors is often debated because of limited evidence, conflicting descriptions, and the fact that many ancient Europeans settled in Africa, some intermarrying with locals during the time of the Roman Empire. The Romanization of ancient northwest Africa began soon after the **Punic Wars** and the incorporation of Carthage into the Roman Empire in 148 B.C.E. Colonization began in earnest with the settling of Marius's veterans at the end of the second century B.C.E., a practice followed by Julius Caesar and Augustus. By the first century C.E., Roman Africans populated the Senate. Africa's economic power, fueled primarily by wheat exports, had translated into political power.

The first African emperor was Septimius Severus (145–211 C.E.). He was born in Lepcis Magna, in modern Libya, and was probably of Liby-Phoenician and Roman ancestry. His grandfather was likely the Septimius Severus praised by the poet Stratius at the end of the first century C.E. One of his cousins, who obtained consular rank, enabled Septimius to enter the Senate. He held posts throughout the Empire.

While he held the post of governor of Upper Pannonia (eastern Austria and western Hungary), the emperor Pertinax (r. 192–193 C.E.) was assassinated by the Praetorian Guard (the personal bodyguard of the emperor). Pertinax was chosen by the Senate to bring order back to the empire after the reign of Commodus (r. 180–192 C.E.). The emperorship was then infamously auctioned by the Praetorian Guard, with Didius Julianus the highest bidder; however, Severus's Pannonian army proclaimed him the new emperor. Severus marched on Rome, not only to eradicate Didius Julianus, but also to convince the Senate and the rest of the Roman elite that he wanted to both avenge Pertinax and assume his mantle of restoring order. Didius was killed by his own bodyguard, and Severus entered Rome without a fight.

Severus's claim did not go unchallenged, however. He did have to fight Pescinnius Niger, a Syrian general with a rival claim to emperorship. Niger was killed within a year, and the east was pacified by 195 C.E. Severus pacified another rival (and fellow African), Clodius Albinus, the governor of Britain. Severus initially named Albinus as Caesar, which denoted Albinus as successor to him.

After defeating Niger, Severus set forth to legitimize his reign. He claimed to be the son of former emperor Marcus Aurelius by adoption. He renamed his eldest son Bassianus Marcus Aurelius Antoninus (better known as Caracalla). He also named him to the position of Caesar. He gave his wife, Julia Domina, the epithet "mother of the camp," a title that previously had been used only by Marcus Aurelius's wife.

Albinus, incensed by the granting of the title to Caracalla, led his army against Severus in 196 C.E. Albinus was defeated and killed near modern Lyons, France, in 197 C.E., and order was restored.

Severus is best known for reforms in the military and legal realms. He increased the pay of the soldiers by half. He made the path to both military promotion and to civilian civil service posts by soldiers more routine. Severus dismissed the old Praetorian Guard and reformed it with soldiers who were promoted from the field. He also allowed for soldiers stationed

The Roman Emperor Septimus Severus (r. 193–211 C.E.), his wife, Julia Domna, and his children Caracalla and Geta. From Egypt, Roman Period, ca. 200 C.E. Bildarchiv Preussischer Kulturbesitz / Art Resource, NY.

in garrisons to marry locals. Severus made these extraordinary moves to inculcate devotion to the emperor. According to tradition, his last words to his sons were, "Get along, pay off the soldiers, and ignore everyone else."

Roman law had yet to be codified (and would not be for another three centuries). Severus relied heavily on a panel of lawyers who held the equivalent of a cabinet post. The lawyers on whom he relied were the three most significant Roman legal minds ever, namely Ulpian, Paul, and Papinian. His reign is known as the golden age of Roman law. The legal bureaucracy expanded during his reign.

Severus had ruled for 18 years by the time he died in York, England, in February 211 C.E. His successor was his eldest son, Caracalla, who secured his position by murdering his younger brother, Geta, in December 211 C.E. (while their mother held the latter, according to tradition). The two were at the time of the death of their father both titled Augustus, meaning both were in theory co-emperors with their father. During the Middle Ages, British historian Geoffrey of Monmouth listed Caracalla (under the name of Bassianus) as an ancient king of Britain.

The most significant event of Caracalla's reign was his proclamation that all freeborn inhabitants of the Roman Empire were now to be considered citizens. This move created uniformity on three fronts. It made all subject to Roman taxation and military levies. It also made a single set of laws applicable for the inhabitants of the empire.

Caracalla visited and participated in a variety of temple rituals for a number of gods throughout the empire. His curiosity can be blamed for the immediate circumstances of his death, as he was murdered by the small bodyguard that accompanied him to a temple in Edessa (in modern Syria) during a lull in his campaign in Mesopotamia. His murder in 217 C.E. brought about the end of the biological descendents of Septimius Severus, although the dynasty continued until 235 C.E.

The Severan dynasty was interrupted after the murder of Caracalla by the 14-month reign of Marcus Opellius Macrinus. Macrinus, likely of Moorish descent, was born in Caesarea Iol in Mauretania (modern Cherchell, Algeria). He held a number of posts during the reigns of the first two Severans. The Senate proclaimed him emperor after the assassination of Caracalla. He was the first emperor who did not come from a senatorial background. His reign unraveled as the Syrian sister-in-law of Septimius Severus, Julia Maesa, paid off an Eastern garrison to support her son (Elagabalus) for emperor. Civil war ensued, and Macrinus was killed as he tried to flee to Rome after a defeat.

The last Roman emperor of African origin was Marcus Aemilius Aemilianus, who ruled in 253 C.E. His origins are obscure, but he was likely born on the island of Gerta, off the west coast of Tunisia. He is called a **Moor** in one source, and a Libyan in another. Either title designates a person of indigenous descent. Most figures who obtained political prominence in the empire were ultimately descended from colonists, who were often of Italian descent.

The event that propelled Aemilianus to the emperorship was his defeat of invading Gothic tribes while he commanded the armies stationed in Moesia. In the wake of his victory, his troops proclaimed him emperor. Whether this elevation was the result of conscious manipulation on the part of Aemilianus or the result of spontaneous emotion is a matter of debate among sources.

What is known is that Aemilianus ruled for three months. After the proclamation of his troops, he made his way to Italy to confront the emperor Gallus and his son and co-emperor Volusianus. The emperors expected to be reinforced by the armies under Valerian, who arrived far too late. Instead, they were killed by their own troops. Valerian's forces arrived to engage Aemilianus, who was killed. Valerian was then proclaimed the new emperor.

The rule of Aemilianus is a paradigm for the era of the Barracks Emperors (235–284 C.E.), as he never left the battlefield to rule. This chaotic period lasted from the end of the Severan dynasty to the advent of Diocletian (284–305 C.E.).

See also: Britain, Blacks in; Italy, Blacks in; Popes, African; *Roar*; Roman Army, Africans in the; Terentius Afer.

Further Reading: Birley, A. R. *Septimius Severus, the African Emperor.* 2nd ed. New Haven: Yale University Press, 1988; Southern, Pat. The *Roman Empire from Severus to Constantine.* New York: Routledge, 2001.

Mark Anthony Phelps

Roman Empire in Africa

The area of western Africa between the Mediterranean coast and the Sahara became an integral part of the ancient Roman Empire after its incorporation, a century-long process that began in the second half of the second century B.C.E. Its impact was primarily economic, but there were also some substantive cultural forces that came from this region.

The region eventually consisted of the provinces of Africa (most of the land that had at one time been controlled by Carthage, incorporated in 146 B.C.E.): Africa Novo, comprising primarily Numidia, the region to the west in modern day Algeria (incorporated 46 B.C.E.); Cyrenaica, the region extending east along the Mediterranean coast from Africa into modern day Libya (incorporated 74 B.C.E.); and Mauretania, the region comprising modern day Morocco (incorporated for the last time in 40 C.E.).

The economic value of the land consisted primarily in the production of grain. This production was spurred by the settling of Roman colonists in the land. By the beginning of the second century B.C.E., retired army veterans (beginning with Marius's troops, with Julius Caesar and Augustus following suit with their veterans) were given land throughout the region. These settlers brought irrigation technology to the region, greatly expanding areas of production. Local populations also took up large-scale agriculture on seeing the wealth it created with the direct access to the markets of Rome. It was claimed that Egypt produced the grain for Rome four months of the year, and Africa produced it for the other eight months. Olive production became significant with the settlement of Roman colonists. The most celebrated of exports from Cyrenaica was a plant known as silphion. Its root was used primarily for medicinal purposes, but it also had some culinary value. Silphion was traded widely in the Greek world, but the plant disappears from history within the first century of Roman occupation, although its memory persisted in literature for centuries.

Another significant economic value in the land lay in its strategic value for shipping. With the advent of Roman domination of the southern Mediterranean coast, Rome no longer had rivals for transport of goods in the region. Further, there were fewer areas that viewed piracy against Roman shipping as a viable economic option. As well, Rome now dominated the sea trade route coming from the Atlantic beyond the Mediterranean.

Last, the region also provided access to game animals of sub-Saharan Africa. This trade became increasingly important during the Imperial era of Rome (31 B.C.E.–476 C.E.), as enormous numbers of animals were required for the plethora of games in Rome and other venues. Ivory was also prized, initially from local elephants, which became extinct in the fourth century C.E.

The economic importance of the region was substantive. The potential for disruption of the grain trade made military maneuvers in the region understandable to the population in Rome. The Roman civil wars of the first century B.C.E. all were fought on African soil as well, with serious repercussions for local leaders who sided with the eventual winners or losers. Romans in Italy considered this region economically integrated into the empire.

The region became heavily Romanized as a result of the settlement there of thousands of veterans and Roman colonists. Carthaginian culture had penetrated the region before the coming of the Romans, and there were Greek colonies in the eastern reaches of the region. As was generally the case in the expansion of Rome, the urban areas were more affected by Roman culture than the rural areas. This was especially true as one traveled farther south, as settled life gave way to the pastoralism of the Sahara and its fringes.

Latin was the language of the cities, Punic that of the villages (with inscriptions attested to the fourth century C.E.), and native dialects were found in mountains and among desert dwellers. Punic social, religious, and political influences were still attested outside the cities for centuries. By the arrival of Christianity in this region in the second century, Punic and native religions were completely Romanized.

Africa's political power was best evidenced in the rise of African Roman emperors. Septimius Severus was the first African to become Emperor of Rome (r. 193–211 C.E.). He was followed by his son, Caracalla (r. 211–217 C.E.). Marcus Opellius Macrinus, a holder of a number of offices under these two, ruled as emperor for just over one year (r. 217–218 C.E.). Aemilius Aemilianus rose to that office later in the century (253 C.E.).

Apuleius (125?–180? C.E.) was the best known Roman writer to emerge from the region before the rise of Christianity. He was born in the Roman colony of Madaurus, Numidia (modern Mdaouroach, Algeria). He is best known for his novel *The Golden Ass*, a satirical adventure as the main character experiences salvation through the Roman/Egyptian mystery cult of Isis after mistakenly being turned into a donkey.

The greatest cultural influence that Africa ever exerted in the course of Western history is the period from the advent of Christianity in the region (the first literary attestation is in the late second century; nothing is attested archaeologically until the middle of the third century) until the invasion of the Vandals and its aftermath (429–435 C.E.). The first literary giant of early Christianity to emerge from the region was Tertullian of Carthage (160–240 C.E.), an often venomous defender of Christian theology.

His disdain of philosophy ("What has Athens to do with Jerusalem?") was a hallmark of his thought, as was his lack of tact.

The greatest Latin theologian was Saint Augustine (354–435 C.E.). He was born in Tagaste, Numidia (modern Souk Ahras, Algeria). Like Apuleius, he was likely of Berber descent. Augustine embraced the Roman Catholic Church while living in Italy. He returned to Numidia, eventually becoming the bishop of Hippo. His best-known works include *The Confessions, On the Trinity, On Christian Doctrine, The City of God,* and a number of treatises explaining theology, as well as defenses against heretical and pagan thought. He was canonized and became the patron saint of brewers, printers, theologians, and those with sore eyes.

Roman Catholic Christianity nearly perished from the face of Africa after the invasion of the Vandals (beginning in 429 C.E.). By the time the initial invasion concluded, churches were left standing only in Hippo, Cirta, and Carthage. The latter church disappeared by 439 C.E. With the advent of the Vandals, North Africa ceased to serve a literary or economic role in the Western Roman Empire.

See also: Italy, Blacks in; Popes, African; Punic Wars; *Roar*; Roman Army, Africans in the; Roman Emperors of African Origin; Terentius Afer.

Further Reading: Cherry, David. *Frontier and Society in Roman North Africa.* Oxford: Clarendon, 1998; Frend, W.H.C. *The Rise of Christianity.* Philadelphia: Fortress, 1984; Raven, Susan. *Rome in Africa.* 3rd ed. London: Routledge, 1993.

Mark Anthony Phelps

Le Roman d'un Spahi (1881)

Le Roman d'un Spahi (1881) is Julien Viaud's (1850–1923) third novel written and the first signed with his pseudonym Pierre Loti. A sub-lieutenant in the French Navy, Viaud served in Senegal in 1873–1874 when the navy supported the Spahis, an elite French colonial force fighting local armed rebellions in the so-called French protectorate. Viaud/Loti was also an idealist whose unhappy Senegalese experience permeates his predominantly autobiographical novel. Set in Senegal, *Le Roman* is a tragic story spanning five years and centering on 22-year-old French Spahi Jean Peyral's life from rural Cévennes.

Displaying the turn of the nineteenth century characteristics of French writing about French colonization, *Le Roman* is generally phobic of black West Africa, which is equated to primitive sexuality and death. Overflowing with racial stereotypes, *Le Roman* infantilizes the Senegalese, assimilating them to perverts and comparing them to monkeys. Indeed, an important part of *Le Roman*'s thematic construct regarding Peyral's moral and cultural deterioration relies on binary symbolisms of skin color and physical descriptions, such as pure whites/impure blacks, with connotations of white moral purity and black moral defect, compounded by depraved, sensual, and vicious biracial women like Cora.

That the black inferiority evident in *Le Roman* was symptomatic of a wider European mindset channeled through popular novels is nowadays unquestionable. Such novels, including *Le Roman*, assisted Europeans in justifying their conquest and rule of Africa and represent a crucial stage in European literature's crystallization of black inferiority, which was sustained in Europeans' minds for more than 50 years. Peyral's ambivalence and alterity, which refers to the cultural construction of "otherness," could be read in this context. He resents having become part African but, at the cost of promotion in the Navy, persistently seeks refuge from alienation in an affair with married Cora, and sex and cohabitation with the black girl, Fatou Gaye.

See also: Colonies in Africa, French; French Army, Blacks in the; Literature, Blacks in French.

Further Reading: Hargreaves, Alec G. *The Colonial Experience in French Fiction: A Study of Pierre Loti, Ernest Psichari and Pierre Mille.* London: Macmillan, 1981; Hughes, Edward G. *Writing Marginality in Modern French Literature: from Loti to Genet.* Cambridge: Cambridge University Press, 2001; Loti, Pierre. *Le Roman d'un Spahi.* Paris: Gallimard/Edition de Bruno Vercier, 2006.

Saër Maty Bâ

Roselmack, Harry (1973–)

Harry Roselmack is a leading French radio and television journalist of Afro-Caribbean descent. He was born in March 1973 in Tours, France, although some accounts state that he was born on the French Caribbean island of Martinique, which was where his parents came from. Roselmack studied history and then completed a postgraduate course in journalism before staring to work with a small French radio station. He also wrote sports reports for the newspaper *La Nouvelle République du Centre-Ouest.* Roselmack then worked with Radio France and finally joined Canal+.

In 2006, the television station TF1 appointed Roselmack the official summer replacement for Patrick Poivre d'Arvor, the anchorman on the evening news. Thus Roselmack became the head of the most popular news bulletin in the country. Part of this move came after French President Jacques Chirac urged the mainstream French media to use more journalists from ethnic minorities. Many French politicians viewed ethnic communities as being marginalized in news coverage. The main reason, however, was a major change in staff at TF1. Thomas Hugues, who had been the summer replacement for Patrick Poivre d'Arvor, left the station for that of a rival. Hugues's departure was followed by that of his wife, Laurence Ferrari, who was another presenter.

Roselmack has long been active in the *Club Averroes,* which was founded in 1997 to improve the diversity of the staff in the French media. He had also occasionally substituted at TF1 during holiday seasons, and many in France greeted his appointment favorably. The daily newspaper *Le Parisien* hailed the appointment, stating that never before had a black journalist been given such an important post in the French media.

Roselmack debuted on July 17, 2006, and became the first black evening news broadcaster for TF1. His program, *Sept à huit* ("Seven to Eight"), has proved extremely popular. It was not long before he started to attract as many as 8 million to 10 million viewers, nearly half of the total evening television viewers. Some press comment soon after the appointment pointed to evidence that Roselmack had been able to include far more news into his show than his predecessor, Patrick Poivre d'Arvor, who preferred commentaries on major stories.

See also: Black History Month; France, Blacks in; May 10 Holiday; Media, Blacks in Contemporary European.

Further Reading: Sloane, Lester. "The News from Paris: There are only three TV anchors who are 'coloring' the French airwaves (Harry Roselmack, Audrey Pulvar, and Christine Kelly)." *Ebony Magazine* 62:10 (August 2007): 94(3).

Justin Corfield

Roumain, Jacques (1907–1944)

Jacques Roumain, a writer, editor, political activist, and ethnographer, was one of the most remarkable Haitian intellectuals of the twentieth century. Throughout his relatively short life, Roumain published numerous works of fiction, poetry, essays, and articles promoting the goals of social justice and cultural respect, while warning against the dangers of racism and color prejudice, fascism, classism, and ethnocentrism, both in Haiti and elsewhere.

Born in Haiti to an aristocratic, light-skinned biracial family, Roumain spent several years in Europe, both as a student and as a political exile. During his adolescence, which was marked by a period of U.S. military occupation in Haiti (1915–1934), Roumain was sent by his family to study in Switzerland, first in Bern and then in Zurich. From Switzerland, Roumain traveled to Spain to study agronomy and became interested in bullfighting. His early prose poem "Corrida" was written in Madrid during this period in 1926. Roumain returned to Haiti at age 20 in 1927, and began writing for, and editing, nationalist periodicals with overtly anti-occupation messages. In 1928, he was arrested, and in 1929, he was imprisoned for contributing to these publications. Shortly after his release, Roumain resumed publishing, only to be arrested and imprisoned again. He was released two months later after a general amnesty was declared for all political prisoners.

In 1930, Roumain's collection of short stories, *La proie et l'ombre* ("The Prey and the Shadow") was published, followed the next year by his novels *Les fantoches* ("The Puppets") and *La montagne ensorcelée* ("The Bewitched Mountain"). In 1934, Roumain founded the Haitian Communist Party and published *Analyse schématique 1932/1934,* an analysis of Haitian society suggesting that Marxism could provide a solution to the numerous social and economic conflicts in Haiti. Roumain's open declaration of his commitment to communist ideas was followed by his arrest and subsequent imprisonment for subversion this same year.

In 1936, Roumain was released from prison and sent into exile. After spending time in Brussels, Roumain and his family settled in Paris. While in Paris, he studied ethnology at the Sorbonne and paleontology at the Museum of Man. He traveled to Spain, where he participated in antifascist activities and wrote his famous antifascist poem "Madrid." In 1939, Roumain briefly studied anthropology at Columbia University in New York City and became close friends with the poet Langston Hughes. In 1940, Roumain traveled to Havana where he met with the poet **Nicolás Guillén.**

In 1941, Roumain returned to Haiti and founded the Bureau of Ethnology. In 1943, he was appointed to a diplomatic post at the Haitian embassy in Mexico, where he finished his poetry collection *Bois d'ébène* ("Ebony Wood") and his highly acclaimed novel about Haitian peasant life, *Gouverneurs de la rosée* ("Masters of the Dew"), shortly before his unexpected death in August 1944. Both works were published posthumously and have been translated into several languages.

See also: Authors in Europe, African American; Colonies in the Caribbean, French; France, Blacks in; Literature, Blacks in French; Spain, Blacks in.

Further Reading: Dash, Michael. "Postcolonial Thought and the Francophone Caribbean." In *Francophone Postcolonial Studies: A Critical Introduction.* eds. Charles Forsdick and David Murphy London: Arnold, 2003, pp. 231–241; Fowler, Carolyn. *A Knot in the Thread: The Life and Work of Jacques Roumain.* Washington DC: Howard University Press, 1980; Laraque, Paul. "Introduction." In *When the Tom-Tom Beats: Selected Prose and Poems.* Jacques Roumain. trans. Joanne Fungaroli and Ronald Sauer. Washington DC: Azul Editions, 1995, pp. 7–12.

Sara Scott Armengot

Russia, Blacks in

The encounter between black Africans and people of black descent and Russia was reflective of the ambivalence with which Russians viewed their place in the Eurocentric world during the **New Imperialism.** Russian identity as a European nation has often been the subject of heated internal debates and widespread suspicion by other Europeans. Imperial Russia did not take part in the trans-Atlantic slave trade and never established colonies in Africa. The last European nation to emancipate its own serfs, Russia had a small but vocal educated class, or *intelligentsia*, whose prominent representatives routinely condemned the depravity of American slavery. In the eyes of many black observers, Russia's absence from the histories of slave trade and European colonialism in Africa contributed to its image as a relatively tolerant society, less affected by the curse of European and North American racism. After 1917, the new Communist rulers of Soviet Russia continued to advocate racial tolerance and acceptance as essential elements of their Marxist ideology. For the Soviets, any expression of racism undermined their own multiethnic project and, as such, was antithetical to the country's new identity and interests. With the rise of the cold war, the rhetoric of antiracism and anticolonialism came to color much of the Soviet Union's interaction with its ideological opponents in the West. With the Soviet economy and society entering a protracted period of stagnation and eventual decline, however, the colorblind ideals articulated by Soviet propaganda were increasingly devoid of genuine meaning and often at odds with the sentiments of the "Soviet street." The disintegration of the Soviet Union was accompanied by increased ethnic tensions and the rise of ethnic nationalisms in the country that had been built on the principles of ethnic coexistence. Black Africans and African Russians residing in late Soviet Union and post-Soviet Russia had to bear the brunt of Russian chauvinism, much of it born out of the society-wide disillusionment with Soviet ideals and values.

PRE-1900.   For many Russians, their connection to Africa is embodied in the genealogy of the country's greatest poet and the national cultural icon, **Alexander**

Pushkin (1799–1937). Pushkin's great-grandfather **Abraham Hannibal** arrived in Russia as a little African slave boy, purchased at an Ottoman slave market by an emissary of Russian Tsar Peter the Great. Hannibal's origins remain murky, but most historians agree that he was most likely born somewhere in Abyssinia, modern-day Ethiopia. Adopted by the tsar, who also served as his godfather, Hannibal entered Russian nobility and made an illustrious career in the Russian military. Hannibal distinguished himself as a talented engineer and reached the rank of general-major. Pushkin did not shy away from his African ancestry and proudly acknowledged it in verse and prose, celebrating the life of his famous progenitor in an unfinished biography, *The Negro of Peter the Great*.

That a person of African descent could be embraced by Russians as the most important cultural symbol underscores how differently they viewed race from most other nineteenth-century Europeans. Few black people ever visited Imperial Russia, but those who did reported encountering generally benign attitudes, in stark contrast to the racism prevalent elsewhere in Europe and North America. One such traveler, an African American woman **Nancy Prince,** spent more than a decade at the Russian imperial court in St. Petersburg during the early decades of the 1800s. Her memoir contains a perceptive analysis of early nineteenth-century Russian society, which she deemed welcoming to blacks. Black American tragedian **Ira Aldridge** found fame on the Russian stage. A close friend of the great Ukrainian bard, Taras Schevchenko, Aldridge toured Russia extensively and attained a cultlike status with the theater goers in St. Petersburg, Moscow, and in the provinces. His popularity with the Russian public had little to do with his race and a lot to do with his acting talents. Yet inadvertently to Russia's educated class, Aldrige also represented a group of people benighted by American slavery. Translated into Russian, Harriet Beecher Stowe's **Uncle Tom's Cabin** became an instant bestseller. Prominent social critics, such as Vissarion Belinsky and Nicholas Chernyshevsky, drew parallels between America's "peculiar institution" and the institution of serfdom in Russia. Belinsky, in his famous *Letter to Gogol* (1847), spoke of Russian serfs as "our white Negroes," and Chernyshevsky sent free copies of *Uncle Tom's Cabin* to the subscribers of his journal, *The Contemporary*. An iconoclastic dissident intellectual, Alexander Herzen, writing from his exile in Britain, contemptibly compared Russia's slave-holding class with the American planters. The two institutions of slavery, Russian and American, were abolished at about the same time (1861 and 1863, respectively). Not surprisingly, a trickle of African American adventurers, performers, musicians, and entrepreneurs began to reach Russia toward the end of the nineteenth century. They were searching for new opportunities in the country that seemingly harbored and practiced less racial prejudice toward black people than other "white" countries.

With the enormous Eurasian landmass open to its imperialist expansion, Russia took no part in the European "Scramble for Africa" during the last two decades of the nineteenth century. Although not immune to the standard Victorian images of Africa that depicted the continent and its people as savage and in need of civilization, Russians felt no obvious need to civilize Africans. Toward the end of the nineteenth century, the country experienced a period of close and intensely emotional contacts with Christian Ethiopia, an independent African country that many Russians considered fraternal because of its Orthodox faith. Russian military advisors, medics, and volunteers were reportedly in the ranks of the Ethiopian army of Menelik II, which inflicted a humiliating defeat on the Italian colonial army at Adwa in 1896. Subsequently, Russians founded a hospital in Addis Ababa that for decades to come would become a fixture of the Ethiopian capital.

1900 TO 1945.   The presence of blacks visiting Russia during the nineteenth century did result in biracial offspring, some of whom became prominent individuals. Mikhail Egypteos, for example, was a biracial general in the Imperial Russian army in the early twentieth century. His father was a black artist commissioned by the Imperial Russian court and his mother was a Russian noblewoman. He graduated from the Tsar Nicholas I Academy in 1881. He later graduated from the Naval Construction Department of the Kronstadt Engineering College and the Naval College. In 1904, Egypteos served as senior naval constructor of the Saint Petersburg dockyard. In 1911, during the reign of Tsar Nicholas II, he was promoted to the rank of major-general.

Russia's connection to Africa again became the focus of public discourse a few years later when, on the eve of World War I, reports surfaced in the Russian press of a strange "African colony" in the Caucuses. An ethnographic expedition to the Abkhasian coast of the Black Sea had come across several villages whose residents had black skin and distinctly African features. These "Black Sea Negroes," as they were sometimes referred to in the press, appeared to have descended from a group of Ottoman slaves who had settled the area back in the sixteenth to seventeenth centuries. Their numbers were small, but their very presence on the territory of the Russian Empire connected it to the general history of global exchanges.

In the aftermath of the Great October Socialist Revolution of 1917, the new Bolshevik regime sought to forge a new Soviet identity, rooted in the ideology of Marxism-Leninism. Because class distinctions were the only meaningful differences between humans recognized by the communists, the new Soviet rulers decried racism as a harmful vestige of capitalism, the system they had set out to destroy. From that point on until the very end of the Soviet Union, the Soviets, at least in their official pronouncements, would continue to make use of the rhetoric of antiracism and anticolonialism. Needless to say, for African Americans living under the Jim Crow laws and the fear of arbitrary lynching, as well as for the African subjects of European colonial administrations, the Soviet Union represented a refreshing alternative to the routine of racial humiliation and colonial domination. As a result, during the first two decades of the Soviet Union's existence, it received plenty of positive publicity in the black press, especially in the United States. Dozens (and probably hundreds) of black "pilgrims," most of them African American and Afro-Caribbean, trekked to the "Red Mecca." Few of them were committed communists, but most shared expectations of a qualitatively new society, free of racism and its attendant oppression. Among those enchanted with the promise of the Soviet Union were some of the most prominent African American intellectuals and cultural figures of the day. Poets **Claude McKay** and Langston Hughes, the famous actor **Paul Robeson,** and the great advocate of **Pan-Africanism, W.E.B. Du Bois,** all traveled to the U.S.S.R. and even resided there for extended periods of time.

Besides these celebrities, there were numerous lesser known individuals who came to the Soviet Union in pursuit of their colorblind dream, but also in search of employment opportunities and the opportunities to contribute to the new socialist experiment in Russia. In 1932, for example, a group of agricultural engineers, most of them the graduates of the historically black Tuskegee University and Hampton Institute, arrived in Soviet Central Asia to help develop new cotton production techniques. Oliver Golden, the leader of the group, and George Tynes, one of the experts, would permanently settle in the U.S.S.R. In doing so, they established the foundations for a small, but culturally and politically significant, **African Diaspora** in the Soviet Union. Oliver Golden's Soviet-born daughter, Lily Golden, would become a prominent Soviet intellectual and a fixture in Moscow cultural elite circles. Lily Golden's daughter, Yelena Khanga (Oliver Golden's granddaughter), would rise to fame as a popular journalist and television celebrity in post–Soviet Russia.

The romance between black radicals and Soviet Russia began to wither away toward the end of the 1930s, as the Soviet Union proceeded to assert itself more as a nation-state than a revolutionary force in world affairs. In 1933, it established diplomatic relations with the United States and subsequently toned down its antiracist propaganda. The Soviets lost some of their earlier clout among black sympathizers when it came to the surface that they had been secretly supplying Italian troops during their 1935 invasion of Ethiopia. The Nazi-Soviet Pact of 1939 came shortly thereafter. The pact was dubbed the "great betrayal" in a famous editorial in the African American periodical, *The Crisis*. Considering the well-publicized racial policies of the Third Reich, the rapprochement with the Nazis undermined the Soviets' antiracist credentials. There is also some evidence, reported by such black residents in the Soviet Union at the time as journalist Homer Smith and mechanical engineer Robert Robinson, that the consolidation of Stalin's dictatorship and the atmosphere of paranoia and fear that surrounded the bloody Soviet purges of the late-1930s affected some of the early black enthusiasts of the Soviet Union. Jomo Kenyatta, the future founder of independent Kenya, left the country disillusioned after a brief stint at Moscow's Communist University of the Toilers of the East (KUTV). **George Padmore,** a prominent Caribbean communist, broke with the Soviets over what he saw as their heavy-handed approach to the issue of race. Padmore would eventually trade his communist convictions for pan-Africanist beliefs. At least one African American communist perished in the cauldron of Stalin's Great Terror. Only recently, Russian archives revealed the fate of Lovett Fort-Whiteman, a black Chicagoan, who died in a remote gulag camp in the late 1930s. By the beginning of World War II, only a few of the original black "pilgrims" to the Soviet Union remained in the country.

POST-1945.   In the aftermath of World War II, much of the former colonial world, including Africa, gained independence from the former colonial masters. The process of decolonization coincided with the rise of the cold war, the historical circumstance that left an indelible mark on the relations betweens the Soviet Union and the newly independent countries of Africa. The Soviets cultivated friendships with the young African states, seeking to present the Soviet development model as a viable alternative to Western capitalism. They also extended material and political support and military training to several liberation movements, especially in southern Africa. Gradually, Africa moved from the periphery of Soviet foreign policy concerns to the center stage of cold war politics. During the cold war decades, the Soviets involved themselves in the Congo crisis of the early 1960s, the Nigerian Civil War of 1967–1970, the Angolan Civil War, the Ethiopian-Somali war of the late 1970s, and a number of other African conflicts. In Africa, the U.S.S.R. sought closer relations with the regimes sympathetic to Marxism, such as Ghana under Kwame Nkrumah, Guinea under Sekou Toure, Ethiopia under Mengistu Haile Miriam, Angola, Mozambique, and others. Increasingly, however, the Soviet Union's approach to Africa combined ideology and pragmatism. For example, during the Nigerian civil war, the Soviets opted to support the pro-Western federalist camp against the secessionist Republic of Biafra. They also established close links with the regime of Gamal Abdel Nasser of Egypt, turning a blind eye to Nasser's merciless persecution of Egyptian communists.

In response to demands of the increasingly global foreign policy, but also as a reflection of a greater openness after the death of Stalin, the U.S.S.R. began to pay more attention to the academic study of Africa and its people. In 1959, a special institution for a comprehensive and interdisciplinary research on Africa (Africa Institute) was founded in Moscow under the aegis of the Soviet Academy of Sciences. Simultaneously, the Soviet Union made a concerted effort to enhance its image in Africa by extending generous educational scholarships to African students. After the 1957 Youth Festival in Moscow, thousands of Third World students started arriving in the Soviet institutions of higher learning. Many of them would enter a new Moscow Friendship University, also known as Lumumba University, specially created to cater to the needs of these students. The appearance of these young, exotic-looking foreigners in the midst of a society largely isolated from the rest of the world had some unintended social and cultural consequences for the Soviet Union. The Soviet officials had clearly hoped that by bringing thousands of African students to the U.S.S.R., they would score a major propaganda victory against their cold war rivals in the West and also consolidate their country's prestige in the Developing World; however, they had failed to foresee the impact of African students on Soviet society. Instead of serving as symbolic ideological allies of the regime, once in the Soviet Union, Africans often functioned as its opponents. In 1963, for example, hundreds of African students participated in an unsanctioned demonstration in Red Square, protesting a suspicious death of a Ghanaian student in Moscow. Africans routinely petitioned university and state authorities for better living conditions, demanding more freedom of movement and expression, and challenging the Soviets to clamp down on the instances of everyday racism. African students presented yet another headache for the regime because they often practiced lifestyles and embraced cultural aesthetics in stark contrast to official Soviet values. Funded by generous state stipends, usually speaking several languages, and having more opportunities for foreign travel than an average Soviet citizen, young Africans in the U.S.S.R. became the conduits of Westernization. They introduced their Soviet friends, spouses, and fellow students to Western fashions, jazz and rock-n-roll records, and the view of the world that was often cosmopolitan and devoid of the ideological rigidity inherent in Soviet education. It is not a coincidence that African themes would come to feature prominently in some of the countercultural production in the late Soviet Union. The ideas of freedom and liberation, which in the course of the decades of vociferous anticolonial and antiracist propaganda had become intrinsically linked to the idea of Africa, challenged the Soviets to think critically about their own condition.

During the period of reforms, generally known as *perestroika* and *glasnost*, ushered in by the last Soviet leader, Mikhail Gorbachev, the Soviet press commentary on Africa grew increasingly negative. Both political commentators and people in the street often attributed the economic decline of the once-powerful Soviet Union to "too much aid for Africa." The eventual dissolution of the U.S.S.R. released the pent-up forces of ethnic nationalisms, including extreme forms of Russian chauvinism. At the time, black Russians and African residents in the Soviet Union found themselves targets of racial slurs and even physical attacks, an unfortunate sociocultural phenomenon that has persisted into the post-Soviet era. Since the late 1990s, on more than one occasion international media has been alerted to an alarming increase in the number of racially motivated attacks in Russia. At the same time, African students continue to arrive in Russia in search of affordable education, and a growing number of African expatriates and Russians of black descent have achieved prominence as educators, journalists, television personalities, musicians, and athletes.

See also: Abolition of Slavery, Russian; Authors in Europe, African American; Soviet Propaganda, Blacks and; Television, Blacks in European.

Further Reading: Blakely, Allison. *Russia and the Negro: Blacks in Russian History and Thought*. Washington, DC: Howard University Press, 1986; Fikes, Kesha, and Alaina Lemon. "African Presence in Former Soviet Spaces." *Annual Review of Anthropology* 31 (2002): 497–524; Golden, Lily. *My Long Journey Home*. Chicago: Third World Press, 2003; Hughes, Langston. *I Wonder as I Wander: An Autobiographical Journey*. New York: Hill and Wang, 1994; Khanga, Yelena. *Soul to Soul: A Black Russian American Family, 1865–1992*. New York: W. W. Norton, 1994; Matusevich, Maxim, ed. *Africa in Russia, Russia in Africa: Three Centuries of Encounters*, Trenton, NJ: Africa World Press, 2006; McClellan, Woodford. "Africans and Black Americans in the Comintern Schools, 1925–1934." *The International Journal of African Historical Studies* 26 (1993): 371–390; Quist-Adade, Charles. *In the Shadows of the Kremlin and the White House: Africa's Media Image from Communism to Post-Communism*. Lanham, MD: University Press of America, 2001.

Maxim Matusevich

S

Saint-Georges, Le Chevalier de (1739?–1799)

Joseph Boulogne, le Chevalier de Saint-Georges, was an eighteenth-century revolutionary figure who embodied superior athletic skill, musical creativity, and courtly charm. With his remarkable accomplishments in music, fencing, and athletics, and his engaging presence, he overcame the disadvantage of his biracial ancestry to become one of the most visible and popular figures in eighteenth-century French aristocratic society.

Adopting the title "Chevalier de Saint-Georges" from his paternal family, Saint-Georges was born in Guadeloupe, possibly in 1739, to a West African slave woman and an aristocratic French plantation owner. Although his date of birth and paternity are disputed, Saint-Georges's father secured for him privileges in France that were rare for people of color in the eighteenth century. He became a student of the fencing master, Texier de La Böessière, and in a few years, his form and athleticism earned him plaudits as France's premier swordsman. Moreover, Saint-Georges regaled audiences with his displays in swimming, skating, riding, and marksmanship.

Alone this would have been an extraordinary story in a society where several thousand people of color, whether enslaved or free, could expect only servile and domestic roles in Paris and the port cities. Saint-Georges, however, also became a violin virtuoso, composer, and conductor of two of France's leading orchestras, the *Concert des Amateurs* and the *Concert de la Loge Olympique*. His own concerti, quartets, and operas were played and admired throughout Europe on programs with those of famous composers Wolfgang Amadeus Mozart and Frantz Joseph Haydn. Saint-Georges also helped to pioneer eighteenth-century music techniques such as the *symphonie concertante* for soloists and orchestra.

With enormous personal appeal to accompany his various talents, Saint-Georges was courted by upper-class French society. He was the first person of color within the ranks of French freemasonry, as he was welcomed into the Lodge of the Nine Sisters of the Grand Orient of France. Counting the French king, Louis XVI, and queen, Marie-

Le Chevalier de Saint-Georges.

Antoinette, and the duc d'Orléans among his many patrons and friends, Saint-Georges was the toast of the Parisian salon world. Yet, as exceptional as he was, Saint-Georges was never beyond the snares of racial prejudice. Although he was often referred to as "the famous Saint-Georges," he was equally "the black Don Juan," and simply, "the mulatto." Regardless of his fame and attention, he was never allowed to forget his origins.

In 1789, Saint-Georges espoused the republican ideals of the French Revolution, eventually fighting for the revolution as organizer and commander of a regiment of 1,000 free blacks. Later, Saint-Georges returned to the Caribbean to greet the **Haitian Revolution for Independence,** which had erupted in the late summer of 1791. Accompanying Julien Raimond, the leading champion of people of color in the French world, in 1796, Saint-Georges found the former colony still in the delirium of emancipation, but also beset with factious strife. Three years later, in June 1799, his own death from abdominal ailments just preceded the end of the century of the Enlightenment that he had helped to glorify.

See also: Abolition of Slavery, French; Colonies in the Caribbean, French; Dumas, Thomas-Alexandre; Enlightenment Philosophers and Race; Enlightenment Philosophers and Slavery; France, Blacks in; French Army, Blacks in the; Slave Trade, French.

Further Reading: Cohen, William B. *The French Encounter with Africans: White Responses to Blacks, 1530–1880.* Reprint ed. Bloomington: Indiana University Press, 2003; Gallaher, John G. *General Alexandre Dumas: Soldier of the French Revolution.* Carbondale and Edwardsville: Southern Illinois University Press, 1997; Guédé, Alain. *Monsieur de Saint-George: Virtuoso, Swordsman, Revolutionary.* trans. Gilda M. Roberts. New York: Picador, 2003; Peabody, Sue. *"There Are No Slaves in France": The Political Culture of Race and Slavery in the Ancien Régime.* New York: Oxford University Press, 1996; Smidak, Emil. *Joseph Boulogne, Called Chevalier de Saint-Georges.* trans. John M. Mitchell. Lucerne: Avenira Foundation, 1996.

William H. Alexander

Salvador, Henri (1917–2008)

Henri Salvador was a famous French singer and songwriter. He was born on the American continent in Cayenne, Guyane (French Guiana) on July 18, 1917. His father was from the French island of Guadeloupe, and his mother was an aboriginal from the Caribbean. The young Salvador spent his childhood in Guiana until 1924, when his family migrated to Paris. Being black, he was fascinated by African American music, and especially jazz in all its forms as epitomized by Louis Armstrong, **Duke Ellington,** Cab

Calloway, and Nat King Cole. While in Paris in the 1930s, Salvador also had the chance to see the legendary guitar player Django Reinhardt play, and Reinhardt remained Salvador's main influence for his guitar style. While in his twenties, Salvador also wanted to be a crooner. His career really began to rise in the mid-1940s, when he received the chance to tour Europe and South America with the famous Ray Ventura Orchestra. Salvador also recorded a few songs (on 78 rpm) for Polydor beginning in 1947.

As a prolific songwriter and virtuoso musician, Salvador was innovative in two ways. During the 1950, he was among the first artists in France to record rock 'n' roll songs and African American classics, either adapting American standards like *"Oh Quand les Saints"* (translated from "When the Saints go Marchin' in"), or even composing original upbeat songs with French novelist Boris Vian (1920–1959). These salient songs (all in French) were first released in 1956 under the comical title: *"Henri Salvador alias Henry Cording and his original rock 'n' roll boys"* on the Philips label. Later, Salvador also composed comical lyrics for songs in which he played a lazy-type character that pretended to be too tired to work in songs like *"Je n'peux pas travailler"* ("I am unable to work"). Another one of his comical songs, *"Blouse du dentiste"* ("The Dentist's Coat"), was orchestrated in the early 1960s by arranger Quincy Jones.

Salvador recorded countless songs in all genres, from jazz and blues to calypso, Afro-Cuban ballads, and MOR (middle of the road). Many of his classics are gathered in *The Long Box*, a compilation that spans six decades. His most famous titles remain *"Le loup, la biche et le chevalier"* ("The Wolf, the Hind, and the Knight"), sometimes known as *"Une chanson douce"* ("A Sweet Song"), a famous lullaby that now is almost part of folklore, and *"Faut rigoler"* ("We ought to laugh"). In *"Faut rigoler,"* he humorously refers to *"nos ancêtres les Gaulois* ("our ancestors, the Gauls"), which was the common way to define the French nation in old history books made in France; this inclusive sentence remains ironic, as most people in Guadeloupe and Guyane are black and therefore without much European roots. Among the other songs Salvador is remembered for is *"Maman, tu es la plus belle du monde"* ("Mom, you are the most beautiful in the world"), which he did not compose, but recorded with huge success in France. He also had a parallel career as a host on French and Italian television during the 1960s.

Salvador made a sort of "comeback" in 2001 with a CD that gave him a new, younger, and wider audience: *Chambre Avec Vue* (*Room With a View*), with soft songs in the "Bossa-Nova" vein. He did a farewell tour until December 2007 and died at the age of 90 on February 13, 2008.

See also: Colonies in the Caribbean, French; France, Blacks in; Music, African Influences on European; Music Industry, Blacks in the European; Television, Blacks in European.

Further Reading and Listening: Salvador, Henri. *Attention ma vie*. Paris: J. C. Lattès, 1994; Salvador, Henri. *Le Long Box*. Paris: Barclay (France)—Universal CD, 2006.

Yves Laberge

Sancho, Ignatius (1729?–1780)

Ignatius Sancho, a former slave, was the first black African prose writer to publish his work in England. In addition, he was also the first black Briton known to have voted in a British election. Sancho also composed music and performed in the theater as an actor, where he attained a degree of celebrity status.

It is believed that Sancho was born aboard a slave ship crossing the Atlantic Ocean from Africa to the Caribbean. In New Granada, one of the Spanish colonies in the Caribbean, his mother died and his father committed suicide. Shortly thereafter, Sancho was taken to Greenwich, England. While still a young man, he met the Duke of Montagu, who supported Sancho's education. In 1749, Sancho ran away from his home and petitioned the Montagu family to take him in. The Montagu family subsequently made Sancho their butler. After the deaths of both the Duke and Duchess of Montagu, Sancho received an annuity of 30 pounds and one year's salary. Sancho quickly became a spendthrift.

Sancho befriended the famous English actor, David Garrick. Garrick suggested that Sancho assume the theatrical roles of Othello and Oroonoko, both theatrical characters of African descent; however, Sancho suffered from a speech impediment that limited his theatrical career.

In 1766, Sancho gained employment as a valet to the new Duke of Montagu, the son-in-law of his earlier patrons. With assistance from Montagu, Sancho and his wife, Ann Osborne, opened a grocery in Westminster in the 1770s. It was in this position that he traded letters with many influential figures including Garrick, the Montagues, Nollekins (a sculptor), and author Laurence Sterne. A large collection of his letters was published in 1782 as *The Letters of the Late Ignatius Sancho, an African*. During this time, Sancho also wrote and published his *Theory of Music*, two plays, and newspaper articles (sometimes under the pen name of Africanus). As a male householder of financial independence, he was able to partake in parliamentary elections of 1774 and 1780.

Ignatius Sancho, 1802. © Mary Evans Picture Library.

Sancho died from the effects of gout in 1780. He was the first black Briton to receive an obituary in a British newspaper. To eighteenth-century abolitionists, Sancho emerged as a symbol of Africans' humanity and potential. It is believed that Sancho served as the inspiration for the character of Shina Cambo in the novel *Memoirs and Opinions of Mr. Blenfield* (1790). In the novel, white men visit the home of a black family as equals, demonstrating blacks as integrated into white English society. In 2007, a plaque was unveiled in Sancho's honor in Greenwich, England, on the remaining wall of the Montague House.

See also: Abolition of Slavery, British; Aldridge, Ira; Britain, Blacks in; Colonies in the Caribbean, British; Literature, Blacks in British; *Oroonoko* (1688); *Othello* (1603); Slave Trade, British; Slave Trade, Spanish.

Further Reading: Gerzina, Gretchen. *Black London: Life before Emancipation*. New Brunswick, NJ: Rutgers University Press, 1995; King, Reyahn, ed. *Ignatius Sancho: African Man of Letters*. London: National Portrait Gallery, 1997; Sancho, Ignatius. *Letters of the Late Ignatus Sancho, an African*. New York: Cosimo Classics, 2005.

Eric Martone

Sarbah, John Mensah (1864–1910)

John Mensah Sarbah, the son of a wealthy Fante merchant and civic leader, was part of the African elite privileged to study abroad in England. Although he began his education at Wesleyan High School, Cape Coast, he completed his secondary studies in England at Wesleyan College, Taunton, Somerset. Sarbah studied law at Lincoln's Inn in London. In 1887, he became the first and youngest barrister from the Gold Coast, gaining admission to the British bar at the age of 23. He used his British education to defend the legal rights of the Fanti people and argued to restore the authority of the chiefs to exercise traditional leadership roles.

In Britain, Sarbah authored several publications, including *Fanti Customary Laws*, with editions published in 1897 and 1904. Its nationalistic impulse educated the British about Fanti customs to foster in them a respect for Fanti traditions. His second major publication, *Fanti National Constitution*, which also upheld the dignity of Fanti customs, was published in London in 1906. Sarbah's pioneering scholarship, which, combining oral history, legal studies, and sociology, was in high demand by Europeans studying West Africa and educated Africans. His other publications included articles in the Liverpool publication *West African Mail* in 1905 and in the *Journal of the African Society*.

When Sarbah returned to the Gold Coast in the late 1880s, he worked to inform people of their rights and helped them fight and negate British colonial domination and ideology. Mensah and other English-trained lawyers, such as Joseph Ephraim Casely-Hayford, were regarded suspiciously by the British because they openly criticized colonial rule. One of Sarbah's major successes that thrust him into a prominent leadership role among West Africans was defeating the Lands Bill of 1897, which would have usurped traditional property rights and allowed the British government to dispose of the people's land without compensation. Sarbah maintained that the British administration had illegally occupied land in the Gold Coast, subjecting the people to direct taxation, an alien concept among traditional Africans. After refusing the legal retainer for his work on the Lands Bill case, Sarbah designated the money should be used to help found the Aborigines's Rights Protection Society. The society helped to prevent the appropriation of indigenous people's lands by the British and other Europeans. An ardent cultural nationalist, Sarbah argued that the traditional customs of the Fanti should be blended with those of the British colonial governments to form an independent nation-state of the Gold Coast.

Following the lead of his father, who had served as a schoolmaster and mission agent for the Wesleyan Missionary Society in Cape Coast, Sarbah advocated developing and promoting education, while fostering pride in indigenous institutions. Sarbah, a former student of the prestigious Methodist all-boys Mfantsipim School (formerly Wesleyan High School), founded in 1876, supplied the new name of the school, which means "countless numbers of Fantes." Today, the school counts among its graduates a number of political leaders, including the former secretary general of the United Nations, Kofi Annan.

See also: Britain, Blacks in; Colonies in Africa, British.

Further Reading: Dumett, Raymond E. "John Sarbah, the Elder, and African Mercantile Entrepreneurship in the Gold Coast in the Late Nineteenth Century." *The Journal of African History* 14 (1973): 653–679; Green, Jeffrey. *Black Edwardians: Black People in Britain, 1901–1914*. New York: Routledge, 1998; Lynch, Hollis R. "Introduction." In Sharbah, John Mensah. *Fanti Customary Laws*. 3rd ed. London: Frank Cass, 1968, pp. v-xiii.

Lena Ampadu

Scandinavia, Blacks in

There are no figures on how many blacks are currently in Scandinavia, as no data concerning ethnicity in Scandinavia have been collected. The description of being "black" in Scandinavia differs somewhat from, for example, being "black" in the United States. To be a black Dane/Norwegian/Swede or an Afro-Dane/Norwegian/Swede usually means having a black parent and a white parent. In Scandinavian countries, however, because transracial and transnational adoptions are a widespread phenomenon, black children can be adopted by white families. Thus many black children have grown up without black role models to identify with or any historical roots. At the same time, they must cope with the necessity to stand their ground and survive in a white world from early childhood. In addition, women and men of African descent have immigrated to Scandinavia to the current era of increasing European multicultural diversity.

In all Scandinavian black communities, giving themselves a name was significant in the process of self-identity. The labels Afro-Danes/Norwegians/Swedes, or black Danes/Norwegians/Swedes, or other self-descriptions help to break the barriers of dominant designations by others, while expressing being black and Scandinavian at the same time. Black Scandinavians cannot fall back on any cultural background of collective memories and traditions. Until recently, the existence and contributions of people of African descent have not been acknowledged adequately. The role they play, both in official historiography and in public discourse, is marked by stereotyped racial clichés.

Scandinavian countries were involved in the Atlantic slave trade, colonization, and missionary work in Africa. For the most part, however, Scandinavian countries have yet to examine their colonial past and their traditions resulting from it. Consequently, they pass such traditions on without major change. As the established patterns in the thinking and acting of white Scandinavians are shaped by these traditions, so is the life and experience of blacks in Scandinavia. In the Scandinavian context, the issue of the colonial past has only recently started to emerge in a fuller context. Conferences and projects in 2006, such as *Rethinking Nordic Colonialism* (Kuratorisk Aktion Berlin/Copenhagen) or *Denmark and the Black Atlantic* (University of Copenhagen), testify to this changing awareness.

People of African descent in Scandinavia are mostly connected by one common experience: They are confronted with racism in their daily lives, both as individuals and as a group, usually being considered transitory or exceptional in a society assumed to be homogenous. The common history of immigration starts in most cases with the experiences of postcolonial migration. This migration was difficult to integrate into the self-image of solidarity and conscientious welfare in the Scandinavian concept of society.

In Denmark, the black Danish journalist Philip Sampson has collected about 400 biographies of blacks living in Denmark from 1600 to 1945, including Moors at courts in the sixteenth century; enslaved people and servants in the seventeenth century; semifree enslaved people in the beginning of the eighteenth century; black Americans coming to Denmark from the mid-eighteenth century as minstrels, musicians, and entertainers; people from the Danish West Indies (now the U.S. Virgin Islands); black jazz artists in the 1920s; and blacks emigrating from Germany in the 1920s and 1930s because of the political situation. Transcending its national context, this work will surely prove to be a milestone in re-accessing black Scandinavian history. In the contemporary political landscape of Norway, Manuela Ramin Osmundsen was the first black woman to receive a prominent political post when she was appointed cabinet minister in 2007.

In Norway, the first efforts to support and empower awareness in order to overcome invisibility, and finally to establish collective activities, have been made in the founding of the **Young Africans in Norway (AYIN)** in 1995. The work of this movement does not just concern itself with the remapping of Norway's history and language, but also with the empowering of self-descriptions, perceptions, and identities for black youths and black people in Norway.

In Sweden, one also finds community structures headed by the *Afrosvenskarnas riksförbundet* that aim at constituting a voice for blacks in Sweden. Such groups strive to empower and to challenge the contemporary reality with statements on numerous topics. In Sweden, Nyamko Sabuni, a black woman, also achieved a prominent political post when she was appointed minister for integration and equality.

Black Scandinavian studies, which has emerged as part of the research on a common black history, continues to grow in the twenty-first century. It faces the challenge to write black history into the dominating historiography.

See also: Abolition of Slavery, European; African Diaspora; Jazz, European Reception of; Larsen, Nella.

Further Reading: Arter, David. "Black Faces in the Blond Crowd: Populist Racialism in Scandinavia." *Parliamentary Affairs* 45 (1992): 357–372; Gullestad, Marianne. "Normalising Racial Boundaries: The Norwegian Dispute about the Term 'neger.'" *Social Anthropology* 13:1 (February 2005): 27–46; Hällgren, Camilla. "'Working Harder to be the Same': Everyday Racism among Young Men and Women in Sweden." *Race Ethnicity and Education* 8:3 (September 2005): 319–342; Pred, Allan. *Even in Sweden: Racisms, Radicalized Spaces, and the Popular Geographic Imagination.* Berkeley: University of California Press, 2000; Sawyer, Lena. "Routings: 'Race,' African

Diasporas, and Swedish Belonging." *Transforming Anthropology* 11:1 (January 2002): 13–35; Weisbord, Robert G. "Scandinavia: A Racial Utopia?" *Journal of Black Studies* 2:4 (June 1972): 471–488.

Nadine Golly

Scientific Racism

Scientific racism refers to nineteenth-century theories or arguments that purportedly used scientific evidence to further notions of evolutionary differences between members of diverse races and/or ethnic groups. Scientific racism draws from such academic disciplines as craniometry, physical anthropology, phrenology, physiognomy, and anthropometry to establish a typology of various human races that revolve around a concept of "race." The popularity of theories that could be classified under the term *scientific racism* increased during the period of European global expansion in the eighteenth and nineteenth centuries. These theories were used to provide ideological justifications for racism and the subordination of certain races or ethnic groups as slaves and/or colonial subjects.

EARLY SCIENTIFIC THEORIES OF RACE.   The modern notion of "race" as human type of classification, using predominantly physical characteristics such as skin color, dates from the eighteenth century. In 1735, a Swedish scientist named Carolus Linnaeus included humans as a species within the primate genus. He subsequently subdivided that species into several different types. Linnaeus's scientific classification efforts were primarily concerned with accounting for the differences between Europeans, Amerindians, Asians, and Africans. Linnaeus attributed to each type certain biological characteristics, which were inherited, and certain cultural characteristics, which were learned. At one end of his classification scale was "Homo European," who had light-colored skin and was governed by laws; at the other end of the scale was "Homo African," who had black-colored skin and was governed by impulses.

Johann Friedrich Blumenbach's *On the Natural Varieties of Mankind* (1776) emerged as one of the most authoritative Enlightenment classifications of races. Blumenbach divided humans into five groups (Caucasians, Mongolians, Ethiopians, Americans, and Malays) based on the known dominant physical characteristics of each type on each of the continents/regions of the known world. In his racial descriptions, Blumenbach emphasized somatic characteristics instead of intellectual or moral ones. He argued that all humans belong to the same species and had a common ancestry. His depiction of a progression from primitive societies to industrialized civilization became popular among later philosophers, including Friedrich Hegel, Immanuel Kant, and Auguste Comte. In addition, such notions of a common ancestry complemented Christian beliefs in the divine creation of Adam and Eve, from which all of humanity descended.

In contrast to such ideas, polygenist theory argued that there were multiple origins of humans, and it was therefore possible to conceive of various biological human races. Although Blumenbach refuted the common claim that Africans were more animalistic (and hence nearer to apes than other men), his work is marked by an ethnocentric bias.

He was the first to trace whites to the Caucasus, but he arrived at this conclusion because of the legendary beauty of its inhabitants. He believed that Caucasians were the first human race, and it was from this race that all others had diverged. Thus with their work, Linnaeus, Blumenbach, and other eighteenth-century ethnologists paved the way for a secular (or scientific) racism.

CRANIOMETRY AND PHYSICAL ANTHROPOLOGY. During the nineteenth century, further research gave racial theories seemingly more legitimacy. Data analyses were conducted from such activities as the measurement of skulls, foreheads, and noses, and the weight of brains. Pieter Camper (1722–1789), a Dutch scholar, was an early proponent of craniometry (the measurement of skulls) to justify racial differences. In 1770, Camper developed the concept of the "facial angle," a measurement to determine intelligence among different species. According to his technique, a "facial angle" was calculated by drawing a horizontal line from the nostrils to the ear of a subject and an additional perpendicular line from the advancing part of the upper jawbone to the most prominent component of the subject's forehead. Camper conclusions reinforced a hierarchic and racist view of humans: he argued that Europeans had an angle of 80 degrees, blacks had an angle of 70 degrees, and orangutans had an angle of 58 degrees.

Drawings from Josiah C. Nott and George Gliddon's *Indigenous Races of the Earth* (1857), which suggested black people ranked between white people and chimpanzees in terms of intelligence.

Other scientists continued such research, including Etienne Geoffroy Saint-Hilaire (1772–1844), Paul Broca (1824–1880), and Samuel George Morton (1799–1851). Morton was a founder of physical anthropology, which involved the collecting of hundreds of skulls from different parts of the globe. Morton sought to classify the skulls according to certain criteria. He argued that he could determine the intellectual capacity of different races based on their cranial capacity, which is the skull's interior volume. Larger skulls were believed to imply larger brains and hence higher capacity for intelligence. Conversely, smaller skulls were believed to imply smaller brains and lower capacities of intelligence. In his examinations of various skulls, Morton determined the point that Caucasians diverged into Africans. He possessed several Egyptian skulls and from these concluded that ancient Egyptians were not black African, but rather white.

EUGENICS. Georges Vacher de Lapouge (1854–1936), a theoretician of eugenics, developed one of the earliest typologies used for the classification of different human races. He published *The Aryan and His Social Role* (1899), an anti-Semitic work that classified humans into different hierarchical races. He believed that the most advanced race was the "Aryan white race," and the lowest type of race was best exhibited by the Jews. William Ripley advanced similar faulty theories in his *The Races of Europe* (1899), which influenced American racist groups.

Joseph Deniker (1852–1918) opposed many of Ripley's ideas. Whereas Ripley (and Vacher de Lapouges) argued that Europe was composed of three races, Deniker argued that there were 10 races in Europe (six primary races and four subraces). One of Deniker's longest-lasting ideas was the designation of a "*race nordique*" ("Northern race").

Madison Grant (1865–1937) built on both Ripley's and Deniker's ideas. Grant used Ripley's notion of three European races and adopted Deniker's notion of a "*race nordique*" (which he transliterated as "Nordic race"), which Grant placed at the top of his racial hierarchy. Grant's Nordic theory became especially popular in Germany during the racial hygiene movement of the early twentieth century. Racial hygiene was historically connected ideas of public health, but with an emphasis on heredity. Francis Galton (1822–1911) was one of the earliest scholars to advocate using social measures to preserve (or enhance) certain biological characteristics. Galton coined the term *eugenics* to describe this process. The popularity of both eugenics and racial hygiene influenced racial policies of the Nazis and their eugenics program in Germany.

RACIAL CATEGORIES.   The idea of "racial differences" implies that there are distinct biological differences between different groups of humans that can be determined by definable physical and/or social features; however, there are no clear, established demarcations of humans who fit coherent sets of physical features. Within any identified racial group are variations of skin color, hair color and texture, body shape, facial structure, etc. Furthermore, there are certain features that transcend more than one racial group.

Although there is no clear link between observable physical and social differences, racial classifications have long presupposed that such a connection exists. The demarcation of socially significant and distinct races, on which racial classifications are based, fetishizes the characteristics that it determines distinctive and artificially fills them with social meaning. Although this does not necessarily imply the division of humans into inferior and superior groups that is how such classifications have historically been used. The practice of assigning importance to physical characteristics such as skin color, eye color, and nose shape have been racialized to give way to racial classifications constricted and based on subjective physical characteristics, which are not historically or socially fixed, rather than on any biological reality.

See also: *Black Athena* Controversy; Cain, Theory of Descent of Blacks from; Enlightenment Philosophers and Race; Enlightenment Philosophers and Slavery; Gall, Franz Josef; Gobineau on Races and Slavery; Hamitic Myth; New Imperialism.

Further Reading: Back, Les, and John Solomos, eds. *Theories of Race and Racism.* New York: Routledge, 2000; Donald, James, and Ali Rattansi, eds. *Race, Culture, and Difference.* New York: Sage, 1992; Fredrickson, George M. *Racism: A Short History.* Princeton: Princeton University Press, 2002; Gates, Henry Louis. *Race, Writing and Difference.* Chicago: University of Chicago Press, 1986; Kohn, Marek. *The Race Gallery: The Return of Racial Science.* New York: Vintage, 1996.

Charlotte Baker

Scotland, Patricia (1955–)

Patricia Janet Scotland, a barrister and politician, became the first woman attorney general for England and Wales in 2007. She was born on August 19, 1955 in Dominica to Antiguan and Dominican parents. Her family migrated to Britain at the age of three. Scotland attended Walthamstow School for Girls. She had a brilliant academic record, earning a law degree at the age of 20 from London University. She specialized in family and children's law from the Middle Temple bar. In her career as an attorney, Scotland took cases pertaining to social justice, immigration, child abuse, mental disorder, domestic violence, and housing.

Scotland became well known in 1991 when she became the first black woman in the legal history of Britain to be appointed as Queen's Counsel. She was also the youngest since William Pitt the Younger (1759–1806). In February 1994, Scotland became the millennium commissioner. Her rise was phenomenal at the time of Tony Blair's tenure as prime minister. She became a bencher of the Middle Temple in 1997 and subsequently a judge two years afterward. Scotland received the coveted position of peer as Baroness Scotland of Asthal in the County of Oxfordshire in 1997. As the parliamentary undersecretary of state at the Foreign and Commonwealth Office from 1999, Scotland looked after the country's overseas territories. A bill was mooted at her behest for ratifying International Criminal Court in Britain. After two years, she became a member of the Privy Council, as well as parliamentary secretary in the Department of Lord Chancellor. Scotland became the first female lawyer to hold the rank of a minister of state in the Lord Chancellor's Department. She had the challenging task of the Department's Bills in the House of Lords.

In 2003, Scotland was the Home Office minister of state for Criminal Justice System and Law Reform. After two years, she became the Home Office minister of state. She also had the additional charge of gender and equality issues of the Trade and Industry Department. Between 2002 and 2003, Scotland was the government's alternate representative to the European Convention. She became the first woman to become attorney general in June 2007 under Prime Minister Gordon Brown. As the highest law enforcement officer of the nation, she reached the pinnacle of glory in her professional career.

Scotland is active in many organizations such as Frank Longford Charitable Trust, British American Project, Thomas More Society, and Women and Children's Welfare Fund. She has not forgotten her Caribbean origin. She is a member of the bar in Dominica and has visited her country of origin.

See also: Black British; Britain, Blacks in.

Further Reading: Adler, Sue, and Catherine Ward. *Baroness Scotland of Asthal: A Profile.* Northwood: Tamarind Books, 2001.

Patit Paban Mishra

Seacole, Mary (1805–1881)

Mary Seacole was a devoted Jamaican nurse of biracial descent during the nineteenth century known for risking her life to save others. Despite the British government's refusal to let her serve as a nurse during the Crimean War due to her ethnicity,

Seacole self-financed her journey to the Crimea, where she ran a hotel to assist the British army's wounded.

Seacole was born Mary Jane Grant in Kingston, Jamaica, in 1805 to a white Scottish officer in the British army and a Jamaican woman who practiced herbal healing and medicine. Seacole's mother also ran a boarding house, Blundell Hall, for injured soldiers. During her adolescent years, Seacole learned herbal cures and traveled throughout the Caribbean and to London. After briefly returning to Jamaica in 1825, she resumed her travels to several places, including Cuba, Haiti, and the Bahamas.

Seacole married Edwin Horatio Hamilton Seacole, a white British merchant, in November 1836. Shortly after her husband's and mother's death in 1844, Seacole took over Blundell Hall until 1851. The next year, she cared for cholera patients in Panana and yellow fever victims in Jamaica. Her success as a nurse encouraged her to tend the wounded in the Crimean War. In 1854, Seacole traveled to London to join the group of nurses established by Florence Nightingale. Despite her skills, the British War Offices refused to employ her because of her skin color. Seacole used her own financial means to reach Crimea and went to Balaclava in 1855. After receiving another refusal to work as a nurse, she built a lodging for ill soldiers named British Hotel. While running the hotel, Seacole also became a battlefield nurse, sold medicine, and gave medical advice. Her dutiful attention and bravery of helping the wounded on the front earned her the title "Mother Seacole" with the soldiers.

Using a large portion of her assets to travel to the Crimea and run British Hotel, Seacole returned to England destitute when the Crimean War ended in 1856. She also earned a poor reputation with Florence Nightingale and some English Victorians for giving alcohol to soldiers and allegedly running a brothel instead of a hotel. Seacole's reputation was restored when an 1856 letter in *The Times* praised her skills and bravery and pushed for her celebration. From July 27 to July 30, 1857, a festival in Seacole's honor was held with more than 1,000 performers; it received support by several Crimean war commanders including Lord Rokeby and Lord Paget. During this same period, she received several honors and medals.

In 1857, Seacole published her autobiography, *The Wonderful Adventures of Mrs. Seacole in Many Lands*. The text became a bestseller and received critical acclaim. Seacole spent the next two decades traveling between Jamaica and England, and attending to patients like the Princess of Wales. After Seacole's death in 1881, her accolades continued. She was voted the Greatest Black Briton in 2004, her portrait hung in the National Portrait Gallery of London in January 2005, and she received an exhibit at the Florence Nightingale Museum in London from 2005 to 2007.

See also: Black British; Britain, Blacks in; Colonies in the Caribbean, British.

Further Reading: Ramdin, Ron. *Mary Seacole*. London: Haus, 2005; Seacole, Mary. *The Wonderful Adventures of Mrs. Seacole in Many Lands*. New York: Oxford University Press, 1988.

Dorsía Smith

Séjour, Victor (1817–1874)

Victor Séjour was an African American writer who wrote in French and made his career in nineteenth-century France, where he achieved notable success and received the prestigious *Légion d'Honneur*. He was born a free Creole in New Orleans, Louisiana in 1817.

His father was a free man of biracial descent from Haiti and his mother was a free woman of biracial descent from the United States. Séjour's parents were relatively prosperous and encouraged their son's education. In 1836, Séjour's parents sent him to Paris to study under fewer racial restraints. Such a practice was common among prosperous Creoles. In Paris, he met **Cyrille Bissette,** who was also black and edited the abolitionist journal *La Revue des Colonies*. Bissette published Séjour's short story, *"Le Mulâtre"* ("The Mulatto," 1837), which condemned slavery. *"Le Mulâtre,"* one of the earliest known pieces of fiction published by an African American writer, tells the story of a slave who exacts revenge on his master for his wife's death only to discover that he has murdered his father. Although the story in general made little impact in the United States at the time (and was not translated into English until the twentieth century), it did have an effect on educated former slaves who became abolitionists, such as **Frederick Douglass.**

In 1841, Séjour wrote "Le retour de Napoléon" ("The Return of Napoleon"), an ode honoring the former French emperor, to celebrate the return of his remains for burial in France. Séjour remained an admirer of Napoleon throughout his life. "Le retour de Napoléon" was reprinted later in the United States as part of *Les Cenelles* (1845), an early anthology of African American poetry. The poem's success brought him admittance to the highest French literary circles, where he met **Alexandre Dumas père,** author of *The Three Musketeers* and himself of African descent.

In 1844, Séjour began his career as a dramatist with the verse play *Diégarias* (*The Jew of Seville*), which was performed at the Théâtre-Français. His success continued with *La chute de Séjan* (*The Fall of Sejanus*, 1849). Séjour's work reflected the influence of Shakespeare and other Renaissance English writers, as well as contemporary writers in France, such as Victor Hugo. For example, *The Jew of Seville* was inspired by Shakespeare's *The Merchant of Venice* and Christopher Marlowe's *The Jew of Malta*. Séjour also wrote a play about the English King Richard III in 1852 that paid homage to Shakespeare's play on the same subject. Séjour's works reflected the intense emotionalism of the French Romantics, and his use of monologue and rhetoric are reminiscent of the work of Hugo. Séjour became a popular and admired dramatist in Paris during the 1850s and 1860s, writing more than 20 performed plays in his career. During this period of success, he brought both his parents to live in France. In 1860, Séjour became a member of the *Légion d'Honneur*.

Shifts in literature and popular taste resulted in the decline of Séjour's popularity. In the 1870s, he was in poor health and with little finances. He died in 1874 in the process of finishing his serialized novel, *Le Comte de Haag* (*The Count of Haag*), which was set in revolutionary France.

See also: Abolition of Slavery, French; Authors in Europe, African American; *Bug-Jargal*; France, Blacks in; *Georges*; *Othello*.

Further Reading: O'Neill, Charles Edwards. "Theatrical Censorship in France, 1844–1875: The Experience of Victor Séjour." *Harvard Library Bulletin* 26:4 (Oct. 1978): 417–441; Perret, J. John. "Victor Séjour: Black French Playwright from Louisiana." *The French Review* 57:2 (Dec. 1983): 187–193; Séjour, Victor. "The Mulatto." trans. Philip Barnard. In *The Norton Anthology of African- American Literature*. ed. Nellie McKay and Henry Louis Gates. 2nd ed. New York: W. W. Norton, 2004.

Eric Martone

Senghor, Léopold Sédar (1906–2001)

Léopold Sédar Senghor was a French writer and the first leader of the newly in-dependent state of Senegal from 1960 to 1980. Born in a coastal village near Dakar in Senegal in 1906, he had the chance to spend his childhood in a relatively wealthy family. He began learning French at the age of seven, when he attended the French missionary school, and later on, when he studied in Paris from 1928. In Paris, Senghor met the young **Aimé Césaire.** During the 1930s, both men began to forge the con-cept of **Négritude,** a positive affirmation of the African identity and culture, with the retelling of Africa as the source of all blacks on Earth. During his school days at the *Lycée Louis-le-Grand* in Paris, Senghor also met Georges Pompidou (who would later become the president of France in 1969). During World War II, Senghor served with the French army for a short time, but he was soon taken prisoner by the Nazi German forces, which occupied France from 1940 to 1942.

From 1945 to 1990, Senghor wrote more than a dozen books, mostly poetry, but also some short essays. Among his most important books is an anthology of young African poetry entitled *Anthologie de la nouvelle poésie nègre et malgache de langue française* (*Anthology of the new Negro and Madagascar poetry in French,* 1948), which was often quoted in French studies.

Senghor is mostly remembered for his term as president of Senegal, which spanned two decades. He had already been active in politics for 15 years when he became the head of the new Senegalese government in 1960. Before Senegalese independence, Senghor was first elected MP (*"député"*) in 1945 to represent the colonial Senegal in the French National Assembly in Paris. He was reelected three times until 1960. Later, while president of Senegal, Senghor organized in Dakar the first World Festival of Negro Arts in 1966. The organization of the festival confirmed his attachment to the arts, literature, and culture. Senghor maintained strong links with the democratic governments of France and remained distant from communist states such as the Soviet Union.

When he retired from politics at the age of 74, Senghor stayed in Normandy, France with his second wife until his death at the age of 95 in 2001. Senghor was among the first "celebrities" from black Africa to obtain many recognitions, distinctions, and lit-erary prices from European institutions. Among many other awards, he received the *Grand prix international de poésie* in 1963, the medal from *Dag Hammarskjoeld* in 1965, the *Cino del Duca* in 1978, the *Athénaï* in Greece in 1985, and the *Intercultura* in Rome in 1987. Senghor was elected a member of the prestigious French Academy on June 3, 1983. In addition, he received more than 35 *"Honoris Causa"* doctorates in Europe, the United States, and Canada. During the World Francophone Summit that reunited the heads of French-speaking states in 1989, he had the privilege to see the birth of an institution that still bears his name, the *Université Léopold Sedar Senghor* in Alexandria, Egypt, which is dedicated to many disciplines, all given in French, to adults over the age of 36.

See also: African Diaspora; Colonies in Africa, French; France, Blacks in; French Army, Blacks in the; Literature, Blacks in French; Pan-Africanism; World War II, Black Participation in.

Further Reading: Kluback, William. *Léopold Sédar Senghor: From Politics to Poetry.* New York: Peter Lang, 1997; Senghor, Léopold Sédar. *The Collected Poetry.* trans. Melvin Dixon. Charlottesville: University of Virginia Press, 1991; Vaillant, Janet. *Black, French, and African: A Life of Léopold Sédar Senghor.* Cambridge: Harvard University Press, 1990.

Yves Laberge

Shakespeare's Sonnets, The Dark Lady of

Several of the sonnets (numbers 127 to 152) of William Shakespeare, the great Renaissance English playwright and poet, refer to a mysterious woman known only as the "Dark Lady." These sonnets are sexual in nature and imply that the speaker has had a torrid affair with the Dark Lady, who is unfaithful to him, possibly with a younger man.

The life of Shakespeare is not well documented and little is known about the details of his personal life. Scholars have long debated the identity of this Dark Lady and have offered many suggestions, including that she was perhaps the writer's mistress. Shakespeare describes the color of the Dark Lady's skin as "dun," which referred to a dull or brown color. One of the popular hypotheses for this mistress's identity is that she was a courtesan called Luce Negro, whom it is believed became acquainted with the writer in the 1590s. Luce Negro was a famous black courtesan in England and ran a brothel in Clerkenwell in London. This Luce may also have been known as Luce Morgan.

See also: Britain, Blacks in; *Othello*; Prostitution in Europe, Blacks and.

Further Reading: Forbes, Thomas R. *Chronicle of Aldgate: Life and Death in Shakespeare's London.* New Haven: Yale University Press, 1971; Harrison, G. B. *Shakespeare at Work.* London: Routledge, 1933; Hotson, Leslie. *Mr. W. H.* London: Rupert Hart-Davis, 1964; Salkeld, Duncan. "Black Luce and the 'Curtizons' of Shakespeare's London." *Signatures* (Winter 2000). Available at: http://www.chiuni.ac.uk/info/Signatures.cfm; Vaughan, Alden, and Virginia Vaughan. "Before Othello: Elizabethan Representations of Sub-Saharan Africans." *The William and Mary Quarterly* 54:1 (1997): 19–44.

Nicole Martone

Shinebourne, Janice (1947–)

Janice Shinebourne (née Lowe) is a prominent Guyanese writer in Britain who wrote novels about the complex web of nationalities in twentieth-century Guyana. She was born in 1947 in Guyana and attended Berbice High School. After leaving school, she became a reporter in Georgetown, Guyana, and then studied at the University of Guyana. During this period, Shinebourne was writing and had already won prizes in the National History and Arts Council Literary Competition. She moved to London in 1970. Shinebourne has studied literature as a postgraduate at the University of London, edited several journals, and worked as a university lecturer. A major cultural activist and author, Shinebourne has also been a Visiting Fellow at New York University and has embarked on reading tours in Europe, the Caribbean, the United States, and Asia.

Shinebourne's first novel, *Timepiece* (1986), is partly autobiographical. The main character, Sandra Yansen, leaves her family and village behind to become a newspaper reporter in Georgetown. Saying farewell to her friends in the village in Berbice, Sandra is divided between her mother, Helen, who likes town life, and her father, Ben, who remains attracted to the village life and country values. Sandra's settling into city life explores the experiences that many other Guyanese felt.

Shinebourne's second novel, *The Last English Plantation* (2001), has the 12-year-old June Lehall confronting her Indian-Chinese heritage at a time of rising political tensions in British Guiana as the colony heads toward independence. The girl wins a scholarship to the local high school and, from there, observes the arrival of British soldiers in a dispute on a nearby sugar plantation. As with Shinebourne's first book, some of the novel draws from her own life and experiences, also showing the rising political consciousness in Guyana and the treatment of the black population. The predicament of the largely Indian heroine contrasts with many other accounts of racial problems in Guyana written by those without Shinebourne's understanding of the Guyanese Indian psyche.

Shinebourne's third book, *The Godmother and Other Stories* (2003), explores colonial and postcolonial themes, with a number of people of African and other heritages struggling to find a role in colonial British Guiana and in independent Guyana.

See also: Britain, Blacks in; Civil Rights Movement in Twentieth-Century Great Britain; Colonies in the Caribbean, British; Literature, Blacks in British.

Further Reading: Gafoor, Ameena. "The Depiction of Indian Female Experience in the Contemporary Novel of the Anglophone Caribbean." *Guyana Chronicle* (April 27, 2003); King, Bruce. *The Oxford English Literary History, 1984–2000: The Internationalization of English Literature.* New York: Oxford University Press, 2004; Scott, Helen. *Caribbean Women Writers and Globalization: Fictions of Independence.* Burlington, VT: Ashgate, 2006.

Justin Corfield

Sierra Leone

Sierra Leone is a multiethnic republic situated on the Atlantic coast of West Africa between Liberia and Guinea. The history of modern Sierra Leone is typically traced to 1787, when a group of "Black Poor" from London arrived there to establish a colony for ex-slaves and their descendants from the Americas and Britain. The Sierra Leone settlement was the project of abolitionists, among them **Olaudah Equiano,** who was to have taken part in the 1787 voyage.

The land to which these colonists sailed was no virgin territory. Some of the states, chieftaincies, and other African communities living along the coast had been trading with European merchants since the arrival of the Portuguese in the area in the fifteenth century. One aspect of the social organization of many of the groups in the area was the important role assumed by the male and female secret societies (*Poro* and *Sande/ Bundu*, respectively) in politics.

The 1787 experiment failed and most of the would-be colonists perished. In 1792, another boatload of settlers arrived from Nova Scotia, Canada. These settlers were American blacks who had fought on the British side in the American Revolution for

Independence on the promise of freedom from the British Crown. In 1800, a third wave of immigrants arrived, this time Jamaican "Maroons," who were slaves that had escaped from slavery and established independent communities in the mountains of Jamaica.

In 1808, Britain took control of the settlement ("Freetown") from the Sierra Leone Company and declared Freetown and its surrounding areas a Crown Colony. The previous year, Britain had abolished the slave trade. With abolition, the British navy established a patrol off the coast of West Africa to enforce its ban against the slave trade. Freetown served as the base of the British patrol, and the slaves liberated from intercepted slavers were resettled in Sierra Leone. The tens of thousands of these "recaptives," as they were called, constituted the largest single group in the settler community, greatly outnumbering the Nova Scotians and Maroons. The settlers, as a whole, are known as *Krio* (formerly "Creole").

Although most *Krio* are identified with Christianity and harbingers of Western civilization, a significant proportion of "recaptives" were Muslim and maintained their religious affiliation through the years. Islam in the area dates from at least the eighteenth century and probably before, when Muslim Mande and Fulani began settling in parts of present-day northern Sierra Leone; conversions by locals ensued.

During the era of European imperialism in Africa, Sierra Leone was as a major center for British rule in West Africa. Fourah Bay College, the first Western-style school of higher education in British West Africa, was established in Sierra Leone in 1827. From Sierra Leone, administrators, doctors, lawyers, and missionaries especially traveled throughout the West African subregion, sometimes settling permanently and establishing Sierra Leonean enclaves.

During the "Scramble for Africa," Britain extended its colonial rule from its coastal base into the interior, declaring a protectorate over the interior in 1896. In 1898, the British imposition of a "hut tax" resulted in war between Britain and a number of chiefs in the interior, most notably Bai Bureh. The protectorate and the colony were administered separately until 1951, when the two were brought under a single system. British colonial rule ended on April 27, 1961.

See also: Abolition of Slavery, British; British Army, Blacks in the; Colonies in Africa, British; Crowther, Samuel Adjai; Missionaries in Africa, European; New Imperialism; Slave Trade, British.

Further Reading: Alie, Joe A. D. *A New History of Sierra Leone.* New York: St. Martin's Press, 1990; Fyfe, Christopher. *A History of Sierra Leone.* London: Oxford University Press, 1962; Fyle, C. Macbaily. *Historical Dictionary of Sierra Leone.* Lanham, MD: Scarecrow Press, 2006; Wyse, Akintola. *The Krio of Sierra Leone: An Interpretive History.* Washington, DC: Howard University Press, 1991.

Anene Ejikeme

Slave Revolts in the British Caribbean

Since ancient times, enslaved persons have revolted against their masters. Some of the major slave insurrections in history occurred in the British colonies in the Caribbean. These insurrections had a far-reaching impact on the colonies as well as the mother country. In the Caribbean (West Indian) region, the islands of Anguilla, Antigua, Bahamas, Barbados, Bermuda, British Guyana, British Virgin Islands, Cayman Islands, Jamaica, Montserrat, Nevis, Trinidad, and Tobago were under British domination. Although many of the sporadic revolts were aborted, three rebellions flared up with serious dimensions. These rebellions occurred in Barbados (1816), Guyana (Demerara Rebellion, 1823), and Jamaica (Insurrection of 1831–1832). The Caribbean slave revolts not only compelled British abolitionists to take a radical posture, but also changed the social, economic, and political profile of the colonies.

The enslaved blacks under the leadership of African-born Bussa (d. 1816) revolted in Barbados on April 14, 1816. With the objective of bringing the plantations under the control of the blacks and ending slavery, the insurrection began with the burning of sugarcane in St. Phillip. The insurrection spread to the neighboring regions and the colonial government imposed martial law. The premature beginning of the insurrection resulted in its failure and the government soon regained control. The rebellion was crushed by the West Indian Regiment and militia on April 17 and Bussa was killed. About 4,000 to 5,000 slaves participated in the revolt. After two major battles, the death toll of the rebels was about 1,000. About 144 slaves were executed and about 123 were deported. There was extensive damage to property and sugar plantations. The slaves, however, received some respite by the 1825 Consolidated Slave Law, which gave them the right to property and to testify in court cases. The Bussa, or Eastern Rebellion, also strengthened the cause of abolitionists in Great Britain in their struggle to end slavery. In 1833, the British Parliament abolished slavery in its territories and more than 83,000 slaves were freed in Barbados. Bussa has become a national hero in Barbados.

The 1823 Demerara rebellion occurred in the colony of Demerara-Essequibo, which was incorporated with Berbice eight years afterward to form British Guyana. This massive rebellion, which involved 1,100 to 1,200 slaves across 55 plantations in the East Coast of Demerara, was the result of accumulated slave grievances. Social tension was brewing. Aging slaves had to work for longer hours in the sugarcane plantations (in Demerara-Essequibo, the production of coffee and cotton had been eliminated). Slave owners would not allow slaves to attend the church prayers. The planters also asked slaves to work on Sundays, thereby making it impossible for the slaves to attend churches.

The insurrection began on August 18, 1823 on Plantation Success and spread quickly to other regions of eastern Demerara. The leaders of the revolt, however, were not able to extend their operation to Georgetown and the western Demerara regions. The official retribution was harsh and several hundred slaves were killed. Many were tried for treason. John Smith of Bethel Chapel in Plantation Le Ressouvenir, for example, was condemned to death for instigating the slaves. The majority of the slaves who had taken part in the revolt were not African-born slaves. They were Creoles born locally who were slaves from birth. The insurrection in 1823 shattered the myth that Creoles were docile and accommodative to the life of a slave. Another notable feature of the revolt was that it was the first major insurrection in the British Caribbean in which religion played an important role.

The 1831–1832 slave rebellions on the British colony of Jamaica, known variously as the Baptist War or the Christmas Rebellion, became a contributing factor in dismantling the institution of slavery throughout the British Empire. After Jamaica's acquisition in 1655, the sugar economy had developed rapidly, and there had been an uninterrupted importation of enslaved persons from Africa. Whereas the planter elite had expanded its enterprise, the condition of blacks was miserable.

The 1831–1832 rebellions received an impetus from the reports that the emancipation of enslaved Africans was imminent. Numerous churches had established parishes in Jamaica and the Baptist Mission Society had dispatched Thomas Burchell (1799–1846), William Knibb (1803–1845), and Henry Bleby (1809–1882) as ministers and missionaries. Samuel Sharpe (1801–1832), a literate slave, was allowed to work as a lay minister. The biblical sermon about equality of humankind acted as a catalyst in stirring up the rebellion. The timing of the revolt was perfect. Sugarcane harvesting was done in winter and planters depended on its continuous harvesting for their economic well-being. A black slave had been arrested after he attacked the person who was flogging his wife, who was also a slave.

The rebellion, which resulted in the destruction of more than $3 million worth of homes and sugarcane fields and the deaths of 15 whites, began on December 27, 1831. About 40,000 slaves participated in the revolt near the Monego Bay region. Within three weeks, it was crushed by the militia, who unleashed a reign of terror. Villages and chapels were burned. Many missionaries returned to Britain. About 201 slaves were killed in the revolt and about 326 were executed. Sharpe was the last to be executed and he has become one of the national heroes of Jamaica.

The conditions for blacks did not improve after the abolition of slavery by the Emancipation Act of 1833, however, because of the low rate of wages, high rents of land, and pitiable living conditions. The later October 1865 Morant Bay rebellion was suppressed ruthlessly. Jamaica reverted to the status of a Crown Colony until its full independence in 1962.

See also: Abolition of Slavery, British; Colonies in the Caribbean, British; Haitian Revolution for Independence; Latin American Revolutions, Blacks in; Slave Trade, British.

Further Reading: Beckles, Hilary. *Black Rebellion in Barbados: The Struggle against Slavery, 1627–1838*. Bridgetown: Antilles Publication, 1987; Craton, Michael. *Testing the Chains: Resistance to Slavery in the British West Indies*. Ithaca: Cornell University Press, 1982; Gelien Matthews. *Caribbean Slave Revolts and the British Abolitionist Movement*. Baton Rouge: Louisiana State University Press, 2006; Heuman, Gad J. *"The Killing Time": The Morant Bay Rebellion in Jamaica*. Knoxville: University of Tennessee Press, 1994; Higman, B. W. *Slave Populations of the British Caribbean, 1807–1834*. Baltimore: Johns Hopkins University Press, 1984; Mullin, Michael. *Africa in America: Slave Acculturation and Resistance in the American South and the British Caribbean, 1736–1831*. Urbana: University of Illinois Press, 1992; Viotti da Costa, Emilia. *Crowns of Glory, Tears of Blood: The Demerara Slave Rebellion of 1823*. New York: Oxford University Press, 1994.

Patit Paban Mishra

Slave Trade, British

The British were involved in the trans-Atlantic slave trade for almost 300 years. The Portuguese were the pioneers of the trans-Atlantic trade, but by the eighteenth century, Britain was the leading slave-trading nation. It is estimated that British ships were responsible for carrying between three and four million slaves from Africa to the Americas from the mid-seventeenth century until the passage of the Abolition of the Slave Trade bill in 1807. Slavery in the British Empire was finally abolished in 1833.

The ship that initiated the British slave trade left Plymouth for West Africa in 1562 and was headed by John Hawkins. He was by no means the first to undertake this journey or to engage in trade with the Africans. British explorers, like John's father, William Hawkins, or John Lok, had ventured into Africa a couple of decades earlier and raised the interest of English merchants who were willing to invest in ships and supplies for the journeys in return for expected goods such as gold, ivory, and pepper. In addition, plantations where much labor was needed were already established in the Spanish colonies in the Caribbean, and the Portuguese had been carrying African slaves across the Atlantic since the early sixteenth century. White indentured servants, former convicts, and Amerindians initially made up the work force, but there would soon be a shortage of labor. Overexertion and diseases were a common problem. The Africans were used to working in an extremely hot climate and knew how to raise crops with which the Europeans were not familiar. They appeared to be the sturdy alternative that the plantation owners urgently needed. By the time Hawkins set out for the West African coast, there was thus already an established market for slaves in the Caribbean.

The trade across the Atlantic is often referred to as "the triangular trade" in recognition of the three parts involved. British iron or copper products, such as guns, buttons, and cooking utensils, and textiles, leather, and ceramics were brought to Africa as payment for slaves. The slaves were brought to the sugar plantations on the British colonies in the Caribbean, primarily Barbados and Jamaica, and to the tobacco and cotton plantations in the North American colonies. Sugar, tobacco, and rum were some of the most important goods shipped back to England. British cities like Liverpool, where the majority of the British slave ships were constructed, and Bristol, which had long been a significant seaport, thrived on the slave trade. The main focus of the British trade was the islands of Jamaica, Barbados, and the Leeward Islands of the Lesser Antilles. After the British acquisition of Jamaica in 1655, the island became the major British producer of sugar. By the end of the eighteenth century, there were about 300,000 slaves on Jamaica and the island was responsible for half of the total sugar production within the British Empire.

British monarchs openly endorsed the slave trade. Queen Elizabeth I was keen on expanding the British Empire and supported the voyages into Africa, well aware of their ultimate purpose. In 1660, Charles II endowed the Company of Royal Adventurers into Africa, more commonly known as the Royal African Company, with a royal charter and a monopoly of trading rights with western Africa. During the next 150 years before the slave trade was abolished, Britain emerged as the major slave-trading nation. This was a time when the English developed plantations in the Americas and required a steady supply of African slaves. In the 1713 Treaty of Utrecht, the English won the *asiento*, the contract to import slaves, into the Spanish Caribbean. England had become a major mercantile power and participant in global trade. But at this time, the trade in slaves became increasingly brutal as raiding parties went deep into the African interior and frequently left whole villages devastated in their search for more recruits.

The British slave trade was fundamentally a commercial enterprise. Profit was its main motive, and a weak moral foundation centered on religious and pseudoscientific racial beliefs was created almost as an afterthought. Racial stereotypes were both an innate part of, and a result of, the institution of slavery. Stereotypes of blacks' inferiority were ancient when British slavery began, but they were to be reinforced by the ethnocentrism that was part of British colonialism. As the profit and scope of the trade grew, pseudoscientific theories of the inferiority of black people were used to justify oppression and cruelty on the part of the slave owners. A common fiction was, for example, that the Africans were like animals, unable to experience pain or other emotions in the same way as their masters. It was essentially a trade that corrupted those who conducted it and destroyed the lives of millions of slaves.

That the trans-Atlantic slave trade was based on racial distinctions is only one of its particular characteristics. Although the practice of slavery has ancient roots in European civilization and has been part of the rise of almost all civilizations, whether in classical Greece and Rome, China, Africa or the Middle East, the trans-Atlantic slave trade was in many ways historically unique. The term *chattel slavery* is often used to describe this particularity; it meant that the slaves were the property of their masters and were considered commodities that could be bought and sold at their owner's will. In ancient times, the state of enslavement was often a punishment for the inability to pay debts or other transgressions. When the sentence was served, the slave could become a free person again. Now, slavery became a permanent condition, as children inherited their slave status from their mother.

Another key component of the British slave trade was the social disruption that followed in its wake. Never before had so many people been abducted from their native land, families, and homes and transported to a new continent to live a life in bondage from which they were never to return. It is difficult to give definite figures on the total number of Africans removed from their homelands, but about 10 to 15 million arrived to their destination in the Americas, and about 4 to 6 million died on the journey.

Conditions on the crossing of the Atlantic, known as the Middle Passage, were horrific. Between 10 and 30 percent of the transported Africans never made it to their final destination. Illnesses such as dysentery thrived, and severe dehydration was a general problem. Quite a few captives threw themselves overboard in a desperate attempt to escape their misery. Many refused to eat and insurrections were common, but not often successful. A firsthand account of the atrocities of the Middle Passage is provided by **Olaudah Equiano,** the author of *The Interesting Life of Olaudah Equiano, or Gustavus Vassa* (1789). Equiano's autobiography describes how he was captured by slavers as a young boy in Africa and brought to work in Barbados and Virginia, before he was manumitted and able to lead a free life in England. The book became a bestseller in England and went through several editions. It would be of use in the abolitionist movement, and Equiano is now considered Britain's first black political leader. He describes how the abducted Africans, who were kept in chains in cramped conditions throughout the journey, had to put up with filth, stench, sickness, hunger, floggings, and other forms of punishment for any misbehavior. His narrative also includes a description of the sale of the slaves on arrival at their destination in Bridgetown, Barbados. This was a sordid business characterized by a great commotion in which buyers would rush in and claim their victims. They all tried to get the slaves best suited for their own purpose, paying no mind to whether they separated relatives and friends. Once the slaves had arrived on the plantations, they were in the hands of their master. Even small children were forced to work long hours and were severely punished for any failure to perform according to the master's wishes. The strict colonial slave laws that regulated the relationships between blacks and whites stated, for example, that blacks could be killed for thieving, whereas whites could take a black slave's life with impunity, or possibly risk a fine.

Equiano relates various instances of brutality and torture of the slaves. Slaves were often whipped for misbehaving, for example, or made to wear iron handcuffs, thumbscrews, or iron muzzles on the head, making it difficult or even impossible to speak, eat, and drink. The slaves often did not quietly accept such treatment. There were several slave rebellions that would be part of the process leading to the final emancipation of the slaves. In Jamaica, runaway slaves, called *maroons*, hid in the mountain ranges, where it was difficult for the British to find them, and from where they could stage attacks on their former owners. Examples of slave rebellions in Jamaica were Tacky's rebellion in 1760 and the Jamaican Christmas Rebellion in 1831, also known as Sam Sharpe's Revolt and the Baptist War. In Barbados, Bussa's rebellion of 1816 is famous, and there were numerous other instances of revolt, both in the Caribbean and in North America.

Demands for the British abolition of slavery would be heard increasingly often in the second half of the eighteenth century. Many devout Christians condemned the slave trade on moral grounds. The politician **William Wilberforce,** the lifelong crusader against slavery Thomas Clarkson, and the radical civil servant Granville Sharp, are some of the most ardent and well-known advocates of the abolitionist cause. Together with a group of Quakers, these men formed the **Society for the Abolition of the Slave Trade** in 1787. After 20 years of petitions and argumentation, their efforts were finally rewarded and the slave trade was abolished.

The legacies of the British slave trade are still in evidence today. The social disruption it caused in many African countries partly explains present-day instability. For example, the triangular trade naturally affected demographic patterns. In addition, traditional modes of farming and political organization were disturbed, and local industries were often undermined as a result of the dependence on imported goods. In England, a black population has been resident since the sixteenth century in consequence of the British involvement in the slave trade. By the end of the eighteenth century, London had a structured black community made up of 10,000 to 15,000 people. Most of them were servants returning with their plantation masters, some were musicians or sailors, and a few were students. At the beginning of the twenty-first century, the recognition of this black presence is transforming the meaning of British identity.

See also: Abolition of Slavery, British; Britain, Blacks in; Colonies in Africa, British; Colonies in the Caribbean, Spanish; Common Law, Slavery and English.

Further Reading: Craton, Michael. *Sinews of Empire: A Short History of British Slavery.* London: Temple Smith, 1974; Equiano, Olaudah. "The Interesting Narrative of the Life of Olaudah Equiano, or Gustavus Vassa, the African." In Henry Gates, ed. *The Classic Slave Narratives.*

New York: Penguin, 1987; Gerzina, Gretchen. *Black England: Life Before Emancipation*. London: Allison and Busby, 1999; Martin, S. I. *Britain's Slave Trade*. London: Macmillan, Channel 4 Books. 1999; Thomas, Hugh. *The Slave Trade*. London: Macmillan, 1997; Walvin, James. *Black Ivory: Slavery in the British Empire*. 2nd ed. Malden, MA: Blackwell, 2001.

Lena Ahlin

Slave Trade, Dutch

From 1620 to 1655, the Netherlands was at war with Portugal. The struggle between the two came to be increasingly determined by the needs of the slave trade. Compared with some other European powers, the Dutch were latecomers to Africa. When the Dutch attempted to set up African trading posts, they came into conflict with the Portuguese, who were already well established in Africa. At first, the Dutch were interested in accumulating gold from Africa. After they captured some sugar plantations in northern Brazil, however, they came to rely on slavery to help develop the plantations. The Dutch captured the Portuguese headquarters of São Jorge da Mina, which they renamed Elmina, in 1637 in the hopes of securing a steady supply of African slave labor. When Brazil fell in 1654, the Dutch continued trading slaves, with colonies like Curaçao emerging as a significant slave base.

Amsterdam, which was the capital of Holland, the largest of the seven provinces that comprised the Netherlands, emerged as the most significant trading center in the world by the mid-1600s. As a result, it provided substantial support to the slave trade. The Dutch West India Company (WIC), headquartered in Amsterdam, was one of the largest single slave traders in the history of the slave trade. The WIC was chartered in 1621 and was granted a monopoly on the African slave trade until 1730. Dutch financiers also financially supported Danish, Swedish, and German slavers.

The ports of Vlissingen and Middleburg in the Dutch province of Zeeland came to emerge as the main departure points of slavers. By 1750, slave trading was the most significant commercial activity in Vlissingen. In the late 1500s, the province had staunchly refused to open a slave market in Middleburg on the grounds that Dutch law did not support slavery. Yet attitudes toward slavery had changed and the slave trade and Dutch commerce expanded. Middleburg was the site of the largest independent Dutch slaving company, the Middleburg Commercial Company, which was at its peak in the eighteenth century.

The Netherlands had to import its wood for shipbuilding from abroad. To save money, the Dutch developed the means of making efficient ships from cheap materials. The *fluyt*, or "fly boat," was one such design. The *fluyt*'s ability to hold a vast cargo and its shallow draft made it ideal for slave voyages. As a result, the *fluyt* was a common site across Europe, Africa, and the Americas.

The Dutch captured the British colony of Suriname during the Second Anglo-Dutch War (1667). Under the WIC, Suriname was turned into a plantation slave society. The colony became a primary destination for African slaves seized by Dutch slavers. Although no large-scale slave revolts ensued on Suriname while it was under Dutch control, slaves resisted through "maroonage." Maroons, or fugitive slaves, fled toward the interior and established permanent communities. The size of these communities became substantially high. The maroon communities engaged the Dutch in a type of guerilla warfare. By the 1760s, the Dutch were forced to acknowledge the maroon communities as independent.

Coffy, a slave in the Dutch colony of Berbice (now British Guyana), led a slave rebellion in 1763. An outbreak of yellow fever had swept across the colony, and the slaves saw this as an opportunity to obtain their freedom. Coffy had intended to negotiate a treaty with the white slave owners in the colony that would enable a peaceful coexistence; however, Coffy had a falling out with the other leaders in the rebellion and he committed suicide. The rebellion was crushed in 1764.

In 1623, the WIC gained permission to establish the province of New Netherland in North America. The Dutch themselves were largely unwilling to become settlers. As a result, the colony was developed with mostly foreign settlers. The shortage also encouraged the reliance on slaves. The first African slaves arrived in 1625. From the 1630s onward, the Dutch also controlled most of Brazil, which occupied a central position in the slave trade. After the loss of Brazil in 1654, the Dutch placed their hopes on New Netherland. Slaves were used to build roads, homes, and defenses. Slaves were mostly in demand in the urban townships. Skilled slaves were able to exploit the labor shortage to achieve more freedom than the slaves in the Caribbean. The relaxed slave arrangements enabled slaves to assimilate into the colonial culture more easily than elsewhere, but the British captured the province of New Netherland in 1664.

The Dutch East India Company was established in 1602 to trade with Asia. The company, which had headquarters throughout the Asia region, owned a large number of slaves. The Dutch East India Company occasionally conducted raids on Madagascar for slaves. The company also established an African base at the Cape of Good Hope, which led to the establishment of Cape Colony. The Dutch wished to use slave labor to develop the region; however, the company wished to maintain good relations with the local inhabitants. The company's rival, the WIC, captured its slaves from West Africa; therefore the company could not get its slaves from there. As a result, the company gathered slaves from Madagascar, Mozambique, and Asia.

Toward the end of the seventeenth century, the Dutch faced increased colonial competition from other European powers such as England and France. Although the Dutch slave trade began to decline, independent slavers perpetuated the practice. During the eighteenth century, Spain had liberalized its colonial policies, and Curaçao became less useful as a slaving base. When the British took control of Curaçao in the early nineteenth century, they ended what remained of the area's slave trade. Britain abolished the slave trade in 1807 and began to pressure other countries to follow suit. By the time Curaçao was returned to Dutch control, international sentiment against the slave trade and the institution of slavery was on the rise.

See also: Abolition of Slavery, European; Colonies in the Caribbean, Dutch; Netherlands, Blacks in the.

Further Reading: Emmer, Pieter. *The Dutch Slave Trade, 1500–1850.* Trans. Chris Emery. New York: Berghahn Books, 2006.

E. Agateno Mosca

Slave Trade, French

The French became substantially involved in the African slave trade in the sixteenth century. The French government wished to develop plantation economies in its Caribbean colonies. These islands began to thrive as centers for the exportation of sugar with the addition of capital, credit, technology, and slaves. Rather than trade with other European powers for slaves, the French government assisted in the development of the West India Company, a monopoly company, in 1664. In the 1670s, French fleets seized factories from the Dutch in Gorée and the Senegambia. Bases were established in West Africa to secure a steady supply of slave labor. In 1672, the French government offered bounties for slaves brought to the French Caribbean; such bounties would be increased periodically. Such incentives inspired the establishment of another monopoly company, the Senegal Company, in 1673.

The French government in the seventeenth century set up strict rules for the slave trade, particularly in regard to buying from, or selling to, other European empires. In 1685, Louis XIV signed the **Code Noir** to establish regulations for slavery. By the 1720s, French private traders had broken the monopolies and the French slave trade expanded greatly. The majority of French slaves were taken from West Africa, although French slave traders took slaves from the Indian Ocean area as well. Slaves were taken from Madagascar and Mozambique to work on plantations in the French colonies of Bourbon (now Réunion) and the Ile de France (Mauritius).

The plantations in the French colonies in the Caribbean were run on slave labor. Conditions on the plantations were harsh. The demand for slaves was high, particularly as slaves were often worked to the point of death and replacements were needed. During the transfer of slaves from Africa to the Caribbean, slave revolts often occurred. A notable revolt occurred on the ship *Diamant* in 1774. The slaves managed to seize control of the ship, forcing the captain and his crew to abandon ship off the coast of an island near Gabon.

In France, several cities were involved in the slave trade, particularly Nantes, Bordeaux, Le Havre, La Rochelle, Saint-Malo, Harfleur, and Rouen. The city of Nantes, on the Atlantic coast of France, however, was the major French slaving port. It retained this position until the 1780s. Even after the official end of the slave trade in 1818, illegal trade continued. Beginning in the sixteenth century, the city of La Rochelle expanded because of its trade with the colonies. By the late eighteenth century, slavers accounted for about one-third of the traffic that passed through the medieval towers of the Old Port. The slave trade contributed to the city's commercial power and led to extravagant projects to develop the city.

The port of Lorient, in Brittany, was established in 1664. By 1719, the French West India Company made the port its primary base for shipbuilding and supplies for the Caribbean colonies. The company's monopoly on slave trading lasted until 1725. It then adopted a new system that made the slave trade an even more global enterprise. The company traded in the Indian Ocean for textiles and Cowry shells, which were used as currency in West Africa. The shells were subsequently sold to private traders who used them to acquire slaves in Africa, which were in turn traded in the Americas for sugar. Some ships sailed directly from Lorient to the Caribbean to bring back all the sugar that the slave ships alone could not bring back to France.

The rise of the French slave trade also resulted in the increase in the number of blacks in France, and the French government issued legislation attempting to regulate their presence. In 1571, some slaves were put on auction in Bordeaux, but the *parlement* ordered their release, claiming that slavery did not exist in France. This rule was broken in 1716 when slave owners from the Antilles retained their slaves on French soil. The *Parlement* of Paris refused to register legislation containing the word *slave*. Consequently, the **Free Soil Principle** remained in effect in one-third of France. Beginning in the 1750s, more than 150 slaves petitioned for their freedom. Several monumental court cases, including the 1738 case of Jean Boucaux and the 1759 case of Francisque, inspired several more lawsuits and set precedents for upholding the Free Soil Principle, prompting administrators to adopt new discriminatory legislation.

In 1777, Louis XVI signed the ***Déclaration pour la police des noirs,*** prohibiting the new arrival of blacks and *gens de couleur*, ordering *depots* for slaves accompanying their owners as they traveled to France, and requiring the registration of all blacks in France. In 1778, an *arret du conseil* required all registered blacks to carry identification cards. Failure to comply resulted in deportation to the colonies. Although bans on interracial marriages had been removed from an earlier version of the *police des noirs*, a ban on such unions was declared on April 5, 1778. Yet efforts to extend the *police des noirs* in the 1780s ultimately failed.

During the French Revolution, the revolutionary government issued the Declaration of the Rights of Man and the Citizen. The revolutionary values of "liberty, equality, and fraternity" ultimately led to a discussion of slavery. The **Society of the Friends of the Blacks,** an abolitionist group, petitioned the government to take action. Moderates were willing to extend rights to free blacks, but withdrew support after pressure from white colonial planters and influential slave traders. Free *gens de couleur* (people of color) from Saint Domingue traveled to Paris to request citizenship for *gens de couleur* and the right to be seated as colonial delegates. Both requests were denied. As the revolution became more radical, the *Code Noir* was abolished and, in 1794, slaves were emancipated throughout the French colonies. When Napoleon came to power, however, he reinstated slavery in the colonies as part of his attempts to develop an overseas French Empire.

The British government came to increasingly support a position against the slave trade. British abolitionists influenced their counterparts in France. The French government finally declared the slave trade illegal in 1818, but slave traders continued in secret and also sold their slaves to such foreign markets as Cuba and Brazil.

In the 1830s, the French government made an effort to enforce the illegality of the slave trade. It even signed a treaty with Britain allowing the British navy limited rights to search French ships suspected of engaging in slave trading. Abolitionist Victor Schoelcher became secretary of state for the colonies after the Revolution of 1848. That year, the French government abolished slavery throughout the French colonies. Shortly thereafter, legislation was passed to grant slave owners financial compensation for the loss of their slaves.

See also: Abolition of Slavery, British; Abolition of Slavery, French; Colonies in Africa, French; Colonies in the Caribbean, Dutch; Colonies in the Caribbean, French; Colonies in the Caribbean, Spanish; French Ministry of the Marine; French Revolution, Blacks in the; Slave Trade, Dutch; Slave Trade, Portuguese; Slave Trade, Spanish.

Further Reading: Dorigny, Marcel, ed. *Abolitions of Slavery: From L. F. Sonthonax to Victor Schoelcher, 1793, 1794, 1848.* trans. New York: Berghahn Books, 2003; Jennings, Lawrence C. *French Anti-Slavery: The Movement for Abolition of Slavery in France, 1802–1848.* Cambridge: Cambridge University Press, 2000; Peabody, Sue. *"There are No Slaves in France"—The Political Culture of Race and Slavery in the Ancien Régime.* New York: Oxford University Press, 1996; Stein, Robert L. *The French Slave Trade in the Eighteenth Century.* Madison: University of Wisconsin Press, 1979; Thomas, Hugh. *The Slave Trade: The Story of the Atlantic Slave Trade: 1440–1870.* New York: Simon and Schuster, 1997.

Eric Martone

Slave Trade, Italian

As ancient Rome consolidated its authority within the Italian peninsula and then the Mediterranean region, a proportion of conquered peoples were taken as slaves. Thus slaves came from a variety of places in Europe and the Mediterranean including Greece, Africa, Thrace, Gaul, the Middle East, and the Near East. Slaves were used for several purposes, including labor, entertainment, and sex. Runaway slaves were often crucified. Slave revolts often occurred in ancient Rome, the most significant being the First (135 B.C.E.–132 B.C.E.), Second (104 B.C.E.–103 B.C.E.), and Third (73 B.C.E.–71 B.C.E.) Servile Wars. By the late Republican period, the use of slaves and the slave trade were essential components of the economy.

After the fall of Rome in 476 C.E., Europe was plagued by invasion from Germanic tribes. The Franks, however, managed to establish the Carolingian Empire and restore a degree of order. In the Carolingian Empire, which encompassed much of France, Germany, and Italy, about 20 percent of the population were slaves. Magyars often raided parts of Germany, Italy, and Greece to capture men, women, and children for sale on the slave market. The bulk of the early medieval slave trade was mainly to the Byzantine Empire, based in Greece and at times parts of Italy, and Muslim areas. At that time, the bulk of slaves were taken from Central and Eastern Europe, as well as areas in Central Asia. So many Slavs living in Eastern Europe were taken captive that the word "slave" derived from their name. The slave trade was conducted primarily by merchants of Scandinavian (Viking), Arab, Greek, and Jewish origin. The Roman Catholic Church attempted to intervene, prohibiting the export of Christian slaves (Council of Koblenz in 922, Council of London in 1102, Council of Armagh in 1171).

The Late Middle Ages slave trade was conducted primarily by Italian merchants from Venice and Genoa who dealt with the Mongols, who had expanded their conquests and had pushed into Europe, and Muslims. For example, between 1414 and 1423, about 10,000 Eastern Europeans were sold as slaves in Venice. The city of Genoa was heavily involved in the slave trade and its operations spread from West Asia to North Africa. The wars between the Byzantine Empire and the Ottoman Turks, which ended in 1453 on the Ottoman conquest of Constantinople (now Istanbul) brought large supplies of slaves on both sides. Christians were highly involved in the sale of captured Muslims from West Asia and Africa as slaves, many of which the Mediterranean countries used as galley slaves. In the 1300s, the **Bubonic Plague,** or Black Death, destroyed the European population. The large number of deaths created a deficiency in the supply of labor in the Mediterranean area. A number of Italian merchants prospered by selling slaves in higher numbers. Because labor supplies were scarce and highly needed, the price of slaves rose substantially.

In the fifteenth century, the Portuguese exploration of the African coast marked the beginnings of European colonialism and the African slave trade. In 1452 and 1455, Pope Nicholas V issued papal bulls granting the right to reduce pagans, Muslims, and other non-Christians to slavery. Thereafter direct Italian involvement in the slave trade declined.

See also: Abolition of Slavery, European; Age of Exploration; Italy, Blacks in; Italy, African Invasions of; Moors; Roman Empire in Africa; Slave Trade, Portuguese.

Further Reading: Earle, T. F., and K.J.P. Lowe, eds. *Black Africans in Renaissance Europe.* New York: Cambridge University Press, 2005; Thomas, Hugh. *The Slave Trade: The Story of the Atlantic Slave Trade, 1440–1870.* New York: Simon and Schuster, 1999; Yavetz, Zvi. *Slaves and Slavery in Ancient Rome.* Somerset, NJ: Transaction Publishers, 1988.

E. Agateno Mosca

Slave Trade, Portuguese

West Africa became the main provider of labor for Portuguese plantations that spread from Cape Verde to the colonies in the New World. The Portuguese leaned how to work from within a network of ancient slave routes controlled by the Muslims. The modest start during the 1450s and 1460s, when around 800 slaves were taken to Europe each year mainly to serve as domestic servants, was drastically increased to more than 2,000 individuals per annum in the 1480s an 1490s. After 1500, these numbers rose from 2,600 to 4,500 captives being sold on an annual basis directly to the Americas in the 1530s. The participation of America in the slave trade would later transform not only its routes and outreach but also the sources from where Africans were put in bondage and carried away, many of them crossing the Atlantic never to see Africa again.

Before the Americas became the final destination for the majority of the slaves during the trans-Atlantic slave trade, Spain, Portugal, and its Atlantic islands were the main destinations. In the 1550s, for example, the black population in Lisbon was estimated to account for 10 percent of its entire population. During the same time in Spain, there were more than 5,000 slaves, 4,000 of which were blacks and individuals of biracial descent.

The second half of the sixteenth century saw large structural changes in the setup of the trans-Atlantic slave trade. Portugal decided to move its sugar production from its Atlantic islands (Madeira, Príncipe, and São Tomé) to the northeast of Brazil. An expanding new industry of sugar cane derivates, beyond the sugar itself, established in the Caribbean and Brazil demanded a dedicated operation that absorbed the vast majority of all Africans enslaved and shipped to the New World. In comparative terms, from the 1500s to the 1870s, the Portuguese colony of Brazil received more than 41 percent of the slaves brought from Africa. As early as the 1600s, Brazil's profits from sugar exportations were higher than previous profits derived from the Asian spice trade. The other colonies in the Caribbean, which belonged to the Dutch, French, Spanish, and British together, imported about 48 percent of all African slaves brought to the Americas. About 5 to 6 percent of African slaves went to North America and about 4 percent went to the Spanish colonies in South America.

The Portuguese control over slaves was maintained with rigorous discipline and harsh physical punishments. Common punishments included flogging male or female slaves and then rubbing a mixture of several foul liquids in the wounds. Slaves also suffered extreme punishments that were barbarous, such as being burned alive in furnaces. This environment was in part responsible for the continued need for the importation of new African slaves. The slaves brought to Brazil were often so badly treated that they were literally worked to death or were killed, thereby creating the need for replacements. This situation also caused the amount of newborns from slaves in Brazil to be very low. The need for new slaves forced the Portuguese to expand their slave sources from the west of Africa to the south of the continent, with new areas in Angola and its hinterlands.

The need for slaves was so great that Brazil, Cuba, and some other Spanish colonies effectively clashed with the British government, which was determined to put an end to the slave trade. The strong hand of the British helped to contain the oceanic slave trade but, at the same time, increased the cost of slaves as a result of the illegal commerce of Africans that continued in Brazil and in Cuba. Brazil agreed to conform to the British desire to put an end to the slave trade in 1850, although the institution of slavery lasted until 1888. Cuba agreed to stop the slave trade almost two decades after Brazil.

See also: Abolition of Slavery, Portuguese; Colonies in Africa, Portuguese; Latin American Revolutions, Blacks in; Portugal, Blacks in; Rio Branco Law of Free Birth.

Further Reading: Boxer, Charles Ralph. *The Golden Age of Brazil, 1695–1750: Growing Pains of a Colonial Society*. Berkeley: University of California Press, 1962; Boxer, Charles Ralph. *The Portuguese Seaborne Empire, 1415–1825*. 2nd ed. Manchester: Carcanet/Calouste Gulbenkian Foundation, 1991; Davis, David Brion. *Inhuman Bondage: The Rise and Fall of Slavery in the New World*. Oxford: Oxford University Press, 2006; Klein, Herbert S. *The Atlantic Slave Trade, New Approaches to the Americas*. Cambridge: Cambridge University Press, 1999; Landers, Jane, and Barry Robinson. *Slaves, Subjects, and Subversives: Blacks in Colonial Latin America*. Albuquerque: University of New Mexico Press, 2006.

Augusto Ciuffo

Slave Trade, Spanish

To a large extent, the Spanish slave trade must be linked to its conquest of a large chunk of the American continent, the New World. In 1532, Spain became the first country to transport African slaves to Latin America. The slaves were used for work in mines and plantations. The bulk of the Spanish slave consignment was directed to the Americas up to the end of the trade in the nineteenth century.

Early into the commencement of slave trade in Spanish America, the Spanish monarchy exercised control over the slave trade, at first, as a source of revenue. Through royal legislations, the government granted *asientos* (contracts) to European companies that shipped slaves of a specified quality and origin to Spanish America. The companies that won the *asientos* were monopolies that paid taxes to the royal court. At this stage, the trade was dominated by non-Spaniards, as most of those who won the contracts were the French, Portuguese, and English slave merchants who controlled the trans-Atlantic slave route. This arrangement lasted for about 150 years. Later, the Spanish monarchy attempted to liberalize the slave trade to accommodate Spanish merchants against the foreign monopolies that had hitherto dominated the trade. This was a response to the high demand for slaves for mining and agricultural purposes in the Spanish American territory of Cuba, as well as other territories such as New Granada, Peru, and Chile. Thus in 1789, King Charles III of Spain issued the free slave trade *cedula*.

The free slave trade *cedula* of 1789 made provision for the exemption of Spanish merchants from the payment of duties, and they were also to be adequately compensated for the slaves that they brought. The slaves were deemed pivotal for the development of the Spanish colonies in the Americas and thus for the development of Spain itself. The Spanish monarch followed the rationale that exemptions and privileges in the slave trade would encourage agriculture. Further, taxes were to be paid for the use of slaves for nonagricultural purposes.

Because the slaves were needed for the mine fields and plantations, the legislation made provision for an inspection of incoming ships to ensure that only healthy and able-bodied slaves were brought in. Likewise, the number of women was not expected to be more than one-third of the total slave population in each consignment. Consequently, the large importation of slaves to Spanish America culminated in enormous economic growth and prosperity for Spain and its Spanish-American colonies up to the point of the final abolition of the slave trade in the nineteenth century.

Between the beginning and end of the Spanish slave trade, Spain became a major player in the global trade of slaves. Spanish slave exports were directed predominantly to Spanish colonies in the New World. Of all these territories, Cuba emerged as the main importer of slaves as a result of its growing and sophisticated sugar industry, which accounted for 30 percent of total world production by 1868.

See also: Abolition of Slavery, Spanish; Colonies in the Caribbean, Spanish; Las Casas, Bartolomé de; Moret Law, Spanish; Spain, Blacks in.

Further Reading: Eltis, David. "The Volume and Structure of the Transatlantic Slave Trade: A Reassessment." *The William and Marry Quarterly* 58 (2001): 17–46; Fisher, John. "Commerce and Imperial Decline: Spanish Trade with Spanish America, 1797–1820." *Journal of Latin American Studies* 30 (1998): 459–479; King, James. "Evolution of the Free Slave Trade Principle in Spanish Colonial Administration." *The Hispanic American Historical Review* 22 (1942): 34–56; Murray, D. R. "Statistics of the Slave Trade to Cuba, 1790–1867." *Journal of Latin American Studies* 3 (1971): 131–149; Restall, Matthew, and Jane Landers. "The African Experience in Early Spanish America." *The Americas* 57 (2000):167–170; Schmidt-Nowara, Christopher. "National Economy and Atlantic Slavery: Protectionism and Resistance to Abolitionism in Spain and the

Antilles, 1854–1874." *The Hispanic American Historical Review* 78 (1998) 603–629; Tomich, Dale. "World Slavery and Caribbean Capitalism: The Cuban Sugar Industry, 1760–1868." *Theory and Society* 20 (1991): 297–319.

Ayokunle Olumuyiwa Omobowale

Snow, Valaida (1903?–1956)

Valaida Snow was an African American jazz sensation and entertainer arrested by the Nazis in Europe during World War II (1939–1945) and likely placed in an internment camp. Snow was born in Tennessee in the early twentieth century and was probably of biracial descent. The exact date of her birth is disputed. The situation is complicated further by the fact that she provided different birth dates for herself, including 1900, 1903, and even 1909. Some researchers have suggested 1904 or 1905. Her family was highly involved in music and at an early age, Snow learned to how to sing, dance, and play a variety of musical instruments. After focusing on the trumpet, Snow became a sensation, nicknamed "Little Louis" in Europe after African American jazz great Louis Armstrong.

Snow recorded frequently and toured throughout the United States, Europe, and China on several occasions, both with her own bands and as part of other leaders' bands. During the 1920s, one of the most famous musical reviews that she was associated with was "The Chocolate Dandies." Snow was at the height of her popularity during the 1930s when she became extremely popular in Europe. She was part of the touring review "Blackbirds" and famous musical show "Rhapsody in Black." In addition, during the 1930s, Snow appeared as an actress in several films in the United States and France. Although Snow was a sensation in Europe, she still faced racism and sexism. Furthermore, her role as a jazz bandleader, a role dominated by men, made her a curiosity to American and European audiences.

In 1939, around the outbreak of World War II, Snow, fearing for her safety, left France for Holland. Once it became clear that Holland was about to fall to the Nazi Germany, she headed to Denmark; however, in 1940, Denmark succumbed to Nazi control. The Nazis arrested Snow in Denmark shortly thereafter. The mysteries surrounding her capture, torture, and imprisonment have increased as time has passed owing to a lack of documents and conflicting accounts. According to most sources, Snow remained a prisoner for 18 months at the Wester-Faengle internment camp in Copenhagen. She may have spent a brief period in Westerbork, a transition camp originally used to house Jews before deportation to concentration camps in Eastern Europe. Some sources claim that Snow was imprisoned for theft and misuse of drugs, which was an outgrowth of a developing drug problem. Other sources claim that she was under Nazi house arrest, rather than internment. She was released in the early 1940s, possibly as part of a prisoner exchange, and returned to New York.

Snow spoke little about her experience afterward, and her claims of Nazi abuse were often dismissed during the 1940s and 1950s. Nevertheless, Snow's experience affected her physical and mental health, and she was never the same again. In the 1950s, Snow's career sagged and she had difficulties maintaining success.

See also: Baker, Josephine; Gilges, Lari; Jazz, European Reception of; Nassy, Josef; Nazis and Blacks in Europe; World War II, Black Participation in.

Further Reading: Charles, Mario. "The Age of a Jazzwoman: Valaida Snow, 1900–1956." *The Journal of Negro History* 80:4 (Fall 1995): 183–191; Lusane, Clarence. *Hitler's Black Victims: The Historical Experience of Afro-Germans, European Blacks, Africans and African Americans in the Nazi Era.* New York: Routledge, 2002; Reitz, Rosetta. "Hot Snow: Valaida Snow (Queen of the Trumpet Sings and Swings)." *Black American Literature Forum* 16:4 (Winter 1982): 158–160.

Eric Martone

Society for the Abolition of the Slave Trade

In existence from 1787 to 1807, the Society for the Abolition of the Slave Trade was one of the first organized British antislavery societies. The members launched a large-scale campaign to mobilize national opinion in support of calling on Parliament to declare the slave trade illegal. To accomplish this goal, the abolitionists created a network of political lobbyists. The society actively sought Parliament members who were willing to present their views to government representatives. Further, the group appealed to the British public to put pressure on Parliament to take action through popular agitation techniques, including circulating petitions, distributing literature, boycotting slave produce, and holding public meetings. These tactics proved to be a model for abolitionist organizations in the United States and elsewhere. Their efforts were so successful that in 1807, the British government outlawed the slave trade with its passage of the Slave Trade Act.

Quakers, with their political lobbying experience and financial backing, were instrumental in the formation of the society. In 1783, a small committee of Quakers became one of the first organized groups to launch an attack on the British slave system. Because the slave trade was legal, it could be abolished only by new legislation. To achieve this goal, the Quaker committee lobbied Parliament members by circulating petitions, distributing pamphlets, and establishing a national network of supportive members. These were the same techniques that they had used years earlier in their own defense from persecution. Quakers were not the only people who opposed slavery at this time. They realized that the base of the antislavery effort needed to be broadened to strengthen their support from regional and local bodies, as well as to increase their funding resources. The establishment of the Society for the Abolition of the Slave Trade in May 1787 did just this by combining Quakers and non-Quakers. The members of the founding Committee of Twelve consisted of nine Quakers (some had been members of the 1783 committee) and three non-Quakers: Thomas Clarkson, Philip Sansom, and Granville Sharp. The committee chose Sharpe as the first chair.

The society's objective was to procure and publish information on the abominations of the slave trade and to secure the support of Parliament to legislate its abolishment. Although opposed to both the institution of slavery and the slave trade, the group resolved to confine their attention to ending the trade, which was viewed as the more vulnerable target. The British public was becoming aware of the horror stories of poor ship conditions and mistreatment. In addition, an attack on slavery would have involved interfering with private property, a highly sensitive subject for Parliament, whereas the regulation of trade had always been recognized as one of their functions.

One of the society's first tasks was to establish active auxiliary organizations in the main towns throughout the country. Clarkson took on the task of organizing provincial support during a series of tours in 1787 and 1788. This organizational structure enabled the society to maintain a national network of supporters. At its center stood the London-based national committee and its Parliamentary spokesmen, jointly responsible for formulating policy and coordinating action. The auxiliaries were given the dual roles of circulating antislavery material supplied by the society's leaders in London and collecting gifts and subscriptions on behalf of the central committee. This successful arrangement served as a model for antislavery organizations worldwide.

The group enlisted **William Wilberforce** as their main parliamentary spokesperson. Sympathetic to their cause, he had already put a question about the slave trade before the House of Commons and had proven to be an influential and persuasive orator. Wilberforce advised the society that he would need additional evidence and reports to strengthen their case to Parliament. Clarkson agreed to gather the necessary information during his campaign tours. His investigative reports and analyses proved to be pivotal to the cause. In 1787, Clarkson wrote a 10-page pamphlet entitled "*A Summary View of the Slave Trade and the Probable Consequences of Its Abolition*," which the Society published and had printed in a run of 2,000 copies as its first propaganda pamphlet. Clarkson faced opposition from supporters of the trade that sometimes involved physical risk because the slave trade was a lucrative business that many slavers, as well as port cities depended on for prosperity. One of his most influential works to raise public awareness was the detailed specifications of a slave ship, the *Brookes*, which he and his colleagues secured in 1789. The drawings graphically depicted the deplorable conditions of stowing 609 slaves on the vessel. The group used the drawings to produce powerful political posters and a wooden model that Wilberforce showed to Parliament.

Wilberforce unsuccessfully introduced a bill to abolish the slave trade in 1791, initiating a prolonged Parliamentary campaign in which he continued to introduce a similar motion in subsequent sessions. Parliament, however, refused to pass any legislation on the trade and the outbreak of war with France effectively prevented further debate for many years. The slave trade campaign revived again in 1804. In 1806, a bill providing for the abolition of the trade to the conquered colonies successfully passed both Houses. In 1807, this bill was superseded by a stronger measure, the Slave Trade Act, which forbade the carrying of slaves in British vessels and their importation into any British colony. With the slave trade now declared illegal, the Society for the Abolition of the Slave Trade had completed its work. It was replaced later that year by a new organization, the African Institution, which would focus on combating the slave trade carried on in foreign vessels.

See Also: Abolition of Slavery, British; Britain, Blacks in; British Anti-Slavery Society; Colonies in Africa, British; Colonies in the Caribbean, British; Slave Trade, British.

Further Reading: Anstey, Roger. *The Atlantic Slave Trade and British Abolition 1760–1810.* Atlantic Highlands, NJ: Humanities Press, 1975; Coupland, Reginald. *The British Anti-Slavery Movement.* 2nd ed. London: Frank Cass, 1964; Gray, Richard A. "Thomas Clarkson and the

Anti-Slavery Society." *Reference Services Review* 21 (Winter 1993): 53–66; Hochschild, Adam. *Bury the Chains: Prophets and Rebels in the Fight to Free an Empire's Slaves.* Boston: Houghton Mifflin, 2005; Klingberg, Frank J. *The Anti-Slavery Movement in England.* Hamden, CT: Archon Books, 1968.

Donna Smith

Society of the Friends of the Blacks

The Society of the Friends of the Blacks ("*Société des Amis des Noirs*" or "*Amis des noirs*" in French) was an association created to oppose the French slave trade. The society's story proves that abolition was a long-lasting and complex process in which the abolitionist lobby played a great role during the French Revolution and the Directory.

Founded in Paris in February 1788 by group mostly composed of white abolitionists, The Society of the Friends of the Blacks was the first wave of French antislavery campaigns. The society was led by Jacques-Pierre Brissot (1754–1793), who was advised by Thomas Clarkson (1760–1846), one of the leaders of the abolitionist movement in Britain. Sentiments to end the slave trade had been spreading throughout Europe, particularly in England, and influenced those in France. In the spirit of the Enlightenment ideas of freedom, equality and fraternity; the French Revolution (1789–1799); and the French Declaration of the Rights of Man and Citizen (August 26, 1789), the society believed in the abolition of slave trade and that political rights should be granted to religious minorities. Brissot believed that the society should also campaign against the institution of slavery as well, but the immediate realization of this objective was met with some opposition among abolitionists. The society's first objective was to obtain international cooperation on the abolition of slavery, then to plan a way to phase out slavery in the colonies in two or three generations, and to reorganize the colonial system. This approach was believed to be more successful than the immediate emancipation of the blacks, which was perceived as leading to a fatal economic impact on the colonies and in France.

The society held activities, such as meetings, registers, and speeches. Within the public sphere, it agitated for new government legislation. The outbreak of slave violence in Saint Domingue (which became the **Haitian Revolution for Independence**), however, unhinged the society. Moreover, it soon faced financial difficulties and political divisions as the French Revolution faced colonial issues in contradictory ways. Thus the society faded away in the early 1790s.

The society reformed in 1796 and would last until 1799 under the dominance of **Abbé Grégoire.** The focus then was on the future of the French colonies. The original society counted between 141 and 200 members (even if the most important meetings never reached more than 23 participants) and the second only 92. These members were publicists, philosophers, politicians, and intellectuals and included such well-known figures as the Marquis de Condorcet (1743–1794), Dominique de la Rochefoucauld (1712–1800), Comte Mirabeau (1749–1791), and Thomas Jefferson (1743–1826), who joined the society when he came to Paris. The society also included blacks and individuals of biracial descent, including Julien Raimond (1744–1801) and **Vincent Ogé** (1750/55–1791).

See also: Abolition of Slavery, British; Abolition of Slavery, French; Belley, Jean-Baptiste; Chaumette, Pierre Gaspard; Colonies in Africa, French; Colonies in the Caribbean, French; Enlightenment Philosophers and Slavery; France, Blacks in; Free Soil Principle; Slave Trade, French.

Further Reading: Cohen, William. *The French Encounter with Africans: White Response to Blacks, 1530–1880*. Reprint. Bloomington: Indiana University Press, 2003; Dorigny, Marcel, ed. *Abolitions of Slavery: From L. F. Sonthonax to Victor Schoelcher, 1793, 1794, 1848*. trans. New York: Berghahn Books, 2003; Hunt, Lynn, ed. *The French Revolution and Human Rights: A Brief Documentary History*. Boston and New York: Bedford/St. Martin's Press, 1996; Jennings, Lawrence C. *French Anti-Slavery: The Movement for Abolition of Slavery in France, 1802–1848*. Cambridge: Cambridge University Press, 2000.

Laëtitia Baltz

Soliman, Angelo (1721?–1796)

Angelo Soliman was a former African slave during the eighteenth century who became a royal tutor and celebrity at the imperial court in Vienna, Austria. He was born Mmadi-Make in Africa in around 1721. As a small boy, he was kidnapped and sold into slavery. Soliman's exact origins in Africa remain obscure, for his vague descriptions in later life of his homeland cannot be assigned to any particular geographic area with much certainty. Soliman was probably purchased in a Mediterranean slave market, subsequently being owned by a string of aristocratic Europeans until he became at favorite at the imperial Habsburg court in Vienna.

Soliman worked as a secretary to his master, General Johann Christian Lobkowitz, until his master's death in 1755. He then became the chamberlain of Prince Wenzel Liechtenstein. At court, Soliman was dressed in the Oriental garb commonly worn by other Africans and received the title "Chief Princely Moor."

Eventually, Soliman took advantage of the opportunities at court to become educated, gaining skill in several foreign languages. He served in several diplomatic missions and worked as a tutor to members of the royal Habsburg family. He also became a noted chess player and favorite of Holy Roman Emperor Joseph II.

Soliman joined the freemasons, eventually becoming grand master of his lodge, and an associate of noted composers Wolfgang Amadeus Mozart and Joseph Haydn. In addition, Soliman married an aristocratic widow. It has been suggested that the character of Monostatos in Mozart's opera *The Magic Flute* is based on Soliman. While he was grand master, Soliman revised Masonic ritual, and lodges throughout Europe copied his modifications.

When Soliman died in 1796, the current Holy Roman Emperor, Francis II of Austria, who possessed a morbid collection of stuffed human corpses, claimed the former slave's body and had it flayed and stuffed to be put on display in his private museum along with two other Africans. Soliman's daughter unsuccessfully attempted to regain her father's remains. Soliman's body remained on display in an elaborate costume until the Austrian Revolution of 1848, when it was destroyed, as the museum it was housed in burned down amid the rioting.

See also: Baartman, Saartjie; Central Europe, Blacks in; Courts, Blacks at European Aristocratic; Enlightenment Philosophers and Race; Enlightenment Philosophers and Slavery; Gall, Franz Josef; Scientific Racism.

Further Reading: Northrup, David. *Africa's Discovery of Europe, 1650–1850*. New York: Oxford University Press, 2002.

Eric Martone

Somerset Case

In the Somerset case of 1772, William Murray, Lord Chief Justice Mansfield, ruled that it was unlawful for Charles Stewart, a Boston, Massachusetts, customs official, to transport James Somerset, an African he had bought in Virginia, forcibly out of England. The decision was popularly taken to mean that slavery was illegal in England, but Mansfield had only meant to give a narrow judgment, and even that was not enforced.

James Somerset came to England from Boston in November 1769 with his master, Charles Stewart, who had purchased him in Virginia. Somerset was baptized on February 12, 1771 at St. Andrew's Holborn. He left his master, but on November 26, 1771, was kidnapped and put on board the *Ann and Mary*, a ship bound for Jamaica under Captain John Knowles to be sold. Two days later, however, his godparents, Thomas Walkin, Elizabeth Cade, and John Marlow, obtained a writ of habeas corpus (which protects the individual from arbitrary imprisonment); and Somerset enlisted Granville Sharp (1735–1815), a known sympathizer to the plight of slaves, to the cause.

The case first came to court on February 7, 1772. Judgment was given on June 22. Somerset's case was pleaded by William Davy, John Glynne, Francis Hargrave, James Mansfield, and John Alleyne. They were opposed by John Dunning and William Wallace, whose services were funded by the West India interest. It was argued that, since the expiration of *villeinage*, no positive law relating to slavery existed in England and the law of Virginia was not applicable in England. Furthermore, Somerset could not be accused of breach of contract, because contract law required the two parties to be free to make the agreement. The case attracted much popular attention, as evidenced by the many newspaper reports and the crowds that flocked to Westminster Hall to hear the proceedings.

Lord Mansfield was reluctant to give judgment because of the "inconveniences" that might ensue, given that there were thought to be 15,000 blacks in England at that time. He was careful in his final judgment to make a narrow decision that, as forcible removal from the country was illegal, Somerset should be discharged. Despite Mansfield's best efforts, the case was reported in the press, and internationally, as ending slavery in England. About 200 black men and their ladies, who could afford a ticket price of 5 shillings, celebrated the event at an assembly at a public house in Westminster a few days later.

Some blacks were able to exploit the ruling to gain their freedom, such as one Mr. Dublin, who ran away from his master John Riddell of Bristol Wells, telling fellow servants that "he had received a letter from his Uncle Sommerset acquainting him that Lord Mansfield had given them their freedom and he was determined to leave." Joseph Knight, whose case against his former master, John Wedderburn, resulted in the 1778 ruling that one could not be a slave in Scotland (which had a separate jurisdiction) had read about the Somerset case in the *Edinburgh Advertiser* and took it to mean that he was a free man.

The Mansfield decision did not bring an end to slavery in England, however, as it was not enforced, even it its most narrow sense. Within a year, *The London Chronicle* was to report that an African (immortalized in Thomas Day's poem "The Dying Negro") shot himself to avoid being transported back to the colonies. Furthermore, as late as 1823, one Grace Jones was forcibly removed to Antigua by her mistress.

See also: Abolition of Slavery, British; Britain, Blacks in; Colonies in Africa, British; Colonies in the Caribbean, British; Common Law, Slavery and English; Slave Trade, British; Strong, Jonathan.

Further Reading: Shyllon, F. O. *Black Slaves in Britain.* London: Oxford University Press, 1974; Wise, Steven M. *"Though the Heavens May Fall": The Landmark Trial that Led to the End of Human Slavery.* New York: Da Capo Press, 2006.

Miranda Kaufmann

Sonthonax, Léger Félicité (1763–1813)

Léger Félicité Sonthonax was a politician during the French Revolution (1789–1799) who abolished slavery in the French colonies. He was born into a wealthy French merchant family in 1763 and became a lawyer and later a rising politician during the French Revolution. Sonthonax was sympathetic to the abolition of slavery and joined the **Society of the Friends of the Blacks.**

In April 1792, the French Revolutionary government passed legislation granting full citizenship to all free people of color. Later that year, the French government sent Sonthonax on a mission to the colony of Saint Domingue (now Haiti). Saint Domingue had been plagued by an increasingly complex racial conflict between the white minority that controlled the island, biracial property owners, and the black and biracial majority, which served as slaves and free people. The outbreak of the French Revolution in 1789 only added to this conflict, dividing members of the colony between those who supported the revolution and those who supported the Old Regime. Consequently, violent conflict ensued. Sonthonax's duties were to preserve French control over the island, where a slave rebellion had erupted, and to enforce recent, controversial legislation from the French government granting social equality to free people of color.

On his arrival in Saint Domingue, Sonthonax found that the white and biracial plantation owners had developed a degree of cooperation against the rebelling slaves. Sonthonax exiled whites who refused to obey the law of social equality and contained the slave rebellion. In 1793, however, France declared war on Britain. Sonthonax's efforts to enforce the directives of the French government had created much opposition that could now rally to the side of the British, heightening conflict with the British colonies in the Caribbean. In 1793, Sonthonax radically proclaimed the freedom of all slaves, albeit with certain restrictions. In 1794, the government of France passed an act to make Sonthonax's emancipation of the slaves official and extended the French abolition of slavery to all of its colonies.

The new support that Sonthonax had hoped for from his former opponents with his act of emancipation was not forthcoming, however. The newly emancipated slaves did not flock to his side, and white and biracial plantation owners still opposed him, now with British assistance. After the French government's 1794 act, however, **Toussaint L'Ouverture,** a leader of the rebelling slaves, temporarily sided with French Revolutionary forces.

Changes in the French government prompted Sonthonax's recall to France, where he was required to defend his actions. In 1796, Sonthonax was vindicated of any wrong doing and allowed to return to Saint Domingue. L'Ouverture, however, had consolidated his position and eventually forced Sonthonax to return to France in 1797, where he died in 1813. French General Napoleon Bonaparte, shortly after gaining control of the French government in 1799, reimposed slavery on the colonies, leading to escalated violence that ultimately led to Haitian independence in 1804.

See also: Chaumette, Pierre Gaspard; Colonies in the Caribbean, French; Delgrès, Louis; France, Blacks in; French Revolution, Blacks in the; Haitian Revolution for Independence; Haitian Revolution in Francophone Literature; Ogé, Vincent; Slave Trade, French.

Further Reading: Gaspar, David Barry, and David Patrick Geggus, eds. *A Turbulent Time: The French Revolution and the Greater Caribbean.* Bloomington: Indiana University Press, 1997; Stein, Robert L. *Léger Félicité Sonthonax: The Lost Sentinel of the Republic.* Rutherford: Farleigh Dickinson University Press, 1985.

Eric Martone

Sousa Martins, José Thomás de (1843–1897)

José Thomás de Sousa Martins was a revered biracial doctor in Portugal during the nineteenth century known for his generosity and medical assistance to the poor in Lisbon. During his career, he became a leader in the international community in the field of medicine.

Sousa Martins was born in Alhandra, Portugal in 1843 of mixed African and Portuguese parents. He grew up in Alhandra and attended the local elementary school. At the age of 12, he left Alhandra and traveled to Lisbon, Portugal. His father had died and he moved to live with his maternal uncle, Lázaro Joaquim de Sousa Pereira. His uncle worked in pharmaceuticals, which led to Sousa Martins's interest in medicine.

By 1868, Martins had become a doctor and was made a member of the Society of Medical Science. In 1872, Sousa Martins became a professor in Lisbon. Two years later, he became a doctor at the Hospital de S. José, where he became director of Saint Michael's Ward. From this time until his death in 1897 Sousa Martins was involved in the International Medical Conferences, becoming vice-president of the group in 1897. During his career, he was noted for his efforts to provide medical care for the poor and oppressed in Lisbon.

In 1897, Sousa Martins died after contracting tuberculosis. In death, Sousa Martins has gained a following that lasts to this day. He has become an icon to many people, leading experts to call his followers a quasi-cult. His followers look to his spirit to intervene in their recovery, as they believe that he is an intermediary between them and God. As Portugal has a strong Roman Catholic tradition, some have used his name as if he were a saint. At several locations, his grave, his childhood home, and at the place of his work in Lisbon, statues have been erected. At any time, but mostly on the anniversaries of his birth and death, flowers are laid, candles are burned, and there are many personal notes left in hopes of invoking his power of healing. Many of the messages are engraved in marble tablets left at the foot of his statue. In recognition of his status during his lifetime and in death, his homestead in Alhandra has been turned into a museum.

See also: Portugal, Blacks in.

Further Reading: Alhandra Museum's Web Page: http://www.museusousamartins.org/uksite. html; Rogers, J. A. *World's Great Men of Color*. vol. II. Reprint. New York: Touchstone, 1996.

Robert Nave

Soviet Propaganda, Blacks and

From its early days, the Soviet Union (U.S.S.R.) exerted a considerable effort in promoting and sustaining propagandist campaigns against racism and colonialism. Soviet leaders considered the subjugated nonwhite colonial populations, as well as the American blacks, to be the most obvious victims of global capitalism and therefore the Soviet Union's "natural allies." The state-sponsored campaigns against various manifestations of racism in the West became an integral part of the official public discourse in the U.S.S.R. During the cold war decades, American and West European racism was routinely subjected to devastating critique in the Soviet media. Images of oppressed dark-skinned colonial subjects or African Americans, depicted as deprived of basic human and civil rights, were contrasted with the apparent achievements of Soviet internationalism. The sources of this concerted effort to expose Western racism were both ideological and pragmatic. Soviet Marxist ideology attacked racism as a bourgeois phenomenon, most symptomatic of capitalism's degeneracy. At the same time, Soviet leaders sought to upstage their rivals in the West by cultivating close ties and trumpeting their solidarity with the newly independent colonial nations, including those in Africa. Black Africans and African Americans continued to be featured prominently in Soviet propaganda into the last years of the Soviet rule.

During the first two decades of its existence, in the aftermath of the Bolshevik Revolution of 1917, the Soviet Union attracted scores of black travelers, who trekked to the "Red Mecca" in search of racial equality and ideological fulfillment. Some of these visitors, most of them African Americans or Afro-Caribbeans, arrived in Soviet Russia under the auspices of the newly founded (1919) Communist International, also known as the Comintern. Others came to experience firsthand life under a supposed colorblind communist regime. Such prominent figures of the Harlem Renaissance, such as **Claude McKay,** Langston Hughes, and **Paul Robeson,** all found fame in the U.S.S.R. By all accounts, the Soviet society warmly accepted them because, for the Soviets, they represented the millions of people of color suffering from capitalist oppression. Soviet propaganda celebrated their success in the Soviet Union and played it up to showcase Soviet values. Flagships of Soviet propaganda, such as the communist dailies *Pravda* and *Izvestia*, took every opportunity to expose the real and, sometimes, imaginary horrors of black existence in the West. During the 1930s, thousands of Soviet citizens signed petitions in defense of the so-called Scottsboro Boys, a group of black American teenagers, falsely accused of raping two white girls. The 1935 Italian invasion of Ethiopia gave Soviet media another reason to decry the evils of Western racism. American racism was mocked in a 1936 cinematic classic *Circus*. This feel-good movie told the story of a white American circus performer who travels to the Soviet Union with her little black son. Rejected by American racists, she and her child find love and acceptance among the Soviets. Another popular Stalinist-era film, *Maksimka* (1951), struck a similar theme by depicting a crew of grizzly Russian sailors saving a black slave boy at sea.

Soviet propaganda focusing on racism gained in intensity with the onset of the cold war. In their ideological contest with the United States and its allies, the Soviets rarely failed to excoriate America's mistreatment of its black citizens. Similarly, Soviet newspapers and popular magazines, such as *Krokodil* (*The Crocodile*), *Ogonek* (*The Little Light*), and *Rabotnitsa* (*The Working Woman*) published numerous accounts and cartoons highlighting African struggles against colonial domination. Soviet support for "third world causes" and an intense competition between the superpowers for the "soul" of the developing world informed Moscow's decision to host the 1957 International Youth Festival. The festival brought hundreds of Africans to the previously isolated Soviet Union and presented Soviet citizens with a rare opportunity to interact with the people whose liberation struggle they had been so vociferously supporting for decades.

Soon after the festival, the Soviets undertook two major initiatives to solidify their country's links to the decolonizing Africa. In 1959, the Soviet Academy of Sciences created a special research institution to facilitate a multidisciplinary study of Africa in the U.S.S.R. The Africa Institute continued to churn out Africa experts and to develop intellectual links with African countries into the post-Soviet era. In 1960, the Soviet leadership undertook an ambitious project to cultivate the good graces of the developing world by establishing a new university specifically for the purpose of educating third world students. The Friendship University of Moscow, also bearing the name of the slain Congolese Prime Minister Patrice Lumumba, would gain an international reputation for extending generous educational scholarships to foreign students, many of whom were from Africa.

Simultaneously, the Soviet media extended its coverage of the Civil Rights movement in the United States, appropriating African American struggles for equal rights in the ongoing critique of American political and social system. Although never quite comfortable with the religious message of such civil rights leaders, such as **Martin Luther King Jr.**, the Soviets readily embraced the more radical black activists. Black activist Angela Davis, for example, became a high-profile celebrity in the Soviet Union in the aftermath of her famous 1972 trial.

As the cold war intensified into the late 1970s, so did the Soviets' propaganda effort to adopt Africa's liberation causes. Subsequently, the Soviet Union would deepen its involvement in a number of African conflicts (such as in southern Africa, in Angola, in Mozambique, in the Horn of Africa), siding with the forces deemed more "progressive." Soviet involvement in Africa and the high pitch of propaganda campaigns against racism and neocolonialism would be greatly diminished with the advent of Mikhail Gorbachev's *perestroika*. The 1991 collapse of the Soviet Union also spelled the end of the cold war and thus the end to seven decades of Soviet propaganda campaigns targeting Western racism and colonialism.

See also: Authors in Europe, African American; Briggs, Cyril; Colonies in Africa, British; Colonies in Africa, Dutch; Colonies in Africa, French; Colonies in Africa, German; Colonies in Africa, Italian; Colonies in Africa, Portuguese; Colonies in Africa, Spanish; James, C.L.R.; Russia, Blacks in.

Further Reading: Blakely, Allison. *Russia and the Negro: Blacks in Russian History and Thought*. Washington, DC: Howard University Press, 1986; Eribo, Festus. *In Search of Greatness: Russia's Communications with Africa and the World*. Westport, CT: Ablex Publishing, 2001; Fikes, Kesha, and Alaina Lemon. "African Presence in Former Soviet Spaces." *Annual Review of Anthropology* 31 (2002): 497–524; Khanga, Yelena. *Soul to Soul: A Black Russian American Family, 1865–1992*. New York: W. W. Norton, 1994; Matusevich, Maxim, ed. *Africa in Russia, Russia in Africa: Three Centuries of Encounters*, Trenton, NJ: Africa World Press, 2006; Matusevich, Maxim, ed. "An Exotic Subversive: Africa, Africans, and the Soviet Everyday." *Race and Class*, 49 (2008): 57–81; McClellan, Woodford. "Africans and Black Americans in the Comintern Schools, 1925–1934." *The International Journal of African Historical Studies* 26 (1993): 371–390; Quist-Adade, Charles. *In the Shadows of the Kremlin and the White House: Africa's Media Image from Communism to Post-Communism*. Lanham, MD: University Press of America, 2001.

Maxim Matusevich

Spain, African Invasions of

African invaders have often sought to penetrate Europe through the Iberian Peninsula because of its close proximity to Africa. In the third century B.C.E., the Carthaginians controlled much of what is now southeastern Spain. During the **Punic Wars,** the ancient Carthaginian general, Hannibal, based his Numidian horsemen there for his march on the Italian peninsula in 218 B.C.E. During the period of Roman rule, there were also many soldiers and civilians in Spain from Africa; however, the Umayyad Conquest of the Iberian peninsula in 710 marked a major change in European history.

The Umayyad Conquest of Hispania, then a kingdom of the Visigoths, started when, in 710, the Berber general, Tariq ibn Ziyad, captured the city of Tangier on the southern side of the Straits of Gibraltar. This was quickly followed by raids across the straits, the largest of which was led by Tarif ibn Malluk. In the next year, Tariq ibn Ziyad led 7,000 soldiers (mainly Berbers) onto the Iberian Peninsula. These soldiers encountered a Visigoth army raised by King Roderic of Hispania. In the Battle of Guadalete, on the Guadalete River, the African Muslim forces of Tariq ibn Ziyad routed the Visigoths and took the city of Toledo, sending another force under Mugit al-Rumi to take the city of Córdoba. This left two major cities formerly held by the Christian Visigoths now under Muslim rule.

In 712, Musa ibn Nusayr, the Muslim governor of Northern Africa, also crossed the Straits of Gibraltar. He brought with him a large army of about 18,000 men and captured Medina-Sidonia, Seville, and Mértole. In the next year, Abd al-Aziz ibn Musa, the son of Musa ibn Nusayr, led his forces against Jaén, Murcia, Granada, and Sagunto. Although the campaign captured all those cities, it was hindered when large numbers of Christians in Seville and Toledo revolted against the newly imposed Muslim rule. The revolts were put down harshly, with Toledo badly destroyed in the fighting. By 715, most of modern-day southern Spain was held by the **Moors,** with Abd al-Aziz ibn Musa using Seville as his capital. He also married Egilona, the widow of King Roderic.

Lisbon was captured in 716. In the next year, the Moors established Córdoba as their capital. The Christians, however, rallied around Pelayo, a Visigoth nobleman from Asturias in northwestern Spain, who was probably a former soldier in the service of King Rodrigo. In 718, Pelayo held off the Moors, but the Moors then launched a massive campaign against him and drove him into the mountains in northern Spain. This allowed the Moors to concentrate on attacking Septimania, the kingdom that straddled the modern Spanish-French border. In 720, the Moors took Barcelona and Narbonne. In the next year, however, when they attacked southern France, the Frankish soldiers surrounded the large Moorish army and defeated it at the battle of Toulouse. The battle was one of the worst military defeats in medieval Moorish history and was followed by the defeat of the Moors by Pelayo at the battle Covadonga in 722. This victory is often seen as the beginning of the *Reconquista*, by which Pelayo and his descendants would later retake the whole of Spain from the Moors.

In spite of these defeats, with further reinforcements arriving from Africa, the Moors were able to continue their advances into northern Spain and France. A Moorish army under the command of Abdul Rahman Al Ghafiqi defeated Duke Eudo (or Odo) of Aquitaine at the battle of Bordeaux in mid-732. The Moorish victory, however, was followed by a massive Frankish counterattack in which Charles Martel, "The Hammer," defeated 60,000 Moorish soldiers at the battle of Tours (sometimes called the battle of Poitiers). This victory blunted the Moorish advance into France, but left them in control of the Iberian peninsula. In 739–740, a major Berber revolt in Spain and northern Africa led to a Moorish-dominated Spain and Morocco, with the Syrian soldiers of Kulthum being defeated and dispersed. Although the descendants of Pelayo continued to fight, it was not until the fall of Granada in 1492 that the whole of Spain was once again in Christian hands.

In 756, the Umayyad Emirate of Córdoba was established by Ad bar-Rahman I. Three years later, however, the Moors lost control of Narbonne. King Pepin the Younger drove all the remaining Moorish armies back across the Pyrenees. Several revolts against Umayyad rule in the Iberian Peninsula followed. Some of these were launched by rival Muslims, especially Syrians, who were defeated at the Battle of Bembezar in 774. Others were led by Abbasids, with yet more by Christians. Indeed, in 778, the Franks from modern-day France under Charlemagne were able to attack Zaragoza, but were forced to withdraw. Charlemagne did take Barcelona in 800.

Moorish rule in Spain and Portugal, which lasted until the fifteenth century, witnessed many changes. It resulted in the migration to the Iberian peninsula of many Moors and others from Africa. It saw the construction of large mosques and palaces, such as the Grand Mosque of Córdoba, built from 785 in the grounds of a former Visigothic church, and the Alhambra at Granada. For the Moors, the Iberian Peninsula, became a great center of learning and culture, with universities, medical schools, and law schools. An exchange of culture and inventions took place.

Gradually, however, the Moors, certain of their continued rule over most of the Iberian peninsula, became overconfident. They started fighting with each other, leading to a fragmentation of the region and the appearance of a number of independent Moorish kingdoms. This led to power struggles, which the Christian kingdoms were able to exploit, although they also had their differences with each other. The emergence of Rodrigo Diaz de Vivar, or "El Cid," in the 1070s and 1080s led to a rallying of many of the Christians. El Cid managed to exploit the differences between them, and also between the various Moorish kingdoms, to great advantage. With help from English crusaders, the Portuguese were able to reassert themselves and retake Lisbon. By this time, El Cid was in control of Valencia, and Moorish cities started to fall to the Christians gradually over the forthcoming centuries. In 1487, the Christians captured Málaga. A few years later, the Christians captured the city of Granada, the last Muslim-controlled city on the Iberian Peninsula, thereby making Queen Isabella of Castile and her husband, King Ferdinand II of Aragon, rulers of the city on January 2, 1492.

See also: Italy, African Invasions of; Moor's Head Symbol; Portugal, Blacks in; Spain, Blacks in.

Further Reading: Collins, Roger J. H. *The Arab Conquest of Spain, 710–797*. Oxford: Basil Blackwell, 1994; Dozy, Reinhart. *Spanish Islam: A History of the Muslims in Spain*. London: Frank Cass, 1972; Fletcher, Richard A. *Moorish Spain*. Berkeley: University of California Press, 1994; Harvey, Leonard P. *Islamic Spain, 1250 to 1500*. Chicago: University of Chicago Press, 1990; Watt, W. Montgomery. *A History of Islamic Spain*. Edinburgh: University Press, 1965.

Justin Corfield

Spain, Blacks in

As a result of its geographic location, the southern coast of Spain is less than 10 miles from Africa, the two separated by the Strait of Gibraltar. During the course of Spanish history, blacks migrated from Africa to Spain as conquering soldiers, slaves, freemen, and immigrants. Consequently, Spain has often emerged as the meeting place between African and European cultures. This intermingling of cultures has had a profound influence on Spanish culture.

During the **Punic Wars,** the ancient African city of Carthage used Spain as a base in its battles with Rome. Many of the soldiers in the Carthaginian army were black Africans. Later, the Roman army, which was stationed and received conquered property throughout the Empire, including Iberia, counted black Africans among its members.

African invasions of Spain in the 700s resulted in large portions of the Iberian Peninsula falling under the control of Muslim African forces. French forces managed to prevent the Muslims from pushing farther into Western Europe. The Muslims, or **Moors,** however, retained parts of Spain until the Spanish Christian forces rallied to expel them completely in 1492. Moorish control of Spain brought the migration of Moors and others from Africa to the Iberian Peninsula. As a result, Spanish culture became a fusion of different cultural traditions. Large Islamic mosques and palaces were built throughout Spain. The Moors transformed Spain into a center of learning and culture in the Mediterranean world.

Spain had been involved in the trade of Moors and other peoples as slaves in the Iberian Peninsula. Spain was also active in exploring the possibility of African alliances to fight the Muslims. In the early 1300s, for example, an Ethiopian delegation arrived in Europe to seek an alliance. In the 1400s, the ruler of the Spanish kingdom of Aragon considered a marriage with an Ethiopian princess to secure an alliance.

The depiction of black characters in Spanish literature testified to the African presence in Spain. In the seventh century, the *Etymologiae*, an encyclopedic work by Saint-Isidore of Seville, gave geographic information on Africa and described Africans as dark because of the continent's hot weather and the sun's intensity there. In the 1300s, Don Juan Manuel's *El Conde Lucanor* featured a prominent black servant character. *La Vida de Lazarillo de Tormes*, written by an anonymous author in 1554, depicted one of the first interracial love stories in European literature. The love story revolves around Antona Perez, a Spanish peasant girl, and Zaide, an African Moor who works as a stableman In the Renaissance Era, Andrés de Claramonte's *El Valiente Negro de Flandes* features the former black slave **Juan de Merida,** who joins the Spanish army.

After the expulsion of the Moors in 1492, the newly unified Spain became involved in the **Age of Exploration.** After Columbus's discovery of the Americas, Spain focused on establishing an empire in the New World. Many black conquistadors and black settlers from Spain were involved in the founding of the Spanish American empire. Some of these blacks achieved status and wealth.

The lack of white women in the Spanish colonies in the Caribbean and Latin America resulted in the rise of biracial offspring of all social rankings. A strict racial categorization developed based on the percentages of one's black and white ancestry. Many individuals of biracial descent traveled from the Americas to Spain during the sixteenth to nineteenth centuries. Some of these individuals were servants or students, but many were also from the middle and upper classes.

In Renaissance Spain, the presence of both free and enslaved blacks in previous and current centuries resulted in several blacks and individuals of black descent rising in prominence. Some notable blacks in Renaissance and early modern Spain included the painters **Juan de Pareja** and **Sebastian Gomez,** as well as **Juan Latino,** the noted scholar and poet.

The Spanish slave trade developed around Spain's American colonies, which were built on the use of slave labor. Initial attempts to enslave the Amerindians did not generate the volume of slaves needed. Africans became used increasingly during the early sixteenth century and continued until the nineteenth century. Under pressure from Britain and the decline of Spain as a world power, the Spanish abolition of slavery and the slave trade finally occurred in the nineteenth century.

In the 1930s, during Spain's Civil War, individuals from various parts of the world flocked to Spain, either as journalists, writers, or to fight against General Franco's attempt to become dictator. Some of these international figures, such as **Nicolás Guillén,** were black and came from former Spanish colonies. African Americans in the Spanish Civil War formed their own unit.

In the postwar era, immigrants from the former Spanish colonies in Africa, such as Equatorial Guinea, and North Africa have increased the presence of blacks in Spain. Illegal African immigration to Europe is quite frequent. Because of its proximity to Africa, Spain is often the site where illegal immigrants attempt to enter Europe. Spain is concerned with efforts to curb illegal immigration from Africa, which is often attempted under dangerous circumstances. The increase of African immigrants, both legal and illegal, in Spain has resulted in race riots, such as those in 2000.

See also: Abolition of Slavery, Spanish; Colonies in Africa, Spanish; Colonies in the Caribbean, Spanish; Conquistadors, Black; Courts, Blacks at European Aristocratic; Immigration to Europe, Illegal African; *Ladinos,* Black; Meneses, Cristóbol de; Moor's Head Symbol; Moret Law, Spanish; Ortiz, Leonardo; Pirates, Blacks and Mediterranean; Race Riots in Europe; Renaissance, Blacks in the; Roman Army, Africans in the; Slave Trade, Spanish; Spanish Army, Blacks in the; Spanish Civil War, African Americans in; Xenophobia and Blacks in Europe.

Further Reading: Seminario, Lee. *The History of the Blacks, the Jews, and the Moors in Spain.* Madrid: Playor, 1975.

Eric Martone

Spanish Army, Blacks in the

Black soldiers in the Spanish army date to the beginning of modern Spain and the conquest of the Iberian Peninsula from the Muslims. Black soldiers took an active role as conquistadors in the Spanish conquest of the Americas. They were later formed into separate companies to defend the Spanish colonial empire from foreign invaders and as special border companies in Spain itself. By the twentieth century, both the colonies and a separate black identity had been lost, but black soldiers continued to serve in the Spanish Army. Battalions of dark-skinned Berber tribesmen helped Francisco Franco in the 1930s defeat the Republicans during the Spanish Civil War. The end of Spain's colonial empire in Africa has resulted in the virtual end to separate black units in the Spanish army.

Black warriors fought for the Muslims before they were defeated by the Spanish. By 1492, the population of blacks in Spain was considerable. Although most were slaves, many were free blacks or of biracial descent. All were familiar with Spanish and Spanish culture. They suffered under various restrictions, because the Spanish authorities did not fully trust them. Many were converted Christians whose faith was questionable to authorities. Free blacks were limited in the professions that they could follow and the organizations to which they could belong. Free blacks were not allowed to carry weapons for their own defense, even in areas where crime was rampant.

Many blacks saw the New World as an opportunity. The first blacks recorded as settling in the Americas were some who accompanied Nicolas de Ovando to Hispaniola in 1502. Although some blacks were domestic servants, others were intended to help keep the Amerindian population subdued. Many of Ovando's blacks ran away and established their own free settlements in the mountains. Even so, hundreds of other blacks soon arrived in the Caribbean as slaves or free men.

At least some blacks participated in the noted conquistador Cortes's conquest of the Aztecs in modern Mexico. One unfortunate, named Francisco de Eguia, is believed to have spread smallpox among the defenders of Tenochtitlan, the Aztec capital, facilitating the conquest. Another, Juan Garrido, left a biography of his deeds in a petition to the Spanish king. These black conquistadors fought for the Spanish against the Amerindians. Historians believe many had fought in earlier campaigns on Caribbean islands. As experienced soldiers, they were highly prized by Cortes and his commanders. All were considered **ladinos,** who were blacks familiar with Spanish culture. Some had lived in Spain, whereas others had been captured in African wars before being sent to Mexico.

Rewards for fighting with the Spanish could be great. If they were not already free men, they were freed. They were also given government positions with a salary. These positions were usually lower ranking, such as a crier or gatekeeper, which in Spanish culture was usually identified with blacks. Some exceptions were made, however. Juan Valiente, a slave probably born in Africa who spent some time in the Caribbean, was active in the conquest of Peru and Chile. Although not formally freed, he received the rank of captain, was given an estate, and an *encomienda* (estates), which required local Amerindians to labor for him and share their produce.

As the Spanish became more established, many blacks intermarried with Amerindian women. These biracial individuals continued to play an important role in the later conquests in South and Central America. They also were used to enforce laws among Amerindians under Spanish colonial rule. By the seventeenth and eighteenth centuries, free biracial individuals were the most numerous people with African backgrounds. Known as *pardos*, they were formed into separate militia companies. These companies were usually stationed at strategic points to defend against European raiders such as the Dutch or British. The *pardo* companies often had black or biracial officers. By the last half of the eighteenth century, *pardo* officers received equal rights to white officers, including access to promotions and exemption from tribute to the crown. In some Spanish colonies, *pardos* formed a majority of the militia that defended the colony. Thousands later fought on both sides during the Latin American revolutions during the nineteenth century.

In Spain itself, the importation of black slaves became insignificant during the sixteenth century. Interracial marriage led to the end of a separate group of people with African heritage. An exception could be found during the eighteenth century in southern Spain. African slaves from the Portuguese region of Alentejo escaped across the border to gain their freedom in Spain. Most settled in the towns of Gibraleon and Niebla in western Andalusia. The Spanish government organized independent companies composed of former black slaves and used them to patrol the border in this region.

By the twentieth century, few blacks remained in the Spanish army. The Spanish Empire had been reduced to Spanish Morocco, Western Sahara, and Equatorial

Guinea. When Berber tribes rose in revolt in 1909, the Spanish army had difficulty restoring order. A reorganization was undertaken in 1911 to create a professional, long-serving army. A battalion of indigenous troops was organized in Morocco with Spanish officers. Known formally as *Regulares,* these African troops quickly became an elite unit. Spanish officers with the *Regulares* were regarded as leaders within the army. When the Rif War broke out in Morocco in 1921, most *Regulares* remained loyal. They played an important role in defeating the rebels.

The *Regulares* expanded to five *Grupos,* based on Melilla, Tetuan, Ceuta, Alhucemas, and Larache. In addition to keeping order in Africa, they were sent in 1934 to put down an uprising by Asturian miners. The dark complexions and brutality of the *Regulares* earned them the nickname "**Moors**" from the Spanish people. The Spanish government was criticized by internal and external observers for using the Africans against whites.

In July 1936, much of the Spanish army revolted against the government. Francisco Franco took command of the Army of Africa, which he had once led. Using aircraft loaned by German Nazi leader Adolf Hitler and Italian dictator Benito Mussolini, many *Regulares* were flown to Spain. The *Regulares* were the shock troops that led Nationalist forces to the outskirts of Madrid. Their presence caused many government supporters to flee without fighting. The urban fighting that followed caused many casualties among the African troops without much gain. The *Regulares* were soon withdrawn. They spent much of the remainder of the war occupying conquered territory. The fear the *Regulares* had once caused turned to racial hatred and caused many Republicans to fight harder.

After the war, the *Regulares* returned to Spanish Morocco. When Morocco became independent in 1956, most were transferred to the new country. Although a single regiment of *Regulares* remains in the Spanish army, it is no longer an exclusively black organization. Black recruits are uncommon and are now integrated into the rest of the Spanish army.

See also: Age of Exploration; Colonies in Africa, Spanish; Colonies in the Caribbean, Spanish; Conquistadors, Black; Interracial Marriages, European Laws Banning; Latin American Colonial Revolutions, Blacks in; Spain, African Invasions of; Spain, Blacks in; Spanish Civil War, Africans Americans in the.

Further Reading: Archer, Christon I. *The Army in Bourbon Mexico, 1760–1810.* Albuquerque: University of New Mexico Press, 1977; Balfour, Sebastian. Deadly Embrace: *Morocco and the Road to the Spanish Civil War.* New York: Oxford University Press, 2002; Beevor, Antony. *The Battle for Spain: The Spanish Civil War, 1936–1939.* New York: Penguin Books, 2006; Restall, Matthew. *Seven Myths of the Spanish Conquest.* New York: Oxford University Press, 2003.

Tim J. Watts

Spanish Civil War, African Americans in the

Civil war erupted in Spain in July 1936, after an uprising led by Francisco Franco and several other generals against the Spanish Republic, which was led by a "Popular Front" of liberal and leftist parties. Nazi Germany and Benito Mussolini's fascist Italian government provided massive aid to Franco's nationalists, and tens of thousands of volunteers from around the world traveled to Spain to fight on behalf of the Republic. Among the 40,000 international volunteers were 3,000 U.S. citizens, including approximately 100 blacks. A large majority of the American volunteers served in battalions that came to be known as the Abraham Lincoln Brigade.

Most African Americans who fought to defend the Spanish Republic were organized by the Communist Party USA, which had a substantial black membership in the 1930s, in large part a result of its advocacy of civil rights at a time when African Americans had few political allies. Some of the international volunteers, such as Harry Haywood, had risen to leadership positions within the Communist Party; others were sympathetic to the party but not necessarily members.

Black Americans also had opportunities within the Lincoln Brigade that were not yet open to them in the U.S. armed forces. For example, Oliver Law, assigned to lead a Lincoln Brigade battalion in 1937, became the first black officer to command an integrated American military force. Law, who was killed in action in July of the same year, had served six years in the U.S. Army, but was denied promotion and remained a private. Other African American volunteers served as pilots, an occupation from which they were virtually excluded at home, either in civilian or military life.

Prominent African -American artists, writers, and intellectuals such as Langston Hughes and **Paul Robeson** lent their talents and prestige to the anti-Franco effort. Hughes wrote several poems about the war and interviewed many black volunteers while reporting from Spain for the *Baltimore Afro-American* newspaper. Other African American writers and spokespeople also linked the defense of the Republic with the struggle against racism at home and colonialism in Africa. Leading black newspapers, including the *Pittsburgh Courier* and the *Chicago Defender*, editorialized in defense of the Republic, and popular black entertainers raised money for the anti-Franco effort. The Harlem Musicians' Committee for Spanish Democracy, for example, enlisted the services of famed musicians such as Count Basie and Fats Waller.

As the cold war set in shortly after the conclusion of World War II, the U.S. government initiated a widespread persecution of leftwing political activists, especially those associated with the Communist Party. Pierre Duvalle, Oscar Hunter, and other African American "internationalists" were harassed by agents of the Federal Bureau of Investigation at their workplaces; others were called before Congressional committees. Several black veterans of the Spanish Civil War, such as Ray Durem, left the United States to avoid further repression. The upsurge in civil rights activism of the 1950s and 1960s, however, eventually led to some recognition of African Americans who had fought in Spain. The city of Chicago, for example, proclaimed an "Oliver Law and Abraham Lincoln Brigade Day" in 1987.

See also: Spain, Blacks in; Spanish Army, Blacks in the.

Further Reading: Carroll, Peter. *The Odyssey of the Abraham Lincoln Brigade: Americans in the Spanish Civil War.* Stanford: Stanford University Press, 1994; Collum, Danny Duncan, ed. *African-Americans in the Spanish Civil War: "This Ain't Ethiopia, But It'll Do."* New York: G. K. Hall, 1992; Eby, Cecil. *Comrades and Commissars: The Lincoln Battalion in the Spanish Civil War.* University Park: Pennsylvania State University Press, 2007; Yates, James. *Mississippi to Madrid: Memoir of a Black American in the Abraham Lincoln Brigade.* Seattle: Open Hand Publishing, 1988.

John M. Cox

Spratlin, Valaurez Burwell (1897–1961)

Valaurez Burwell Spratlin was a renowned historian who conducted much research into the history of blacks in Europe and the Americas during the early twentieth century. Spratlin was born in December 1897 in Colorado. His father, who was from Alabama, was an African American physician in general practice in Denver, and his mother was a teacher from New Orleans, Louisiana. Spratlin attended the University of Denver, earning both his bachelor's and master's degrees there. Spratlin also developed an interest in playing the piano and remained a keen enthusiast of music and opera.

From 1920 until 1921, Spratlin worked at Armstrong Manual Training High School (later Armstrong High School), one of the two African American high schools in Washington, and then taught at the State College of West Virginia. In 1927, Spratlin traveled to Europe, returning to New York in September. He had a deep interest in Spanish and Portuguese colonial history, and on his return, he started working at Howard University as director of the department of Romance languages, a position he held until his death. Spratlin also started work for his doctorate at Middlebury College, completing it in 1931.

Over succeeding years, Spratlin used his university vacations to travel extensively in Latin America and the Caribbean. In 1945, Spratlin was awarded the National Order of Honor and Merit of Haiti, and eight years later was invested with the Order of Vasco Nuñez de Balboa in Panama. Spratlin's pioneering book on Juan Latino *Juan Latino: Slave and Humanist*, was published in 1938. The book focuses on the life of **Juan Latino,** the famous black figure of the Spanish Renaissance. Spratlin's other works included *Slave Painters in Spain* (1937), in which he made a major study of **Sebastian Gomez.** In 1949, he wrote to *The New York Times* complaining about racial discrimination in theaters in Washington, D.C. Spratlin also reviewed many books for *The Journal of Negro History*, *The Journal of Negro Education*, and other journals. He was a member of the American Association of Teachers of Spanish and Portuguese.

See also: Pareja, Juan; Portugal, Blacks in; Renaissance, Blacks in the; Spain, Blacks in.

Further Reading: Ferrer Canales, José. "Valaurez Burwell Spratlin (1897–1961)." *Hispania* 45:3 (September 1962): 446–450.

Justin Corfield

Storm, Theodor (1817–1888)

The novellas of Theodor Storm are among the finest in German literature. Although Storm is better known for novellas such as *Immensee* (1849) and *The Dykemaster* (*Der Schimmelreiter*, 1888), which are set on the North Sea Plain, he also wrote about international themes. Storm's 1865 novella, *Von Jenseits des Meeres* (*From Across the Sea*), is a conventional love story exploring the trope of a beautiful biracial woman and contains some obvious and conscious racist passages. Jenni was sent by her white father, a rich plantation owner in the Caribbean (West Indies), to

Germany to be educated and to visit his family. It is unspecified how her father, who later appears on the scene as a cruel and dominating man, has made his fortune. He is the prototypical colonial master, used to commanding and getting his way. The colonial background needs no explanation because it is obvious that through hard work and ruthless behavior, he amassed a fortune and fathered a child with a beautiful dark-colored woman. When 12-year-old Alfred meets his white-complexioned cousin, it is implied that her beauty and "naturally" passionate character have their origin in her dark mother's heritage. In a scene reminiscent of many American slave narratives, the young girl is literally handed over to the boy to be his companion. The German word "*gespielin*" alludes to a sexual relationship that foreshadows later developments.

When Jenni and Alfred meet again 10 years later, Jenni is a mature, beautiful, and seductive woman. The narrative is steeped in allusions, direct and indirect, to her race; she is repeatedly called Alfred's "*räuberbraut*," or "robber-bride." Alfred seems to detect a primordial wildness in her that attracts him. The narrator is credited with real affection and love for her, seemingly without any concern for her black heritage. Jenni herself, however, is aware of the racial barrier. In a noble gesture, she wants to prevent Alfred from committing the sin of marriage with her.

Jenni rebels against her father's rule and his deeply prejudiced view of her mother's race. Her return to the West Indies, and her visit with her mother, is by far the most problematical part of the story. The plot now foregrounds the racist assumptions. Jenni has become a stranger and she is shocked by her mother's behavior. She cannot cope with the open passion, the colorfulness, and the lack of restraint in her mother's boarding house. Two full pages abound in descriptions that spell her horror. She is unsettled by the realization that she is part of this race, that her blood contains traces of the animal-like noises of the people in the West Indies. By presenting the scenes in the West Indies from the point of view of the young girl, rather than that of her white father or lover, Storm disguises the racism behind it as criticism of one of their own. It is the voice of despair of a young girl caught between a deeply ingrained racism and a perception of herself as different. As with so many other novels and plots of the nineteenth century, interracial relationships are accepted on an individual basis, but do not lead to any heightened tolerance against the race itself. In Storm's story, Jenni fares well in the end and is allowed to marry her beloved. In many other stories, some of them set in Germany, many of them set in the United States, the girl has to die a tragic death.

See also: Germany, Blacks in; Interracial Marriages, European Laws Banning; Literature, Blacks in German and Central European; Von Kleist, Heinrich.

Further Reading: Pastor, Eckart. "Theodor Storms Novelle 'Von jenseits des Meeres' oder: Überlegungen zur Frage, ob 'es möglich ist, einen Mohren weiß zu waschen." *Theodor Storm— Narrative Strategies and Patriarchy/Theodor Storm: Erzählstrategien und Patriarchat.* ed. David A. Jackson and Mark G. Ward. Lewiston: Edwin Mellen, 1999, pp. 61–84; Storm, Theodor. "Von Jenseits des Meeres." *Gedichte, Novellen, 1848–1867.* ed. Dieter Lohmeier. Frankfurt: Deutscher Klassiker Verlag, 1987, pp. 649–693.

Hanna Wallinger

Strong, Jonathan (1747?–1773)

Jonathan Strong was a former slave who became involved in a major court case in eighteenth-century England concerning slavery and the slave trade. He had been a slave in Barbados before being brought to London While in London, his master, David Lisle, beat him savagely with a pistol in 1765. Strong's head was swollen severely and he was nearly blinded in the assault. Although Strong was barely able to walk, Lisle abandoned him in the street; however, Strong made his way to William Sharp, a surgeon known to treat London's poor free of charge. Sharpe's brother, Granville Sharp, an abolitionist and government clerk, questioned Strong about his injuries, which had almost led to his death. William Sharp assisted Strong in gaining admittance to a hospital, where he was treated for his injuries for four months. After Strong was released from the hospital, the Sharps assisted him in gaining employment running errands.

Strong was baptized on July 22, 1765, when he was about 18 years old. During the eighteenth century, popular belief posed that the act of baptism rendered African slaves free. Theological ideas had been used to support slavery on the grounds that blacks were divinely cursed. If blacks became Christian, many believed that this also meant that the slave could no longer remain in forced servitude. Consequently, many slaveholders refused to allow their slaves to be baptized, and many British colonies passed laws outlawing freedom by baptism. In 1729, both the attorney general and solicitor general confirmed the legality of outlawing freedom by baptism in the Yorke-Talbot ruling. Nevertheless, popular belief persisted. After baptism in England, a slave was no longer a "slave," but rather a "servant" and could no longer be bought or sold. Many slaves brought to England, therefore, were baptized.

By chance, Lisle encountered Strong after abandoning him a few years previously and followed his former slave home. Lisle attempted to recapture Strong and gained £30 for him, payable when Strong was aboard a West Indian (Caribbean) vessel set for departure. Lisle then hired two men to capture Strong and bring him to a London jail until a West India vessel was ready for departure. Strong sought Granville Sharp for aid. Consequently, Sharp took Strong's case to court. On September 18, 1767, Sir Robert Kite, the lord mayor, discharged Strong on the grounds that he had not committed any crime. In the court, the captain of the ship attempted to seize Strong, but he was prevented from being carried off.

The Jamaican planter who had purchased Strong attempted to sue the Sharps on the grounds that they had deprived him of his rightful property. The Sharps furthered the position that since Strong was in England, he was no longer a slave. During the suit, the Yorke-Talbot ruling of 1729 was brought up, confirming that despite his baptism, Strong was still a slave and not free by baptism. Consequently, a master could rightfully force his slave to work in the Caribbean. In 1768, however, the courts ruled in Strong's favor, as Lisle lacked funding to continue the case, which received national publicity. The case helped set the principle that any slave was free upon setting foot on English soil. Sharp used the case to further the abolitionist cause and took up the cases of other slaves such as Thomas Lewis and James Somerset. Strong, however, never recovered fully from his beating and died in 1773.

See also: Abolition of Slavery, British; Britain, Blacks in; Cain, Theory of Descent of Blacks from; Colonies in the Caribbean, British; Common Law, Slavery and English; Free Soil Principle; Hamitic Myth; Slave Trade, British; Somerset Case.

Further Reading: Schama, Simon. *Rough Crossings: Britain, the Slaves, and the American Revolution*. New York: Ecco, 2006; Thomas, Hugh. *The Slave Trade: The Story of the Atlantic Slave Trade, 1440–1870*. New York: Simon and Schuster, 1997; Wise, Steven. *"Though the Heavens May Fall": The Landmark Trial that Led to the End of Human Slavery*. New York: Da Capo Press, 2006.

Eric Martone

T

Tanner, Henry Ossawa (1859–1937)

Henry Ossawa Tanner, who spent the last period of his life in self-imposed exile in France, was the first African American artist to gain international acclaim. He was born in June 1859 in Pittsburgh, Pennsylvania. His father was a minister from the African Methodist Episcopal Church and his mother was a private school teacher. The oldest of a large family, Tanner accompanied his family when they moved to Philadelphia. When he was 13 years old, Tanner saw a painter at Fairmount Park and decided to become an artist himself. Using much of his free time to draw, Tanner went to watch other artists at the various art galleries in Philadelphia.

Tanner enrolled at the Pennsylvania Academy of Fine Arts in 1879 and studied under the celebrated painter, Thomas Eakins (1844–1916). Seven years later, Tanner opened his own studio in Philadelphia. He then moved to Atlanta, Georgia, where he opened an unsuccessful photography studio and taught drawing at Clark University. In 1891, Tanner went to France, where he studied under Jean-Paul Laurens. Two years later, back in Philadelphia, Tanner painted one of his most famous paintings featuring African Americans, *The Banjo Lesson.* The painting depicts a small boy in a log cabin learning how to play the banjo from a patient old man. Tanner found the racial discrimination in the United States oppressive and decided to return to France in 1895. He then lived in Paris for much of the rest of his life, although he returned to the United States during 1901 to 1904. In 1900, Eakins painted a portrait of Tanner.

In Paris, Tanner remained a teetotaler and always observed the Sabbath, which distinguished him from many of the other painters there. Tanner's early paintings were on religious themes, including *Daniel in the Lion's Den,* which won an honorable mention in the Paris Salon of 1896. Consequently, Tanner's father seems to have had a major influence on his interest in religion. Tanner continued exhibiting at the Paris Salon in 1897, winning silver medals in 1900 and 1906. His *Raising of Lazarus* (1897) is regarded as one of his best works. During World War I, Tanner served with the Red Cross Public Information Department. Two of his paintings of this period, both of war-time camp scenes, were displayed in the War Museum of the American Red Cross in Washington, DC. Tanner was also involved in painting images of the conflict.

Many of Tanner's paintings were bought by the Atlanta art collector J. J. Haverty, founder of the Haverty Furniture Company. Haverty used his fortune to establish the High Museum of Art, which now holds some of Tanner's best works.

See also: Artists in Europe, African American; France, Blacks in; World War I, Black Participation in.

Further Reading: Bruce, Marcus. *Henry Ossawa Tanner: A Spiritual Biography.* New York: Crossroad 8th Avenue, 2002; Gale, Robert. *The Gay Nineties in America: A Cultural Dictionary of the 1890s.* Westport, CT: Greenwood Press, 1992; Matthews, Marcia. *Henry Ossawa Tanner: American Artist.* Chicago: University of Chicago Press, 1969.

Justin Corfield

Television, Blacks in European

Contemporary television programming has a large impact in shaping and developing national identities and cultures. The depiction of certain group identities on European television influences how such groups are perceived by the country at large and how they perceive themselves. Furthermore, the common and positive depictions of certain minority group identities on television can play a crucial role in integrating minority cultures within the larger mainstream culture of the country. In general, blacks are underrepresented on European television, although many European countries are increasing the black presence on television and are attempting to develop increased programming for blacks.

BRITAIN.   Since the 1980s, British television has made strides to represent cultural and ethnic minorities in its programming. Nevertheless, British television still has a long way to go before a true sense of equality and diversity is attained.

According to recent surveys conducted by the Open University and the University of Manchester on behalf of the British Film Institute, the major British minority groups feel alienated from much of British television culture, particularly soaps. Much of British programming still caters almost exclusively to white, middle-class Britons. The survey found that although minority groups integrate with national culture, aspects of television culture does not integrate ethnic interests or identities. The BBC created a new executive position to review and track programming content to work with the network and independent companies toward improving diversity. The logic behind the initiative was that because the British viewing audience is becoming increasingly diverse, these diverse groups will desire to see themselves and their experiences reflected in television culture. While the focus was, therefore, not on establishing quotas, a 2005 study by the Cultural Diversity Network revealed that although minorities accounted for almost 7.8 percent of Britain's population, they were represented in only 6.6 of the roles on television soaps and 7.5 percent of roles on factual shows.

The BBC has made several efforts, some successful and some not so successful, to provide programming for black Britons in the 2000s. The BBC recently attempted to integrate an African theme into its regular programming. For example, it adapted a ballroom dancing program into a game show entitled *Strictly African Dancing*. The program featured African and Caribbean celebrities who traveled to Africa to train with dance troupes to perform live on television before a panel of judges. Another example is the BBC television show *Holby City*, which chronicled the life of a black British doctor who returned to Ghana to practice medicine. A notable failure was *The Crouches*, a sitcom about a black family.

Nevertheless, minorities are represented on British television and the television industry in a much more proportional rate than on American television. The Writers Guild of America reported that although minorities make up almost 30 percent of the American population, only 12 percent of the writers for American television during the 2005–2006 season were minorities.

FRANCE.   French television rarely portrays cultural and racial minorities. The most visible roles for minorities on French television are as hosts and news personalities. Minority issues are often limited in French television programming, in which minorities are often victims of negative stereotyping.

France has historically been a country of immigrants, which have been used to offset the declining French birthrate. Before World War II, however, most French immigrants were of European descent. During the postwar period, many of the immigrants to France have come from areas formerly under French colonial rule, particularly Africa. Yet, French television often reinforces the notion of a white France devoid of multiethnic diversity. The French population, therefore, is disproportionately represented on television.

The topic of minorities on French television was first studied in 1991 by the Center for Information and Research on International Migrations. The study made several conclusions. First, few professionals of foreign origin appeared on French television. Second, although minorities were visible in news and general information programming, their onscreen presence was limited, and the topics associated them were negative (crime, poverty, unemployment, etc.). Third, minorities, especially blacks, were visible in musical and nonfiction entertainment programming. Fourth, commercials often ignored or presented reduced roles for minorities. Fifth, French shows often relegated minorities to roles as extras or as petty criminals.

In 1999, the *Conseil Superieur de l'Audiovisuel* (Audiovisual Supreme Council, CSA) conducted a similar study. The study reaffirmed that few minority professionals appeared on French television, and revealed that blacks were the minority group most represented of all minorities on French television. Minorities were revealed often as occupying marginal or inconsequential roles. They were depicted in a stereotypical manner and associated with negative phenomena or situations. Furthermore, minorities were not presented as integrated components of a multicultural French society.

The discussion of the issue of minorities and multiculturalism on French television is still, to an extent, taboo in France, and minorities still retain a marginalized role on French television. The notions of affirmative action and quotas are often criticized as running counter to the ideas of French republicanism. North Africans began to push for equality in the 1980s, but blacks from Africa and the Caribbean did not to begin to collectively agitate for equality until the late 1990s. In 1999, Calixthe Beyala, a black writer, even filed a complaint calling for quotas for blacks on French television. Some positive changes have occurred during the 2000s. Minority journalists and news personalities have been recruited to a larger extent. For example, in 2006, **Harry Rosel-mack,** a black news reporter, made headlines in France when he temporarily assumed the lead anchor position on television's most popular news program. In addition, more films have been made with minority actors.

GERMANY.   Blacks also occupy a marginal role on German television, although entertainment remains the most visible field in which blacks appear in German society. For example, **Cherno Jobatey,** an Afro-German, has had a successful career on German television as a host of a popular morning show. Afro-Germans are also seen frequently in musical programming. Some famous Afro-German television personalities include hosts and announcers Nadja Abd el Farrag, Mola Adebisi, and Pierre Geisensetter. Some famous Afro-German actors and actresses include Liz Baffoe, Karin Boyd, Charles Huber, and Ron Williams.

See also: Afro-Germans; Black British; Cinema, Blacks in European; Civil Rights Movement in Twentieth-Century Great Britain; Kiesbauer, Arabella; Massaquoi, Hans-Jürgen; May 10 Holiday; Media, Blacks in Contemporary European; Music Industry, Blacks in the European; Robin Hood Legend, Blacks in the.

Further Reading: Blackshire-Belay, Carol, ed. *The African-German Experience: Critical Essays.* Westport, CT: Praeger, 1996; Bourne, Stephen. *Black in the British Frame: The Black Experience in British Film and Television.* London: Continuum, 2001; Gilman, Sander. *On Blackness Without Blacks: Essays on the Image of the Black in Germany.* Boston: G. K. Hall, 1982; Mazon, Patricia, and Reinhild Steingrover, eds. *Not So Plain as Black and White: Afro- German Culture and History, 1890–2000.* Rochester: University of Rochester Press, 2005; Scriven, Michael, and Emily Roberts, eds. *Group Identities on French and British Television.* New York: Berghahn Books, 2003; Scriven, Michael, and Monia Lecomte, eds. *Television Broadcasting in Contemporary France and Britain.* New York: Berghahn Books, 1999.

Eric Martone

Terentius Afer (195/185?–159 B.C.E.?)

Publius Terentius Afer (also known as Terence) was a former African slave and ancient Roman playwright known for his comedies. Ancient Roman historians debate Terentius's date of birth, placing it at either 195 B.C.E. or 185 B.C.E. Terentius was born in Carthage in North Africa, but he was not Carthaginian as demonstrated by the use of ethnonym *Afer*, which referred to Africans in general, rather than Punicus, which referred exclusively to Carthaginians. Terentius was from a wealthy family that went bankrupt; consequently, Terentius was sold as a slave to a Roman senator, who educated and later freed him. On his release from slavery, he was named Terentius (the name of his former master) and Afer (where he was from); his family's original name is unknown.

Terentius's comedies were first performed circa 170–160 B.C.E. He wrote six known plays, including *Andria* (*The Girl from Andros*, 166 B.C.E.), *Hecyra* (*The Mother-in-Law,*

165 B.C.E.), *Heauton Timorumenos* (*The Self-Tormentor*, 163 B.C.E.), *Eunuchus* (*The Eunuch*, 161 B.C.E.), *Phormio* (161 B.C.E.), and *Adelphoe* (*The Brothers*, 160 B.C.E.). Some famous lines from his work are "Charity begins at home" (*Andria*, act IV, scene I), and "You are harping on the same string" (*Phormio*, act III, scene II). Terentius, whose works were adapted from Greek plays and used many Greek dramatic conventions, wrote in conversational Latin. His work, based on the Greek New Comedy of Menander, can be divided into two groups: close translations of the later Greek comedy writers (particularly Menander), and more original combinations of two or more Greek dramas into a new Romanized play. Terentius became friends with elite Romans, particularly Publius Cornelius Scipio, who served as his patrons.

Terentius died while still a young man, possibly in 159 B.C.E. in Greece or during a sea journey back to Rome. His work received a revival in Europe during the Medieval and Renaissance periods. New Comedy became the precursor to the modern European comedy of manners, demonstrated by such writers as Molière and Oscar Wilde. Earlier European writers, such as Chaucer and Shakespeare, also drew inspiration from Terentius's work.

See also: Italy, Blacks in; Punic Wars; Roman Army, Africans in the; Roman Emperors, African; Roman Empire in Africa.

Further Reading: Terence. *The Complete Comedies of Terence: Modern Verse Translations.* trans. Palmer Bovie, Constance Carrier, and Douglass Parker. New Brunswick: Rutgers University Press, 1974.

Nicole Martone

Terrell, Mary Church (1863–1954)

Mary Church Terrell was a prominent biracial writer and civil rights activist in the United States. She traveled extensively to Europe and was the only black woman to attend the Berlin International Congress of Women in Germany in 1904.

Terrell was born on September 23, 1863, in Memphis, Tennessee. Both of her parents were former slaves. Terrell's father, the son of his white master Charles Church, made a fortune from real estate speculation in Memphis and became the first African American millionaire in the southern states. Terrell went to Oberlin College, where she graduated in 1884. She was one of the first African American women to gain a college degree. Terrell then studied for two years in Europe, where she became fluent in French, German, and Italian.

On Terrell's return to Memphis in 1891, she married Robert Heberton Terrell, a lawyer who was to become the first African American municipal court judge in Washington. Terrell started work as a teacher and was promoted to the position of principal. She was appointed to the District of Columbia Board of Education from 1895 to 1906, and was the first African American woman to hold such a position in the United States. In 1896, along with Josephine Ruffin, she founded the Federation of Afro-American Women. In the same year, Terrell was elected the first president of the National Association of Colored Women, which was responsible for raising money for kindergartens, nurseries, and orphanages. She also founded the National Association of College Women (which later changed its name to the National Association of University Women). In 1904, Terrell spoke at the International Congress of Women in Berlin, Germany. She was the only black woman in attendance. Terrell spoke at the conference in English, French, and German to much acclaim.

Campaigning against racial discrimination, Terrell was present at the organizational meeting of the National Association for the Advancement of Colored People. During World War I, she was involved in picketing the White House for the Congressional Union of Women's Suffrage. After the war, Terrell worked with the War Community Service to help returning African American troops. For the next decade, she worked in the suffrage movement campaigning for the Nineteenth Amendment to the U.S. Constitution, which became law in 1920. Terrell wrote her autobiography, *A Colored Woman in a White World*, which was published in 1940. She was an articulate speaker, highlighting the lynching of African Americans in the southern states, and the discrimination against African Americans in employment and housing.

During the early 1950s, Terrell led a campaign against segregated restaurants in the United States. On February 28, 1950, she and some friends entered a segregated restaurant, where they were refused service. Terrell filed a lawsuit and for the next three years, she and her supporters began a series of boycotts, picketing, and demonstrations against segregated eating places. Eventually, on June 8, 1953, the Supreme Court ruled that regulations allowing restaurants to refuse to serve people on account of their race were unconstitutional.

See also: Civil Rights Movement in Twentieth-Century Great Britain; Du Bois, W.E.B.; Germany, Blacks in; King Jr., Martin Luther; Malcolm X in London; Pan-Africanism; Race Riots in Europe; World War I, Black Participation in.

Further Reading: Andrews, William, Frances Smith Foster, and Trudier Harris, eds. *The Oxford Companion to African American Literature.* New York: Oxford University Press, 1997; Fradin, Dennis, and Judith Fradin. *Fight On! Mary Church Terrell's Battle for Integration.* New York: Clarion Books, 2003.

Justin Corfield

Thompson, Daley (1958–)

Daley Thompson is a **black British** decathlete whose performances during the 1980s made him one of the most successful athletes of all time. Setting world records on several occasions, he was only the second British decathlete in history to win the decathlon twice at the Olympics, winning gold medals in 1980 and 1984. Thompson's flamboyance and personality helped increase the popularity of the decathlon in Britain.

Thompson, born Francis Thompson in London in 1958, is of Scottish and Nigerian descent. He later adopted the name Daley, a form of the African name Adodele given to him by his father. He competed in his first decathlon (which is composed of 10 events: shot put, discus, javelin, long jump, high jump, pole vault, 100 meter run, 400 meter run, 1500 meter run, and the 110 meter hurdles) when he was 16 years old. The next year, Thompson won the AAA title. Despite an unimpressive 18th-place finish in the 1976 Montreal Games, he went on to win the European junior title shortly thereafter. In 1978, Thompson first achieved international fame by winning the Commonwealth title.

In 1980, Thompson competed in the Olympics, winning a gold medal and setting a world record. In 1982, Thompson was the BBC Sports Personality of the Year and set two more world records, one of which occurred when he won his second European title. Despite injuries, he won the initial World Championships in 1983. Thompson set his best score in the decathlon 8,797 in the 1984 Olympics, winning his second gold medal and defeating his rival Jürgen Hingsen. The score remained a world record until 1992. In 1986, he won both European and Commonwealth titles. Thompson attempted to win a third gold medal by competing in the 1988 Olympics, but he was hampered by injury and finished fourth.

Thompson was inducted by Queen Elizabeth II in 1983 as a member of the Order of the British Empire (MBE) and in 2000 as a Commander of the British Empire (CBE). In 1992, he retired from athletics.

See also: Britain, Blacks in.

Further Reading: Rozin, Skip. *Daley Thompson: The Subject Is Winning.* London: Arrow Books, 1984.

Mark Cordery

Tocqueville, Alexis de (1805–1859)

Alexis de Tocqueville was a French political thinker and historian whose *Democracy in America*, published in two volumes in 1835 and 1840, greatly influenced European opinion of the United States and its inhabitants. Racialist thinking infused European thought about blacks, even extending to the normally detached French social scientist de Tocqueville. In the final chapter of volume one of *Democracy in America*, de Tocqueville presents the position of African Americans within the United States of the 1830s. De Tocqueville offered sympathy to African Americans held in slavery, but nevertheless generally believed that a black slave had no family, for to "him a woman is no more than the passing companion of his pleasures, and from their birth his sons are his equals." De Tocqueville ascribed animalistic qualities to African American slaves, calling them an "intermediate between beast and man." He also shared the pseudoscientific belief that blacks could work "without danger" in the tropical environments of the South.

Recognizing the ills of slavery for a democratic society, de Tocqueville made the case that slavery was the "most formidable evil" facing the United States. De Tocqueville argued that slavery posed a pernicious threat to all of Western society; however, like many racialist thinkers of this era, de Tocqueville desired to eliminate slavery more for the benefit of white citizens than black slaves. He pointed to the gradual emancipation and eventual segregation in the North as an ideal way to eliminate slavery and maintain the low status of blacks. Noting the alarmingly high ratios of blacks to whites in the southern states, de Tocqueville feared no easy solution was possible in the South.

So powerful was slavery that de Tocqueville believed, "all marked differences in character between northerners and southerners have their roots in slavery." He presented the examples of Kentucky and Ohio, two states sharing a common border of the Ohio River, but with very different results. In Kentucky, where slavery existed, the laborers were idle and slothful. On the other side of the river in free Ohio, the idealized free labor society of whites and European immigrants produced industry and prosperity. De Tocqueville, who has been called by scholars one of the first proponents of American exceptionalism, thus argued for slavery's elimination under the perception that it would allow for the best possible route to success for his beloved Americans.

For de Tocqueville, the only solution to the slavery problem in America was abolition followed by deportation. De Tocqueville believed that abolition without deportation would inevitably produce a violent conflict between whites and free blacks in the southern United States, possibly leading to the formation of a separate black nation. De Tocqueville held this belief throughout the remainder of his life. In the *Liberty Bell: Testimony against Slavery* (1855), he urged the deportation of blacks, but he acknowledged that segregation, as already conducted in the northern United States, presented the second best option. Although de Tocqueville believed in segregation for blacks, he adamantly opposed the scientific racism theories of Arthur Gobineau in the latter's essay on *The Inequality of Human Races* (1853–1855).

See also: Abolition of Slavery, French; Cain, Theory of Descent of Blacks from; Enlightenment Philosophers and Race; Enlightenment Philosophers and Slavery; Gobineau on Races and Slavery; Interracial Marriages, European Laws Banning; Scientific Racism.

Further Reading: Tocqueville, Alexis de. *Oeuvres Completes. Volume VII: Correspondance Américaine et Européenne.* Paris: Gallimard, 1986; Tocqueville, Alexis de. *Democracy in America.* trans. George Lawrence, ed. J. P. Mayer. New York: Perennial Classics, 2000.

Thomas Balcerski

Tombouctou (1883)

Tombouctou (*Timbuctoo*) is a story by celebrated nineteenth-century French writer Guy de Maupassant that details the adventures of French colonial soldier from Africa named Timbuctoo. In the story, Timbuctoo, arrives in Paris and bumps into two French officers, one of whom he had served under at Bezieres. The officer inquires what Timbuctoo is doing in Paris. Timbuctoo, extremely giddy, informs him that he had made a lot of money opening a restaurant catering to Prussians. After Timbuctoo leaves, the officer explains to his friend how he met Timbuctoo during the Franco-Prussian War (1870–1871). In the war, the officer commanded a garrison at Bezieres that included rowdy, drunken troops from the French colonies, including Timbuctoo. The officer learned that Timbuctoo was supplying the troops with alcohol from a mysterious source, later revealed as coming from a special vineyard. The officer could not comprehend Timbuctoo's African name, and therefore referred to him as Timbuctoo, his native place. One day, some Prussians ventured too closely to Timbuctoo's vineyard, and he and some other French colonial soldiers ambushed the Prussians and paraded their decapitated heads. The officer remarked to his friend how Timbuctoo looted the bodies of anything valuable, placing items in a pocket that stretched from his waist to his ankles. As the fighting progressed, the officer noticed that his African soldiers, including Timbuctoo, became increasingly fat, yet there were no more meat rations. He speculated that the meat derived from the bodies of Prussian soldiers. Timbuctoo developed a fondness for the officer, offering him presents and even bringing him a mysterious filet to eat. When Bezieres fell, the French soldiers fled or were captured. The French officer later found Timbuctoo at the head of a restaurant bearing a sign stating that he was an army chef and former cook to the emperor. Timbuctoo continued to feed the Prussians from the same "mysterious" meat source that he and his African companions ate from, which inspired Timbuctoo to laugh. After concluding his tale, the officer remarks to his friend that Timbuctoo's restaurant was the first step of revenge for the Franco-Prussian War.

The story *Tombouctou* is full of racist stereotypes and is representative of the late nineteenth-century attitude toward blacks. In the story, Timbuctoo is described as "an enormous negro, dressed in black, with a paunch beneath his jean waistcoat, which was covered with charms." We learn that this pocket is for Timbuctoo to hide stolen goods; therefore this description presents Timbuctoo, and hence blacks, as thieves whose primary motivation for action is profit. Furthermore, as Timbuctoo walks, his face was "shining as if it had been polished," revealing "dazzling white teeth" that shown "like a crescent moon in a black sky." The story also makes note that the giddy Timbuctoo gesticulates as he walks, causing Parisians to think that he is crazy. Consequently, Timbuctoo is depicted as mischievous and childlike, apt to pull pranks, and frequently in trouble. This image is further solidified through the officer's own remarks that Africans possessed "characteristics of overgrown frolicsome children."

Consequently, because the story depicts Africans as childlike, Europeans are depicted as paternal, attempting to teach the Africans how to behave in a "civilized" manner. The French officer believes that Timbuctoo "worshipped" him because of his leadership. The officer even recounts how Timbuctoo kisses his white commander's hand, which is "according to negro and Arab custom." Therefore the story depicts Africans as happily subservient to their white masters and teachers. Such depictions justified racism and the subjugation of the African people through colonialism. While the story depicts the job of Europeans to civilize Africans, the story simultaneously mocks Timbuctoo for trying to speak French, for the character of Timbuctoo speaks in broken French that causes everyone who is French to laugh.

The French characters also demonstrate disrespect for African culture. Timbuctoo is referred to as a "brute," and his African companions-in-arms are referred to as "savages." Africans are depicted as drunks, undisciplined, and cannibals. The French officer makes no attempt to learn Timbuctoo's African name, jokingly remarking that it was something like "Chavaharibouhalikranafotapolara." Such a nonsensical jumble of letters is meant to imply that the Africans spoke "gibberish." He then gives Timbuctoo a new name, similar to the way Europeans renamed Africans captured as slaves.

See also: Colonies in Africa, French; France, Blacks in; French Army, Blacks in the; Literature, Blacks in French.

Further Reading: De Maupassant, Guy. *The Complete Short Stories of Guy de Maupassant.* trans. New York: Halcyon, 1947.

Eric Martone

Trouillot, Hénock (1923–1988)

Hénock Trouillot, an important Haitian historian and novelist, was born on January 19, 1923 in Haiti. He was the second son of Emmanuel Trouillot and Marianne (née Alvarez). Trouillot was also the great-grandson of Duveneau Trouillot, a senator of the Republic of Haiti. From a family much interested in history, Trouillot immersed himself in Haitian history, spending many years working in the National Archives and in the museums and libraries around the country. During his career, he wrote a number of important books on Haitian history and historiography. His first book, *Historiography of Haiti* (1953), was coauthored with Cattes Pressoir and his brother, Ernst.

Trouillot subsequently wrote *La Condition des Nègres Domestiques à Saint-Domingue* (1955), *Economie et Finances de Saint-Domingue* (1965), *Dessalines; ou, Le sang du Pont-Rouge* (1967), *La Vengeance du Mapou* (1967), and *Le Gouvernement du Roi Henri Christophe* (1974). Over many years, he had become a critic of what became known as "mulatto hegemony," claiming that Haitian literature was becoming used (or as he would argue, abused) by a small elite to repress other people. Further, Haitian literature had become characterized by its defense of the African origins of the people. These ideas permeated through Trouillot's work, which coincided with the changes in Haitian politics introduced by François Duvalier and Jean-Claude Duvalier, who tended to use the "mulattoes" as scapegoats to gain political support.

Trouillot died on September 13, 1988. His older brother, Jean-Jacques Dessaline Ernst Trouillot (1922–1987), jurist and historian, was the coauthor of the *Biographical Encyclopedia of Haiti*. His son, Michel-Rolph Trouillot, is a historical theorist and anthropologist at the University of Chicago. His second wife, Ertha Pascal-Trouillot, a lawyer, was appointed to the Haitian Supreme Court by the government of Henri Namphy. She went on to serve as president of Haiti from March 1900 until February 1991.

See also: Colonies in the Caribbean, French; Haitian Revolution in Francophone Literature; Literature, Blacks in French.

Further Reading: Degraff, Michel. "Linguists' Most Dangerous Myth: The Fallacy of Creole Exceptionalism." *Language in Society* 34 (2005): 533–591; Nicholls, David. *From Dessalines to Duvalier: Race, Colour and National Independence in Haiti*. Piscataway: Rutgers University Press, 1995.

Justin Corfield

Turquia, Nugaymath (?–1099)

Nugaymath Turquia led a contingent of 300 female Moorish archers, called "Amazons" in the stories of the Spanish hero El Cid, during the historic Almoravid siege of Valencia in 1099, which led to the death of El Cid himself.

The *Romance of El Cid*, the main epic story about the Spanish military hero Rodrigo Diaz de Bibar ("El Cid") against the invading Muslims from Africa, mentions that there were Berber women fighting the Christian Spanish, but it does not record much about them. A slightly more detailed description, which includes the reference that they were led by a female warrior called Nugaymath Turquia, can be found in the *Primera Cronica General* of Afonso X, king of Castile and Léon, which was completed in about 1289. The account describes Turquia's actions at the siege of Valencia and also mentions that the women had originally come to the Moorish king on a pilgrimage to seek a pardon. The women then joined the Moorish army, with the women in battle always being armed with Turkish bows and carrying cuirasses. They also had most of their heads shaven except for a topknot (the hairstyle worn for their original pilgrimage).

In the siege of Valencia in July 1099, about 100 of the Moorish women following Turquia into battle were killed by El Cid's men. During the fighting, El Cid was hit by an arrow, but legend does not relate whether it was fired by one of the Berber women under Turquia. When the body of El Cid was strapped to his horse and sent out in death to lead his men against the **Moors** in a final charge, Turquia and what remained of her supporters rallied and managed to kill large numbers of El Cid's men before they were eventually overcome and Turquia herself was killed.

Initially, scholars studying the *Primera Cronica General* suggested that the women could be Turks, with the name Nugaymath Turquia being translated as "little star of Turkey." It was certainly possible for people from Asia Minor to have been involved in the fighting in southern Spain. Linguistic and historical research by L. P. Harvey and others, however, pointed to the idea that Turquia was originally a Tuareg, a nomadic pastoral group of people from the Sahara, and her name in Arabic, Nugaymath al-Tarqiyya, means the "star of the Tuareg archers." Her origin as a Tuareg certainly seems more probable and is now accepted by most scholars.

See also: Spain, African Invasions of; Spain, Blacks in.

Further Reading: Harvey, L. P. "Nugaymath Turquia: Primera Cronica General, Chapter 956." *Journal of Semitic Studies* 13:2 (1968): 232–241; Norris, H. T. *The Berbers in Arab Literature.* London: Longman, 1982; Van Sertima, Ivan. *The Golden Age of the Moor.* New Brunswick, NJ: Transaction Publishers, 1992.

Justin Corfield

Tuskegee Airmen

African American aviation units were established by the United States Army during World War II in response to pressure from the black community for equal access to military training and service. The men trained mostly at segregated facilities, and they served in segregated units in northern Africa and Italy, flying the P-39, P-40, P-47, and P-51 Mustang. Their outstanding record proved that African Americans were courageous and effective in aerial combat.

The 99th Pursuit Squadron was activated on March 22, 1941, at Chanute Army Air Field (AAF), Illinois, in response to pressure from African American political leaders, newspapers, and individuals. In July 1941, the Army Air Corps established a segregated pilot training facility, Tuskegee Army Air Field (TAAF), near Tuskegee Institute, the historically black Alabama college. Five men graduated in the first class of pilots in March 1942, including Benjamin O. Davis, Jr., a 1936 graduate of West Point. Davis later commanded the 99th Pursuit Squadron, the 332nd Fighter Group, and the 477th Bombardment Group.

Racial discrimination was always present. It was nearly a year before the combat-ready 99th was ordered to North Africa, flying its first mission in June 1943. White commanders soon recommended that the unit be removed from combat for alleged unsatisfactory performance, but the men were provided additional time to prove themselves.

The 332nd Fighter Group arrived in Italy in January 1944 and was first stationed in southern Italy, but was finally based at Ramitelli Air Base. The unit was assigned strafing missions and later bomber escort over southern and central Europe. Downed pilots were sometimes assisted by local residents. By the end of the war, the men had completed more than 15,000 combat sorties, including 200 escort missions and many thousands of ground attack sorties. They destroyed more than 260 enemy aircraft, as well as the only destroyer sunk solely by machinegun fire. A total of 66 men were killed in the combat zone and 32 became prisoners of war, where they were treated equally with their white colleagues.

The 477th Bombardment Group, activated in January 1944, never deployed overseas. The men of the 477th challenged segregation on army installations within the United States, including the illegally segregated officers' clubs at Freeman Field, Indiana.

The decorated combat veterans of the 332nd returned from the war to a segregated America and a segregated military, where they were still treated as second-class citizens. The army's flying training school at Tuskegee graduated 992 single- and twin-engine pilots, who, along with the ground crews, bombardiers, navigators, and administrative personnel, came to be known as the Tuskegee Airmen. In July 1948, United States President Harry Truman issued Executive Order 9981 calling for "equality of treatment and opportunity for all persons in the Armed Services without regard to race," and in 1949 the Air Force desegregated.

In March 2007, the Tuskegee Airmen were awarded the Congressional Gold Medal in recognition of their military accomplishments that served as an inspiration for military desegregation (S 392, 109th Cong., 1st sess.).

See also: Italy, Blacks in; Nazis and Black POWs; World War II, Black Participation in.

Further Reading: Davis, Benjamin O., Jr. *An Autobiography. Benjamin O. Davis, Jr.: American*. Washington, DC: Smithsonian Institution Press, 1991; Dryden, Charles W. *A-Train: Memoirs of a Tuskegee Airman*. Tuscaloosa: University of Alabama Press, 1997; Gropman, Alan. *The Air Force Integrates, 1945–1964*. 2nd ed. Washington, DC: Smithsonian Institution Press, 1998; Jefferson, Alexander, with Lewis Carlson. *Red Tail Captured, Red Tail Free: The Memoirs of a Tuskegee Airman and POW*. New York: Fordham University Press, 2005.
Tuskegee Airmen, Inc. Web Site: www.tuskegeeairmen.org.

Rosemary F. Crockett

Uncle Tom's Cabin in London

After its publication in 1852, London theaters readily adapted American writer Harriet Beecher Stowe's novel *Uncle Tom's Cabin* for the stage, thereby trying to capitalize on the commercial success of the book. The novel, which became tremendously popular in Britain, inspired an antislavery petition and was translated into British melodrama.

Numerous dramatizations appeared and were produced by London theaters of all kinds, reflecting the cross-class appeal of the story. On the whole, the British adaptations made up a distinct tradition that altered the material of the novel to suit the specific cultural, as well as theatrical, framework. Generally, the most violent and Gothic scenes from *Uncle Tom's Cabin* were selected to attract an audience expecting this kind of spectacle. Some plays even depicted slave revolts and the downfall of American slavery.

All stage adaptations were necessarily politically charged and frequently represented popular British views on slavery and the United States. Many dramatizations not only showcased the moral superiority of the British over Americans, but also displayed a certain degree of theatrical tourism by emphasizing the foreignness of the United States, or even attempting to create an overarching impression of America. Although an abolitionist standpoint was favored, London's *Uncle Toms* did not always articulate a clear and unambiguous attitude toward slaves or "the peculiar institution," making the plays agreeable to spectators of different political opinions.

British licensing laws caused the productions to leave out those scenes of *Uncle Tom's Cabin* that promoted Christianity and referenced religion: Little Eva was sometimes omitted and Uncle Tom's faith only hinted at. In other plays, these two characters were given a Cockney accent and thus turned into the audience's representatives on stage. In this way, British laborers may have identified with the slaves, but only a few parallels between the working poor and American slaves were drawn. Overall, the dramatizations did not show any overt concern with workers and were only slightly interested in women. In the main, interracial sex was much more an issue and many of the novel's subtleties were lost during the adaptation process.

London's *Uncle Tom's* also relied heavily on the British blackface tradition. In Britain, blackface often was enacted on the streets and was viewed as cross-class (family) entertainment in theater, where it functioned as a sign of theatricality. Many dramatists exploited the blackface moments and scenes in their adaptations without including their original ironic context. They also incorporated minstrel-like material with which the viewers were already familiar (e.g., songs by the Ethiopian serenaders). Especially among London's lower classes, the *Tom* plays were a prominent and popular phenomenon. Because of this, theater critics felt the need to comment on this "Uncle Tom Mania," but were critical of most plays for not meeting the standards of high culture.

See also: Abolition of Slavery, British; Britain, Blacks in.

Further Reading: Meer, Sarah. *Uncle Tom Mania: Slavery, Minstrelsy, and Transatlantic Culture in the 1850s.* Athens: University of Georgia Press, 2005; Waters, Hazel. *Racism on the Victorian Stage: Representations of Slavery and the Black Character.* Cambridge: Cambridge University Press, 2007.

Katharina Gerund

Ustinov, Peter (1921–2004)

Peter Alexander Ustinov was a humanitarian and Academy Award–winning British actor and director. His ethnic background was quite diverse and included French, Italian, German, Russian, and Ethiopian ancestry. As a result of his African ancestry from the monarchs of Ethiopia, the country asked him to serve as a spokesperson for Ethiopia in the media, serving as a cultural liaison between Africa and the West. As a result of the culture and racial attitudes of his era, Ustinov was reluctant to publicly acknowledge his interracial ancestry until well into his career.

Ustinov was born in London in 1921. His parents were Nadia Benois, a Russian painter and ballet designer, and Iona, Baron von Ustinov, a German subject of Russian and German descent who had fought in World War I (1914–1918) as a pilot. The couple had met while Iona was on business in Russia. After their marriage, they moved to London. In the 1930s, Iona worked in London at the German Embassy as a press officer. In addition, he worked as a correspondent for a German news agency. He later served in M15 (British Security Service, Counterespionage) as an agent and runner, and became a British citizen.

Ustinov descended from Russian nobility on his paternal side. His paternal grandfather was an officer in the tsar's army who was exiled because of his religious beliefs. Ustinov's mother was of Russian, French, Italian, and Ethiopian ancestry. Jules-César Benois, one of her ancestors, had been a chef who had fled to Russia from France during the French Revolution. He later worked as chef to Tsar Paul. Ustinov's mother was also descended from the Ethiopian royal family, thereby making him one-eighth Ethiopian. Ustinov's great-grandfather, a Swiss military engineer, married the daughter of Ethiopian emperor Tewodros II. The emperor had many Europeans in his service in an attempt to westernize Ethiopia. The most valued of these Europeans were forbidden to leave the country. The marriage to Tewodros's daughter was therefore a form of compensation and a means to ensure loyalty.

Ustinov was proud of his multicultural descent and became fluent in English, French, German, Italian, Russian, and Spanish, while also learning Greek and Turkish. He was educated at Westminster School and made his stage debut in 1938 after receiving training in acting as a teenager. Ustinov served in World War II as a private and made several propaganda films for the war effort.

During his acting career, Ustinov received two Tony Award nominations in 1958 for his play "Romanoff and Juliet," a cold war satire; two Golden Globes; an Academy Award for his role in *Spartacus* (1960); and another Academy Award for his role in *Topkapi* (1964). Thus Ustinov is possibly the first recipient of an Academy Award to be of African descent. He starred in several celebrated films and portrayed many memorable characters, including six films as Agatha Christie's famous Belgian detective, Hercule Poirot, and the voice of the anthropomorphic lion, Prince John, in Walt Disney's animated film, *Robin Hood* (1973).

Ustinov was highly involved in humanitarian and educational efforts. From 1968 until his death in 2004, Ustinov served as a goodwill ambassador for UNICEF, the United Nations Children's Fund, frequently assisting the poor in several areas including Africa. He was a humanist laureate and a member of the International Academy of Humanism. In addition, Ustinov functioned as the World Federalist Movement's president from 1991 until 2004. In 1992, Ustinov became chancellor of the University of Durham. Previously, in the 1970s, he had served as rector of the University of Dundee. In addition, the Vrije Universiteit in Belgium awarded Ustinov an honorary doctorate. In 1975, Queen Elizabeth II awarded Ustinov the CBE (Commander of the Order of the British Empire), paving the way for his knighthood in 1990.

Because of his high profile in the entertainment and humanitarian arenas, the Ethiopian legation to Canada, in cooperation with the Department of Multicultural Affairs in Quebec, requested on several occasions for Ustinov to serve as a spokesman for Ethiopia to the media. Ustinov had performed a similar function for the Soviet Union during the height of the cold war, serving as a cultural link between the Soviet Union and the Western powers. The racial climate of the era, however, hindered Ustinov's efforts to assist Ethiopia. In his autobiography, he refused to acknowledge his African ancestry, claiming that his great-grandmother was a Portuguese woman at the Ethiopian court. Many years later, he finally acknowledged his descent from the Ethiopian royal family in a radio interview.

Ustinov died in 2004 from heart failure. As a testament to his humanitarian efforts, the Executive Director of UNICEF spoke at Ustinov's funeral as a representative of the secretary general of the United Nations.

See also: Britain, Blacks in; Civil Rights Movement in Twentieth-Century Great Britain.

Further Reading: Miller, John. *Peter Ustinov: The Gift of Laughter.* London: Weidenfeld and Nicolson, 2003. Ustinov, Peter. *Dear Me.* London: Heinemann, 1977.

Eric Martone

Vieira, António (1608–1697)

António Vieira, a Jesuit missionary and Portuguese diplomat during the seventeenth century, is renowned in the Lusophone world for his eloquent oratory and unrivaled written prose. Vieira is also well known for his staunch denunciations of the cruelty of slave masters, his interest in indigenous Brazilians and "New Christians," and his belief in a central, prophetic role for Portugal in Christian world history.

Vieira, whose paternal grandmother was a woman of color, most likely of African origin, was born in Lisbon and moved to Bahia, Brazil with his family when he was six years old. Against his family's wishes, Vieira joined the Society of Jesus, commonly known as the Jesuits, in 1623. As a novice studying at the Jesuit College in Bahia, he received what he believed to be a divine revelation from Mary, the mother of Jesus. Thereafter, he dedicated himself to missionary work. He developed his literary and oratory skills while preaching to the Portuguese, enslaved Africans, and indigenous Brazilians in Bahia. Vieira learned the Tupi-Guarani language of Brazil and shared the Jesuit enthusiasm for learning languages spoken by non-Christian communities. He was ordained in 1635.

The Restoration ended Spanish rule of Portugal in 1640, and in 1641, Vieira traveled to Portugal, where he became an adviser to King João IV. In the service of the Portuguese king, Vieira performed diplomatic missions in Paris, The Hague, London, and Rome. In 1648, Vieira spent eight months in Amsterdam and engaged in discussions with the Rabbi Menasseh ben Israel on the relationship between Judaism and Christianity. He returned to Brazil in 1652, but after publicly denouncing slave masters for their cruelty, he was briefly forced to leave Brazil for Portugal from 1654 to 1655.

After returning to Brazil, he worked with indigenous Brazilians for six years, until he was again forced to return to Portugal along with other Jesuits in the area. Under King Afonso VI, successor to João IV, Vieira was condemned by the Portuguese Inquisition and imprisoned from 1665 to 1667. This sentence was later reversed, and Vieira moved to Rome, where he lived comfortably from 1669 to 1675. His first volume of sermons was published in 1679 in Portugal. From Portugal, Vieira returned in 1681 to Brazil, where he died in 1697.

Vieira preached against the mistreatment of all enslaved people throughout his life, but he never openly opposed the enslavement of African people or their descendents. He maintained the belief that enslaved Africans in Brazil were in a better position than those of Africans in Africa. Vieira fervently advocated for the rights of indigenous Brazilians and was a voice of reform in much the same way as the Spaniard **Bartolomé de Las Casas** had been in the sixteenth century.

See also: Abolition of Slavery, Portuguese; Age of Exploration; Portugal, Blacks in; Slave Trade, Portuguese.

Further Reading: Boxer, Charles Ralph. *A Great Luso-Brazilian Figure: Padre António Vieira, S. J., 1608–1697.* London: Hispanic and Luso-Brazilian Councils, 1957; Cohen, Thomas. *The Fire of Tongues: António Vieira and the Missionary Church in Brazil and Portugal.* Stanford: Stanford University Press, 1998; Cohen, Thomas, and Stuart Schwartz, eds. *Luso-Brazilian Review* 40:1 (Summer 2003).

Sara Scott Armengot

Villa-Lobos, Heitor (1887–1959)

Heitor Villa-Lobos was a Brazilian composer whose music raised the profile in Europe of South American classical music and the African rhythm incorporated into his compositions. Born in Rio de Janeiro in 1887, Villa-Lobos was the son of a wealthy musician, amateur astronomer, and book collector whose family came from Spain. He grew up at a time when Brazil was changing dramatically, abolishing slavery in 1888 and becoming a republic in the next year. European compositions dominated the music scene in Brazil, and Villa-Lobos initially studied music surreptitiously. He learned how to play the cello, guitar, and clarinet. When Villa-Lobos was 12 years old, his father died. After leaving school, Villa-Lobos was able to find work playing in theaters and cinemas in Rio de Janeiro.

In 1905, Villa-Lobos decided to travel around the interior of Brazil and became interested in the native Brazilian music scene. His travels had a great influence on his life and his future music. Villa-Lobos later wrote of his capture and subsequent escape from cannibals; many people believe these accounts were exaggerated, if not entirely fabricated. He became interested in the music of the former African slaves in remote Brazilian settlements and made copious notes of the rhythms during this period. Back in Rio de Janeiro, Villa-Lobos incorporated some of this music into his own work. From 1915 until 1921, he was involved in composing a number of pieces for chamber concerts.

Although Villa-Lobos was fascinated by African music, much of the style of music that he followed involved classical themes. He met Sergei Diaghilev, Russian art critic and patron, during the Russian Ballet tour of Brazil in 1917. Villa-Lobos also became friends with pianist Arthur Rubenstein. In 1923, Villa-Lobos went to Paris,

France, where he planned to play some of his new music, and remained there for one year. He returned to Paris in 1927 and remained until 1930. During these two visits, Villa-Lobos managed to raise his profile and that of Brazilian music and African rhythms.

Back in Brazil, Villa-Lobos turned his hand to "patriotic" music with a number of compositions that gained him much acclaim under the dictatorship of President Getúlio Vargas. Such compositions made Villa-Lobos's work famous throughout Brazil. After World War II, he decided to travel to Europe again. Villa-Lobos was now able to be a full-time composer, writing concertos for the guitar, harp, and harmonica. He also composed some film music.

See also: France, Blacks in; Music, African Influences on European; Portugal, Blacks in.

Further Reading: Appelby, David P. *Heitor Villa-Lobos: A Life (1887–1959)*. Lanham, MD: Scarecrow Press, 2002; Peppercorn, L. M. *The World of Villa-Lobos*. Aldershot, England: Scholar Press, 1996.

Justin Corfield

Von Kleist, Heinrich (1777–1811)

Heinrich von Kleist was an important poet, dramatist, novelist, and short story writer of the German Romantic movement. In his 1811 *Die Verlobung in St. Domingo* (*The Engagement in San Domingo*), he explores the topic of racism and imperialism, and the trope of the tragic biracial heroine, the nearly white woman with a torn personality, driven by divided loyalties and tragically succumbing to a history built on black and white opposition. The novella is set in 1803 during the **Haitian Revolution for Independence.** The young Swiss officer Gustav von Ried seeks refuge on an estate controlled by a black man, Congo Hoango, and his biracial wife, Babekan. Babekan's beautiful daughter, Toni, who looks white, heroically saves Gustav's life, but is killed in the course of events by Gustav, who then commits suicide.

Congo Hoango is a *"fürchterlicher alter Neger"* who killed his master and his family, although they have treated him well. He is described as cruel, unthankful, and barbaric, and he embodies the inferior physical appearance and consequent mental degeneracy of the African well known to the German reading public of that time. Kleist's narrator mentions that in his youth on the Gold Coast, Hoango was a righteous person; therefore his enslavement is blamed for having produced this meanness and cruelty in him. It is emphasized, however, that his master behaved well and in a friendly way toward him, and that this has corrupted rather than improved his character. Hoango is described as not capable of benefiting from the system of slavery that the slave holders see as right and superior. Kleist chooses not to write a criticism of slavery itself, but rather focuses on the presumably innate barbarism in a slave. Babekan is the equally cruel, deceptive, and mean woman. Her mixed racial origin and the cruel treatment she received from her former master have made her bitter and vindictive toward white people. Babekan's light-colored, beautiful daughter, Toni, is part of the plotting against Gustav and his family and friends; however, she is torn between her loyalties because she is deeply in love with Gustav.

In this story, Kleist's narrator invites the reader to condemn the less than human and barbarian acts committed by Congo Hoango and his family against white people in general. It is not so clear, however, whether Kleist himself endorses this view. In the substantial body of criticism about this novella, several critics have paid attention to Kleist's own attitude toward the French Revolution, his imprisonment in Strasbourg in the same prison that had held Haitian slave rebel **Toussaint L'Ouverture** some years earlier, and his obvious attempt to displace an argument against the French onto the black Haitians. On close textual analysis, much irony is apparent on the side of the narrator who creates a distance between his own view and the attitude of the reader. It becomes obvious that Hoango has ameliorating character traits (he loves his children, for example), that Babekan is fully justified in her desire to revenge herself, and that Gustav is more scheming than appears at first sight. And yet, despite all narrative attempts to present at least a somehow complex constellation of characters, there can be no denying that race and racist attitudes are prominently displayed.

Displaying the "natural" supremacy of the white European, Gustav, for example, thinks that the revolt is so cruel because the blacks could not cope with freedom. They have regressed into a state of frenzy. In the most often mentioned episode of the novella, he tells the story of a young slave woman who took revenge on her master by infecting him with yellow fever. The deceptiveness of the freed slaves and hence their moral degeneration and state of uncivilized barbarity are thus particularly referred to.

See also: *Bug-Jargal* (1820); Colonies in the Caribbean, French; Germany, Blacks in; Haitian Revolution in Francophone Literature; Literature, Blacks in German and Central European.

Further Reading: Angress, R. K. "Kleist's Treatment of Imperialism: *Die Hermannsschlacht* and 'Die Verlobung in St. Domingo.'" *Monatshefte* 69:1 (1977): 17–33; Fleming, Ray. "Race and the Difference It Makes in Kleist's 'Die Verlobung in St. Domingo." *The German Quarterly* 65:3–4 (1992): 306–317; Gilman, Sander. "The Aesthetics of Blackness in Heinrich von Kleist's 'Die Verlobung in St. Domingo.'" *Modern Language Notes* 90 (1975): 661–672.

Hanna Wallinger

Walcott, Derek (1930–)

Derek Alton Walcott is an acclaimed West Indian (Caribbean) poet and postcolonial writer who won the Nobel Prize for Literature in 1992. He was born on January 23, 1930 in Saint Lucia in the West Indies. Both of his grandmothers were former slaves. Walcott's father, a Bohemian watercolor painter, died when Walcott and his twin brother were only a few years old. Consequently, Walcott's mother, a teacher at the local Methodist school, raised him. He studied at Saint Mary's College, Saint Lucia, and then at the University of the West Indies in Jamaica. Walcott moved to Trinidad in 1953.

Walcott's first published work was *25 Poems*, a collection of poetry, published in 1948. The next year he published his second collection of poems, *Epitaph for the Young: XII Cantos*. Walcott then gained enough confidence to complete plays. His first play, *Henri Christophe: A Chronicle in Seven Scenes* (1950), focused on the life of one of the leaders of the **Haitian Revolution for Independence**. Subsequent plays included *Harry Dernier: A Play for Radio Production* (1951), *Wine of the Country* (1953), *The Sea at Dauphin: A Play in One Act* (1954), *Ione* (1957), *Drums and Colours: An Epic Drama* (1958), and *Ti-Jean and His Brothers* (1958).

In 1959, Walcott became involved in the founding of the Trinidad Theatre Workshop, which was later involved in producing many of his plays. From 1966 until 1997, Walcott wrote 15 more plays: *Malcochon* (1966); *Dream on Monkey Mountain* (1967); *In a Fine Castle* (1970); *The Joker of Seville* (1974); *The Charlatan* (1974); *O Babylon!* (1976); *Remembrance* (1977); *Pantomime* (1978); *The Isle Is Full of Noises* (1982); *The Last Carnival* (1986); *Beef, No Chicken* (1986); *A Branch of the Blue Nile* (1986); *Steel* (1991); *Odyssey: A Stage Version* (1993); and *The Capeman* (1997). Many collections of Walcott's poems have been published; his most famous collections were *The Caribbean Poetry of Derek Walcott and the Art of Romare Bearden* (1983) and *Selected Poems* (2007).

As a postcolonial writer, Walcott was critical of the role of European colonialism in the West Indies. His epic poem, *Omeros*, deals with the complex interplay between African, Amerindian, and European cultures and heritage in the West Indies. It uses some of the style of the Greek poet Homer and includes the West Indian heritage in London, England, and the American West.

See also: Colonies in the Caribbean, British; Literature, Blacks in British.

Further Reading: Breslin, Paul. *Nobody's Nation: Reading Derek Walcott*. Chicago: University of Chicago Press, 2001; Hamner, Robert, ed. *Critical Perspectives on Derek Walcott*. Washington, DC: Three Continents, 1993.

Justin Corfield

Waters, Billy (1778?–1823)

Billy Waters was a black African sailor who became famous as an eccentric street musician and actor in eighteenth-century London known as the "king of beggars." Waters wore a soldier's uniform with feather in his hat and had a wooden peg leg, having lost his leg in war, while he played his fiddle in the West End, entertaining onlookers. Waters was one of the many black personalities featured in Pierce Egan's book *Life in London* (1821), which was adapted into a popular stage play. Waters even played himself in some performances.

Many runaway slaves tended to flee to London's East End, where they congregated in overcrowded lodgings surrounded by brothels and hangouts for thieves and sailors. Many of them lacked marketable skills. Most blacks who found gainful employment in London during the eighteenth century worked as servants, soldiers, sailors, musicians, actors, or peddlers. Others, who could not find employment, resorted to prostitution, begging, and thievery. Waters served as a sailor and lost his leg before settling in London. Although he received a pension, it was too meager to support his family, which included a wife and two children.

Waters became a street musician in London. Playing his fiddle, he was a common sight outside the Adelphi Theatre, in the Strand. Waters's peculiar antics gained attention from passersby who were amused. He became a celebrity within the local underworld.

In 1820, Pierce Egan began publication of a monthly journal, *Life in London*. His articles were later collected in his book *Life in London, or The Day and Night Scenes of Jerry Hawthorn Esq. and His Elegant Friend Corinthian Tom* in 1821 and included a famous caricature of Waters by cartoonist George Cruickshank. The tales told of life on the streets and that of London's poor. Such efforts were among the first in British journalism to cover common life rather than politics and the elite. Included were several black personalities including Waters, African Sal, her baby Mungo, and Massa Piebald, another sailor who became a beggar whose real name was Charles M'Ghee. The book was adapted into a successful stage play by William Moncrieff that was performed in Britain from 1821 to 1823 and then in New York in 1823.

Waters's notoriety led to roles on the stage. He appeared as himself in Moncrieff's play *Tom and Jerry, or Life in London* at the Adelphi and Caledonian Theatres. He spoke his lines in a strong African accent and sang a song, which included the following lyrics: "That all men are beggars, 'tis very plain you see; only some they are of lowly, and some of high degree."

Soon afterward, Waters became ill and spent his final days at Saint Giles's Workhouse. Without work, he pawned his fiddle to raise money for his family. While at the workhouse, because of his notoriety, a party of beggars elected him as "king." He died in 1823 around the age of 45. Later, Waters was immortalized in the Billy Waters figurines produced by Staffordshire Potteries.

See also: Britain, Blacks in.

Further Reading: Edwards, Paul, and J. Walvin. *Black Personalities in the Era of the Slave Trade.* Baton Rouge: Louisiana University Press, 1983.

Eric Martone

Wedderburn, Robert (1762–1835/36?)

Robert Wedderburn, a radical born to a slave woman in Jamaica, campaigned for an end to slavery and the oppression of the working class. His fiery comments and provocative speeches led to his being charged with treason and to several terms in prison. Wedderburn's refusal to accept the subordinate role that his society subscribed to his race helped raised British consciousness of the problems of slavery and the working class, as well as the need for freedom of speech.

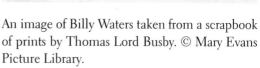

An image of Billy Waters taken from a scrapbook of prints by Thomas Lord Busby. © Mary Evans Picture Library.

Wedderburn was born in Kingston, Jamaica, in 1762. His mother, Rosanna, was an African-born slave. His father, a sugar planter named James Wedderburn, was part of a well-known Scottish family. Wedderburn's mother was sold by his father while she was pregnant to Lady Douglas. A condition of the sale was that the child would be free when born. Wedderburn was baptized into the Anglican Church and received a minimal amount of schooling. He witnessed his mother and grandmother being whipped for violations of rules, and he became an opponent of the slave system.

When he was old enough, Wedderburn enlisted in the Royal Navy and left Jamaica. He may have been involved in a mutiny at the Nore. Wedderburn arrived in London in 1778. He survived by doing menial jobs, as well as some petty thievery. Eventually, he established himself as a tailor. Little is known about his activities until 1813. In that year, Wedderburn was licensed as a Unitarian preacher. He accepted the Unitarian ideal that social problems were created by man and that man could correct those problems. He became a familiar figure among lower class radicals.

Wedderburn was influenced by Thomas Spence, whom he met shortly before Spence's death in 1814. Spence was apparently buried by 40 disciples, including Wedderburn, who pledged to spread his ideals and work for a revolution. They formed the Society of Spencean Philanthropists. In 1818, Wedderburn and Thomas Evans, leader of the Spenceans, were licensed to operate a "Church of Christian Philanthropists." Wedderburn soon quarreled with Evans and opened his own chapel in Soho in 1819. His sermons quickly became famous for their libertarian ideas. Wedderburn's chapel was regarded by the authorities as a center of sedition.

Wedderburn often compared black slaves to British factory workers. To him, the slave masters and the factory owners were the same. He called for a change in society, by violent means if necessary. A spy named John Castle was hired by the police to attend meetings at which Wedderburn was present. In September 1819, Castle reported that Wedderburn prompted a discussion of whether a slave had the right to murder his master. His listeners understood the question to include whether workers had the right to kill factory owners. Castle's report included the comment attributed to Wedderburn that "before six months were over, there would be slaughter in England for their liberty." He also called on the workers to learn how to use "the gun, the dagger, the cutlass and pistols." Wedderburn believed that simultaneous uprisings by slaves in the West Indies (Caribbean) and workers in Britain would overthrow the existing system.

Wedderburn was arrested for blasphemous libel and tried in May 1820. He was convicted and sentenced to two years in prison. When he was released, he wrote an autobiography entitled *The Horrors of Slavery* (1824) with the assistance of radical lawyer George Cannon. Wedderburn's book helped to make the working class more aware of slavery's evils and is credited with assisting the movement to outlaw slavery.

Wedderburn maintained his radical politics during the 1820s and 1830s. He was arrested and convicted in 1831 for keeping a brothel. His last recorded public appearance was in March 1834, when he was among the audience at a speech by Robert Taylor at the Theobalds Road Institute. He is believed to have died in 1835 or 1836.

See also: Abolition of Slavery, British; Britain, Blacks in; British Army, Blacks in the; Colonies in Africa, British; Colonies in the Caribbean, British; Cuffay, William; Slave Trade, British.

Further Reading: Hoyles, Martin. *The Axe Laid to the Root: The Story of Robert Wedderburn.* London: Hansib Publishers, 2004; Linebaugh, Peter, and Marcus Buford Rediker. *The Many-Headed Hydra: Sailors, Slaves, Commoners, and the Hidden History of the Revolutionary Atlantic.* Boston: Beacon Press, 2000; Wedderburn, Robert, and Iain McCalman. *Horrors of Slavery and Other Writings.* New York: Marcus Wiener, 1991.

Tim J. Watts

Weimar Republic, African Activists in the

From the outset of the colonial conquest by the German Kaiserreich, Africans in Cameroon and the other African colonies resisted not only by violence but also by organizing and conducting different forms of political opposition. After unsuccessfully sending a delegation to Berlin, Cameroonian chiefs wrote a petition to the German Imperial Chancellor complaining about the mistreatment by the German Governor von Puttkamer in 1905. It listed more than 20 points of discontent with the colonial administration and asked for changes. Several petitions by Cameroonians and Togoans followed during the next few years. The political activities of Africans living in Germany intensified after the country lost its colonies at the end of World War I.

On May 1, 1918, the *Afrikanische Hilfsverein e.V.* ("African Beneficial Association") was founded in Hamburg. Ernst Anumu, a Togoan businessman, served as the chairman of the association. On the surface, this association functioned as a nonpolitical support group that helped its members deal with the everyday problems of living in a foreign country. The members lived throughout Germany, and the association actually advanced the integration of people of African descent independent of national or ethnic affiliation.

One of the leaders of Afro-German political movement was Martin Dibobe, born in Cameroon in 1876, who had come to Germany in 1896 for the German Colonial Exhibition in Berlin. Dibobe stayed in the capital and was trained as a train driver for the Berlin Public Transport Company. He was a representative for the Cameroonians in Germany and wrote a 32-point petition, dated June 27, 1919, to the Weimar National Assembly. In a letter accompanying the petition, Dibobe protested against the rape of the colonies and requested a German government that recognized the initial treaty between the Deutsche Reich and the Cameroonian authorities, which according to Cameroonian understanding, guaranteed their independence. Provided that their demands were met, the Cameroonians were willing to manifest their loyalty to the German Republic. Among other things, the petition asked for the German Code of Civil Law to be introduced to Africa with the same effect as in Germany and for the abolishment of corporal punishment in the colonies.

As a result of the difficult living conditions of **Afro-Germans** in the 1920s, the work of the African Beneficial Association came to a halt by the end of 1924. Henceforth, the home of Liberian consul Momulu Massaquoi served as a meeting place for Afro-German political activists. There they met with black intellectuals, such as **W.E.B. Du Bois,** Marcus Garvey, and **George Padmore,** who was supposed to play a central role in the Africa oriented policy of the Comintern. After Massaquoi left for Liberia at the end of 1929, the *"Negerbüro"* ("negro bureau") of the *Internationale Gerwerkschaftskomitee der Negerarbeiter* ("International Trade Union Committee of Negro Workers") became the center of African political activities in Germany. The First International Conference of Negro Workers was organized in Hamburg by James W. Ford (1893–1957), a prominent African American Communist, and took place illegally in July 1930. The International Trade Union Committee of Negro Workers began to publish the radical journal *The Negro Worker.* In 1931, Padmore, who had been a leading member of the Comintern in Moscow, was in charge of the *"Negerbüro."*

Joseph Ekwe Bilé and Victor Bell, who were among the signatories of the 1919 petition formulated by Martin Dibobe, were the founding members of the German Section of the League for the Defense of the Negro Race in 1929. The main organization had been created in 1924 by the Senegalese Lamine Senghor and its headquarters were located in France. In 1930, the League had 30 members and its main purpose was to form a union for all Africans working and living in Germany. Their mission was to organize workers in their home countries, which mostly consisted of the former German colonies Togo and Cameroon. Bilé was active as an agitator and participated in the First International Conference of Negro Workers, where he had a speech criticizing the French and British colonial authorities in Cameroon. Bilé gained respect among the German communists and presumably joined the German Communist Party (KPD) as a functionary. His activities with the German communists led to a breakup between him and other members of the League for the Defense of the Negro Race.

After the Nazis came to power in 1933, all political activities of Africans in Germany came to an abrupt end. The few who continued their political activities had to fear for their lives. The Afro-German **Lari Gilges,** a young communist from Dusseldorf, was murdered by members of the SS in June 1933. Among the first to be arrested was Padmore, secretary of the International Trade Union Committee of Negro Workers in Hamburg. He and many of those who had been politically active were then deported from Germany. Those who stayed, mostly those from the former German colonies, tried to live their lives without attracting any attention from the authorities.

See also: Colonies in Africa, German; Duala Manga Bell, Rudolf; Germany, Blacks in; Mpundu Akwa; Nazis and Blacks in Europe.

Further Reading: Lusane, Clarence. *Hitler's Black Victims: The Historical Experience of Afro-Germans, European Blacks, Africans, and African Americans in the Nazi Era.* New York: Rouledge, 2003; Martin, Peter. "Anfänge politischer Selbstorganisation der deutschen Schwarzen bis 1933." In Marianne Bechhaus-Gerst and Reinhard Klein-Arendt, eds. *Die (koloniale) Begegnung.* Frankfurt: Peter Lang, 2003, pp. 193–206.

Marianne Bechhaus-Gerst

Wells, Nathaniel (1779–1852)

Nathaniel Wells, the son of a Welsh merchant and his black slave, inherited his father's Caribbean estates in Saint Kitts and became a wealthy proprietor in Britain and the Caribbean. Wells became a British magistrate and Britain's first black sheriff.

Nathaniel's father, William Wells, from a prosperous family in Wales, moved to Saint Kitts in the Caribbean, where he became a successful slave trader and plantation owner. After the death of his wife, he fathered numerous illegitimate children by several different slaves, including Juggy, who gave birth to Nathaniel. William Wells looked after his illegitimate children and their mothers, granting them freedom and sums of money to help them become established on their own. In the case of Nathaniel Wells, William had him baptized and freed in 1783, later sending him to Wales to be educated in preparation to attend Oxford University. On his graduation, Wells seems to have been accepted by members of his social class, at least in the area around Chepstow in Wales. Wells established himself as a landowner in his own right in Britain and became a magistrate, or judge. Consequently, Wells held legal authority over white Britons at a time when most black people in the British colonies held hardly any legal rights.

Wells inherited the bulk of his father's sugar plantations in Saint Kitts, governing them as an absentee owner. The estates were leased out to local managers, who controlled the way the estates were operated. At least one of these managers was particularly brutal to his slaves, and he was targeted by British abolitionists for excessive brutality. Wells retained possession of his plantations and slaves until 1833, when slaves were emancipated in Saint Kitts and Wells received financial compensation from the government.

Wells married the only daughter of the prosperous Charles Este, former chaplain to King George II. In 1802, Wells purchased Piercefield house and estate from Colonel Mark Wood and continued to expand it into a lavish home. Despite Well's success, it seems that he was still subjected to racism. An excerpt from a document by Wood in *Black Presence: Asian and Black History in Britain, 1500–1850*, sponsored by the British National Archives, states that, "Mr. Wells is a West Indian of large fortune, a man of very gentlemanly manners, but so much a man of colour as to be little removed from a Negro."

During the early 1800s, Wells was likely the wealthiest person of black descent in Britain. He followed up his appointment as justice of the peace in 1803 by becoming, in 1818, the sheriff of Monmouthshire and the deputy lieutenant of the County. He was also an absentee plantation owner in Antigua and became governor of Saint Vincent in the Caribbean.

In 1850, because of ailing health, Wells sold Piercefield. He also married a second time and had 22 children.

See also: Abolition of Slavery, British; Britain, Blacks in; Colonies in the Caribbean, British; Slave Trade, British.

Further Reading: *Black Presence: Asian and Black History in Britain, 1500–1850* (Online Exhibit from the British National Archives): http://www.nationalarchives.gov.uk/pathways/blackhistory/; Debrunner, Hans. *Presence and Prestige, Africans in Europe: A History of Africans in Europe Before 1918*. Basel: Basler Afrika Bibliographien, 1979; Shyllon, Folarin. *Black People in Britain, 1553–1833*. Oxford: Oxford University Press, 1977.

Eric Martone

Wharton, Arthur (1865–1930)

Arthur Wharton was the first black professional footballer (soccer player) in the world and is a member of the English Football Hall of Fame. He was born in the Gold Coast (now Ghana) in 1865. Both of Wharton's parents were of biracial descent; his father, a Protestant minister, was of Grenadian and Scottish descent, and his mother, a member of the Fante royal family of Ghana, was of Scottish and Ghanaian descent. In 1884, Wharton moved to England for training as a Protestant missionary at Cleveland College, Darlington. He abandoned his religious studies, however, and became a full-time athlete, competing as a "gentleman amateur."

Wharton excelled in all athletics. In 1886, he won the 100-yard sprint in the Amateur Athletics Association national championship in London. In 1887, Wharton set a record cycling time between Preston and Blackburn. In addition, Wharton played cricket as a member of local teams in Yorkshire and Lancashire. Wharton, however, turned his attention to football. Amateur player Andrew Watson, the first black footballer in the United Kingdom, paved the way for blacks in football slightly more than a decade before Wharton, who became the first amateur black footballer to turn professional.

Wharton began his football career as a goalkeeper for the Darlington Football Club. At that time, the FA Cup was the primary competition, along with district and county matches. While at Darlington, Wharton was selected to the Newcastle and District team, which was then the best in the city. He gained attention for his eccentric playing style, remaining in crouching position at the side of the goal before charging out to save the ball. While at Darlington, he was spotted by the Preston North End, which signed him to their team. Wharton was part of their team that played the FA Cup semifinals in 1886–1887, while still turning out for Darlington.

In 1888, he left football to become a professional runner in Sheffield. Wharton returned to football in 1889 and signed with Rotherham, where he played for six years. He then played for Sheffield United for a season. Wharton played for a year at Stalybridge, but had a disagreement with management. He then played for their rivals Ashton-under-Lyme in 1897, playing with them until they went bankrupt in 1899. Consequently, Wharton returned briefly to Stalybridge. He then returned to the Football League in 1901, signing with Stockport County in 1901–1902. On the team, Wharton played goal and occasionally outfield as a winger.

Wharton retired from football and descended into alcohol abuse. During his career, he had never received any major recognition. He spent the last 15 years of his life working as a laborer and died in poverty in 1930. He was buried initially in South Yorkshire in an unmarked grave. In 1997, however, Football Unites-Racism Divides, an antiracism group, campaigned for a gravestone for Wharton; and in 2003, he was inducted into the English Football Hall of Fame.

See also: Batson, Brendon; Britain, Blacks in; Colonies in Africa, British.

Further Reading: Official Web Page of *Football Unites, Racism Divides:* http://www.furd.org/; Vasili, Philip. *Colouring Over the White Line: The History of Black Footballers in Britain.* Edinburgh: Mainstream Publishing, 2000; Vasili, Philip. *The First Black Footballer, Arthur Wharton, 1865–1930: An Absence of Memory.* London: Frank Cass, 1998.

Mark Cordery

Wheatley, Phillis (1753–1784)

Phillis Wheatley was the first African American woman to publish an original book. In 1773, her *Poems on Various Subjects* was printed in England after it was rejected by publishers in the British American colonies. She was born in 1753 in Gambia, Africa, and brought to North America when she was seven or eight years old. In July 1761, she was sold to John and Susanna Wheatley of Massachusetts. She took her surname from her master and her first name from *Phillis*, the ship that brought her to America. In North America, the merchants who bought her ensured that she was educated and their daughter, Mary, taught the slave girl how to read and write. Wheatley became proficient in English, geography, history, Latin, and religious education. She became interested in poetry and soon started writing her own poems.

Throughout her poetry, Wheatley, whose owners had converted her to Christianity, praised the divine through verse and viewed her conversion as a path to spiritual salvation. Wheatley's earliest recorded poems were *On Messrs Hussey and Coffin* (1765), *An Address to an Atheist* (1767), and *An Address to the Deist* (1767). Her first published poem appeared in the *Newport Mercury* in 1767. Wheatley's first major work was her poem, *On the Death of Rev. Mr. George Whitfield* (1770). The poem, which revolves heavily around Christian moralism in an elegiac style with classical, religious, and literary allusions, became the talk of Boston. White colonial settlers could not believe that a slave was capable of writing such a complex and beautiful poem. Consequently, two years later, Wheatley was examined in court to verify that she did indeed write the poems. After a public examination, it was clear that she was the author.

The support that Wheatley gained ultimately led to the publication of her first collection of poems. Her collection of poetry, *Poems on Various Subjects, Religious and Moral*, was submitted to various publishers in Boston; however, each of them declined to print the book. Wheatley became unwell and was prescribed "fresh sea air." As a result, she traveled with her master's son to London. In England, Wheatley gained the patronage of Selina Hastings, Countess of Huntington, and others who assisted in helping publish her poetry collection. Despite owning estates abroad that contained slaves, Huntingdon encouraged the writings and independence of former slaves who promoted religious viewpoints in accordance with her own beliefs. Some of the former slaves whom she promoted included **Olaudah Equiano** and **Ukawsaw Gronniosaw.** Consequently, in 1773, Wheatley's poetry collection was published in London.

Wheatley's popularity as a poet in both North America and England resulted in her being freed in October 1773. American revolutionary leader George Washington met her in March 1776. In response, Wheatley wrote a poem entitled *To His Excellency George Washington* and became a strong supporter of United States independence during the American Revolutionary War.

Wheatley married John Peters, a free black grocer, and they had three children, two of whom died as infants. Peters tried his hand at a number of jobs, but he was hampered in his career prospects by his lack of education. His wife, desperate to publish another book of poetry, was unable to find a publisher; for the death of the Wheatley family, her former owners, eliminated her ability to transcend into white society. Peters deserted her and soon Wheatley was working as a servant. In 1784, she had fallen on hard times and was living in a boarding house in Boston, where she died in childbirth in 1784 at the age of 31.

See also: Abolition of Slavery, British; Britain, Blacks in; Literature, Blacks in British; Slave Trade, British.

Further Reading: Gates, H. *The Trials of Phillis Wheatley: America's First Black Poet and Her Encounters with the Founding Fathers.* New York: Basic Civitas Books, 2003; Hunter, Jane Edna. *Phillis Wheatley: Life and Works.* Cleveland: National Phillis Wheatley Foundation, 1948; Renfro, G. Herbert. *Life and Works of Phillis Wheatley.* Salem: Ayer Company, 1993; Shockley, Ann Allen. *Afro-American Women Writers, 1746–1933: An Anthology and Critical Guide.* New Haven: Meridian Books, 1989.

Justin Corfield

Wilberforce, William (1759–1833)

William Wilberforce, a member of the British Parliament and vocal supporter of reform in eighteenth- and nineteenth-century England, was one of the driving forces behind Great Britain's abolition of the slave trade.

Wilberforce was born in Yorkshire, England, in 1759 and grew up in a wealthy family. From childhood, Wilberforce was sickly, although, even at a formative age, he impressed others with his ability to communicate. When he was only 10 years old, his father died. Wilberforce then lived for a number of years with his uncle, who introduced him to Evangelical Christianity, a force that would drive Wilberforce's life work. His uncle also later died. These two tragedies, combined with the death of Wilberforce's grandfather, left him with a vast inheritance. At the age of 17, Wilberforce enrolled in St. John's College in Cambridge.

At Cambridge, Wilberforce was far from studious and he spent much of his time gambling, playing cards, and drinking. He made a number of important connections, however, that would help during his legislative career. Indeed, at the age of 21, in 1780, Wilberforce secured a position in the House of Commons. In 1785, he experienced a religious conversion and became an Evangelical Christian. With this renewed sense of purpose and with the backing of many other Evangelical Christians, Wilberforce aimed to end slavery.

In 1790, Wilberforce spoke before Parliament and condemned the slave trade as morally unethical, although he met little success. After the chaos of the French Revolution, the Parliament moved in a decidedly conservative direction, and abolition would receive little support or attention through the rest of the 1790s. During this period, Wilberforce married Barbara Ann Spooner.

In the first years of the nineteenth century, support for abolition began to grow again. Wilberforce aimed to outlaw participation in the slave trade for all British subjects, regardless of a ship's affiliation. In 1807, the bill passed the House of Lords. In the House of Commons, members of Parliament, rather than use their time to debate, instead praised and congratulated Wilberforce. All knew that it was his unwavering support, especially through the difficult 1790s, that made possible the Slave Trade Act of 1807.

The Slave Trade Act failed to end the slave trade, however. Foreign vessels and even some British ships ignored the law. By the early 1820s, Wilberforce's health was failing, and he could no longer actively work toward further abolition. Yet it was not legislation but popular support that pushed final abolition through. Public opinion was so strongly against slavery that in 1833, the Whig government was prepared to pass a new, more comprehensive abolitionist bill. Wilberforce received word of this, and he died three days later. A month later, the Slavery Abolition Act passed. The law generously compensated slave owners, but it marked the end of slavery throughout the British Empire.

See also: Abolition of Slavery, British; Britain, Blacks in; Slave Trade, British.

Further Reading: Hague, William. *The Life of the Great Anti-Slave Campaigner.* London: Harper Press, 2007; Tomkins, Stephen. *William Wilberforce: a Biography.* Grand Rapids, MI: William B. Eerdman's Publishing, 2007.

Joshua M. Rice

Woodson, Carter G. (1875–1950)

Carter Goodwin Woodson was a prominent African American historian and journalist who founded the *Journal of Negro History* (now the *Journal of African-American History*), which has resulted in much scholarship covering many aspects of African history and heritage throughout the world, with strong emphasis on Latin America and Europe as well as North America and the Caribbean. Furthermore, Woodson founded **Black History Month,** a month-long celebration of black contributions and achievements in society that has been adopted in the United States and several European countries, including Britain and Germany.

Woodson was born in December 1875 in Virginia. He was the son of former slaves and one of a large family. Woodson's father had worked with the Union soldiers during the American Civil War, moving to West Virginia after he heard that a high school for African Americans was under construction in Huntington.

Although Woodson was desperate to go to school, he was not able to maintain regular attendance, for he had to work as a miner in the coalfields in Fayette County. He learned much at home, however, and gained his diploma from Douglass High School. He was allowed to teach in Fayette County, becoming, in 1900, the principal of Douglass High School. Woodson earned a bachelor's degree in literature from Berea College in Kentucky and, from 1903 to 1907, worked in the Philippines as a school supervisor. He then earned his master's degree from the University of Chicago in 1908 and his doctorate in history from Harvard University in 1912.

Always interested in African American history, Woodson joined Jesse Moorland in 1915 to found the Association for the Study of Negro Life and History (which later became the Association for the Study of African American Life and History). Woodson also became active with the National Association for the Advancement of Colored People and, in 1916, founded the *Journal of Negro History*. Woodson managed to get out the first issue by himself. The journal, which is still published, changed its name to the *Journal of African-American History* in 2002. Woodson also became a regular columnist in African American leader Marcus Garvey's weekly magazine, *Negro World*.

Woodson wrote many books, including *The Education of the Negro Prior to 1861* (1915), *A Century of Negro Migration* (1918), *The Negro in Our History* (1922), and *The History of the Negro Church* (1927). He was working on the six-volume *Encyclopedia Africana* at the time of his death on April 3, 1950. Woodson donated 5,000 items to the Library of Congress, some of which were used in a 1992 exhibition there entitled *Moving Back Barriers: The Legacy of Carter G. Woodson.*

Further Reading: Conyers, James, ed. *Carter G. Woodson: A Historical Reader.* New York: Garland, 2000; Logan, Rayford. "Carter Godwin Woodson." *Journal of Negro History* 35 (1950): 344–348.

Justin Corfield

World War I, Black Participation in

The French, American, and British armed forces in particular deployed thousands of blacks in Europe during World War I as combat soldiers or support troops. The

French army used the largest contingent of black men in the frontlines. The United States Army formed two black divisions under mostly white command, but deployed African Americans primarily in support duties. The British army was reluctant to use black troops in combat with European nations and therefore used most of its black units deployed in Europe in supportive roles. France, Britain, and Germany all used black soldiers in combat outside of Europe.

FRANCE.   The French army recruited 181,512 men in western and central Africa, 45,803 men in Madagascar, and several thousand men in French Somalia. Some of these forces secured regions of the French empire, notably French North Africa, and conquered the German colony Cameroon in 1916. Strong black African forces also fought in mainland France, on the Gallipoli Peninsula, and in Macedonia. A large number of black Africans was drafted for war-related work in mainland France. These soldiers helped fill vacant spots in industry and agriculture and provided crucial supportive services such as unloading ships and constructing defensive fortifications. On the western front, black troops (primarily *tirailleurs sénégalais*) participated in almost all of the major battles of the war. They played an important role in securing the French defenses in September 1914, and fought in the first Battle of Ypres in November and December 1914. In 1915, black African troops made up approximately half of the French contingent landing on the Gallipoli Peninsula in the Ottoman Empire; for half a year, 18,000 West Africans in vain battered Ottoman defenses, suffering 8,000 casualties. The appalling French losses on the western front dictated a return of the black forces to France, where they fought in the battles of Verdun (1916), the Somme (1916), the Chemin des Dames (1917), Reims (1918), and during the final offensives in the fall of 1918. Several units of French black soldiers also fought against the Bulgarians and Austro-Hungarians in Macedonia (1916–1918).

The record of the black French troops is controversial. Advocates of the black forces had argued that many Africans were ideal assault troops because they belonged to martial races whose nervous system made them less sensible to fear. Critics charged, however, that the black Africans had proven undisciplined, ineffective, and prone to panic under fire. Clearly, black French troops fought with courage and distinction in many places throughout the war, but they were often hampered by poor training, leadership, and equipment. On the western front, moreover, black units were highly vulnerable to pulmonary disease during the winter. The French army command, therefore, decided to withdraw the black troops from the front during the winter months and let them train and rest in the warmer regions of southern France. It also made some tactical changes: whereas it had initially sent larger black units into battle without much support, it later adopted a more effective "panache" system, whereby small black units were mixed with white units and fought in a larger, more heterogeneous unit. Still, in 1917, the French recruitment of black soldiers almost collapsed after the recruitment campaigns in West Africa had triggered local revolts. The French army was desperate for manpower, however, and a major reorganization of recruitment under the leadership of the Senegalese deputy to the French National Assembly, **Blaise Diagne,** yielded a record number of West African recruits in 1918. Some historians argue that the French army increasingly deployed its black troops as shock troops in the most dangerous spots to save the lives of white soldiers, but other historians see no major differences in deployment. The

Germans accused the black French soldiers of atrocities. Responding to the charge that Germany was conducting the war in a barbaric manner, German propaganda depicted the black French soldiers as savage hordes let loose against "civilized" Europeans by cynical Western statesmen. French propagandists, in appreciation of the terror black troops could strike in the hearts of German soldiers, did not always contradict these accusations and presented the alleged wildness of black troops as a positive feat. In some battles, blacks and Germans seem to have killed their prisoners.

UNITED STATES. The American army was still segregated when the United States declared war on Germany in April 1917. African Americans were recruited in large numbers, but the army was reluctant to deploy them as frontline troops and to station them in Europe. Most African American recruits, even those trained for combat, were therefore used in labor battalions, some of which were sent to France. Only two black frontline divisions were formed, the 92nd and 93rd Infantry, and deployed on the western front during the last months of the war under the command of predominantly white officers. The 93rd Infantry was integrated into a French division and, equipped and led by the French army, fought well. The 92nd Infantry was temporarily loaned to the French but fought mostly under American command. It suffered from poor training, leadership, and equipment. Many U.S. Army commanders shared the widespread racist prejudice that African Americans were not intelligent enough to fight in a modern war and worried that earning military glory in combat units would boost African Americans' claims to civil rights and political power. African American soldiers often perceived the French army as more respectful toward blacks than was the U.S. Army.

BRITAIN. The British government, concerned about a loss of authority in the colonies, shared the reservations about using black troops against white nations (it even opposed the planned stationing of the American 92nd Infantry Division on British soil). The British army deployed most of its own black troops, which were recruited in British Africa and the Caribbean, in non-European theaters of the war. Blacks from the British Southern African colonies fought together with Indian and white South African troops against the German East African protective force, which itself consisted mostly of black soldiers. In the Middle East, the British army used African and Caribbean units against the Ottoman armies. If black British units were sent to Europe, they usually received supportive tasks. The British West Indies (Caribbean) Regiment, for example, unloaded supply ships in Italy in 1918. Poor pay and working conditions, in addition to the humiliation of not being sent to the frontline, led to a mutiny.

Whereas black soldiers participated in most campaigns of the Western powers, they faced much racism clouded as doubts about the quality of their performance, the wisdom of their deployment, and allegations of atrocities. Blacks encountered particularly high obstacles if they desired to become officers, at least in the American and British armies, and there was a consensus that white men should never have to serve under a black officer. In the long run, the experiences of blacks in World War I helped to boost political expectations for more civil rights in the United States and for more autonomy in the colonies of the European powers.

See also: British Army, Blacks in the; Bullard, Eugene; Colonies in Africa, British; Colonies in Africa; French; Colonies in Africa, German; *Des inconnus chez moi*; Diallo, Bakary; French Army, Blacks in the.

Further Reading: Astor, Gerald. *The Right to Fight: A History of African Americans in the Military.* Novato, CA: Presidio, 1998; Barbeau, Arthur, and Florette Henri, *The Unknown Soldiers: Black American Troops in World War I.* Philadelphia: Temple University Press, 1974; Conklin, Alice. A *Mission to Civilize: The Republican Idea of Empire in France and West Africa, 1895–1930.* Stanford: Stanford University Press, 1997; Echenberg, Myron. *Colonial Conscripts: The Tirailleurs Sénégalais in French West Africa, 1857–1960.* Portsmouth, NH, and London: Heinemann and James Currey, 1991; Killingray, David. "Race and Rank in the British Army in the Twentieth Century." *Ethnic and Racial Studies* 10 (1987): 276–290; Koller, Christian. "*Von Wilden aller Rassen niedergemetzelt*". *Die Diskussion um die Verwendung von Kolonialtruppen in Europa zwischen Rassismus, Kolonial- und Militärpolitik (1914–1930).* Stuttgart: Franz Steiner, 2001; Lunn, Joe. *Memoirs of the Maelstrom: A Senegalese Oral History of the First World War.* Portsmouth, NH: Heinemann, 1999; Michel, Marc. *Les Africains et la Grande Guerre: l'appel à l'Afrique (1914–1918).* Paris: Karthala, 2003; Rives, Maurice, and Robert Dietrich. *Héros méconnus, 1914–1918, 1939–1945.* Paris: Association Frères d'Armes, 1990.

Raffael Scheck

World War II, Black Participation in

As in **World War I,** the French, American, and British armies used black soldiers in World War II. The French mobilized a large force from its African colonies. These soldiers fought in the defense of France in 1940, often suffering massacres and abuses at the hands of their German captors. From 1940 onward, the Free French forces continuing to fight Germany also enlisted African soldiers. Until the end of 1944, blacks made up a large part of these forces, fighting in Syria, North Africa, Italy, and mainland France. The U.S. armed forces sent African soldiers to Italy, France, Belgium, and Germany. It deployed the majority of its black soldiers in auxiliary roles. Nevertheless, some of its units fought with great distinction. The British armed forces used few black soldiers in Europe, entrusting the guarding and the defense of its empire to many units drafted in the African colonies.

FRANCE.   The introduction of the draft in French West Africa after World War I had established a steady recruitment system in France's most important sub-Saharan colony. More than 100,000 *tirailleurs sénégalais* were mobilized in French West Africa in 1939–1940, and smaller contingents from French Central Africa and Madagascar also made their way to mainland France. The French government made a special effort to enlighten African recruits about the blatant racism of Nazi Germany and to interpret the war as a defense of the values of French civilization, above all, racial tolerance. Some African units were already stationed in France at the outbreak of hostilities and were quickly moved to the border. Given that the western front remained quiet for the time being, the black units, following the practice established in World War I, were withdrawn to camps in the warmer south of France during winter 1939–1940. Meanwhile, reinforcements from Africa arrived.

When the German offensive started on May 10, 1940, most black units were near the border again or in transit to the frontline. Many black soldiers were involved in heavy combat with German troops within a few days. A unit from Madagascar and two West African regiments fought heroically against German forces during their breakthrough in northeastern France, but to no avail. Black African units later experienced the hardest fighting during the second wave of the German offensive, starting on June 5, 1940 along the Somme River. Surrounded and out of ammunition, black soldiers often resisted for a long time, even during the last days of the campaign. The German troops, believing Nazi propaganda that black soldiers were mutilating German prisoners, killed several thousand black soldiers after capture and in some cases decided not to take any black prisoners at all. Abuses and massacres continued in the makeshift POW camps throughout the summer of 1940 before conditions stabilized and treatment of POWs improved. Nearly 16,000 black French prisoners were still in German army camps in occupied France in the middle of 1941, but several thousand of them were dismissed in the following years because of to illness.

The French collaborationist Vichy regime under Marshall Philippe Pétain continued to employ black soldiers among the forces guarding its African colonies and the French mandate in Syria. Meanwhile, the Free French forces under General Charles de Gaulle also began recruiting black Africans, especially after the defection of French Central Africa to de Gaulle in the summer of 1940. In Syria, black soldiers fighting for de Gaulle defeated the Pétainist protective force that also included many black soldiers. In Madagascar, troops loyal to Pétain fought a bitter defensive battle against a British invasion in 1942. When the U.S. Army and the British army landed in French North Africa in November 1942, they encountered some resistance from black troops under the command of Pétainist officers. Vichy's gradual loss of control over the empire swelled the ranks of the black units in the Free French armies, which played a major role in slowing German Field Marshal Erwin Rommel's last big offensive in North Africa in 1942, and joined in the invasion of Italy (July 1943) and southern France (August 1944).

In the fall of 1944, black units played a major role in liberating the southern and eastern parts of France from Provence to Alsace. At the end of the year, however, they were withdrawn from the frontline and transferred to camps in southern France, a move that many Africans now perceived as a humiliating measure meant to reserve the ultimate glory of invading and defeating Germany to white French troops. Many black soldiers (former POWs, resisters, and members of the Free French forces) found themselves deeply frustrated at this stage of the war because of inadequate living quarters, missing pay, and continued discrimination. Several riots and mutinies occurred, the most spectacular of which happened in Thiaroye outside of Dakar in Senegal.

UNITED STATES.   The United States drafted approximately 1,100,000 African Americans into its armed forces during World War II. As in World War I, however, many white commanders were reluctant to send African Americans into theaters of war and into combat. Most African Americans were therefore assigned to service units, and only about half of the recruited soldiers were ever sent overseas. It did not help that many allied countries, including Australia, opposed the stationing of African American units on their soil. The U.S. armed forces were still segregated in 1941, but civil rights groups mobilized much pressure to end segregation. In 1944, the navy gradually abolished segregation for practical reasons, and the army in some emergency situations also disregarded it.

Among the most important units deployed in the European theater of war was the 92nd Infantry Division (re-created after Word War I), which fought in Italy from October

1944 to the end of the war. The 2nd Cavalry Division, also an African American unit, was assigned to service roles in North Africa even though it was a combat unit. The African American 761st Tank Battalion, however, was allowed to fight and did so with great distinction. Known as the Black Panthers, the battalion landed in France in October 1944 and participated in the Battle of the Bulge (December 1944 to February 1945). After breaching the Siegfried Line on the western border of Germany, it reached Austria at the end of the war. During the Battle of the Bulge, the U.S. Army called for volunteers among the African American service units behind the front to shore up its endangered defenses. Approximately 4,500 African American soldiers volunteered for frontline duty, and 2,500 of them were quickly trained and sent into battle. At the onset of the Battle of the Bulge, 11 black soldiers were murdered by a German Waffen-SS unit in Wereth (Belgium) on December 17, 1944. Perhaps the most famous group of African American soldiers in Europe was the **Tuskegee Airmen,** African Americans trained at the U.S. Army Air Force school in Tuskegee, Alabama. Deployed foremost in the 332nd Fighter Group, the Tuskegee Airmen became highly accomplished fighter pilots. They participated in combat in North Africa in 1943 and later in Italy. In addition, some African American women from the Women's Army Corps were sent to Britain in early 1945. Some African American forces fought in the Pacific theater of war, both in the Army (notably the 93rd Infantry Division) and in the Navy. Overall, black soldiers in the U.S. armed forces still faced much prejudice and discrimination; that some black units fought very well helped to undermine segregation, however, and the political climate was less favorable to it than it had been in the previous world war. The larger scale of American military involvement in World War II, and its longer duration, also went a long way to erode segregation by exposing not only the injustice, but also the inefficiency of segregation.

See also: British Army, Blacks in the; Colonies in Africa, British; Colonies in Africa, French; Éboué, Félix; French Army, Blacks in the; Nazis and Black POWs; Nazis and Blacks in Europe; World War I, Black Participation in.

Further Reading: Buchanan, Albert R. *Black Americans in World War II.* Santa Barbara: ABC-Clio, 1977; Echenberg, Myron. *Colonial Conscripts: The Tirailleurs Sénégalais in French West Africa, 1857–1960.* Portsmouth, NH, and London: Heinemann and James Currey, 1991; Koller, Christian. *"Von Wilden aller Rassen niedergemetzelt". Die Diskussion um die Verwendung von Kolonialtruppen in Europa zwischen Rassismus, Kolonial- und Militärpolitik (1914–1930).* Stuttgart: Franz Steiner, 2001; Lawler, Nancy Ellen. *Soldiers of Misfortune: Ivoirien Tirailleurs of World War II.* Athens: Ohio University Press, 1992; MacGregor, Morris, Jr. *Integration of the Armed Forces, 1940–1965.* Washington, DC: Center of Military History, United States Army, 1985; Moore, Christopher Paul. *Fighting for America: Black Soldiers—The Unsung Heroes of World War II.* New York: Ballantine Books, 2005; Morehourse, Maggi M. *Fighting in the Jim Crow Army: Black Men and Women Remember World War II.* Lanham, MD: Rowman and Littlefield, 2000; Rives, Maurice, and Robert Dietrich. *Héros méconnus, 1914–1918, 1939–1945.* Paris: Association Frères d'Armes, 1990; Scheck, Raffael. *Hitler's African Victims: The German Army Massacres of Black French Soldiers in 1940.* New York: Cambridge University Press, 2006; Thomas, Martin. *The French Empire at War 1940–45.* New York: Manchester University Press, 1998.

Raffael Scheck

Wright, Richard (1908–1960)

Richard Wright was an African American writer whose novel, *Native Son*, and subsequent autobiographical work, *Black Boy*, garnered him critical acclaim in national and international contexts. Wright's corpus addressed the visceral and existential reality of black life in the American system of Jim Crow segregation, discrimination, and racism. His work was well received in the United States, but it received particular attention in France as a result of a growing European interest in African American literature and culture. Wright was one of the first African American writers invited to Paris as a guest of the French government. While in Paris, Wright met, befriended, and developed enduring intellectual relationships with prominent persons in French scholarly circles, including philosophers Jean-Paul Sartre and Simone de Beauvoir. Wright's presence provided these French thinkers with firsthand information about the reality of race relations in the United States, encouraging their own empirical and theoretical investigations into the subject. Beauvoir traveled in the 1940s throughout the United States and published *America Day by Day*. Similarly, Sartre was inspired to travel to the United States and write an essay, "Return from the United States: What I Learned about the Black Problem." Wright's articulation of American racial oppression helped inspire Europe as a whole to think more about the history of racial oppression in the world, and the relationship between racial oppression and African American lives.

Wright was born in 1908 on a small plantation in Roxie, Mississippi. His family moved several times during his early life, from Roxie to Memphis, Tennessee, to West Helena, Arkansas. During this series of moves, Wright's father left the family, and his abandonment was a turning point in Wright's young life that would eventually land him, along with his younger brother, in an orphanage and away from his mother for 10 years. After graduating from high school in Mississippi, Wright moved back to Memphis to pursue a writing career. The collectivity of his experiences in Memphis and the rural south inspired his two critically acclaimed novels, *Native Son* and *Black Boy*, along with numerous articles, including "The Ethics of Living Jim Crow." Frustrated with his experiences of segregation and racism in the South, Wright migrated to Chicago just two years after moving to Memphis. Despite his fantasies of Chicago as a promised land for African Americans, Wright found the city to be mired in what he saw as the same problems of racism, African American pathology, and social disappointment as the rural South. Wright sought an answer to the problems of racism in African American life and African American families. Although Wright's experiences of Chicago were not as he expected, he settled there for 10 years, joined the Chicago John Reed Club (a literary club), and later became affiliated with the Communist Party. During his time with the Reed Club, Wright published many essays, short stories, and poems in their magazine, *Left Front*.

Wright left Chicago in 1937 for New York. While Wright lived in New York, his reflections on his experiences in the South, his observations of the oppression of African American populations in Chicago, and his membership in the Reed Club led him to question the relationship between African American poverty and racial oppression, and African Americans and the Communist Party. In *12 Million Black Voices*, Wright drew on the theories of the Chicago School of Sociology to examine the condition of the black poor in segregated spaces in northern urban centers. Wright's essay, "I tried to be a Communist" expressed his disappointment with the Communist Party in its lack of a solution to the problems of African Americans.

Scholarship on Wright has focused on his relationship to existential philosophy, especially that of Sartre. What has been undertheorized in scholarship is his own organic, indigenous, existential thought developed early in his intellectual career. Wright's novel, *The Outsider*, considered the most existential novel of his corpus, was written in London, England before his formal engagement with French existential thinkers. Throughout Wright's intellectual career, he expressed concern for individual freedom and the influence of environment. For Wright, there were two main concerns in his corpus: the possibility of individual freedom in a society that oppresses him and the possibility of a core self from which one cannot be alienated. Both of these concerns dealt with the issue of whether an individual can develop a personality outside of, and against, that which a society attempts to place on him. Inversely, Wright posed the question of whether society determines individual personality. These existential concerns were primary for Wright in that it went to the heart of his reflections on his life in the rural South, urban South, and in the urban North. Wright was concerned with whether African Americans could have individual freedom in a racist society. He tried to negotiate these two concerns, leading him to pose existential questions in his work.

In France, Wright found a receptive audience for his work, as well as a less oppressive living environment. His novels and essays appealed to French intellectuals, who were concerned about the nature of human freedom and responsibility, specifically having to do with the relationship between individuals, their environment, and the state. Europe's fascination with existentialism, and France in particular, was due to the recent events of World War II and Nazi Germany. In the aftermath of the German invasion of several European countries, including France, Europeans began to question the nature of human freedom and responsibility, and the role of environment and the state to limit this freedom and responsibility. Sartre, who wrote about the freedom and responsibility of the individual, emerged in the early 1940s as one of the leading philosophers of existentialism with his publication of *Being and Nothingness* and several essays, the most significant of which was "Existentialism Is a Humanism." Beauvoir's relatively less obtuse work, *The Second Sex*, was published in the latter half of the 1940s and grappled with issues of women's oppression in France and Europe. Wright's work appealed to both Sartre and Beauvoir in that it combined Sartre's esoteric theorization with Beauvoir's interest in the concrete in literary form. Wright developed a close intellectual relationship with both Sartre and Beauvoir. With Sartre, Wright found a thinker with whom he could discourse seriously about the human condition and the possibility of freedom therein. With Beauvoir, Wright found a thinker with whom he shared the concrete lived experience of oppression.

During Wright's decade in France, he expanded his analysis of oppression, from African Americans of the rural South and urban North in the United States, to people of color throughout the world. He traveled to Ghana (then still the Gold Coast), Indonesia, and throughout Europe, visiting Spain, Germany, and Scandinavia. While in

Spain, Wright reflected on his travels in Indonesia and Ghana, and the nature of oppression and its effects on oppressed peoples. His novel, *Pagan Spain*, was concerned with the origins of European enslavement of African people, and the psychology of oppressed people. While in Germany and Scandinavia, Wright lectured on the history of Africa, the psychological problems of oppressed people, and African American literature. Toward the end of his life, Wright's published *White Man, Listen*, a series of essays on racial injustice. *Eight Men, Lawd Today*, and *American Hunger* were published posthumously.

Wright's development of an African American literary voice to tell an American narrative of oppression and overcoming of oppression inspired an entire generation of African American novelists, as well as entire generation of European thinkers.

See also: Authors in Europe, African American; France, Blacks in.

Further Reading: Fabre, Michel. *From Harlem to Paris: Black Writers in France, 1840–1980.* Urbana: University of Illinois Press, 1993; Gates, Henry Louis, and K. A. Appiah, eds. *Richard Wright: Critical Perspectives Past and Present.* New York: Amistad Press, 1993; Gayle, Addison. *Richard Wright: Ordeal of a Native Son.* Garden City, NY: Anchor Press/Double Day, 1980; Mackssey, Richard, and Frank E. Moorer, eds. *Richard Wright: A Collection of Critical Essays.* Englewood, NJ: Prentice-Hall, 1984; Rowley, Hazel. *Richard Wright: Life and Times.* New York: Henry Holt, 2001; Walker, Margaret. *Richard Wright: Daemonic Genius.* New York: Amistad Press, 1988; Wright, Ellen, and Michel Fabre, eds. *The Richard Wright Reader.* New York: Harper and Row, 1978.

James B. Haile

Xenophobia and Blacks in Europe

Since the 1980s, racism and xenophobia, which is a fear or contempt of that which is foreign or unknown, particularly of strangers or foreigners, have increased in Europe. In the wake of the Islamic terrorist attack on September 11, 2001, in the United States and subsequent attacks in Britain and Spain, xenophobia has primarily manifested itself as a fear of all Muslims, some of whom are also black Africans. Anti-Semitism has persisted, as well as negative perceptions and actions toward Roma (derogatorily known as gypsies). In addition, immigration and asylum-seekers to Europe have been on the rise. Many of the immigrants and refugees to Europe are foreign, often originating from Asia, Africa, or the Caribbean. Many, particularly from Africa, sneak into Europe illegally. Minority groups in Europe are often associated with such negative phenomenon as unemployment, poverty, and crime. Many black Europeans unfortunately face the threat of physical violence, discrimination, and verbal harassment. Far-right and neofascist groups have helped spread the growth of xenophobia and racism; however, memories of the horrors of the Nazi Holocaust have thus far kept such fears in check.

Fear of increased numbers of foreigners, many from Africa, has made many European Union (EU) members question existing asylum laws to deny European access to large numbers of refugees. In the years after 1992, EU members generally resorted to the practice of allowing refugees to be sent back to their countries of origin if it was determined to provide guarantees for refugees' safety. In some cases, readmission agreements had already been made requiring countries to take back their repatriates. European fear of an uncontrolled influx of foreigners encouraged xenophobic electioneering, as foreigners were seen as a danger and their invasion as out of control.

Although the EU insists on the inclusion of equal rights in the law of all its members, equal rights are not always put into practice. In the early 2000s, the rise of far-right groups, such as the *Front National* in France; and the BNP and United

Kingdom Independence Party (UKIP) in Britain; the *Alleanza Nazionale* and the *Alternativa Sociale* in Italy; the *Liga Polskich Rodzin* (Polish League of Families), *Prawo i Sprawiedliwosc* (Law and Order) and *Samoobrona* (Self Defense) in Poland; the *Lijst Pim Fortuyn* in Denmark; the *Vlaams Blok* in Belgium; and the Freedom Party in Austria, used xenophobic and racist rhetoric to score votes in national or European elections, although with varying degrees of success. Some successful far-right groups have included the Freedom Party, which managed to briefly make up part of the governing coalition in Austria in 2001 and the *Front National* in France, whose presidential candidate, Jean-Marie Le Pen, managed to make it to the final round of candidates in 2002. In general, however, such far-right groups have not been able to dominate any European country's government, or the European parliament, thus far. Yet many mainstream conservative political groups have adapted the new right's anti-immigration discourse.

In general, the EU has sought to eliminate racism, xenophobia, and all forms of hate and intolerance. In the EU Race Equality Directive (Directive 2000/43/EC), distinctions were made between "direct" and "indirect" discrimination based on racism and xenophobia. "Direct" discrimination was defined as having occurred when "one person is treated less favourably than another is, has been or would be treated in a comparable situation on grounds of racial or ethnic origin." On the other hand, "indirect" discrimination was defined as occurring when "an apparently neutral provision, criterion or practice would put persons of a racial or ethnic origin at a particular disadvantage compared with other persons, unless that provision, criterion or practice is objectively justified by a legitimate aim and the means of achieving that aim are appropriate and necessary." The wording of the law legally enables indirect discrimination under certain conditions. In the following fictitious example to illustrate such conditions, if a doctor's office needed to hire a medical assistant, the assistant would be required to wear coverings over his or her hands and mouth for health reasons. The law would discriminate against individuals or groups who forbid the covering of hands and mouth in this way. The doctor's office can justify discriminating against this group because the primary and legitimate aim is the safety of their patients and such a requirement is reasonable and necessary under standard safety regulations.

In 2000, the EU signed a Charter of Fundamental Rights and played a key role in the United Nations' 2001 World Conference Against Racism. The EU also established a monitoring center on racism, xenophobia, and anti-Semitism in Vienna to study the rise of extreme-right groups in attempts to understand how they gain support and how to isolate them. Other organizations, such as the European Network Against Racism, have developed to encourage the equal treatment of all Europeans.

In the late 2000s, the EU agreed to new rules to criminalize racism and xenophobia; however, the measures were mostly symbolic. Under the new rules, members of the EU had to establish minimum jail terms for those who publicly incite violence or hatred toward any individual or group "defined by reference to race, color, religion, descent or national or ethnic origin." The legislation did not establish any minimum fines and left it up to national courts to define what constituted publicly inciting violence or hatred. The EU also banned the use of Nazi symbols and made it illegal to deny crimes of genocide, crimes of humanity, and war crimes if these crimes have been defined as such by international courts and if the statements are meant to incite violence or hatred.

See also: Immigration to Europe, Illegal African; Nazis and Blacks in Europe.

Further Reading: Baumgartl, Bernd, and Adrian Favell, eds. *New Xenophobia in Europe.* London: Kluwer Law International, 1995; Holmes, Douglas. Integral *Europe: Fast Capitalism, Multiculturalism, Neofascism. Princeton*: Princeton University Press, 2000; Lahav, Gallya. *Immigration and Politics in the New Europe: Reinventing Borders.* Cambridge: Cambridge University Press, 2004; McClintock, Michael. *Everyday Fears: A Survey of Violent Hate Crimes in Europe and North America.* New York: Human Rights First, 2005.

Eric Martone

Young Africans in Norway (AYIN)

Young Africans in Norway (AYIN) was founded in 1995 as a youth nongovernmental organization in Norway. AYIN's purpose was to help teenagers who are black African or of black African descent combat racial discrimination and to create multicultural awareness in Norwegian society. AYIN received attention for its efforts to launch a critical debate over how black Africans and those of black African descent are identified in Norway. Terms such as *negro, mulatto, half-caste, darkie,* and other terms deemed derogatory were still in common accepted usage during the 1990s. In 1997, AYIN produced an informational brochure in an attempt to educate the Norwegian public about racism in language and why such terms were offensive to minority Norwegians. AYIN's efforts did result in less usage of such terms by teachers and the media.

See also: Abolition of Slavery, European; Afro-German Women (ADEFRA); Campaign Against Racial Discrimination (CARD); Initiative of Blacks in Germany (ISD); Pamoja; Representative Council of Black Associations (CRAN); Scandinavia, Blacks in.

Further Reading: Arter, David. "Black Faces in the Blond Crowd: Populist Racialism in Scandinavia." *Parliamentary Affairs* 45 (1992): 357–372; Gullestad, Marianne. "Normalising Racial Boundaries: The Norwegian Dispute about the Term *'neger.'*" *Social Anthropology* 13:1 (February 2005): 27–46; Weisbord, Robert G. "Scandinavia: A Racial Utopia?" *Journal of Black Studies* 2:4 (June 1972): 471–488.

E. Agateno Mosca

Z

Zulu War (1879)

The Anglo-Zulu War of 1879 was a conflict between the British Empire and the native Zulu tribe for control of South Africa. The war was part of the European "scramble for Africa" and British attempts to expand its colonial empire.

The war followed a British ultimatum on December 11, 1878, demanding that the Zulu leader, Cetewayo, grant the British a virtual protectorate over Zululand. On January 11, 1879, the British commander, General F. A. Thesiger, Viscount Chelmsford, led 5,000 British and 8,200 African native troops into Zululand. They marched in three widely dispersed columns while Cetewayo raised a force of 40,000 Zulu warriors.

The Africans who served with the British did so in a number of capacities. Recruited in Natal, many were from tribes that had traditionally been hostile to the Zulus, making them loyal supporters of the British. Chelmsford raised three regiments of the Natal Native Contingent. Lieutenant-Governor Sir Henry Bulwer opposed the use of levy units, however, which he felt might worsen relations between the various African tribes, as did others in Natal who feared the arming and training of Africans. Initially, it was hoped that the entire Native Contingent could be issued with red coats, but this was impossible to achieve. Instead, the Native Contingent received red cloth to tie as headbands. In the end, only a tenth of the contingent was issued with firearms (often obsolete models), with most of the rest armed with spears and shields. There were also the men of the Natal Native Horse. They wore European clothing with a red hatband for identification and were armed with carbines, although some carried spears on the back of their horses. The Natal Native Pioneers formed a 273-strong unit divided into five companies and was used for reconnaissance and skirmishing by all three columns. British commander Sir Henry Evelyn Wood used the other African units in the northern theater of the Zulu War. These were also Swazi warriors, who traditionally hated the Zulus. Added to these were the Zulu supporters of African Prince Hamu kaNzibe, who supported the British. These combined African forces formed what became known as Wood's "irregulars."

Facing the British forces was a large Zulu force, highly organized and operating in a number of skilled regiments formed from the moment the boys had reached puberty. As a result, most men were serving with others of the same age, although imprecise records and the filling of places caused by casualties did lead to some divergences from this trend. The Zulus were well trained and followed orders given by the *induna enkulu,* or field commander, who was appointed by the Zulu king from his own family or from his close advisers. The appointments were always for the length of the conflict, after which the commanders returned to their peacetime roles. The men in the army were armed with rifles or spears, the latter used for throwing or thrusting as circumstances dictated.

In January 1879, Viscount Chelmsford led the central column of the British forces of 1,800 Europeans and 1,000 Africans to establish a camp at Isandhlwana. Early the next morning, while Chelmsford was leading half of the Europeans in an attempt to intercept the Zulus, 10,000 Zulus attacked the British base, killing most of the British forces. Only 55 Europeans and 300 Africans survived. After their victory at Isandhlwana, half the Zulu force turned and attacked the nearby encampment at Rorke's Drift, where 85 British soldiers who had escaped from Isandhlwana held off six major Zulu attacks, with a loss of 17 killed and 10 severely wounded.

On his return to Isandhlwana, Chelmsford found the destroyed camp and hundreds of dead bodies strewn across the battlefield. He retreated toward Rorke's Drift, the defense of which was hailed in the British press as one of the greatest victories of the British Empire, with 11 Victoria Crosses subsequently awarded. The other British advance columns also did not fare as well. Colonel C. K. Pearson was forced to take refuge at Eshowe, where the British forces held out from January 28 until April 4, when Chelmsford broke the siege. The mounted force from the northern column was attacked at the Battle of Hlobane on March 28, with the main force attacked the next day. The British government hastily dispatched large numbers of reinforcements and Chelmsford went on the offensive again at the end of May.

On June 1, the Zulus ambushed a British column and killed Louis Bonaparte, son of the former French Emperor Napoleon III. The death of the "Prince Imperial," as the young man had been known, focused world attention on the conflict. By this time, the exploits of the British columns were described daily in the British press.

Eventually, British numbers, weaponry, and planning led to success. Chelmsford led 4,200 Europeans and 1,000 native Africans to the Zulu capital. There, at the battle of Ulundi, on July 4, more than 10,000 Zulus attacked the British. The British immediately formed a defensive square with the Natal Native Corps placed at its center. The Zulus attacked the square from every side, with about 100 British casualties being sustained. The Zulus lost 1,500 killed and many more severely injured. Such losses forced the Zulus to retreat from the field. Cetewayo, the Zulu king, fled, but was captured and deposed on August 28. On January 29, 1883, however, Cetewayo was restored to power and fought a civil war against his rival for the throne. Cetewayo was defeated in December 1883, but Dinuzulu, a son of Cetewayo, becoming the next king. The Zulu War marked the end of an independent Zulu nation and enabled the British to further their control over South Africa, which became a vital part of the British Empire.

See also: Boer War; British Army, Blacks in the; Colonies in Africa, British; New Imperialism.

Further Reading: Barthorp, Michael. *The Zulu War.* Poole, Dorset: Blandford, 1980; Knight, Ian. *British Forces in Zululand, 1879.* Oxford: Osprey, 1991; Knight, Ian. *The Zulu War, 1879.* Oxford: Osprey, 2003; Lloyd, Alan. *The Zulu War.* London: Hart-Davis MacGibbon, 1973; Wilkinson-Latham, Robert. *Uniforms and Weapons of the Zulu War.* London: Batsford, 1978.

Justin Corfield

Zwarte Piet

Zwarte Piet (Black Pete) is a character in European folklore that accompanies Sinterklaas (Saint Nicholas) as he brings gifts to children in celebration of his feast day on December 6. The character of Zwarte Piet is popular in the Netherlands and parts of Belgium, where he has emerged as a central character in Dutch/Flemish holiday traditions. The figure of Sinterklaas is derived from a medieval bishop from Anatolia who was made a saint by the Byzantine Church. The bishop is remembered in an annual celebration widely celebrated in the Low Lands in which celebrants give each other gifts and write poems in jest. Children are taught to believe that they will receive gifts from Sinterklaas and Zwarte Piet if they have behaved during the year. Zwarte Piet is one of a variation of several companions of Saint Nicholas in Germanic traditions sometimes associated with Satan or devils. He is portrayed often as a mischievous character, and in earlier traditions, distributing punishment to naughty children in the form of physical beatings or stuffing them in a large sack, where they would be whisked away to some unknown place of torment. According to modern legend, Zwarte Piet is a **Moor** of African descent commonly depicted in colorful pantaloons, feathered cap, and Renaissance-style page dress. In contemporary Dutch celebrations, the character of Zwarte Piet is depicted in blackface, which is a style of theatrical makeup used to depict a racist archetype of those of African descent. Consequently, such practices have provoked accusations of racism and the promotion of intolerance.

In the Germanic tradition, Saint Nicholas is accompanied by a sinister figure frequently carrying a stick or whip and a sack, usually dressed in black rags or fur, and bearing a black face and black hair. In many such depictions, the character resembles rustic depictions of the Santa Claus character in early American folklore. The traditions of the Saint Nicholas feast derive from the pre-Christian customs of Europe that emphasized nature. In the Sinterklaas tradition before the nineteenth century, Zwarte Piet acted both as a foil to the good Saint Nicholas and as a depiction of the triumph over evil as the devilish Piet was held in chains and under the domination of the saint. Some of the most recognized companions of Saint Nicholas in central and northern Europe include *Knecht Ruprecht, Krampus, Klaubauf, Pelznickel, Rumpelklas, Bullerklaas, Julgubben, Hanstrapp,* and *Père Fouettard.* It is uncertain whether all such characters are variations of the same tradition or a mixture of various traditions. Zwarte Piet is connected to, and yet distinct from, these companions.

Earliest depictions of Zwarte Piet depict him as a hairy, chained, black, devilish monster. Holiday customs varied according to the idiosyncrasies of individual families.

Zwarte Piet (Black Pete) with Sinterklaas (Saint Nicholas). Courtesy of Isis Wegman.

In general, Sinterklaas tested the children on their catechism while Zwarte Piet intimidated them. Children who performed well were rewarded; those who performed poorly were beaten. Sinterklaas usually intervened to save the children from being taken away in Zwarte Piet's sack. In other versions, children would be asleep and would wake to find their shoes filled with sweets, sticks, or ashes. Children who misbehaved often received ashes or a stick, understanding it as a warning to behave; otherwise Zwarte Piet would return to dole out punishment. In some traditions, Zwarte Piet's blackness is explained by his traveling through chimneys; therefore his face is covered in soot.

In 1845, Jan Schenkman wrote *Saint Nicholas and his Servant*, which greatly influenced the legend of Zwarte Piet. In the book, Zwarte Piet is presented as an Indian servant of the gift-giving Sinterklaas. In an 1850 version of the book, Sinterklaas's servant has an African origin. In subsequent editions, Zwarte Piet is depicted in a Renaissance page costume. The book remained in print until the middle of the twentieth century, greatly influencing contemporary Dutch celebrations of the holiday. Stories developed to explain the origin of the character, including that he was an African orphan saved from slavery by Sinterklaas.

As the legend evolved, Sinterklaas was said to arrive in Holland from Spain. Consequently, his assistant became a Moor and the naughtiest children would be stuffed in his sack and taken to Spain. Such connections derive from the time when the Spanish Habsburg royal family also ruled the Netherlands during the early modern period, as well as the longstanding Muslim influences on traditionally Christian Europe. Zwarte

Piet's costume resembles those worn by the Spanish at the time of William of Orange, who initiated an uprising for Dutch independence against the Habsburgs in the early modern period. Until well into the twentieth century, Zwarte Piet was depicted as a comical fool, consistent with colonial traditions. In the emerging multiethnic Europe, the character was modified into a more respectable character and multiplied, so that there are several Zwarte Pieten assisting Sinterklaas.

In the present Netherlands, a great spectacle is organized around Sinterklaas's arrival from Spain in a steamboat full of gifts, Zwarte Piet, and his horse, an idea found in Schenkman's book. They are welcomed by bells and a huge crowd of children and parents, which is filmed for television. In recent years, the character of Zwarte Piet has caused controversy. The origin of the character is perceived by some as a form of racism that promotes a negative view of dark-skinned individuals as fools and lacking intelligence. Zwarte Piet's role as a subservient figure is especially sensitive within the context of the pivotal Dutch role in colonization and in the development of the Atlantic slave trade. Since the end of the twentieth century, there have been several attempts to modify Zwarte Piet, replacing his traditional black makeup for a variety of colors to render him acceptable to a diverse population, but such efforts have failed to attract mass support.

See also: Abolition of Slavery, European; Colonies in Africa, Dutch; Netherlands, Blacks in the; Slave Trade, Dutch.

Further Reading: Fox, Anna, and Mieke Cal. *Zwarte Piet*. London: Black Dog, 1999; Russ, Jennifer. *German Festivals and Customs*. London: Wolff, 1982; Siefker, Phyllis. *Santa Claus, Last of the Wild Men*. Jefferson, NC: McFarland, 1997.

Eric Martone

Resource Guide

SUGGESTED READING

Alt, William, and Betty Alt. *Black Soldiers, White Wars: Black Warriors from Antiquity to the Present.* Westport, CT: Praeger, 2002.

Andell, Jacqueline. *Gender, Migration, and Domestic Service: The Politics of Black Women in Italy.* Bulington, VT: Ashgate, 2000.

Andrews, William. *To Tell a Free Story: The First Century of Afro-American Autobiography, 1760–1865.* Urbana: University of Illinois Press, 1986.

Barthelemy, Anthony Gerard. *Black Face, Maligned Race: The Representation of Blacks in English Drama From Shakespeare to Southerne.* Baton Rouge: Louisiana State University Press, 1987.

Berliner, Brett. *Ambivalent Desire: The Exotic Black Other in Jazz-Age France.* Amherst: University of Massachusetts Press, 2002.

Birmingham, David. *Portugal and Africa.* New York: Palgrave Macmillan, 1999.

Birnbaum, Lucia. *Black Madonnas: Feminism, Religion, and Politics in Italy.* Boston: Northeastern University Press, 1993.

Blackett, R.J.M. *Building an Antislavery Wall: Black Americans in the Atlantic Abolitionist Movement, 1830–1860.* Baton Rouge: Louisiana State University Press, 1983.

Blackshire-Belay, Carol, ed. *The African-German Experience: Critical Essays.* Westport, CT: Praeger, 1996.

Blakely, Allison. *Blacks in the Dutch World: The Evolution of Racial Imagery in a Modern Society.* Bloomington: Indiana University Press, 1993.

———. *Russia and the Negro: Blacks in Russian History and Thought.* Washington, DC: Howard University Press, 1986.

Bourne, Stephen. *Black in the British Frame: The Black Experience in British Film and Television.* London: Continuum, 2001.

Boxer, C. R. *Race Relations in the Portuguese Colonial Empire, 1415–1825.* Oxford: Oxford University Press, 1963.

Bridgman, Jon, and David Clarke. *German Africa: A Select Annotated Bibliography*. Stanford: Hoover Institution on War, Revolution, and Peace, 1965.

Brock, Colin. *The Caribbean in Europe: Aspects of the West Indies Experience in Britain, France, and the Netherlands*. London: Routledge, 1986.

Campbell, James. *Paris Interzone: Richard Wright, Lolita, Boris Vian, and Others on the Left Bank, 1946–60*. New York: C. Scribner's Sons, 1995.

Campt, Tina M. *Other Germans: Black Germans and the Politics of Race, Gender and Memory in the Third Reich*. Ann Arbor: University of Michigan Press, 2004.

Carretta, Vincent. *Unchained Voices: An Anthology of Black Authors in the English-Speaking World of the Eighteenth-Century*. Lexington: University of Kentucky Press, 1996.

Cazenave, Odile. *Afrique sur Seine: A New Generation of African Writers in Paris*. New York: Lexington Books, 2005.

Chapman, Herrick, and Laura Frader, eds. *Race in France: Interdisciplinary Perspectives on the Politics of Difference*. New York: Berghahn Books, 2004.

Christophe, Marc. "Changing Images of Blacks in Eighteenth Century French Literature." *Phylon* 48:3 (1987): 183–189.

Cohen, William. *The French Encounter with Africans: White Response to Blacks, 1530–1880*. Reprint. Bloomington: Indiana University Press, 2003.

Colatrella, Steven. *Workers of the World: African and Asian Migrants in Italy in the 1990s*. Trenton, NJ: Africa World Press, 2001.

Conklin, Alice. *A Mission to Civilize: The Republican Idea of Empire in France and West Africa, 1895–1930*. Stanford: Stanford University Press, 1997.

Cook, Mercer. "The Negro in French Literature: An Appraisal." *The French Review* 23:5 (March 1950): 378–388.

Cullen, Paul. *Refugees and Asylum-Seekers in Ireland*. Cork: Cork University Press, 2000.

Dabydeen, David, ed. *The Black Presence in English Literature*. Manchester: Manchester University Press, 1985.

Davis, David Brion. *The Problem of Slavery in the Age of Revolution, 1770–1823*. Ithaca: Cornell University Press, 1975.

———. *The Problem of Slavery in Western Culture*. New York: Oxford University Press, 1988.

Davis, Robert C. *Christian Slaves, Muslim Masters: White Slavery in the Mediterranean, the Barbary Coast and Italy, 1500–1800*. New York: Palgrave Macmillan, 2003.

Debrunner, Hans. *Presence and Prestige, Africans in Europe: A History of Africans in Europe Before 1918*. Basel: Basler Afrika Bibliographien, 1979.

Diop, Cheikh Anta. *The African Origin of Civilization: Myth or Reality?* Chicago: Lawrence Hill, 1974.

Donnell, Alison, ed. *Companion to Contemporary Black British Culture*. London: Routledge, 2002.

Dorigny, Marcel, ed. *Abolitions of Slavery: From L. F. Sonthonax to Victor Schoelcher, 1793, 1794, 1848*. trans. New York: Berghahn Books, 2003.

Duffield, Ian. "Blacks in Britain: Black Personalities in Georgian Britain." *History Today* (Sept. 1981): 34–36.

———. "Identity, Community and the Lived Experience of Black Scots From the Late Eighteenth to the Mid-Nineteenth Centuries." *Immigrants and Minorities* 11:2 (1992): 105–129.

Dunbar, Ernest. *Black Expatriates: A Study of American Negroes in Exile*. New York: Dutton, 1968.

Earle, T. F., and K.J.P. Lowe, eds. *Black Africans in Renaissance Europe*. New York: Cambridge University Press, 2005.

Echenberg, Myron. *Colonial Conscripts: The Tirailleurs Sénégalais in French West Africa, 1857–1960*. Portsmouth, NH and London: Heinemann and James Currey, 1991.

Edwards, Paul, and James Walvin. *Black Personalities in the Era of the Slave Trade*. Baton Rouge: Louisiana State University Press, 1983.

El-Tayeb, Fatima. "'If You Can't Pronounce My Name, You Can Just Call Me Pride': Afro-German Activism, Gender, and Hip-Hop." *Gender and History* 15:3 (Nov. 2003): 460–486.

Ellis, David. "Free and Coerced Transatlantic Migrations: Some Comparisons." *American Historical Review* 188:2 (1983): 251–280.

Emmanuel Eze, ed. *Race and the Enlightenment: A Reader*. Cambridge: Blackwell, 1997.

Epstein, Steven. *Speaking of Slavery: Color, Ethnicity, and Human Bondage in Italy*. Ithaca: Cornell University Press, 2001.

Fabre, Michel. *From Harlem to Paris: Black American Writers in France, 1840- 1980*. Urbana: University of Illinois Press, 1991.

Fanning, Bryan. *Racism and Social Change in the Republic of Ireland*. Manchester: Manchester University Press, 2002.

Farrell, Fintan, and Philip Watt, eds. *Responding to Racism in Ireland*. Dublin: Veritas Publications, 2001.

Fehrenbach, Heide. *Race after Hitler: Black Occupation Children in Post-war Germany and America*. Princeton: Princeton University Press, 2005.

Field, Frank, and Patricia Haikin. *Black Britons*. Oxford: Oxford University Press, 1971.

Fikes, Robert. "Blacks in Europe, Asia, Canada, and Latin America: A Bibliographical Essay." *A Current Bibliography on African Affairs* 17:2 (1984–85): 113–128.

Fletcher, Richard. *Moorish Spain*. 2nd ed. Berkeley: University of California Press, 2006.

Foner, Nancy. "Race and Color: Jamaican Migrants in London and New York City." *International Migration Review* 19:4 (1985): 708–727.

Foney, E. L. "A Visual Arts Encounter: African Americans and Europe." *The International Review of African American Art* 11:4 (1994). Available at: http://museum.hamptonu.edu/iraaa_publication.cfm.

Fryer, Peter. *Staying Power: The History of Black People in Britain*. London: Pluto Press, 1984.

Garner, Steve. *Racism in the Irish Experience*. London: Pluto Press, 2004.

Genovese, Eugene. *From Rebellion to Revolution: Afro-American Slave Revolts in the Making of the Modern World*. Baton Rouge: Louisiana State University Press, 1979.

Gerzina, Gretchen H. *Black London: Life Before Emancipation*. New Brunswick: Rutgers University Press, 1997.

———, ed. *Black Victorians, Black Victoriana*. New Brunswick: Rutgers University Press, 2003.

Gilman, Sander. *On Blackness Without Blacks: Essays on the Image of the Black in Germany*. Boston: G. K. Hall, 1982.

Gilroy, Paul. *The Black Atlantic: Modernity and Double Consciousness*. London: Verso, 1993.

———. *"There Ain't no Black in the Union Jack": The Cultural Politics of Race and Nation*. Reprint. Chicago: University of Chicago Press, 1991.

Gould, Philip. *Barbaric Traffic: Commerce and Antislavery in the Eighteenth-Century Atlantic World*. Cambridge: Harvard University Press, 2003.

Gray, John, ed. *Black Theatre and Performance: A Pan-African Bibliography*. Westport, CT: Greenwood Press, 1990.

Grimm, Reinhold, and Jost Hermand, eds. *Blacks and German Culture*. Madison: University of Wisconsin Press, 1986.

Hargrove, Hondon B. *Buffalo Soldiers in Italy: Black Americans in World War II*. Jefferson, NC: McFarland, 1985.

Hellie, Richard. *Slavery in Russia: 1450–1725*. Chicago: University of Chicago Press, 1982.

Hiro, Dilip. *Black British, White British: A History of Race Relations in Britain*. Rev. ed. London: Grafton Books, 1991.

Hochschild, Adam. *Bury the Chains, Prophets and Rebels in the Fight to Free an Empire's Slaves*. Wilmington, MA: Houghton Mifflin, 2004.

Hodges, Carolyn. "The Private/Plural Selves of Afro-German Women and the Search For a Public Voice." *Journal of Black Studies* 23:2 (1992): 219–234.

Innes, C. L. *History of Black and Asian Writing in Britain, 1700–2000*. Cambridge: Cambridge University Press, 2003.

Jackson, John, and Nadine Weidman. *Race, Racism, and Science: Social Impact and Interaction*. Santa Barbara: ABC-CLIO, 2004.

Jacobs, Sylvia M. *The African Nexus: Black American Perspectives on the European Partitioning of Africa, 1880–1920*. Westport, CT: Greenwood Press, 1981.

Jenkinson, Jacqueline. "The Black Community of Salford and Hull, 1919–21." *Immigrants and Minorities* 7:2 (1988): 166–183.

———. "The Glasgow Race Disturbances of 1919." *Immigrants and Minorities* 4:2 (1985): 43–67.

Jennings, Lawrence C. *French Anti-Slavery: The Movement for Abolition of Slavery in France, 1802–1848*. Cambridge: Cambridge University Press, 2000.

Jules-Rosette, Bennetta. *Black Paris: The African Writers' Landscape*. Urbana: University of Illinois Press, 1998.

Katznelson, Ira. *Black Men, White Cities: Race, Politics, and Migration in the United States, 1900–1930, and Britain, 1948–1968*. London: Institute of Race Relations/Oxford University Press, 1973.

Kaul, Mythili, ed. *Othello: New Essays by Black Writers*. Washington, DC: Howard University Press, 1997.

Kenney, William H. "'*Le Hot*': The Assimilation of American Jazz in France, 1917-1940." *American Studies* 25:1 (1984): 5–24.

Kesteloot, Lilyan. *Black Writers in French: A Literary History of Negritude*. New ed. Washington, DC: Howard University Press, 1991.

Kesting, Robert. "Forgotten Victims: Blacks in the Holocaust." *Journal of Negro History* 77:1 (1992): 30–36.

Killingray, David. "Race and Rank in the British Army in the Twentieth Century." *Ethnic and Racial Studies* 10 (1987): 276–290.

Kolchin, Peter. *Unfree Labor: American Slavery and Russian Serfdom*. Cambridge: Harvard University Press, 1987.

Lawler, Nancy Ellen. *Soldiers of Misfortune: Ivoirien Tirailleurs of World War II*. Athens: Ohio University Press, 1992.

Lewis, Shireen. *Race, Culture, and Identity: Francophone West African and Caribbean Literature and Theory from Négritude to Créolité*. New York: Lexington Books, 2006.

Little, Kenneth. *Negroes in Britain: A Study of Racial Relations in English Society*. Revised ed. London: Kegan Paul, 1972.

Lorimer, Douglas. "Black Slaves and English Liberty: A Re-Examination of Racial Slavery in England." *Immigrants and Minorities* 3:2 (1984): 121–150.

———. *Class, Colour, and the Victorians: A Study of English Attitudes Toward the Negro in the Mid-Nineteenth Century*. Leicester: Leicester University Press, 1978.

Lusane, Clarence. *Hitler's Black Victims: The Historical Experiences of Afro-Germans, European Blacks, Africans, and African Americans in the Nazi Era*. London: Routledge, 2002.

McClellan, Woodford. "Africans and Black Americans in the Comintern Schools, 1925–1934." *International Journal of African Historical Studies* 26:2 (1993): 371–390.

McCloy, Shelby. *The Negro in France.* Lexington: University of Kentucky Press, 1961.

McGregor, Morris, Jr. *Integration of the Armed Forces, 1940–1965.* Washington, DC: Center of Military History, United States Army, 1985.

McKernan, James. "Value Systems and Race Relations in Northern Ireland and America." *Ethnic and Racial Studies* 5:2 (1982): 156–174.

McVeigh, Robbie. "The Specificity of Irish Racism." *Race and Class* 33:4 (1992): 31–45.

Malik, Sarita. *Representing Black Britain: Black and Asian Images on Television.* London: Sage Publications, 2001.

Mark, Peter. *Africans in European Eyes: The Portrayal of Black Africans in Fourteenth and Fifteenth Century Europe.* Syracuse: Maxwell School of Citizenship and Public Affairs, 1974.

Marks, Sally. "Black Watch on the Rhine: A Study in Propaganda, Prejudice and Prurience." *European Studies Review* 13 (1983): 297–334.

Marques, Joao Pedro. *The Sounds of Silence: Nineteenth-Century Portugal and the Abolition of the Slave Trade.* trans. Richard Wall. New York: Berghahn Books, 2006.

Matusevich, Maxim, ed. *Africa in Russia, Russia in Africa: Three Centuries of Encounters.* Trenton, NJ: Africa World Press, 2006.

Mazon, Patricia, and Reinhild Steingrover, eds. *Not So Plain as Black and White: Afro-German Culture and History, 1890–2000.* Rochester: University of Rochester Press, 2005.

Miller, Christopher. *Theories of Africans: Francophone Literature and Anthropology in Africa.* Chicago: University of Chicago Press, 1990.

Morgan, Philip, and Sean Hawkins, eds. *Black Experience and the Empire.* New York: Oxford University Press, 2004.

Morrison, William. *Blacks in Ancient Greece.* Santa Barbara: Bellerophon Books, 2000.

Mtubani, Victor C. D. "The Black Vote in Eighteenth-Century Britain: African Writers Against Slavery and the Slave Trade." *Phylon* 45:2 (1984): 85–97.

Murithi, Timothy. *The African Union: Pan-Africanism, Peacebuilding and Development.* Burlington, VT: Ashgate, 2005.

Myers, Norma. "Servant, Sailor, Soldier, Tailor, Beggarman: Black Survival in White Society 1780–1830." *Immigrants and Minorities* 12:1 (1993): 47–74.

Northrup, David. *Africa's Discovery of Europe, 1650–1850.* New York: Oxford University Press, 2002.

Obenneier, Karin. "Afro-German Women: Recording Their Own History." *New German Critique* 46 (1989): 172–180.

Oguntoye, Katharina, May Opitz, and Dagmar Schultz. *Showing our Colors: Afro- German Women Speak Out.* trans. Anne Adams. Amherst: University of Massachusetts Press, 1991.

Oliver, Paul, ed. *Black Music in Britain: Essays on the Afro-Asian Contributions to Popular Music.* Milton Keynes, UK: Open University Press, 1990.

Owuso, Kwesi. *Black British Culture and Society: A Text Reader.* New York: Routledge, 1999.

Pakenham, Thomas. *The Scramble for Africa.* New York: Avon Books, 1992.

Paul, Kathleen. *Whitewashing Britain: Race and Citizenship in the Postwar Era.* Ithaca: Cornell University Press, 1997.

Peabody, Sue. *"There are No Slaves in France"—The Political Culture of Race and Slavery in the Ancien Régime.* New York: Oxford University Press, 1996.

Peabody, Sue, and Tyler Stovall, eds. *The Color of Liberty: Histories of Race in France.* Durham, NC: Duke University Press, 2003.

Phillips, Mike. *London Crossings: A Biography of Black Britain.* London: Continuum, 2001.

Poikane-Daumke, Aija. *African Diasporas: Afro-German Literature in the Context of the African-American Experience.* London: Lit Verlag, 2007.

Pommerin, Reiner. "The Fate of Mixed Blood Children in Germany." *German Studies Review* 5:3 (1982): 315–323.

Popeau, Jean Baptiste. *Dialogues of Negritude: An Analysis of the Cultural Context of Black Writing.* Durham, NC: Carolina Academic Press, 2003.

Potts, E. Daniel, and Annette Potts. "The Deployment of Black American Servicemen Abroad During World War Two." *Australian Journal of Politics and History* 35:1 (1989): 92–96.

Powell, Eve Troutt, and John O. Hunwick, eds. *The African Diaspora in the Mediterranean Lands of Islam.* Markus Weiner, 2002.

Pred, Allan. *Even in Sweden: Racisms, Radicalized Spaces, and the Popular Geographic Imagination.* Berkeley: University of California Press, 2000.

Preto-Rodas, Richard. *Negritude as a Theme in the Poetry of the Portuguese-Speaking World.* Gainsville: University of Florida Press, 1970.

Pryce, Everton A. "The Notting Hill Gate Carnival: Black Politics, Resistance, and Leadership, 1976–1978." *Caribbean Quarterly* 31:2 (1985): 35–52.

Raphael-Hernandez, Heike, ed. *Blackening Europe: The African American Presence.* New York: Routledge, 2003.

Reese, Joan. "Two Enemies to Fight: Blacks Battle For Equality in Two World Wars." *Colorado Heritage* 1 (1990): 2–17.

Restall, Matthew. *Seven Myths of the Spanish Conquest.* New York: Oxford University Press, 2003.

Rogers, J. A. *World's Great Men of Color.* 2 vols. Reprint. New York: Touchstone, 1996.

———. *Sex and Race: Negro-Caucasian Mixing in All Ages and All Lands.* New York: J. A. Rogers, 1940.

Russell, Francis. "Liberty to Slaves: Black Loyalists in the American Revolution." *Timeline* 4:2 (1987): 2–15.

Saunders, A. *A Social History of Black Slaves and Freedmen in Portugal, 1441–1555.* Cambridge: Cambridge University Press, 1982.

Schäfer, Wolf. "Global History and the Present Time." In *Writing Prometheus: Globalisation, History, and Technology,*. ed. Peter Lyth and Helmuth Trischler, 103–125. Aarhus, Denmark: Aarhus University Press, 2004.

Scheck, Raffael. *Hitler's African Victims: The German Army Massacres of Black French Soldiers in 1940.* New York: Cambridge University Press, 2006.

Scobie, Edward. *Black Britannia: A History of Blacks in Britain.* Chicago: Johnson, 1972.

Seminario, Lee Anne Durham. *The History of the Blacks, Jews, and Moors in Spain.* Madrid: Playor, 1975.

Sertima, Ivan Van, ed. *African Presence in Early Europe.* Somerset, NJ: Transaction Publishers, 1986.

Sesay, Amadu, ed. *Africa and Europe: From Partition to Interdependence or Dependence?* London: Croom Helm, 1986.

Sherwood, Merika. *After Abolition: Britain and the Slave Trade Since 1807.* London: I. B. Tauris, 2007.

Shyllon, Folarin. *Black People in Britain, 1553–1833.* Oxford: Oxford University Press, 1977.

Small, Stephen. *Racialized Barriers: The Black Experience in the United States and England in the 1980s.* London: Routledge, 1994.

Smith, Graham. *When Jim Crow Met John Bull: Black American Soldiers in World War II Britain.* London: I. B. Tauris, 1987.

Snowden, Frank. *Blacks in Antiquity: Ethiopians in the Greco-Roman Experience.* Cambridge, MA: Belknap Press, 1970.

Sollors, Werner. *Neither Black Nor White Yet Both: Thematic Explorations of Interracial Literature.* Cambridge: Harvard University Press, 1997.

Spratlin, V. B. "The Negro in Spanish Literature." *The Journal of Negro History* 19:1 (January 1934): 60–71.

Stevens, Christopher. *Soviet Union and Black Africa.* London: Palgrave Macmillan, 1976.

Stouffer, Allen P. "Black Abolitionists in Britain and Canada." *Canadian Review of American Studies* 19:2 (1988): 249–252.

Stovall, Tyler. *Paris Noir: African Americans in the City of Light.* Boston: Houghton Mifflin, 1996.

Stovall, Tyler, and Georges Van Den Abbeele, eds. *French Civilization and Its Discontents: Nationalism, Colonialism, Race.* Lanham, MD: Lexington Books, 2003.

Sweet, James. *Recreating Africa: Culture, Kinship, and Religion in the African-Portuguese World, 1441–1770.* Charlotte: University of North Carolina Press, 2006.

Tabili, Laura. *"We Ask for British Justice": Workers and Racial Difference in Late Imperial Britain.* Ithaca: Cornell University Press, 1994.

Taylor, Julie. *Muslims in Medieval Italy: The Colony at Lucera.* New ed. Lanham, MD: Lexington Books, 2005.

Thomas, Dominic. *Black France: Colonialism, Immigration, and Transnationalism.* Bloomington: Indiana University Press, 2006.

Thomas, Hugh. *The Slave Trade: The Story of the Atlantic Slave Trade: 1440–1870.* New York: Simon and Schuster, 1997.

Walvin, James. *Black and White: The Negro in English Society, 1555–1945.* London: Allen Lane, 1973.

——. *Black Ivory: Slavery in the British Empire.* 2nd ed. Malden, MA: Blackwell, 2001.

——. *The Black Presence: A Documentary History of the Negro in England.* New York: Schocken Books, 1972.

Washington, Joseph. *Anti-Blackness in English Religion, 1500–1800.* Lewiston, NY: Edwin Mellen Press, 1985.

Whitfield, James. *Unhappy Dialogue: The Metropolitan Police and Black Londoners in Post-war Britain.* Portland, OR: Willan Publishing, 2004.

Whyte, Iain. *Scotland and the Abolition of Black Slavery, 1756–1838.* Edinburgh: Edinburgh University Press, 2006.

Winders, James. *Paris Africain: Rhythms of the African Diaspora.* New York: Palgrave Macmillan, 2006.

WEB SITES

Black in Britain. http://blackinbritain.co.uk/ This Web site hosts a variety of news and pieces of interest for black Britons.

Black European Studies. http://www.best.uni-mainz.de/ This Web site, hosted by the Johannes Gutenberg University in Mainz, Germany, follows current scholarship and conferences on black European studies. It also allows scholars to share information about their research and forthcoming publications in the topic.

Black Presence: Asian and Black History in Britain, 1500–1850. http://www.nationalarchives.gov.uk/Pathways/black history/ This online exhibit from the British National Archives traces the history of the early modern black presence in Britain.

Blacks during the Holocaust. http://www.ushmm.org/wlc/article.php?lang=en&ModuleId=10005479 This Web site, hosted by the United States Holocaust Memorial Museum, presents an overview of the Nazi persecution of blacks in Europe.

SUGGESTED FILMS

100 % Arabica (Director: Mahmoud Zemmouri, 1997). This French feature film (available with English subtitles) presents a comedic take on the struggles of African immigrants living in the housing projects located on the outskirts of Paris. *Respectable Trade* (Director: Suri Krishnamma, 1998). This lavish BBC mini-series, based on the historical novel by Philippa Gregory, is an eighteenth-century drama about the African slave trade in Bristol, England.

Alexandre Dumas fils (A&E Biography). This episode from the television documentary series on the Arts and Entertainment Network details the life of French author Alexandre Dumas *fils*, author of *The Lady of the Camelias*. His great-grandmother was an African slave.

Alexandre Dumas père (A&E Biography). This episode from the television documentary series on the Arts and Entertainment Network details the life of French author Alexandre Dumas, author of *The Three Musketeers*. His grandmother was an African slave.

Alexander Pushkin (A&E Biography). This episode from the television documentary series on the Arts and Entertainment Network details the life of nineteenth-century Russian author Alexander Pushkin, who was descended from an African slave.

Amazing Grace (Director: Michael Apted, 2006). This feature film chronicles the nineteenth-century efforts of William Wilberforce to pass a law in parliament to abolish the British trans-Atlantic slave trade.

Ben Okri (A&E Biography). This episode from the television documentary series on the Arts and Entertainment Network details the life of British Caribbean author Ben Okri.

Black and White in Color (Director: Isaac Julien, 1992). This documentary film chronicles the history of black people in British television.

Black Girl (Director: Ousmane Sembene, 1966). This black and white French feature film (available with English subtitles) details the life of a black girl from Senegal who becomes a servant in contemporary France.

Black Dju (Director: Pol Crutchen, 1995). *Black Dju* (in French and Portuguese with English subtitles) follows Dju Dele Dibonga's quest from Cape Verde to Luxembourg to find his father. The main character experiences racism and harassment from immigration authorities on his arrival in Europe.

Black Knight (Director: Gil Junger, 2001). This comedic film, inspired by Mark Twain's *A Connecticut Yankee in King Arthur's Court*, substitutes the "Connecticut Yankee" with African American comedian Martin Lawrence as a modern-day man transported to medieval Camelot. The film also takes its inspiration from the numerous black knights that have become a component of the Arthurian legend, such as Morien, Palamedes, and Feirefiz.

Black Orpheus (Director: Marcel Camus, 1959). This Portuguese film (available with English subtitles) updates the ancient Greek myth by featuring an all-black cast and setting the tale during Carnival in Brazil.

Black Survivors of the Holocaust (Director: David Okuefuna, 1997). Known outside of the United States as *Hitler's Forgotten Victims*, this monumental documentary focuses on the Afro-German experience of persecution in Nazi Germany and includes interviews with individuals who had experienced the era.

Blacks Britannica (Director: David Koff, 1978). This documentary film traces the role of blacks in British society within a historical perspective.

Borders (Director: Mostefa Djadjam, 2002). This French feature film (available with English subtitles) chronicles the attempts of seven sub-Saharan Africans to illegally enter Europe in the hopes of having a better life.

Burning an Illusion (Director: Menelik Shabazz, 1981). This film feature follows the life a young black woman in London, whose experiences make her question her identity, torn between the white European society that she has grown up in and the black African society of her ancestors.

Catch a Fire (Director: Menelik Shabazz, 1995). This docudrama recounts the life and legacy of Deacon Paul Bogle, a nineteenth-century Jamaican black advocate of civil rights. The 1865 Morant Bay Rebellion left a lasting racial impression on Victorian Britain.

Colin Jackson (A&E Biography). This episode from the television documentary series on the Arts and Entertainment Network details the life of the black British athlete Colin Jackson.

Colour Blind: The Murder of Stephen Lawrence (Director: Paul Greengrass, 1999). This British television film, based on a true story, dramatizes the murder of a young black Briton by a group of white hooligans. The subsequent investigation is botched by the police department and reveals the racial tensions in contemporary Britain.

Congo: White King, Red Rubber, Black Death (Director: Peter Bate, 2003). This feature film (in French and Dutch with English subtitles) chronicles the abusive administration of the Congo under King Leopold II of Belgium. The subtitled American DVD release also includes the documentary *Boma-Tervuren: The Journey*, which focuses on the exhibition of several Congolese at the 1879 World's Fair in Brussels.

Diane Abbott (A&E Biography). This episode from the television documentary series on the Arts and Entertainment Network details the life of black British politician Diane Abbott.

Flyboys (Director: Tony Bill, 2006). This feature film follows the exploits of the Lafayette Escadrille, a collection of volunteers, mostly American, who fought as part of the French air force during World War I. A prominent member of the group was African American pilot Eugene Bullard, who became a noted French celebrity and military hero, despite remaining an unknown in America.

Four Feathers (Director: Shekhar Kapur, 2002). This blockbuster film, based on the novel by A.E.W. Mason, depicts the British in the Sudan during the era of nineteenth-century colonialism and explores issues of race and racism.

Frantz Fanon (A&E Biography). This episode from the television documentary series on the Arts and Entertainment Network details the life of black Francophone author Frantz Fanon.

Glass Ceiling [Le Plafond de Verre]. (Director: Yamina Benguigui, 2004). This documentary (in French with English subtitles) chronicles the struggles of black and Arab Africans as they seek employment in modern France.

Hope in My Heart: Oral Poetry—May Ayim (1997). This documentary features the work of poet May Ayim (May Opitz), one of the founders of the Afro-German Movement.

The Josephine Baker Story (Director: Brian Gibson, 1991). This HBO Emmy award-winning feature film chronicles the life of African American entertainer Josephine Baker, who became a celebrity in jazz-age France.

Mestizo (Director: Mario Handler, 1989). This Spanish feature film (available with English subtitles), set in Venezuela, follows the attempts of Jose Ramon, the son of a Spanish aristocrat and a black fisher-woman, to define his identity.

Le Mozart Noir: Reviving a Legend (Media Headquarters Film and Television Inc., 2003). This documentary chronicles the life and music of the famous black composer, swordsman, and soldier of the French Revolution.

Names Living Nowhere (Director: Dominique Loreau, 1994). This docudrama (in French with English subtitles) follows the adventures of an African *griot*, or storyteller, as he travels to Brussels and reveals the struggles of Belgian African immigrants.

Othello (Director: Oliver Parker, 1995). An excellent cinematic adaptation of Shakespeare's play set in Italy featuring Laurence Fishburne in the title role and Kenneth Branagh as Iago.

Otomo (Director: Frieder Schlaich, 1999). This German feature film (available with English subtitles), based on a true story, re-creates the attempts of a West African man to seek asylum in Germany and the manhunt that follows. The film exposes racism at all levels toward Africans in German society.

Papa's Song (Director: Sander Francken, 1999). This Dutch family drama (available with English subtitles) touches on race relations in the Netherlands.

Playing Away (Director: Horace Ove, 1986). This feature film follows a charity cricket match between a white team from a small English village and a black West Indian team from London. Underlying the game is intense racial tensions.

Roar (Executive Producer: Shawn Cassidy, 1997). This television series features a black character named Tully who assists the hero in his quest to unite the Irish clans and expel the ancient Roman invaders.

Robin Hood: Prince of Thieves (Director: Kevin Reynolds, 1991). This blockbuster film was the first to feature a black Moor as a member of Robin Hood's outlaw band in medieval England. Most subsequent film and television versions now include a black character, which was parodied in Mel Brook's spoof, *Robin Hood: Men in Tights* (1993).

Samuel Coleridge-Taylor (A&E Biography). This episode from the television documentary series on the Arts and Entertainment Network details the life of British composer Samuel Coleridge-Taylor.

Samuel Adjai Crowther (A&E Biography). This episode from the television documentary series on the Arts and Entertainment Network details the life of Samuel Adjai Crowther, an Anglican missionary from Africa.

Tasumi (Director: Daniel Kollo Sanou, 2003). This French comedic film (available with English subtitles) chronicles the struggles of an African World War II veteran to obtain his deserved pension.

Toussaint L'Ouverture (A&E Biography). This episode from the television documentary series on the Arts and Entertainment Network details the life of Francophone revolutionary leader Toussaint L'Ouverture.

Tropiques Amers (Director: Jean-Claude Flamand-Barny, 2007). This French mini-series, set in French Caribbean colony of Martinique during the eighteenth century, is a drama revolving around a French plantation owner, his aristocratic wife, and his black mistress. The film reflects the inhumanity of the institution of slavery and sexual exploitation of female slaves. The mini-series debuted in May 2007 as part of the national celebrations in France to commemorate the abolition of slavery.

Waalo Fendo: Where the Earth Freezes (Director: Mohammed Soudani, 1998). The dialogue of this feature film, set in Milan, Italy, is in Wolof, an African dialect (available with English subtitles). The film follows the attempts of two brothers from Senegal to immigrate to Italy and start a new life, but they are met with a harsh reality.

Index

About the Editor and Contributors

EDITOR

Eric Martone is instructor of history in the School of Professional Development at the State University of New York at Stony Brook and a history teacher at John F. Kennedy High School in Waterbury, Connecticut. He has a master's degree in global history from Iona College, a master's degree in European history from Western Connecticut State University, and is currently a doctoral candidate in the Department of History at the State University of New York at Stony Brook. He has published articles on European history, essays on teaching methods, and numerous articles for historical references.

CONTRIBUTORS

Adebusuyi Isaac Adeniran teaches in the Department of Sociology and Anthropology at Obafemi Awolowo University in Nigeria. He is finishing his doctorate in sociology.

Mary Afolabi Adeolu holds a master's degree in history from the University of Ibadan in Nigeria.

Lena Ahlin has a doctorate in English from Lund University in Sweden. Ahlin's dissertation dealt with the representations of Europe in African American literature, particularly in the works of James Weldon Johnson, Jessie Fauset, and Nella Larsen. Ahlin's research interests include the role of "race" in Swedish modernity.

Robbie Aitken is a research fellow in the German Department at the University of Liverpool in England.

William H. Alexander is professor of history at Norfolk State University. He specializes in modern European intellectual and cultural history, and comparative world history.

Lena Ampadu is associate professor of English at Towson University, where she directs the African and African American Studies program. Her research focuses on comparative traditions of the literature of women of African descent.

Sara Scott Armengot is a doctoral candidate in the Department of Comparative Literature at Pennsylvania State University. Her area of specialization is Inter-American literature.

Saër Maty Bâ is research fellow at the National Institute for Excellence in the Creative Industries, Bangor University (UK). His research interests blur boundaries between film, media, cultural studies, and black Diaspora studies. He has a particular interest in the visual and sonic cultures of the "Black Atlantic," primarily Francophone Africa, the Francophone Caribbean, France, Britain, and the United States.

Charlotte Baker is a lecturer at Lancaster University in England. Her research interests center broadly on twentieth-century French and Francophone African fictional writing.

Thomas Balcerski is a graduate student in the Department of History at the State University of New York at Stony Brook.

Laëtitia Baltz is a doctoral candidate at the Bordeaux Institute of Political Studies in France specializing on the links between politics, culture, and human rights; identity; and Africans and blacks.

Marianne Bechhaus-Gerst is professor of African Studies at the University of Cologne in Germany specializing in the history of Africans in Germany, German colonial history, and the images of Africa and Africans in German popular culture. Her books include *Treu bis in den Tod. Von Deutsch-Ostafrika nach Sachsenhausen–eine Lebensgeschichte* (2007), *Koloniale und postkoloniale Konstruktionen von Afrika und Menschen afrikanischer Herkunft in der deutschen Alltagskultur* (coauthor, 2006), *AfrikanerInnen in Deutschland und schwarze Deutsche–Geschichte und Gegenwart* (coauthor, 2004), and *Die (koloniale) Begegnung. AfrikanerInnen in Deutschland 1880–1945 — Deutsche in Afrika 1880–1918* (coauthor, 2003).

Gábor Berczeli is a doctoral candidate in Budapest, Hungary.

Brett A. Berliner is associate professor of history at Morgan State University. He has written on the reception of black Africans in France in the 1920s and the rejuvenation movement.

Amanda Bidnall is a doctoral candidate at Boston College. She focuses on modern British and imperial history, in particular the cultural politics of Caribbean artists in postwar England.

Allison Blakely is professor of European and comparative history and the George and Joyce Wein Professor of African American Studies at Boston University. His publications include *Russia and the Negro: Blacks in Russian History and Thought* (1986) and *Blacks in the Dutch World: The Evolution of Racial Imagery in a Modern Society* (1994).

Jennifer Westmoreland Bouchard is a doctoral candidate in the Department of French and Francophone Studies at the University of California at Los Angeles.

Pierre H. Boulle is professor of history (post-retirement) at McGill University in Canada. He is the author of numerous articles on colonial commerce, the slave trade, slavery, and race, principally in France in the early modern period. His books include *Esclavage et Race dans la France d'Ancien Régime* (2007).

Tristan Cabello is a doctoral candidate in history at Northwestern University and in American studies at the Universite Denis Diderot—Paris VII. His research and publications focus mainly on the history of gay communities in the United States and Europe.

Marcia Chatelain is Reach for Excellence assistant professor of Honors and African-American Studies at the University of Oklahoma Honors College.

Augusto Ciuffo is a professional journalist, filmmaker, and academic. His main areas of research are African and Brazilian cinemas, race relations, urban slave riots, and ethnicity and Diaspora issues.

Mark Cordery is a student at Central Connecticut State University in New Britain. His research interests include ancient Greece and Rome, and sports history.

Robert A. Cordery is research fellow at Pitney Bowes Inc. Prior to joining Pitney Bowes, he earned a doctorate in physics from the University of Toronto and held teaching positions at Rutgers University and Northeastern University. He has published numerous academic articles and has over 100 patents.

Justin Corfield teaches history and international relations at Geelong Grammar School in Australia. He has authored numerous books on aspects of colonial history.

John M. Cox is assistant professor of European History at Florida Gulf Coast University. His research and teaching interests include the Holocaust, fascism and antifascism, and social and working-class history.

Rosemary F. Crockett, the daughter of an original Tuskegee Airman, graduated from Harvard University after a career as a foreign service officer.

Tommy J. Curry is a doctoral candidate in philosophy at Southern Illinois University at Carbondale. His areas of interest include critical race theory and Africana philosophy.

Holger Drössler is currently finishing his graduate studies at the Ludwig-Maximilians-University in Munich, Germany. His thesis analyzes West German discourse on Afro-German "occupation children" between 1945 and 1960 from a trans-Atlantic perspective.

Anene Ejikeme teaches history at Trinity University in San Antonio, Texas.

Allyson Nadia Field is completing a doctoral degree in comparative literature at Harvard University. Her research focuses on race and representation in cinema.

Gérard Gengembre is professor of French literature at the University of Caen in Normandy, France specializing in nineteenth-century studies. He has published numerous articles and books, including *La Contre-Révolution ou l'Histoire désespérante* (1989), *Balzac: Le Napoléon des lettres* (1992), *Le Romantisme en France et en Europe* (2003), and *Napoleon: The Immortal Emperor* (2003).

Katharina Gerund is a doctoral fellow in American studies at Bremen University in Germany. Her dissertation project deals with the German reception of African American women's cultural production and the trans-Atlantic exchanges involved.

Gretchen Holbrook Gerzina is Kathe Tappe Vernon Professor in Biography and chair of the Department of English at Dartmouth College. She has published several books and articles on blacks in England and in English literature, including *Black London* (1997) and *Black Victorians/Black Victoriana* (editor, 2003). Her most recent book, *Mr. and Mrs. Prince* (2008), focuses on the life of Mary T. Prince, the first African American poet, and her husband.

Rachel Gillett is a doctoral candidate in the Department of History at Northeastern University. Her dissertation examines the intersection between jazz, race, and gender in interwar Paris.

Nadine Golly is teaching and working on a doctoral project at the Justus-Liebig-University in Giessen, Germany, on the emigration of Afro-German children to Denmark. Golly's research interests are blackness and critical whiteness, racism, (post)colonialism, migration, cultural politics, resistance, biographies, and memory in the context of black Diaspora in Europe (particularly Denmark, Sweden, and Germany).

Annette Gordon-Reed is professor of law at New York Law School and professor of history at Rutgers University. Her publications include *Thomas Jefferson and Sally Hemings: An American Controversy* (1997) *and Race on Trial: Law and Justice in American History* (editor, 2002).

James B. Haile is a doctoral candidate in the Department of Philosophy at the University of Memphis. His research has engaged the intersection of black American existential thought and Continental existential thought, and a project that situates Ralph Ellison as a black American existentialist thinker and positions *Invisible Man* in conversation with traditional existentialist thought.

Mark Hanna is assistant professor of early American history at the University of California at San Diego. His dissertation, entitled "The Pirate Nest: The Impact of Piracy on Newport, Rhode Island and Charles Town, South Carolina, 1670–1740," explains why piracy was actively supported by maritime communities on the periphery of European empires.

Jennifer Heuer is assistant professor of history at the University of Massachusetts at Amherst. Her research interests include modern France, Europe, and gender history. She is the author of *The Family and the Nation: Gender and Citizenship in Revolutionary France* (2005).

Lawrence F. Hundersmarck is Edward J. Mortola Scholar and professor of philosophy and religious studies at Pace University in Pleasantville, New York. He has published on a wide range of topics about the history of Christianity.

Dawn P. Hutchins is an independent scholar. Her research areas include the history of the family unit and Native American history, specifically focusing on southeastern tribes and gender roles.

Deborah Janson is associate professor of German in the Department of Foreign Languages at West Virginia University. Her scholarly interests focus on post-Wende and GDR literature, including the theme of national and personal identity in works by minority and East German writers. In addition to publications in these areas, she has written about the literature of the German Enlightenment and Romantic periods.

Jeannette Eileen Jones is assistant professor of history and ethnic studies at the University of Nebraska at Lincoln and the Deutsche Bank Junior Scholar-in-Residence Fellow at the Heidelberg Center for American Studies at the University of Heidelberg in Germany.

S. Marina Jones is a doctoral candidate in the Department of History at the University of North Carolina at Chapel Hill. Her research interests include modern European and gender history, the African Diaspora, and race relations.

Joyce A. Kannan is an independent researcher in London, England. She has a doctorate in history from the University of London and has taught courses on African history.

Paul H. D. Kaplan is professor of art history in the School of Humanities at the State University of New York, Purchase College. He is the author of *The Rise of the Black Magus in Western Art* (1985) and many essays on Africans in European art.

Miranda Kaufmann is a doctoral student at Christ's Church, Oxford studying Africans in Britain, 1500–1640.

Bénédicte Laberge is a student at the Polyvalente de Charlesbourg in Quebec City.

Yves Laberge is a cultural historian. The author of numerous scholarly articles, he is the associate French editor for the journal *Canadian Ethnic Studies/Études ethniques au Canada* and the series editor for the book series *"L'espace public"* and *"Cinéma et société"* at the Presses de l'Université Laval, Québec City.

Christine Levecq is assistant professor in the humanities at Kettering University. She specializes in African American and African Diaspora literatures. She is the author of *Slavery and Sentiment: The Politics of Feeling in Black Atlantic Antislavery Writing, 1770–1850* (2008).

Tobe Levin teaches at the University of Maryland University College, Europe and at the University of Frankfurt. She serves as editor-in-chief of *Feminist Europa* and has translated Fadumo Korn's *Born in the Big Rains: A Memoir of Somalia and Survival* (2006).

Karen A. Macfarlane is an independent scholar. Her doctoral dissertation at York University in Canada illuminated ethnic minorities and criminal justice in eighteenth-century London.

Thomas Martin teaches history at Shippensburg University. His research has dealt with Renaissance humanism and its mutations when applied to the problem of Ireland in the sixteenth century.

Nicole Martone teaches composition and developmental writing at Naugatuck Valley Community College and English at John F. Kennedy High School, both in Waterbury, Connecticut. Her research interests include Shakespeare, the Renaissance, and ancient Greek literature.

Maxim Matusevich teaches in the Department of History at Seton Hall University. His books include *No Easy Row for a Russian Hoe: Ideology and Pragmatism in Nigerian-Soviet Relations, 1960–1991* (2003) and *Africa in Russia, Russia in Africa: Three Centuries of Encounters* (editor, 2006).

Alexander Mikaberidze teaches European history at Louisiana State University at Shreveport. His publications include the *Russian Officer Corps in the Revolutionary and Napoleonic Wars, 1792–1815* (2004), *The Czar's General: The Memoirs of a Russian General in the Napoleonic Wars* (2005), *Historical Dictionary of Georgia* (2007), and *The Battle of Borodino: Napoleon versus Kutuzov* (2007).

Patit Paban Mishra is professor of history at Sambalpur University in India specializing in world history with particular reference to South Asian and Southeast Asian history.

E. Agateno Mosca is an independent scholar living in Connecticut. His main areas of research include Italian history and the history of Christianity.

Laura Murphy is a doctoral candidate in the Department of African and African American Studies at Harvard University. She is writing a dissertation on representations of the trans-Atlantic slave trade in West African literature.

Robert Nave is a social studies teacher at Terryville High School in Connecticut.

Ayokunle Olumuyiwa Omobowale teaches sociology at the University of Lagos in Nigeria. He has a special interest in the areas of development, political, rural, and medical sociology.

Sue Peabody is professor of history at Washington State University at Vancouver. Her research interests include France and modern European colonialism from 1450 to 1800. Her publications include *There are No Slaves in France: The Political Culture of Race and Slavery in the Ancient Regime* (1996), *The Color of Liberty: Histories of Race in France* (co-editor, 2003), and *Slavery, Freedom and the Law in the Atlantic World: A Brief History with Documents* (co-editor, 2007). She is currently working on a book entitled *Free Soil: Slavery, Freedom, Statehood and the Law in the Atlantic World* and is president of the French Colonial Historical Society.

Mark Anthony Phelps is a doctoral candidate at the University of Arkansas, where he is finishing his dissertation in ancient Mediterranean history.

Heike Raphael-Hernandez is professor of English at the University of Maryland University College, Europe. Her books include *Blackening Europe: The African American Presence* (editor, 2003), *AfroAsian Encounters: Culture, History, Politics* (co-editor, 2006), and *The Construction of a Utopian Aesthetic for African-American Literature: Ernst Bloch's Principle of Hope and Contemporary African-American Women Authors* (2008).

Joshua M. Rice is a graduate student at the University of Nebraska at Kearney. His research centers on the cultural aspects of Native American and European relations via Christian missions.

Cambridge Sena Ridley specializes in urban studies of Paris and New York in the midnineteenth century.

Kristen Roupenian is a doctoral student in English literature at Harvard University. Her work focuses on the politics of language choice in East African fiction.

Raffael Scheck is associate professor and chair of the Department of History at Colby College. His publications include many articles and books on German right-wing politics, including *Hitler's Black Victims: The German Army Massacres of Black French Soldiers in 1940* (2006).

Alyssa Goldstein Sepinwall is associate professor of History at California State University at San Marcos. A specialist in French history, she is the author of *The Abbé Grégoire and the French Revolution: The Making of Modern Universalism* (2005).

Maryam Sharron Muhammad Shabazz is a doctoral student at Howard University. Her research focuses on Afro-Asian communities.

Kenneth L. Shonk, Jr. is a doctoral candidate in the Department of History at Marquette University specializing in modern European history, with a geographic emphasis on Ireland and a thematic emphasis on nationalism, gender, and intellectual history.

Donna Smith is associate professor of library services at W. Frank Steely Library of Northern Kentucky University in Highland Heights, where she is the assistant head of technical services.

Dorsía Smith teaches English at the University of Puerto Rico at Río Piedras. Her primary interests include Caribbean and African American literature.

Jessica Callaway Smolin is a doctoral candidate in the Department of Comparative Literature at Harvard University and specializes in nineteenth- and twentieth-century Brazilian and American literature. Her research focuses on the literature of the Brazilian abolitionist movement.

Ruth Starkman is professor of philosophy and comparative literature at the University of San Francisco. She has published on Germany, German philosophy, race relations and ethics, and Riefenstahl and the 1936 Olympics.

Tyler Edward Stovall is professor of history at the University of California at Berkeley. His research interests are twentieth-century France and the history of race. His books include *Paris Noir: African Americans in the City of Light* (1996), *The Color of Liberty: Histories of Race in France* (co-editor, 2003), *French Civilization and Its Discontents: Nationalism, Colonialism, Race* (co-editor, 2003), and *Josephine Baker: Image and Icon* (co-author, 2006).

Charlotte Szilágyi is a doctoral candidate in the Department of Comparative Literature at Harvard University. Her dissertation focuses on frame narratives and otherness in nineteenth- and twentieth-century German, Jewish-American, and African American literature.

Ayanna Thompson is assistant professor of English and Women and Gender Studies at Arizona State University. She specializes in depictions of race in the Renaissance. Her books include *Colorblind Shakespeare: New Perspectives on Race and Performance* (editor, 2006) and *Performing Race and Torture on the Early Modern Stage* (2007).

Kira Thurman is a doctoral candidate in modern European history at the University of Rochester. Her studies focus on German cultural history in the nineteenth and twentieth centuries.

Ayotunde Titilayo teaches population and research methodology courses at Obafemi Awolowo University in Nigeria. His interests are in qualitative research methods with a bias in child and maternal health, social epidemiological research relating to adolescents' sexual health, and population development.

Teruyuki Tsuji is a visiting professor at Nova Southeastern University. His research has focused on transnational identity construction and its relations with religious practices in both contexts of the Caribbean and of West Indian migrant communities in South Florida.

Hanna Wallinger is associate professor of American Studies at Salzburg University in Austria. She is author of *Pauline E. Hopkins: A Literary Biography* (2005), *Transitions: Race, Culture, and the Dynamics of Race* (editor, 2006), *Critical Voicings of Black Liberation in the Americas* (co-editor, 2003), *Daughters of Restlessness: Women's Literature at the End of the Millennium* (1998), as well as numerous articles. Her main fields of research include African American studies and women's studies.

Tim J. Watts is the subject librarian for history at Hale Library, Kansas State University. His research interests include early modern and modern European history, military history, and popular perceptions of libraries and librarians.

Richardine G. Woodall teaches at York University in Canada. Her research interests are the literatures of the English Renaissance, particularly Shakespearean drama. Arising out of her interests in postcolonial and feminist studies, her research frequently focuses on the overlap of race and gender in literary texts.